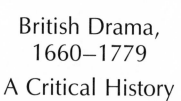

British Drama, 1660–1779

A Critical History

Twayne's
Critical History
of
British Drama

◇

British Drama, 1660–1779
A Critical History

◇

Frances M. Kavenik
University of Wisconsin–Parkside

Twayne Publishers
An Imprint of Simon & Schuster Macmillan
New York

Prentice Hall International
London   Mexico City   New Delhi   Singapore   Sydney   Toronto

Twayne's Critical History of British Drama Series

British Drama, 1660–1779: A Critical History
Frances M. Kavenik

Twayne Publishers
An Imprint of Simon & Schuster Macmillan
866 Third Avenue
New York, NY 10022

PR
701
, K38
1995

Library of Congress Cataloging-in-Publication Data

Kavenik, Frances M., 1944–
    British drama, 1660–1779 : a critical history / by Frances
M. Kavenik.
        p.   cm. — (Twayne's critical history of British
    drama)
        Includes bibliographical references and index.
        ISBN 0-8057-4533-5
        1. English drama—18th century—History and criticism.
    2. English drama—Restoration, 1660–1700—History
    and criticism.   3. Literature and society—England—
    History— 18th century.   4. Literature and society—
    England—History—17th century.   5. Theater—England—
    London—History—18th century.   6. Theater—England—
    London—History—17th century.   I. Title.   II. Series.
    PR708.S46K38   1995
    822'.409—dc20   94-26538
                                                                CIP

10 9 8 7 6 5 4 3 2 1

Printed in the United States of America.

To
Harold R. Hutcheson
and
Walter B. Scott,
teachers, mentors, and friends

contents

Preface and Acknowledgments   *ix*

1   *Introduction: The Contexts and Conditions of Drama*   *1*

2   *The Carolean Period: 1659–1685*   *26*

3   *The Last of the Stuarts: 1685–1714*   *65*

4   *The Hanoverian Accession to Garrick's: 1714–1747*   *115*

5   *The Age of Garrick: 1747–1779*   *158*

6   *Conclusion*   *203*

Chronology   *211*

Notes and References   *223*

Selected Bibliography   *251*

Index   *265*

preface and acknowledgments

In the first half of the twentieth century, particularly in the post–World War I climate of world-weary cynicism, plays of the late seventeenth and eighteenth centuries were rescued from the disrepute of the Victorians and Edwardians to appear on stage alongside the works of George Bernard Shaw and Noel Coward, while the musicals of Irving Berlin and Cole Porter were being staged and filmed. Although some critical interest in this earlier drama was also revived at that time, it was not until the 1950s and 1960s that scholarship on them began to change, with the work of Thomas Fujimura, Norman Holland, the first volumes of *The London Stage* project, and scholarly editions like the *California Dryden* that replaced the sparsely annotated editions from the first half of the century. Accompanying and dependent upon such editions and scholarship were the works of critics who have appeared in the last 30 years, such as Arthur H. Scouten, Emmett L. Avery, Eric Rothstein, Susan Staves, Robert D. Hume, and Judith Milhous. These critics have all been curious about the social, cultural, and psychological impact of the theater on the drama, and their writings have served to advance our knowledge and understanding of both. The work of these and other similarly dedicated writers figures prominently in this study.

Literary studies generally have moved in the last few decades to see texts as products of history that also have the potential to influence that history. Critics of twentieth-century literary forms often call such work "popular culture" studies when applied to film or television, but we have been reluctant to use even the more dignified "culture studies" for the seventeenth and eighteenth centuries, lest it lump us with those who talk seriously about sitcoms, soap operas, and movies. At the same time, we may secretly acknowledge that, factoring in the variables, late seventeenth- and eighteenth-century comedies, heroic plays, tragicomedies, and tragedies were the genre films and soap operas of their day, enthralling their audiences and speaking to their needs and desires, offering entertainment, excitement, and escape. They were also capable, as films or advertising are today, of creating or reforming their audiences' needs and desires. Without much apology, therefore, I offer on the following pages a "popular culture" discussion of this drama that attempts to incorporate the theater and audiences that bred it.

These audiences, unlike polite modern ones, were direct and forceful about making their feelings known; they didn't wait for the Nielsen ratings to come out. As Arthur H. Scouten puts it, even "sophisticated Augustan theatregoers . . . did not have the slightest intention of putting up with a play that bored them, that they disliked, or that they thought failed to make sense."[1] They shouted, they hissed, they used noisemakers such as catcalls, they left in midact or midscene; in extreme cases, they rioted to show their disapprobation. Conversely, if they liked a play, they came again and again, particularly for the author's or actor's benefit night, and made special requests for revivals. Their taste, for good or ill, formed the drama and theater of their time and was in turn formed by it.

The methods used in this study are not unique, but deserve some comment. They extend the methods used by Eric Rothstein and me in *The Designs of Carolean Comedy* (1988), which deals with repertory development in comedy in a narrower time frame. After an introductory section on the theater, in chapters 2–5 I have divided the 1660–1779 period into four roughly equal parts of 25 to 33 years, largely for convenience but also because each of the four segments so demarked has features that distinguish it from the ones preceding and following it. Each of the four eras begins with a political or theatrical event and covers a period in which important change occurred in the drama. The ascension of Charles II and the reopening of the theaters in 1660 ended with the union of the two theaters and the political controversies of the early 1680s; the accession of James II in 1685 began a period that included a great deal of experimentation, the splitting of the United Company, and the Collier Controversy; the accession of George I in 1714 led into a period in which the theaters came into their own once again, with more · plays produced and theaters operating than ever before, but culminating in the Licensing Act of 1737 and its aftermath; Garrick's assumption of the managership of Drury Lane in 1747 created a new kind of solid prosperity in the playhouses, conservative innovation, and ensemble acting. Within each time span, I have looked at all the popular plays, but particularly at those likely to start trends or denote shifts in generic conventions, usually the most popular of the new plays. From those I have selected a few plays to discuss in detail, showing specifically how they used existing generic conventions in new ways and passed those features along to the next wave of playwrights, how they used the theater of their time and thrived in response to their audiences' needs and demands. I have tried, in short, to define dramatic development in terms of the experience of the plays as theatrical products.

In order to talk about such development in an active repertory, I have used terms like *Fletcherian* and *Shakespearean*, which indicate not just the plays of John Fletcher and William Shakespeare in the repertory but modal characteristics of the older drama that reappear in new plays as ways of treating characters, types of plotting, setting, and other variables. I have avoided terms like *comedy of manners* or *neoclassical*, which do not seem definable in the same way and therefore are not useful for my purposes. Where terminology, such as *sentimental comedy*, was a part of the rubric of the time, I have tried to fix its meaning as carefully as possible in its contemporary and present-day definitions. Performance figures and other data I have derived from *The London Stage*.

Over the years this manuscript has been "in progress," I have been fortunate in having the support of my family, friends, and colleagues, such as the librarians at the University of Wisconsin–Parkside, who facilitated my research and found answers to a variety of questions, and my friend Felicia Boyle, who read the final version and made helpful suggestions. To Eric Rothstein, who offered a critical eye and ear at every stage of the "progress," my debt is incalculable.

Introduction

the contexts and conditions of drama

Late seventeenth- and eighteenth-century British drama was public art whose lifeblood was the cash paid at the box office by Londoners prepared to be entertained, stimulated, soothed, and sometimes even enlightened by what they saw on stage. As public art, the drama was especially sensitive to the contingencies of time and place, current events and controversies, while as a moneymaking industry, it had its own set of contingencies. It depended on the pooled efforts of authors, actors, and managerial personnel, as well as on a set of changing social roles and expectations in the audience. In incorporating all these influences, I will be treating this drama as a medium of popular culture whose main function was to please its contemporary audiences, and will be assuming that entertainment was the primary if not exclusive motive of the writers, actors, and producers of any given era. Dr. Samuel Johnson confirmed this reality in his prologue written for the opening of the Drury Lane theater in 1747 under the management of David Garrick: "The stage but echoes back the public voice. / The drama's laws the drama's patrons give, / For we, who live to please, must please to live."[1] But even a simple formula has its corollaries and caveats. What passes for entertainment can change shape radically over the course of some six score years, and so it did in the late seventeenth and eighteenth centuries. What was a "guilty pleasure" to a theatergoer in 1675 produced more guilt than pleasure in his or her counterpart in 1750, and what moved a member of the audience of 1760 to sympathetic tears would probably have provoked his or her counterpart in 1660 to tears of mirth. Thus, the textual and textural changes in the popular drama between 1660 and 1779 reflect the changing theatrical expectations of that drama's audiences.

Focusing on expectations and the way the drama presents images attractive to theatergoers allows us to see audiences as varied rather than monolithic. From its very beginnings, as Emmett L. Avery and Arthur H. Scouten point out in their introduction to the first volume of *The London Stage*, "the Restoration audience was not of the single complexion which some subsequent theatrical historians have emphasized. The range of social classes, professions, and cultural attainments was fairly great, and the taste of the spectators as well as their motives in attending the playhouses varied considerably" (*LS*, 1:162). Thus, I will try to acknowledge the diversity within a given audience rather than treating it as univocal and Cyclopean.

Diversity is, in fact, key to understanding the kind of dramatic development associated with the most vital periods of late seventeenth- and eighteenth-century drama. Where a competitive theatrical climate has new plays vying with proven repertory favorites in a particular theater as well as with the repertories of other theaters, success often means wresting a limited audience away from the opposition, and the reward is concrete box-office returns. Whenever and wherever it occurs, such repertory development is both conservative and innovative.[2] Any popular new play both reproduces the qualities audiences found pleasing in older plays and rings changes on those patterns so that, at least for a time, it outbids its predecessors for attention. Unlike the products of noncompetitive periods, as when the theater companies were united from 1682–94 and 1707–14, new plays created in a genuinely competitive climate are more apt to experiment in this way. There are also more new plays during such competitive periods and more new playwrights encouraged to test their imagination and skills. Like other forms of popular culture, such a repertory can respond quickly to any significant change in the sociopolitical climate, whether it be patriotic fervor, anti-Catholic prejudice, or mercantile sensibility. The theaters' reactions, however, are not always predictable. At times between 1660 and 1779, events outside the theater had a significant impact on the kinds of plays produced and their reception; at other times, not. John Loftis encourages us to look beneath the surface of these latter plays for what they say about the shared beliefs that animated them: "In creating the imaginary and self-contained worlds of their plays, the dramatists imposed an order on the experience they depicted, and in so doing they revealed widely held attitudes toward social and political relationships. The drama may tell us more about the habits of thought in its authors—and those of the audiences on whose favor they depended—than about the world that provided its subject."[3] In analyzing the popular drama, I will try to be alert to these attitudes and attempt to determine how the theater, as a medium of living culture, was affected by and perhaps affected them.

At the same time, we need also be aware that this drama was created not for the streets of London but for its stages. The physical environment of the theater, the costumes and scenery, the financial and management practices of various eras, and the individual and collective efforts of managers, actors, writers, scene designers, singers, dancers, and musicians were formidable influences on what kinds of drama could and would exist at any time. For these theatrical conditions, *The London Stage* editors and those who have followed them have done an admirable job of setting out the known facts and making educated guesses about the rest, and the student or scholar wanting more than the broad outlines sketched in the ensuing discussion should go to those sources for more detailed discussions.

Theater Buildings

The physical space and shape of a theater determines a number of variables about the drama written to be performed in it. In Shakespeare's Globe, the combination of open-air center, raised platform, and relatively bare stage made him supply verbally what was lacking visually. Alternatively, the indoor theaters of the nineteenth century, though they housed similarly huge audiences, distanced both stage and performance from the audience and brought into being a species of drama that sacrificed nuance and gesture for stereotype and spectacle. The theaters of the late seventeenth and eighteenth centuries operated somewhere in between, with a kind of close relationship between actor and audience perhaps never seen again, but with a full range of scenes, machines, and music as factors of production and audience expectation, part of what George Winchester Stone has called the "whole show" (*LS*, 4:24).

These theaters were linked with, yet different from, their predecessors. By edict of Parliament, the theaters were closed in 1642, such entertainments being anathema to the Puritan government; one of Charles II's first public acts when the monarchy was restored in 1660 was to issue two royal patents meant to give their owners exclusive rights to put on theatrical performances in London. In between occurred the longest hiatus in the continuous presentation of drama on the London stage since the opening of The Theater in 1576. It was not, to be sure, a complete hiatus; various kinds of activities went on covertly during those 18 years that could be identified as theatrical.[4] Particularly in the late 1650s, after royalist Sir William Davenant (1606–68) returned to London from his exile abroad, his name became associated with certain kinds of musical evenings, advertised as "concerts" (permitted by the government) but in fact operatic theatrical performances. By 1659 he was operating in London under a "Tolleration," along with other companies headed by John Rhodes, William Beeston, and one referred to only as the "old actors." Davenant was thus ideally placed to receive one of the two royal patents from the king, and he and Thomas Killigrew (1612–83)—operating, respectively, the Duke's Company and the King's Company—became the first in a long line of owner-managers and theatrical entrepreneurs who would help define the shape and scope of dramatic entertainment in the next 120 years. The two men found most of the old theater buildings burned down or turned to different purposes.[5] They made provisional use of existing small indoor theaters, but between 1661 and 1663 they developed something much better for their purposes.

First Davenant converted an indoor tennis court[6] into the Lincoln's Inn Fields theater so that he could use scenes and machines more extensively than Killigrew's theater on Vere Street could. Opening with Davenant's own *The Siege of Rhodes* in June 1661, Lincoln's Inn Fields adapted many new features into the rectangular plan, with a thrust stage that covered as much as half of the available auditorium space, a substantial forestage acting area flanked by two doors at each side of the stage, at least one trap, and a significant rear stage with movable side wings and back wings. A "music room" was placed either above the scene opening in the center or to one side overhead, as in the Elizabethan playhouses. Within the auditorium itself, the center sloping area filled with benches formed the pit, and there were two or three levels of side boxes and at least one and perhaps two gallery levels at the back and one at the sides. The royal box was at stage level in the center of the back of the auditorium, called the front boxes, the best seating in the house for hearing and seeing the performance. Maximum capacity for either theater was about 600 spectators, comparable to the capacity of a large movie theater in the late twentieth century.[7]

Of all these innovations, movable scenery was probably the most important, and a month later Samuel Pepys noted that the Vere Street audiences had thinned considerably. Soon Killigrew, to offset Davenant's competitive advantage, was planning a new theater, this one built from scratch, and his Theater Royal opened in Drury Lane in May 1663. Personal accounts indicate this theater was the first to have shaped its auditorium into a semicircular "fan" pattern, with the musicians placed under and in front of the stage rather than above or at the sides.[8] Successive seventeenth-century theaters were built in 1671 (Dorset Garden) and 1674 (Drury Lane),[9] and were designed to hold larger audiences than their predecessors. Dorset Garden could accommodate about 1,200 spectators, while Drury Lane, after manager Christopher Rich reduced the thrust stage by some four feet in the 1690s and allowed members of the audience to sit on the stage itself, held about 1,000, approximately the capacity of today's mainstream Broadway theaters.

Three new theaters were built during the eighteenth century. Sir John Vanbrugh's Queen's (later King's) theater in the Haymarket opened in 1705, physically larger than Dorset Garden or Drury Lane, with such "vast Columns, . . . gilded Cornices," and "immoderate high Roofs," according to Colley Cibber, that "scarce one Word in ten could be distinctly heard in it" (quoted in Leacroft, 102), even though the capacity of the theater was probably about the same as for the reconstructed Drury Lane. But when John Rich built a new theater at Lincoln's Inn Fields in 1714, its capacity was about 1,400, as was that of the theater in Covent Garden he built in 1732 with the money he made from *The Beggar's Opera*. Though Rich's theater building in Covent Garden was more than twice the length and three times the width of Davenant's original conversion of Lincoln's Inn Fields, much of the extra space was taken up on one side by green rooms, scene rooms, and offices, and the fore- and backstage remained proportionally about two-thirds the size of the internal space. From the forestage to the front boxes, the distance was about 30 feet, slightly less than the width of a modern tennis court, and to the highest seating in the shilling galleries, about 40 feet; thus, no spectator was more than 50 feet from the stage, for example, the width

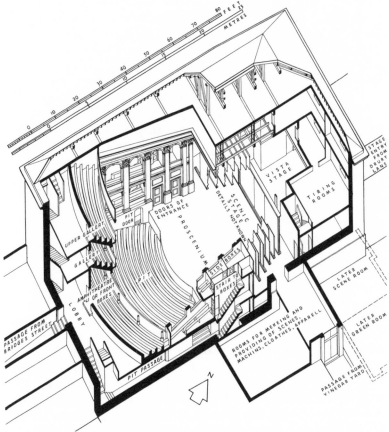

The Theatre Royal, Drury Lane, Wren, 1674: scale reconstruction. *From Richard Leacroft,* The Development of The English Playhouse *(1973); reproduced by permission of Eyre Methuen, Reed Consumer Books Ltd.*

of a modern basketball court. Wren's original fan-shaped design continued to be used throughout the period even for smaller theaters like Henry Giffard's Goodman's Fields because it possessed ideal sightlines and acoustics for almost all audience members. Any tampering with the design tended to unbalance both perspective and audio. Even Christopher Rich's reduction of the stage by about four feet disadvantaged those in the far side boxes (Leacroft, 111–12),[10] and ironically it was those very side boxes which tended to take the added numbers as the auditorium seating capacity was gradually increased throughout the eighteenth century.

Successive alterations by John Rich, Garrick, and others increased

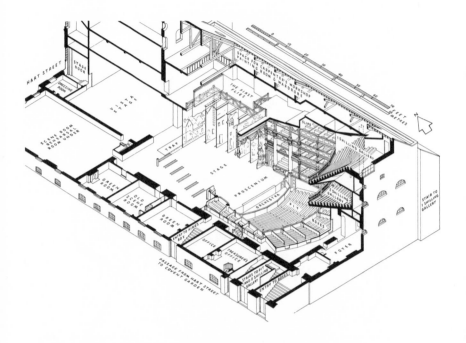

Covent Garden 1732: scale reconstruction. *From Richard Leacroft,* The
Development of The English Playhouse *(1973); reproduced by permission of Eyre
Methuen, Reed Consumer Books Ltd.*

audience capacity within the original walls, to about 2,000 by the 1770s.[11]
Although considerably more than in the original Drury Lane or Dorset
Garden theaters in the seventeenth century, these capacities were still
considerably less than those of the new theaters built in the late eighteenth
and nineteenth centuries. Indeed, one witness to both the eighteenth-
and the nineteenth-century theaters, Richard Cumberland, looked back
in 1806 nostalgically to the heyday of Garrick's reign:

> Since the stages of Drury Lane and Covent Garden have been so
> enlarged in their dimensions as to be henceforward theatres for
> spectators rather than playhouses for hearers, it is hardly to be
> wondered at if their managers and directors encourage those repre-
> sentations, to which their structure is best adapted. The splendor
> of the scenes, the ingenuity of the machinist and the rich display
> of dresses, aided by the captivating charms of music, now in a
> great degree supercede the labours of the poet. There can be

nothing very gratifying in watching the movements of an actor's lips, when we cannot hear the words that proceed from them; but when the animating march strikes up, and the stage lays open its recesses to the depth of a hundred feet for the procession to advance, even the most distant spectator can enjoy his shilling's-worth of show. What then is the poet's chance? Exactly what the parson's would be, if the mountebank was in the market-place, when the bells were chiming for church.

On the stage of old Drury in the days of Garrick the moving brow and penetrating eye of that matchless actor came home to the spectator. As the passions shifted, and were by turns reflected from the mirror of his expressive countenance, nothing was lost; upon the scale of modern Drury many of the finest touches of his art would of necessity fall short. The distant auditor might chance to catch the text, but would not see the comment, that was wont so exquisitely to elucidate the poet's meaning, and impress it on the hearer's heart.[12]

The expansionist fervor of the nineteenth century was set in the 1790s when both Drury Lane and Covent Garden were rebuilt. A spectator in the new Drury Lane of 1794, John Byng, was moved to call for divine intervention: "Restore me, ye overruling powers to the drama, to the warm close, observant, seats of Old Drury where I may comfortably criticise and enjoy the delights of scenic fancy: These now are past! The nice discriminations, of the actors face, and of the actors feeling, are now all lost in the vast void of the new theater of Drury Lane" (quoted in Langhans, 53). But for nearly a century, his pleas went unanswered.

Scenery, Lighting, and Machines

Scenery and other effects were not invented for the post-1660 stage but derived from the early seventeenth-century court masques created primarily by architect and stage designer Inigo Jones (1573–1652). When Davenant began theatrical productions in 1656, he teamed up with Jones's nephew and fellow designer John Webb (1611–72), and after the restoration at Lincoln's Inn Fields, Davenant and Webb chose to combine the scenic features of Caroline public and court theaters, the thrust stage of the former and the picture stage of the latter. Almost all of the acting took place on the forestage, with entrances and exits through the two sets of proscenium doors on either side of the stage. Balconies above these doors were also used as playing space, particularly in Spanish plays like *The Adventures of Five Hours* (1662) or those likewise derived from Roman comedies like Shakespeare's *The Comedy of Errors*. The proscenium walls could represent interior or exterior walls or, oddly, "could even represent an interior while the exterior was simultaneously shown on the wings and back shutters."[13]

As this suggests, at least initially scenery was used less as realistic backdrop than for its own sake. The area behind the proscenium, almost twice as deep as the forestage, initially contained a frontispiece and three side wings on each side, parallel to the line of the stage itself, with a group of shutters at the back. The wings decreased in height from front to back, and the stage surface rose from the front to the back shutters. The assumption is that wings and shutters ran in grooved tracks top and bottom and that several sets of shutters enabled the back of the scene to be changed, or that they could all be pulled apart to reveal a scene set behind. This was the "discovery area," also called the "scene," often used in comedies that required a fast shift of place or room. During the Carolean period (1660–85), the near-simultaneity of action indigenous to the popular drama of John Fletcher and its imitators was enhanced by scenic shifts of this sort. Later, by the mid-eighteenth century, "shutters could be run on behind any wing positions" (Visser, 74), thus allowing more variation between separate "discoveries" or the swift changes of setting particularly suitable for the frantic pace of farce or pantomime.

Discoveries of various kinds were used for a variety of purposes, for instance, when a set piece of some elaborateness or shock value was called for, whether Juliet's tomb, the temple setting of *The Indian Queen* (1664), or the prison scene of *The Mourning Bride* (1697). This space could be extended to the depth of the back wall, and Garrick extended it even farther, opening the wall itself for *Henry VIII* in 1761 to expose the street behind the theater. For such long scenes, the perspective was maintained in gradually diminishing scenic vistas. In the early theaters, a second set of shutters suspended above the first and worked independently allowed "heavenly" discoveries particularly useful for operatic or fantasy productions. Visser notes that by the mid-eighteenth century, wings could be set at oblique angles as well as parallel to the stage front; these oblique wings, unlike the parallel wings operated by stage personnel, were operated by machines under the stage. Both systems were in use by the late seventeenth century and through the eighteenth century, along with drop scenes operated by rollers. There were, however, clear limitations to this

method. Its "fixity of design," as Visser points out, made "the part of the
stage behind the proscenium . . . ultimately inhospitable to the actor,
who could not move up or down it without threatening the perspective
effect" (85). This problem was countered to some extent by the use of
set scenes, "pieces" such as rocks or mountains with concealed ramps
that individuals or armies could descend, caves into which they could
disappear, or platforms from which they might speak, turning the area
behind the proscenium into acting space, and coinciding with or perhaps
hastening the retreat from the forestage that occurred gradually during
the eighteenth century.

   Although early scene designers, even the famous ones like John
Webb, worked largely unacknowledged except by fellow theater profes-
sionals, as the work of such designers became more important during
the eighteenth century, they became more well known. "Covent Garden
could take pride in the work of John Inigo Richards and Nicholas Thomas
Dall, while Drury Lane correspondingly drew attention to the creations
of its Robert Carver" (Nicoll 1980, 137), and the names of these designers
began appearing in playbills and published editions of plays. After Garrick's tour of the continent in the early 1760s, he returned to revamp
the lighting at Drury Lane, an effort that in turn made changes in scenic
design possible. For Drury Lane's production of *Harlequin's Invasion* in
1768, designer Domenico Angelo worked with transparencies in a new
way, so that scenes changed character when lighted from the back rather
than the front. As described by Angelo's son, his father "caused screens
to be placed diagonally which were covered with scarlet, crimson, and
bright blue [fabric], which, having a powerful light before them, but
turning them towards the scenes, reflected these various colours alternately, with a success that astonished and delighted the audience. Indeed,
the whole stage appeared on fire."[14] Perhaps the most famous of the scene
designers during the Garrick era was Phillip James de Loutherbourg. For
Garrick's *A Christmas Tale* in 1773, de Loutherbourg made magic on
stage:

> [A]s Floridor visits Camilla while the evil spirits whom he was left
> to guard escape, the stage directions note that "the objects in
> the garden vary their colors." The audience was startled by the
> varicolored lights. One spectator described it thus: "It was a sud-
> den transition in a forest scene, where the foliage varies from green
> to blood colour. This contrivance was entirely new; and the effect
> was produced by placing different coloured silks in the flies, or

> side scenes, which turned on a pivot, and with lights behind,
> which so illumined the stage, as to give the effect of enchantment.
> (Dircks, 66)

Although Nicoll notes that de Loutherbourg invented very few of the effects he used, his innovations on existing techniques gave new vibrancy to the late eighteenth-century stage.

Besides moving scenery, machines effected descents from above and ascents from below the stage, and were apparently functioning on the earliest Carolean stages.[15] The noise of the machinery producing such "risings" was generally masked by the thunder-and-lightning effects appropriate to such supernatural impositions. The larger traps upstage could raise scenery, beds, and other properties as well as actors, whereas "flaps" backstage were used only for scenery. Machines creating descents from above were more complex, allowing not only vertical movement but diagonal and horizontal "flyings," whether of the witches in Davenant's *Macbeth* (1663) or the elaborate "palaces of the Gods" scenes in Thomas Betterton's *The Prophetess* (1690). Like today's film stunt work, the more complex the effects and machinery, the more dangerous, and only dummies were used in flyings after a serious accident in 1736.

Like traps, sound effects dated from Shakespeare's time. Thunder was created by rolling balls down a "thunder run," a wooden trough situated above either the stage or the auditorium; in the latter case, the movement shook the auditorium for an even more lifelike effect. Effects of wind and rain were used to create storms in plays like Dryden and Davenant's version of *The Tempest* (1667) or Fletcher's *The Sea Voyage* (1622) throughout their long life in the repertory.

When plays began in the afternoon, as they did at the beginning of the Carolean period, lighting was largely supplied by daylight from the windows, supplemented by candles in chandeliers in the auditorium, on the forestage, and behind the proscenium, with oil-powered footlights used as early as the 1670–71 season. Since the auditorium was not darkened during the performance, a benighted stage could only be suggested in these early theaters by actors carrying torches or "dark lanthorns." Candles and lamps were also placed on the backs of wings and on lighting poles between the wings and footlights, with oil lamps gradually replacing candles up through the mid-eighteenth century. When Garrick abolished the forestage chandeliers in 1765–66, the backstage required additional lighting, probably ground lighting, and footlights were added or enhanced. These changes enabled the stage to be darkened by masking the wing lights, raising the chandeliers, and lowering, literally, the footlights through traps. Lightning was usually achieved by lighting and smoke effects, but occasionally more hazardous fire or fireworks were used—with tanks of water nearby in case of accident.

Music and Dance

Along with visual and sound effects, music and dance also became more important with the increase in entr'acte entertainments around the turn of the century, although they had also existed in the earliest Carolean productions: "Between 1660 and about 1705 scarcely a play was mounted that was not accompanied by vocal and instrumental music—often in abundance—newly composed by the best masters."[16] While most new plays provided opportunities for a song or dance—comedies turned farcical bits into dances, tragedies used songs to set a melancholy mood—spectacular productions particularly exploited these capabilities: John Dryden and Sir Robert Howard's *The Indian Queen*, Davenant's *Macbeth*, Dryden and Davenant's *The Tempest*. We can assume that at least part of the interest in sorcery and necromancy displayed in a number of comedies from Dryden's *An Evening's Love; or, The Mock Astrologer* (1671) to Aphra Behn's *The Rover, Part 2* (1681) during the 1670s and early 1680s may be attributed to the opportunity such characters and scenes afforded for music, dance, and special effects.

The first famous composer connected with the seventeenth-century theater was Henry Purcell, active during the 1680s and 1690s, and his presence seemed to inspire playwrights like Dryden to integrate music more fully into their drama, while even a nonmusical comedy like William Congreve's *The Old Batchelor* (1693) benefited from Purcell's overture (called first and second music) and his two songs strategically placed in the last act.[17] Almost all comedies, both old and new, ended with a festive celebration of song and dance, the visible embodiment of newfound harmony. By the end of the seventeenth century, these closing dances had become so elaborate that they were almost separate from the play, perhaps helping to develop the audience's taste for separate entertainments and afterpieces.

On the whole, we can assume that such interpolations of music and dance were of variable quality, much like those in classic Hollywood musicals. In the hands of more than competent playwrights and composers, they could genuinely add to the play or film, and/or a good performer could elevate a song or dance beyond its merits, but only at times was there a true wedding of talent in text, song, dance, and execution. In the seventeenth century, one such matrimony produced the operatic version of Dryden and Howard's *The Indian Queen*, originally produced in 1664, which in 1694–95 had music added by Purcell and entered into a second substantial "run." As Price points out (200–2), most of the musical additions are incidental; only the elaboration of Queen Zempoalla's portentous dream sequence in act 3, scene 2 is an integral part of the plot and mood, foretelling her eventual fall and suicide. Although such completely integrated scenes were rare, Price notes that scenes of music and dance became more frequent and longer in nonmusical plays around the turn of the century, at the same time that interludes of music and/or dance and afterpieces were becoming more common and just before Italian opera came along to introduce another kind of competition. In fact, opera and pantomime, introduced by manager-performer John Rich at Lincoln's Inn Fields after 1714, together served to divorce music and dancing from serious drama and comedy, permitting drama to "shed the musical burden it had borne since 1660" (Price, 233).[18] Songs and incidental music remained, but they no longer threatened to overwhelm the plays that contained them.

Financial Management, Operations, and Procedures

The finances and operations of theatrical production changed relatively little between 1660 and 1779, such that the customs and procedures established just after the Restoration remained, with variations, throughout the period.[19] The two original patents given to Killigrew and Davenant by Charles II gave them financial control over their companies, plus the ability to pass on the patent itself through inheritance or sale.[20] Despite some periods of disruption, especially during the hard times between 1685 and 1714, the two original patents remained extant except for the years 1709–14 when Christopher Rich was "silenced," and in 1779 they were held by the owners at Drury Lane and Covent Garden.[21] At various times between 1660 and 1779, other theaters operated under a license, usually granted for a temporary period by the monarch via the

Lord Chamberlain's office to an individual, although the license William III gave to the actors rebelling from the United Company in 1695 was unrestricted. In the 1760s and 1770s, Samuel Foote was licensed to operate at the Haymarket only in the summer while the two patent theaters were closed, and the license expired with his death. Despite these differences, while in operation licenses were treated as if they were patents, giving managers absolute control over their companies.

To gain extra money, owner-managers might seek outside investors, particularly when they needed substantial capital investment to build new theaters or extensively renovate existing ones.[22] Investors were usually repaid with a flat sum, or "rent," for each day of operation, and perhaps a free seat for every night of performance. Vanbrugh in 1705 offered investors in his new opera house no money but lifetime passes and the ability to make special requests about programming instead. Although a company at any time might have a number of shares owned by individual investors, the majority controlling interest was always in the hands of the owner-manager or managers. A few leading actors in the company might also own another kind of share, entitling them to a portion of the profits, but such shares were nontransferable. More pertinently, as Milhous points out (1980, 6–12), power over the company and control over operations varied with individual owners' styles and capabilities. Of the two original patentees, Davenant was both competent and able to share operational control; after his death in 1668, the Duke's Company continued smoothly under the leadership of his designated assistants, actors Henry Harris and Thomas Betterton. Killigrew, on the other hand, was inept but unwilling to share power, and his actors rebelled. The tyrannical Christopher Rich, who managed the United Company after 1693, used the powers of the patent to lower salaries arbitrarily and alter the stage without consulting or considering his actors. When his main actors walked out and were given a license to perform elsewhere, the company they formed acted initially as a cooperative, then under a manager with limited powers until the license was transferred to William Congreve and Sir John Vanbrugh in 1704. The most stable theatrical periods tended to be when the owners were managers and involved with daily operations, like Davenant, John Rich, and Garrick; unstable periods mainly had absentee or incompetent owners like the Killigrews, Christopher Rich, and Richard B. Sheridan.[23]

The main source of any company's operating capital was gate receipts. From the gross returns on any acting day, the management subtracted "house charges" or daily expenses to be used for salaries, scenery, costumes, and other house expenditures. During the Carolean period, these charges were about £25 a day, rising steadily to about £105 by 1776. Nonsharing actors and other personnel were paid from these house charges, including the prompter, treasurer, doorkeepers, boxkeepers, dressers, musicians, and dancers—all part of the permanent company.[24] There was a substantial difference between the highest-paid actors and the lowest, and between actors and other personnel, with shareholding actors and managers in a different category altogether. Through the eighteenth century, though actors' salaries rose steadily, they also declined in proportion to total expenses. The main persons, and the best paid, in any given company at any time were the manager, who chose and mounted plays, supervised rehearsals, and held sway over daily operations, combining the roles of producer, director, and stage manager in the modern theater; the prompter, who assisted the manager and was responsible for copying of parts and overseeing performances; and the treasurer, who collected income, paid bills, and kept records.

Another significant expense was for new plays, and since old plays cost nothing and new plays were also risky, managers tended to favor the old in the repertory unless competition or other factors forced them to do otherwise.[25] Overall, decisions about the repertory were made by the owner or manager, though he might share the responsibility with some of the leading actors. Once a new play was chosen, its author was permitted to cast the play from among the company, especially since he or she had often written parts with specific actors in mind. After rehearsals overseen by author, manager, and prompter,[26] the play premiered; if it reached the third night, the author received gate receipts less house charges, and the same might be true for the sixth night and, after the turn of the century, for the ninth and even twelfth nights.[27] After its premiere run, the play became the property of the acting company, although after a few years it apparently entered the public domain and could be acted anywhere.

Benefit performances also cut into the total house income. Begun at Lincoln's Inn Fields after 1695 by the rebel actors to supplement their meager salaries, benefits became standard practice at all theaters shortly after the beginning of the eighteenth century. Since these benefits took place in the spring, Milhous points out, "managers had to make their profits before Easter, even though the company played on through May and into June" (1980, 16; see also *LS*, 2:96–102). Benefits were arranged not just for star actors, but also for "house servants" such as the treasurer and prompter, while the pit doorkeepers and boxkeepers had collective benefits.[28] Though subject to some abuse and clearly favoring established performers over newcomers, the benefit performance was a healthy innovation. Emmett L. Avery notes, "A worthy actor could double his yearly salary at a single benefit, and the lesser personnel of a playhouse would have great difficulty in visualizing an adequate substitute if they were deprived of participation in the system" (*LS*, 2:102). The benefit system also established linkages between author, player, and audience which were vital and direct, rewarding service and encouraging achievement and ambition in younger performers and new playwrights.

On the credit side of the playhouse ledger, in addition to gate receipts, shareholders', and other investors' contributions were the not insubstantial gifts of clothing for costumes from royalty and other aristocratic patrons. Monarchs and their extended families also supported the theaters by direct payments[29] and command performances at Hampton Court, although the highest cash subsidies during the Georgian period went to the opera, which needed them the most. Moreover, the attendance of royal family members at a given public performance, well advertised in advance, almost always guaranteed full houses. Royal patronage brought a measure of security that went beyond money. It is not coincidental that during the reigns of those monarchs who had little or no interest in the theater—William and Mary, Anne—the theater experienced its worst crises, and that the ascension of the Hanoverians in 1714 began the long road to prosperity and good health for the London stage as well as for the Commonwealth of Britain.

Performers and Performing

Although we are mainly concerned with actors, a variety of performers gave life to the late seventeenth- and eighteenth-century theater; Philip H. Highfill, Jr., lists "actors, singers, dancers, musicians, . . . acrobats, equestrians, sibilists, ventriloquists, monologists, pyrotechnists, magicians."[30] Our problem is to get a fix on something that, before the era of film, was an ephemeral art; even musical performances of that era can be duplicated in the study or salon.[31] Yet we know that the acting and productions of any age give particular life to a dramatic piece—Burbage's Hamlet was not Betterton's, Betterton's was not Garrick's—and that the audience's social milieu and taste are both formed by and, insofar as they are an active agent in the process, help to form what occurs on stage. Contemporary commentary and criticism are not very useful in helping reconstruct such performances. The word *nature*, for example, appears regularly in such discussions, but what is natural to one age invariably seems artificial to the next. Finally, there is the human factor. Even though climate, training, and other externals are important, actors of genius, like authors or composers of genius, are born, not made.

The late seventeenth and eighteenth centuries were blessed with a long line of male and female actors who became famous, became powerful, became rich, and even, with Garrick, became respectable. At the beginning of the Carolean period, the stage inherited a long performance tradition carried over by pre-Commonwealth actors like Charles Hart and Michael Mohun; it also inherited a tradition of actors as "vagabonds" that was exacerbated by the addition of female actors sometime late in 1660. [32] Few critics, fortunately, were as virulent in their denunciations as the writer of *The Players Scourge* in 1757: "Play-actors are the most profligate wretches, and the vilest vermine, that hell ever vomited out; . . . they are the filth and garbage of the earth, the scum and stain of human nature, the excrements and refuse of all mankind, the pests and plagues of human society, the debauchers of mens [*sic*] minds and morals" (quoted in Highfill, 144). Whereas attacks on actors existed from the earliest times to the end of Garrick's reign, they tended to decline in frequency and fervency over time.

Initially in the 1660s, despite Mohun and a few other pre-Commonwealth actors, the main problems were recruitment and training, especially of female actors, who came to the profession by various means, usually from fairly respectable families who had fallen on hard times, though Nell Gwyn was a barmaid turned orange girl, operating a concession in the theater. [33] Throughout the seventeenth century, the companies seem to have maintained "nurseries" to instruct would-be actors; with the proliferation of theaters in the 1720s and 1730s, manager Henry Giffard instituted similar training programs (*LS*, 3:80–81), and at various times in the eighteenth century, actor Charles Macklin offered apprenticeships under his tutelage. Later still, managers sent scouts out into the provinces and to Dublin to spot new talent. [34]

It seems surprising that such a haphazard system would contrive to find, foster, and reward actors capable of holding audiences enthralled night after night, with as many as 70 different plays per season of 160 to 180 performances, [35] but such was the case. From the earliest years of Charles Hart, Nell Gwyn, John Lacy, and Rebecca Marshall, to the reign of the "three B's—Thomas Betterton, Elizabeth Barry, and Anne Bracegirdle—at the Lincoln Inn's Fields Company, with Colley Cibber, Anne Oldfield, and Robert Wilks at Drury Lane, on down to Garrick,

Susannah Cibber and Kitty Clive at Drury Lane versus John Rich, Peg Woffington, and Spranger Barry at Covent Garden, star actors were feted and fawned over as film or rock stars are today. Some left the stage after a few years, whether for more respectable professions or royal beds; others had careers that lasted 30 to 40 or more years (Macklin's acting career spanned 66 years). Though they were virtually indentured servants, liable to fines for nonperformance and generally unable to change to a competing theater to better their lot, actors could make good money compared with that payable at comparable "trades." Anne Oldfield certainly fared better than the man who discovered her, author George Farquhar, who wrote her best roles.

How good were these actors? What was their acting like? These are the kinds of questions for which we can unearth only approximate answers. The tools of a stage actor's trade are always the same—voice and body—but in the relatively small, thrust stage theaters of the late seventeenth and eighteenth centuries, he or she could use facial expressions or even the eyes more advantageously than in later, larger theaters. Types of drama also influenced acting performance. The set speeches and high rhetoric of rhymed couplets in heroic drama called for "rant," a style that seemed to be reborn in James Quin, while pathetic tragedy required a more musical "cadenced" delivery, both derived from oratorical styles of the day. Macklin and Garrick, by all accounts, introduced a very different style of acting from that of Quin, and when the two styles came together onstage, as in Richard Cumberland's recollection of an eighteenth-century performance of *The Fair Penitent*, the results could be odd: "Quin presented himself . . . with very little variation of cadence, and in a deep full tone, accompanied by a sawing kind of action, which had more of the senate than of the stage in it, he rolled out his heroics with an air of dignified indifference. . . . I first beheld little Garrick, then light and alive in every muscle and in every feature, come bounding on the stage, and pointing at the wittol Altamont and heavy-paced Horatio—heavens, what a transition!—it seemed as if a whole century had been stept over in the transition of a single scene" (quoted in Highfill, 165). As this quotation suggests, physical movement was as important as voice in distinguishing acting styles.

While a long-lived actor might amass 100 or more repertory roles in the course of his or her career, actors often preferred, or were preferred by audiences in, certain kinds of parts. Susannah Cibber excelled in playing tragic, pathetic heroines, whereas the more robust Kitty Clive was formed for brisk comedy. Female actors were often chosen as much for their physical attributes, such as good legs to titillate the audience in "breeches parts," as for their acting. They also had to be multitalented in ways that male actors did not: Cibber's singing was as admired as Moll Davis's dancing, and roles were written or reprised to exploit these abilities. As pantomime and musicals became more important in the repertory, actors' singing and dancing abilities became even more essential. An actor's physical size and shape also seem to have had some influence on casting, but not always: "Garrick prudently doffed aside a few characters, like Othello, which did not seem to sort with his diminutive size, but in general his artistry made the question seem unimportant. He was not particularly bothered by the fact that his leading ladies were often a head taller" (Highfill, 171).

Audiences

In a study that emphasizes repertory development and a theater responsive to its patrons, the most intriguing questions are about the late seventeenth- and eighteenth-century audiences, and while some facts can be determined, others are highly speculative.[36] Recent critical approaches, summed up in Harry William Pedicord's "The Changing Audience," temper the long-held assumptions about aristocratic, coterie audiences in even the Carolean theater: "There are sufficient grounds for thinking that audiences did change in quality and taste during these forty years, especially in the 1670s and 1690s, though the change might also be thought of as one in which the stage educated its public."[37] Comments from diaries and other sources show a great variety of people attending the theater from its earliest beginnings—royalty and courtiers, gentlemen and -women, foreign visitors, wealthy merchants and their wives, middle-class tradesmen, apprentices, lawyers, Freemasons, soldiers, sailors, and a sprinkling of pickpockets and prostitutes—while evidence from prologues and epilogues also suggests playwrights aiming at a diverse audience. Pedicord cites Garrick's prologue to Arthur Murphy's *All in the Wrong* (1761):

> What shall we do your different tastes to hit?
> You relish satire *(to the pit)* you ragouts of wit—*(to the Boxes)*
> Your taste is humour and high-season'd joke *(First Gallery)*
> You call for hornpipe, and for hearts of oak. *(Second Gallery)*
> (Pedicord 1954, 121)

The prologue to Thomas Baker's *The Humour of the Age* (1701), more
than a half-century earlier, makes a similar claim:

> Therefore this Poet to secure his own,
> Seeing the various Humours of the Town,
> Has got some Fancy to please every one.
> To gain the Court, he calls the City, Fools,
> To please the Citts, the Court he ridicules;
> To win the Beaux, that nice i'th'Box appear,
> He laughs at Gall'ry Things that ape an air.
>   (cited in Hughes 1971, 82)

Both of these prologues suggest distinctions based on the seating
arrangements in the audience, which from the early Carolean period was
segregated by ticket prices. During the late seventeenth century, boxes
cost 4 shillings, the pit 2s/6d, and galleries 1s/6d and 1s, while throughout
the eighteenth century, prices were standardized at the somewhat higher
rate of 5s, 3s, 2s, and 1s. Prices were higher for the opening of a spectacular production, lower in the lesser or nonpatent theaters. Also, part of
the admission price was refunded if one left before the afterpiece, while
the "half-price" tradition (also referred to as "after money") allowed people
to get into the theater after the third act of the main piece for half the
cost of usual admission.[38] Yet while scarcely an aristocratic audience, it
was not representative of the London populace. Pedicord convincingly
argues that, at eighteenth-century wages, even a shilling was beyond the
means of the working class, journeymen and laborers whose long hours
of work also prevented their attending late afternoon or early evening
performances (1954, 20–28). Until the closing years of the eighteenth
century, the "masses" obviously sought other forms of entertainment.

Within the theater, choice of seating was not entirely determined
by cost, and Hughes (1971, 169ff.) cautions against assuming a class-
segregated audience.[39] Those who wanted primarily to see and hear the
play seem to have congregated in the middle gallery or the boxes, while
those who wanted to be seen and heard sat in the boxes, the pit, and,
after 1685 and before 1762, the stage itself. Lively young gentlemen and
-women tended to favor the stage, the pit, or the boxes; citizens and their
wives preferred the lower and middle galleries; prostitutes inhabited the
"green boxes"; and critics, whether professional or self-styled, were usually in the pit or lower gallery. The upper or "shilling" gallery over time

became the province of apprentices, footmen, and rowdy young men, although rowdiness was not confined to the lower classes or certain areas of the theater.

By today's standards, late seventeenth- and eighteenth-century audiences were noisy and volatile throughout the 120 years. Riots of the sort that destroyed the theater interior and threatened life and limb were infrequent, but minor disturbances such as throwing fruit and vegetables, hissing and catcalling, and other performance-stoppers went on pretty regularly (see Hughes 1971, chap. 2). Yet Pedicord cautions us to distinguish between behavior that went on before the play and during the secondary entertainments, and behavior that accompanied the main piece. By and large, he concludes, "These people went to theaters to see and to hear. And see and hear they did to their entire satisfaction. We can approve the report of von Archenholz: 'When the play begins, all noise and bombardment ceases, unless some especial provocation gives rise to further disturbances; and one is bound to admire the quiet attentiveness of such an estimable folk'" (1954, 63). Hughes puts the issue in a larger context: "Two tendencies were developing simultaneously. First, there was the growing consciousness of the individual's right to express himself, not always accompanied, as Tocqueville had warned, by a sense of responsibility but more often by a love of mischief and self-display. Simultaneously, there was a quieter but actually far more important growth of tolerance for what appeared intolerable to foreigners" (1971, 65).

Criticism

It would be tidy to subdivide the dramatic criticism of the late seventeenth and eighteenth centuries into the theoretical or academic and the practical or immediate, in the same way that we might divide film or drama criticism today, but it would not be legitimate. During what is sometimes called the Age of Criticism, there was too much of the practical in the theoretical, too much immediacy and purpose in all dramatic criticism, to isolate it from the living theater of the time. John Dryden, the first and perhaps the best of the age's critics, is a good case in point. As Arthur C. Kirsch puts it, Dryden

> neither analyzes a text intensively nor speaks portentously about literary form or theory. His criticism is almost entirely occasional:

prefaces, dedications, prologues, epilogues, written to explain or
justify his own works. He changes his mind, often, and has little
patience with theoretical positions for their own sake. His interests
are practical to the point of being technical. In the modern critical
pantheon these are not virtues, and we are tempted to explain them
away either by reducing Dryden to an amateur who wrote graceful
prose and entertaining shoptalk or by magnifying him into a skeptic
who contradicted himself on the basis of consistent philosophical
premises. But Dryden was not a philosophical skeptic, and he certainly was no amateur. He was a great literary critic. . . .[40]

Most of Dryden's critical essays were published as prefaces to particular
plays recently produced on the stage, and even the freestanding ones, *Of
Dramatic Poesy* (1668) and "Heads of an Answer to Rymer" (1677), were
engaged with justifying current dramatic practices, particularly his own.
In brief, Dryden consistently argues for modern drama over classical or
neoclassical, including the restrictive "rules" and decorum advanced by
the French and advocated by Thomas Rymer in his *Tragedies of the Last
Age* (1677); he favors rhymed couplets as a medium for heroic tragedy
(though he later reversed himself); he generally prefers the home-grown
and "vehement" over the austere, foreign, and ancient. Interestingly,
much of what Dryden laid out, though unsystematic and personal, was
echoed in his eighteenth-century successors, especially during the 1770s
when defenses of English comedy against French rules and sentiment
reappear. Finally, Dryden's legacy to succeeding generations of critics
was his implicit trust in and respect for the audience's taste and judgment;
he did not seek to interpose his ideas on theirs, though he did not
mindlessly follow theirs either: "The liking or disliking of the people gives
the play the denomination of good or bad, but does not really make or
constitute it such. To please the people ought to be the poet's aim,
because plays are made for their delight; but it does not follow that they
are always pleased with good plays, or that the plays which please them
are always good" ("Defense of An Essay," Kirsch, 79).[41]

At about the turn of the century, two developments changed the
substance and face of criticism: the moralists' assault on the stage and
the rise of the periodical press. Critics in the narrower sense had existed
since the beginning of the Carolean theater, and playwrights were particularly leery of those who banded together to "damn" a play at its premiere.
Authors' prefaces to the printed versions of their plays often claim that
the play was treated unfairly because of such factions "formed before the
drama had a hearing on stage" (*LS*, 1:172). But those critics of the stage

who surfaced near the end of the seventeenth century, many of them members of the Societies for the Reformation of Manners, were different; many of them believed that the theater in and of itself was "immoral" and contributed to the degradation of society.

Their most eloquent spokesman was Jeremy Collier, still remembered today for A *Short View of the Immorality and Profaneness of the English Stage* (1698). Although he later admitted the truth, Collier purported in this work to be interested in reforming the stage, not eliminating it, and he based his attack on the ancient critical dictum, restated in Sir Philip Sidney's *Defense of Poesy* (1583), that the purpose of drama was didactic, "to recommend Virtue and discountenance Vice."[42] Collier claimed, and rightly so, that late seventeenth-century dramatists were more interested in the "delight" side of "to teach and to delight," and that this had led them to portray lewd and profane characters and actions as successful and heroic. Collier cast his net wide, excoriating not only genuine excesses in comedies, but relatively benign kinds of performances: music he deemed "almost as dangerous as Gunpowder" because it "play[ed] People out of their Senses" (Harwood, 2–3). Nonetheless, Collier and his fellow moralists had considerable impact on the production of plays and the writing of new plays during his time.

Though Collier died in 1726, his ideas, though not his witty expression of them, were picked up in the eighteenth century by moralists like William Law, whose *Unlawfulness of Stage Entertainment Fully Demonstrated* was in its fourth edition by 1759, and the anonymous *An Address to Persons of Fashion concerning Some Particulars relating to Balls, with Hints on Plays, Card Tables, Etc.* (1761) and *The Stage the Highroad to Hell* (1767) (*LS*, 4:200). Perhaps the best known and most influential of Collier's numerous progeny, however, was Sir Richard Steele. Unlike Collier, Steele steered a middle course, seeing much that needed to be rectified in the theater from a moralist's viewpoint, but wanting to effect those changes which would make it tolerable. Along with his critical writings, Steele's own plays, culminating in *The Conscious Lovers* (1722), fostered the kind of theater he supported, and the success and long stage life of that play suggests that his middle position enjoyed broad-based support.

The views of Collier and the other moralists were also argued and argued against in the periodicals that began to appear after the turn of the century. Although the dailies had neither space nor inclination to present theatrical news until the 1720s (*LS*, 2:170–71),[43] the biweeklies, weeklies, and monthlies like the *Tatler* (1709–11) and the *Spectator* (1711–12) Steele and others wrote for did offer a venue for occasional pieces on the theater that commented both on specific plays and on the state of the theater and drama more generally. According to Avery (*LS*, 2:173–78), much of this periodical criticism focused on the weakness of the present drama as opposed to that of the past, often accompanied by attacks upon opera, farce, and pantomime as vile foreign imports. Such a piece appeared in the *Universal Spectator* (10 April 1731): "In the present Condition of Theatrical Entertainments, the true End of the Stage is almost wholly lost; we go not thither to see Folly exposed, but to see it acted; whence the Paradox is solved, That the most applauded Pieces for some Years past in our Theaters, have not been the Composition of *Poets*, but of *Dancing-Masters*" (quoted in *LS*, 2:175). At the same time, other periodical writers praised such offerings as bringing new life and creative energy to the contemporary theater.

The passage of the Licensing Act in 1737, which restricted both the number of London theaters and the plays produced in them, seemed to stimulate supporters and detractors of the stage equally, and the last two-thirds of the century saw a proliferation of criticism in periodicals like the *British Journal*, *Grub Street Journal*, and *Theatrical Review*, as well as pamphlets. Though this criticism largely focused on actors and acting styles, it did not end there: "The close scrutiny given the actors carried over to a fresh examination of the plays themselves, to the accuracy of the playing texts, to the intentions of the original author, to comparative values of different treatments of similar themes, and to all that we now consider valid critical interest in drama as opposed to mere theater" (*LS*, 4:201). At the same time, Stone cautions against taking adverse criticism in press or pamphlet too seriously: "The *Theatrical Campaign* pamphlet (1767) offers on nearly every one of its forty-four pages instances of what one may, perhaps, call more discriminating criticism than that exhibited by London's twelve thousand weekly play-goers, but which in almost every instance went unheeded by both manager and public" (*LS*, 4:206). The audience, as always, had the final say.

The final and perhaps most powerful kind of "criticism" was that wielded by the state. The terms under which theatrical patents and licenses were tendered to individuals or groups included the right of the Crown to censor new plays via the Lord Chamberlain's office.[44] Specifically, sometime before it was to be performed, a new play had to be submitted to and could not be produced unless it was "passed" by that office. (It could, however, be published or, even if edited by the censor, be published in its original form.) This procedure was in force long before Charles II took the throne in 1660, as Winton points out: "In theory the Master of the Revels, a member of the royal household under the general jurisdiction of the Lord Chamberlain, was empowered to regulate rather strictly what the theater companies produced. In practice, before the interregnum, he had done so" (288). Indeed, Charles II's first Master of the Revels, Sir Henry Herbert, had held that office since 1623. Yet this power to refuse a license to a play, as opposed to editing parts of it, was exercised only intermittently during the reign of Charles II except during the Exclusion Crisis in the early 1680s.[45] With the Licensing Act of 1737, however, the Lord Chamberlain's powers were reasserted, with specific details about when plays were to be submitted, that is, two weeks before their intended premiere. Although most often used to suppress renegade performances and theaters, these powers were also used to refuse permission to some plays until they were rewritten to exclude material considered injurious to the ruling party (see Loftis 1980, 272–4).

In addition to the Lord Chamberlain's office, censoring could take place through the civil courts, and these were largely indictments against theater personnel and performances at fairs. The "Middlesex jury" was particularly active at the beginning of the eighteenth century, at the instigation of the Societies for the Reformation of Manners arresting actors as "Rogues, Vagabonds, Sturdy Beggars, and Vagrants" (Winton, 292). Unlike the political censorship during the Exclusion Crisis or the Walpole era, these courts, like the Societies which used them to harass actors, were primarily concerned with blasphemy and obscenity. As the century advanced, censorship of any kind from on high dwindled almost out of recognition; the process of self-censorship took control as the theaters responded to audiences prepared to make their feelings known.

Conclusion

Theatrical conditions affected much that went on in drama between 1660 and 1779. The kinds of plays that were fostered or produced, their success or failure, depended as much on what was possible or profitable as it did on individual writers and their capabilities. The sexual themes and tensions of many Carolean comedies and tragedies would not have been written had not female actors been available to embody them, and scenic effects had much to do with the creation of new forms such as heroic drama and pantomime. While the text played an integral role in the late seventeenth- and eighteenth-century theater, it was only a part of the collaborative process that enabled many generations of Londoners to experience and interact with their own living culture.

2

The Carolean Period

1659–1685

The reign of Charles II, the Carolean period, began in celebration and ended in crisis, with many Londoners fearing a resurgence of the divisiveness that had brought open civil strife within recent memory. The initial euphoria of the Restoration wore off all too soon, and the Exclusion Crisis of the late 1670s and early 1680s demonstrated that the healing process went only so far to bridge the gap between the separate worlds inhabited by powerful forces vying for ascendancy. And while Charles II never entirely lost control of the government even during the Exclusion Crisis, his victory over the parliamentary forces led by the Earl of Shaftsbury clarified that English political solidarity rested more on the king's personal skill as a politician and manipulator than on the monarchical system itself.

All of these traumas and political questions were played out in the drama of the time, particularly the serious forms—tragedy and heroic drama. Often concerned with usurpation and Machiavellian maneuverings at court, they seemed to represent the hopes and fears of the alert Londoners who constituted the theater audiences. Plays that

centered on the qualities of a good ruler could be interpreted as cautionary messages to that ardent theatergoer Charles, while their continued
assertion of the need for authority and order, especially in the late
1670s, seemed to be issuing warnings to the rest of the populace of the
chaos that threatened. Yet just a few years earlier, the drama was asserting a very different message—that it was safe and satisfying to flout
authority. Both comedies and early heroic plays show, again and again,
prosperous endings for young people who revolt against unreasonable
rulers, parents, and guardians, and who follow their own impulses to
glory and glorious sexual and verbal freedom. It is to this period that
the plays of William Wycherley, Sir George Etherege, and the Howards
belong, as do some works by John Dryden, Aphra Behn, and Thomas
Shadwell. How, in such a short span of years, had the drama changed
so much?

If we look only to the external political world, we will be misled,
for drama as living theater responds less to reality than to perceptions of
reality in its audiences. It also responds to internal theories, voiced or
unvoiced, about what drama is or should be. What we find, then, is that
during certain parts of the Carolean period, drama was what might be
called "desire-based," that is, intent on giving audience members pleasing
images of themselves in safe ways, playing out their fantasies on stage.
Figures such as the male and female rake, or the usurper who turns out
to be the true king, are projections of latent wishes for freedom and
power, and skilled dramatists made these projections guilt-free by means
of carefully designed characters and plots. They also enhanced the affective qualities of their plays exponentially, so that audience members
might feel themselves enthralled and then purified while in the theater.
Moral actions, endings, and characters existed to placate those audience
members who needed them, even though for many they were largely
specious and unnecessary. Hobbesian survival tactics[1] were played out
each afternoon in stage versions of contemporary drawing rooms and
malls, or exotic foreign locales; superior intellect, physical prowess, and
linguistic eloquence enabled some characters to win the prizes and stump
their competitors. Love and war were alike—games and combats to be
enjoyed by both participants and spectators.

By late in the Carolean period, the voices of political reality had
forced serious drama to make accommodations, as at the end of the
century social reality would make inroads in comic drama. But the early
Carolean forms and their exhuberance would linger on much longer in
the repertory, well into the eighteenth century, when they would finally

be driven out by a recognizably different kind of London audience with different expectations for dramatic entertainment.

Tragicomedy: Secret Love

> QU.:   *As for my self I have resolv'd*
> *Still to continue as I am, unmarried:*
> *The cares, observances, and all the duties*
> *Which I should pay an Husband, I will place*
> *Upon my people; and our mutual love*
> *Shall make a blessing more then Conjugal,*
> *And this the States shall ratifie.*
>   (Secret Love, 5.1.456–62)

> FLOR.:   *La ye now, is not such a marriage as good as*
> *wenching,* Celadon?
>
> CEL.:   *This is very good, but not so good,* Florimell.
>   (Secret Love, 5.1.560–62)[2]

These paired renunciations—one of conjugal love, the other of unlimited freedom—mark the final climactic scene of John Dryden's *Secret Love; or, the Maiden Queen* (1667), a play that brilliantly combined the appeal of late 1660s heroic drama—high style, grand settings, grander persons and passions—and witty comedy in its two plots. In the humorous plot, Celadon and Florimell epitomize the clever, coolheaded, energetic young sophisticates who might be expected to hang around the court, whether the Queen of Sicily's or Charles II's, while the Queen of the high plot is the ideal ruler, combining passionate grandeur with noble self-sacrifice. The parallel renunciations serve to accentuate the substantive difference between the play's "high" and "low" actions: that personal desires must give way to public needs for rulers but not for others. Thus, whatever the realities of Whitehall and the Court of St. James, the monarchial ideal was awake and thriving in the public mind and on the public stage. As described by Nicholas Jose, this ideal included a return to stability, a fresh start on healing the divisions that had plagued English society for more than two decades.[3] While panegyric poetry was the form of literature that most directly responded to this public desire for healing, the drama had its part.

Though authors' names did not yet appear on playbills, the audience watching the first performance of *Secret Love* at the King's Company theater in Bridges Street, Drury Lane, was probably aware that it was the work of John Dryden (1631–1700), already proving himself one of the most prolific and versatile of the new Carolean playwrights. Building on his successes with the heroic *The Indian Queen* (1664) and *The Indian Emperor* (1665), Dryden was ready for another hit, and the company at Bridges Street was ready to share it with him. The cast of *Secret Love* included the best King's Company players in roles designed to show off their particular talents, and the stage design was suitably elaborate, though not so exotic as for *The Indian Queen* or *The Indian Emperor*. This production of *Secret Love* thus demonstrates how far the theater had come in the relatively short time since the Restoration.

Nonetheless, it was still in the process of reconstituting itself after the long hiatus of the interregnum. The two theater managers, Killigrew and Davenant, had overcome formidable obstacles, including the lack of theaters, actors, technicians, and "trained" audiences.[4] Innovations such as movable scenery and the use of female actors to play female parts had proved good drawing cards for those new audiences, but external circumstances such as the London Fire and the Great Plague of 1665–66 had closed the theaters for months at a time and interrupted the momentum of regular performances. Faced with so many problems, the managers would not have considered the lack of new plays and playwrights their first priority. For a time, they were content to draw upon a storehouse of old plays, many by Sir Francis Beaumont and John Fletcher, and, as can be seen by the list of most popular plays, audiences were satisfied enough to see new productions of old favorites like *The Maid's Tragedy* (1610) and *The Scornful Lady* (1613). But the key to successful competition between rival theater companies so closely matched in talent and capability was innovation, and Killigrew and Davenant soon perceived that only brand-new plays would help establish a competitive edge.[5] Thus, we see overall a heavier proportion of new popular plays during this 25-year period than ever again, about 60 percent. Predictably, the first of such plays, like Thomas Porter's *The Villain* (1663) or Sir Robert Howard's *The Surprisal* (1665), simply offered new plots very much in the Fletcherian mold, but by the mid-1660s, genuinely new subgenres had also begun to emerge: witty comedies with contemporary characters (Howard's *The Committee*, 1665), heroic plays with exotic historical settings (Roger Boyle, Earl of Orrery's *Mustapha*, 1665), Spanish plays that put heroism into a contemporary foreign setting (Sir Samuel Tuke's

Most Popular Plays: 1659–1685
(Plays with Nine or More Performances
with Performance Numbers in Parentheses)

COMEDY
*The Adventures of Five Hours** (21)
The Alchemist (10)
Bartholomew Fair (11)
*The Committee** (10)
*The Country-Wife** (4)[†]
The Cutter of Coleman Street[‡] (13)
Epicoene (13)
*An Evening's Love** (12)
Love in a Maze (10)
Love Lies a'Bleeding (10)
*The Plain-Dealer** (6)[††]
*The Rover** (3)[††]
The Scornful Lady (13)
*She Would if She Could** (11)
*Sir Martin Mar-all** (27)
*The Sullen Lovers** (12)
The Tempest[‡] (32)
*The Wits** (13)

TRAGEDY
The Bondman (10)
*The Conquest of Granada** (9)
*Don Carlos** (12)
Hamlet (11)
*The Indian Emperor** (14)
*The Indian Queen** (11)
Macbeth[‡] (17)
The Maid's Tragedy (9)
The Moore of Venice (9)
*Mustapha** (10)
Rollo, Duke of Normandy (11)
The Siege of Rhodes (19)
The Traitor (6)[†]
*Venice Preserved** (4)[†]
*The Villain** (16)
Vittoria Corombona (5)[†]

TRAGICOMEDY
*The Comical Revenge** (14)
The Humorous Lieutenant (19)
*Marriage A-la-Mode** (4)[†]
*Secret Love** (17)

HISTORY
Henry VIII (12)

OPERA
Psyche** (13)

NOTES
*New play
[†]More popular than numbers would indicate
[‡]New revision of pre-1660 play

Adventures of Five Hours, 1663). By 1667, Dryden, the fledgling play-wright, had tried writing in all the new modes, with variable success, in *The Wild Gallant* (1663), a wit comedy; *The Indian Queen* and *The Indian Emperor*, heroic dramas; and *The Rival Ladies* (1664), a Spanish play.

By the time of *Secret Love*, he was experimenting further, this time with a complicated mixture of heroic and comic actions in two plots which, although they touched upon one another at times, were essentially separate. He was not absolutely original in this; the "split plot tragicomedy," as Robert D. Hume has called it,[6] had already appeared and been successful in the repertory in old plays like Fletcher's *The Humorous Lieutenant* (1619) and new plays like Etherege's *The Comical Revenge* (1664). But *Secret Love* combined the familiar and the unfamiliar so well that it earned its status as a "hit" play of the 1666–67 season.

Although Dryden, along with some other playwrights, was perfectly aware and indeed at the vanguard of current theories about literary merit, structure, and purpose, his theories invariably followed his own and others' practices.[7] For example, his *Of Dramatic Poesy*, written in 1668, was essentially an exegesis of his own and his fellow playwrights' success in producing an indigenous mode of tragedy[8] called heroic drama, which delighted contemporary London audiences with its intricate design and extravagance. Yet for all its newness, heroic drama, the source of the high plot in *Secret Love*, was at base a repertory product, a combination of the attractive qualities of previous seasons' successful tragedies, which were predominantly by or derived from plays by Fletcher, such as *The Maid's Tragedy*, and his Jacobean or Caroline imitators—such as John Webster's *Vittoria Corombona; or, the White Devil* (1612) and James Shirley's *The Traitor* (1631)—along with the only Shakespearean tragedies popular during this period: *Othello, Hamlet,* and *Macbeth*.[9] Despite their differences, all these popular tragedies share some common features: all are, or purport to be, grounded in historical "fact"; all aim to teach their audiences morality; all include deaths, display passions, and use high rhetoric; all emphasize conflicts between honor and political maneuvering; and all end with the hero's vindication. Structurally, the Fletcherian tragedies and, to a lesser extent, the Shakespearean ones offer multiple climaxes and plot turns which keep the audience guessing; Fletcherian tragedy also provides "protean" characters, who are "monsters and saints, living abstractions and combinations of irreconcilable extremes," and who "elude our grasp by changing shape from moment to moment."[10] Such characters are able to serve the elaborate plot configurations more readily than more solid characters would.

The antecedents of heroic drama are even more evident in another group of plays popular on the early Restoration stage, most of which postdate Fletcher and Shakespeare: Philip Massinger's *The Bondman* (1624) and *The Virgin Martyr* (1621), Davenant's *Love and Honour* (1646) and *The Siege of Rhodes* (1656). Whereas in Fletcherian drama, character is subservient to plot, these plays are firmly focused on the heroic character itself, usually represented in one or more figures; the plot, in effect, exists to display character.[11] The heroic hero (male or female) is the best that nature produces—powerful, passionate, eloquent, and attractive, he or she stands above the play's other characters and, to some extent, even above the action to become an example and an inspiration. Such an ideal of inspiration and imitation is at the heart of epic theory as interpreted by Davenant in his prefaces to works like *Gondibert, An Heroick Poem* (1650) and *The Siege of Rhodes:* "since Nature hath made us prone to Imitation, by which we equall the best or the worst, how much those Images of Action prevail upon our mindes which are delightfully drawn by Poets."[12] Davenant made it clear that his purpose was to create indigenous English epics, whether in poetic or dramatic form, and to "advance the Characters of Vertue in the shapes of Valor and conjugal Love."[13]

Because of when Davenant's heroic plays were written and his epic theory advanced, some critics have suggested a link with the interregnum and with its hero Cromwell, who had so recently demonstrated that will and might often did not coincide with established legal authority. Hence, perhaps, the intense interest after the Restoration in literary forms, epic and heroic drama, that reflect conflict or reconciliation of high ideals and worldly success. As Susan Staves writes, "The heroic drama indulges in a fantasy of pure honor while simultaneously acknowledging such honor to be impossible. Its early protagonists are creatures of wish-fulfillment dreams. They always behave well and always preserve honor intact under kaleidoscopically shifting circumstances—and are thus quite unlike the vast majority of real royalists who endured the Civil War. . . . Characters like Boyle's Mustapha behave as their creators and their audiences would like to have behaved, but, for the most part, did not" (51–52). But not all the heroes of heroic drama behaved as well as Mustapha did, and Dryden was significantly responsible for the alternative, a more erratic and exciting hero.

The plots of the heroic plays in the repertory, whether inherited from the Commonwealth period or written during the early Carolean period itself, are a curious blend of climactic action, often on a battlefield or in the midst of political upheaval, punctuated by rhetorical displays: exhortations, debates on the fine points of love and honor, set pieces of various kinds. The heroes do not develop, but reveal their inner qualities in the crises the dramatist has constructed for that purpose; they are magnificently humorless, self-conscious without being self-aware, and separated from the rest of humanity by their character and role. They are not models in the sense that their specific behavior is to be imitated, but they are meant to be attractive and inspirational figures, in the tradition of what Eugene Waith calls "the Herculean Hero":

> [This hero] belongs to the realm of the semi-divine, the wonderful, the mysterious. Though he is a man, he is so far removed from the ordinary that the generic classification hardly contains him. His origins may lie in religious ritual; his life is imbued with meanings only half understood. His exploits are strange mixtures of beneficence and crime, of fabulous quests and shameful betrayals, of triumph over wicked enemies and insensate slaughter of the innocent, yet the career is always a testimony to the greatness of a man who is almost a god—a greatness which has less to do with goodness as it is usually understood than with the transforming energy of the divine spark. That is not to say that tales about the hero excuse his moral defects, but rather that they point to a special morality. What matters most is something difficult to define, which pushes the hero to the outermost reaches of the human and even beyond. To the Greeks, this quality, which makes the hero a dream-image of what a man might be, was *árete*, the ideal of the nobility, the *aristoi*. The Romans called it *virtus*, a word related to both *vir* and *vis*, "man" and "energy."[14]

Implicit in Waith's delineation is that such heroes, whether male or female, subscribe to a "masculine" code of honor.

As one might expect from this description, morality is often a problem in heroic drama, where conventional behavior and Christian values are often at odds with heroic "grandeur." Dryden begs the question in various ways in his heroic plays: by setting his heroes in a non-Christian universe (*The Indian Queen*), by offering multiple heroes (*The Indian Emperor*), or by blatant deux ex machina conversions and final reconciliations. In the heroic plot of *Secret Love*, he employs all these devices with enhanced skill to ask the questions, How does individual heroism benefit society? In what ways must rulers be both capable and virtuous? What is the relationship between political responsibility and personal freedom? The questions, however, are more important than the answers, since an operating premise of all heroic plays, especially Dryden's, is "that the exaltation of the self [can] lead to morally acceptable action."[15] Furthermore, Dryden and other heroic dramatists were extremely elastic about their version of "morally acceptable."

Which brings us back to *Secret Love*. Again, it was probably the popular success of *The Comical Revenge* and *The Humorous Lieutenant* that suggested to Dryden the possibility of writing a double-plot play with separate serious and humorous actions, and his gamble paid off. The diarist Samuel Pepys, who saw it at least five times, indicated where the audience had focused its attention: "though I have often seen [*Secret Love*], yet [it] pleases me infinitely, it being impossible, I think, ever to have the Queen's part, which is very good and passionate, and Florimel's part, which is the most comicall that ever was made for woman, ever done better than they two are by young Marshall and Nelly" (24 May 1667; *LS*, 1:109). Although Pepys's remarks indicate his appreciation of *Secret Love*'s regular plot, the main attraction was the two central actresses and their leading roles in the two plots, which also determined the affective center of the play.

The high or heroic plot of *Secret Love* centers on the Queen of Sicily, who is secretly in love with Philocles, one of her subjects. Her royalty, reticence, and political acuity prevent her from declaring herself to him, and he, of course, never dreams she loves him. Two complications of this central dilemma are that (a) her subjects want her to ensure the succession by marrying Prince Lysimantes and (b) Philocles is in love with Lysimantes's sister, Candiope. After revealing her secret to her confidante Asteria, the Queen tests Candiope and Philocles, and when they prove constant, forbids their marriage. The lovers run off, and she sends Lysimantes to arrest them, but instead he and Philocles join forces and capture the citadel, making the Queen their prisoner. Lysimantes tries to force her to marry him by threatening to expose her secret, but she outmaneuvers him by letting the lovers marry, declaring Lysimantes her successor, and rededicating herself to her subjects and eternal virginity. The revolution, then, is successful in that everyone gets something: Philocles gets Candiope; Lysimantes, the kingdom; and the Queen, her restored "glory."

Derived from Madeleine de Scudéry's *Artamène; ou, Le Grand Cyrus*,[16] a French romance, the serious plot closely resembles those of other contemporary heroic plays. It is filled with elevated language, whether blank verse, couplets, or "something approximating verse" (*CD*, 9:336), and has larger-than-life characters and events. Initially, this plot seems to resemble Orrery's heroic plays more than Dryden's previous ones because of its central heroine,[17] its reliance on language over action, and its presentation of a courtly world in place of the political battlefields of *The Indian Queen* and *The Indian Emperor*. Yet this resemblance is more apparent than real, for Dryden's Queen is the very opposite of the strict exemplary females that Orrery produced, whose virtue was unquestioned and who were never seriously tempted to forgo it. The Queen of Sicily, like Dryden's male figures such as Montezuma of *The Indian Queen* or Guyomar of *The Indian Emperor*, is torn by conflicting passions, desires, and obligations, and she is rigorously and endlessly tested to emerge, finally, victorious over her inner and outer "enemies." Like Dryden's male heroes, she exemplifies the highest achievements of humankind, and the play shows the difficulty of attaining them.

In the Queen, then, Dryden is again presenting an active developing hero, although the play's conflicts are more verbal and psychological than in *The Indian Queen* or *The Indian Emperor* and its setting is the court rather than the camp. In these and other heroic plays, the hero's battle for self-control and his or her attempts to make the "right" (i.e., heroic) choices are offset and analogized by actual battles for political control. The balance between outer responsibilities and inner conflicts is resolved by the plot in accordance with the hero's character. In the serious action of *Secret Love*, Dryden concentrates on the inner struggle more than the outer (to the extent that the taking of the citadel, though performed offstage, strikes a rather jarring note), and we spend most of the time watching the Queen's psychic turmoil, her contradictory impulses, and her temporary losses of control. On the one hand, such treatment restores Fletcherian affectiveness to heroic action, by heightening climaxes and rendering character emotionally. On the other hand, it suggests Dryden's continued interest in the hero's psychology.

The Queen first attracts our attention when she reveals her secret to Asteria, admitting how this passion is causing her physical and mental deterioration. As the play unfolds, it reveals this truth in climactic confrontations enhanced by Dryden's use of affective rhetoric to draw a detailed portrait of the tormented Queen. Though the medium is prose rather than heroic couplets, Dryden employs many of the same techniques here as in his tragedies. For example, in act 4, scene 2, after the citadel has been taken, the Queen's reactions range from regal acceptance to near hysteria to despair:

AST.:   O vertue, impotent and blind as Fortune!
           Who would be good, or pious, if this Queen
           Thy great Example suffers?

QU.:   Peace, *Asteria*, accuse not vertue;
           She has but given me a great occasion
           Of showing what I am when Fortune leaves me.

AST.:   *Philocles*, to do this!
          Qu. I, *Philocles*, I must confess 'twas hard!
          But there's a fate in kindness
          Still, to be least return'd where most 'tis given.
          Where's *Candiope*?

AST.:   *Philocles* was whispering to her.

QU.:   Hence Screech-owl; call my Guards quickly there;
          Put 'em apart in several Prisons.
          Alas! I had forgot I have no Guards,
          But those which are my Jaylors.
          Never till now unhappy Queen:
          The use of pow'r, till lost, is seldom known;
          Now I would strike, I find my Thunder gone.
                                                (4.2.50–68)

As Fletcher often did, Dryden heightens the sentiments of the opening lines into apostrophe, using the weighted terms *vertue* and *fortune* and underscoring the Queen's position as "great Example." The Queen's response aptly picks up the sounds and key words of the introduction, as she responds nobly to the challenge, and even the introduction of Philocles's name elicits only the sad paradox of "kindness . . . least return'd where most 'tis given." It is all the more startling, then, when Candiope's name linked with his produces a passionate outburst, underscored with harsh sounds: "Hence Screech-owl," immediately followed by the despairing notes of powerlessness. In the space of 19 lines, Dryden moves from the surface of noble sentiments to the harsh reality of usurpation, as the Queen is forced to confront it emotionally.

In its ability to reproduce and engender emotion, this scene is Fletcherian. But unlike such scenes in Fletcherian drama, it also constitutes a climax of developing character—the nadir of the Queen's emotional imbalance. Dryden's Queen combines the virtuous qualities of his earlier male heroes with the emotional ones of heroic villainnesses such as Zempoalla and Almeria. Her passionate and vindictive outbursts, alternating with lofty sentiments and dedications to glory, enable Dryden to incorporate the conflicts within the heroic temper. By allowing the political dimension of the play to recede into the background, Dryden focuses on the individual hero, showing the pitfalls of the self-serving ethic he has elsewhere lauded. Although he reconciles the struggle conventionally by showing the Queen's reassertion of control as beneficial to herself and society, her success is saturated with loss. Unlike Montezuma of *The*

Indian Queen, who develops and expands his awareness in the course of the play, the Queen of Sicily learns only to subvert her passions and curtail her freedom. Whereas Montezuma could find private fulfillment with Orazia along with public fulfillment as king, the Queen can satisfy only the greater of these two goals at the expense of the lesser.[18] She is caught in the gender trap of reconciling personal needs and public role in ways that male heroic heroes never are, and Dryden brilliantly exploits the conflict. He could, after all, have depicted the Queen's need for an heir as her paramount concern; instead, it is pure lust that motivates her. He could have reconciled her to a marriage with Lysimantes, however second-rate; instead, he leaves her austere and lonely. In short, Dryden could have made the choices easier or the Queen's character more pliable; instead, he gave her a tiger's heart and a golden cage. As a result, Dryden raises the affective level of the serious action and complicates the basic structure and conventions of heroic drama by exacerbating rather than reconciling the conflict between public virtue and individual *virtu*, highlighting it even further by the presence of the second plot and its characters.

The humorous plot of *Secret Love* presents the lively courtship of Celadon and Florimell. Returning to Sicily after his travels, Celadon begins courting Florimell, the Queen's Maid of Honor, along with Olinda and Sabina, two sisters. Florimell is prepared to make him a courtly lover for her own amusement, but Celadon is too fickle to pass the test of constancy and too witty or too honest to act it convincingly. So Florimell takes matters into her own hands, dressing as a gallant to humiliate him by seducing Olinda and Sabina, thus proving herself the "better man." In the end, despite (or because of) his failure as an ideal lover and hers as a decorous virgin, they are reconciled and their mutual capitulation is rendered in the form of a highly entertaining proviso scene.[19] Although the humorous action borrows some of its incidents and dialogue from various French romances, it is essentially a plot of Dryden's own devising.[20] Despite its courtly setting, in fact, the courtship action, heroes, and repartee of this plot closely resemble those found in popular contemporary comedies like Sir Robert Howard's *The Committee* (1662), the Duke of Newcastle's *The Country Captain* (1661), Dryden and Newcastle's *Sir Martin Mar-all* (1667), or James Howard's *All Mistaken* (1665). As in the serious plot, Dryden replaces the physical action of these competing plays with vigorous language and psychological movement.

Most discussions of the humorous plot have properly focused on its hero and heroine and their relationship to other such couples in Carolean comedy. All agree that they are more refined and witty than most of their contemporaries, and therefore significant in the development of indigenous comedy during the Carolean period. They are, in many ways, the archetypal "gay couple" identified by John Harrington Smith as antagonistic lovers who battle their way through a courtship process.[21] When looking for analogues and antecedents for their lively pair in the repertory, one finds them in many older Fletcherian comedies, such as *The Scornful Lady* and *The Wits*, where males and females engage in confrontations of various sorts. One also looks to the plays of Ben Jonson for social characters who make it their business to cozen others, whether for gain (*The Alchemist*) or for fun (*Epicoene*). In the 1671 Preface to *An Evening's Love*, Dryden in fact refers to the characters of *Epicoene*: "Dauphine (who, with the other two gentlemen, is the same character with my Celadon in the *Maiden Queen*, and with Wildblood in this)," and Truewit, "the best character of a gentleman which Ben Jonson ever made" (CD, 9:208, 207). Slightly earlier, in 1668, Dryden had produced a discussion of *Epicoene/The Silent Woman* in his "Of Dramatic Poesy: An Essay," wherein he compliments Jonson: "he has here described the conversation of gentlemen in the persons of True-Wit and his friends, with more gaiety, air, and freedom, than in the rest of his comedies," and describes the "main design" as "perfection" (Kirsch 1966, 52). In this way, Dryden sought to gain both literary and social prestige for his own characters created in the image of Jonson's.

But what about Florimell—the other component part of the "gay couple"? Here we must look beyond influence to the internal needs of *Secret Love* and its parallel plots. First, the setting and serious plot of *Secret Love* forced Dryden to create a more exclusively verbal, less farcical hero and heroine than he or other Carolean dramatists had previously wrought. The play's language is therefore much wittier than what he had produced in *The Wild Gallant*. Wit may appear purely linguistically in the form of satiric descriptions such as Celadon's "how like a fool a man looks, when after all his eagerness of two Minutes before, he shrinks into a faint kiss and a cold complement" (1.2.25–28); or it may show in a quick retort such as Florimell's "ignorance is the Mother of your devotion to me" (1.2.67–68). The most elaborate of such encounters between Celadon and Florimell is the proviso sequence that ends the humorous plot; it begins with Florimell's assertion that Celadon can't marry Olinda or Sabina, the tall and short sisters, and builds from there:

FLOR.: If you marry her Sister you will get Maypoles, and if you marry her you will get Fayries to dance about them.

CEL.: Nay then the case is clear, *Florimell*; if you take 'em all from me, 'tis because you reserve me for your self.

FLOR.: But this Marriage is such a Bugbear to me; much might be if we could invent but any way to make it easie.

CEL.: Some foolish people have made it uneasie, by drawing the knot faster then they need; but we that are wiser will loosen it a little.

FLOR.: 'Tis true indeed, there's some difference betwixt a Girdle and a Halter.

CEL.: As for the first year, according to the laudable custome of new married people, we shall follow one another up into Chambers, and down into Gardens, and think we shall never have enough of one another.—So far 'tis pleasant enough, I hope.

FLOR.: But after that, when we begin to live like Husband and Wife, and never come near one another—what then Sir?

CEL.: Why then our onely happiness must be to have one mind, and one will, *Florimell*.

FLOR.: One mind if thou wilt, but prithee let us have two wills; for I find one will be little enough for me alone: But how if those wills should meet and clash, *Celadon*?

CEL.: I warrant thee for that: Husbands and Wives keep their wills far enough asunder for ever meeting: one thing let us be sure to agree on, that is, never to be jealous.

FLOR.: No; but e'en love one another as long as we can; and confess the truth when we can love no longer.

(5.1.507–35)

Verbally, Florimell and Celadon jockey for control in the wit combat: attributing motives to each other that are then denied, appropriating the other's words or sounds by giving them a new twist in a quick response. In this exchange, we see Dryden's refinement of the couple that by 1667 had become standard repertory fare, not only in older Fletcherian comedies but in new plays like Howard's *Committee*, Newcastle's *The Country Captain*, and Thomas St. Serfe's *Flora's Vagaries* (1663); Dryden simply does it better. Again, his characters' verbal facility is one of

Dryden's major contributions to Carolean comedy. His predecessors and his own *Wild Gallant* relied mainly on farce in the form of physical action and its verbal equivalent; his successors, on wit. These devices are, moreover, used with real ingenuity in *Secret Love* and ultimately suggest either an idyllic scene of marital bliss based on honesty or a realistically brief passion, depending on how one interprets the "love/ long/longer" of Florimell's last retort.

The other important components of the Carolean "gay couple," besides verbal power, are social freedom and sexual appetite. Dryden gives these qualities to both participants, not just the male, and by restricting venue to a courtly or city environment where women have more power, he levels the playing field for the love game. Social rules exist, to be sure, but part of the game is getting around them; stellar performers of both sexes contrive to satisfy their appetites without becoming outcasts. To achieve such parity, Dryden eliminated blocking the figures—parents and unworthy suitors—of previous comedies to focus attention on the lovers and their own internal obstacles to matrimony. Celadon and Florimell are a highly sophisticated pair of lovers, wise in the ways of court and courtship both. Whereas earlier Carolean lovers had depended on farcical tricks to win one another and were often found in absurd postures (Careless languishing in jail in *The Committee*, Alberto in *Flora's Vagaries* falling down drunk in the gutter), Florimell and Celadon trap and punish each other more subtly. She gives him enough rope to hang himself, and he parries the inescapable truth of her accusations of infidelity with impudence, barefaced lies, and charming insouciance. Clearly, their devotion to the rules of courtly romance is on the surface only; even while Florimell sets him the task of a year's constancy, she knows he will not, cannot, fulfill it. Celadon goes through the motions of paying court to Melissa's daughters, while he admits to himself his heart is otherwise engaged. Even as the courtly rules dictate they must cast one another off, they are contriving an elaborate set of new rules to bind themselves together, a situation Dryden uses again in *An Evening's Love* between Wildblood and Jacinta.

Even more than in the high plot, the woman's role is paramount here. The movement of the plot is largely through Florimell: hers is the generalship that directs the progress of their love affair; she is the one who deflects and challenges Celadon's assumptions about women and constancy, although both characters undergo almost simultaneous epiphanies in act 3. Even while Celadon lies to Florimell in order to keep a date with Olinda and Sabina, he admits the game has him in thrall: "Yet

I love *Florimell* better than both of 'em together;—there's the Riddle on't; but onely for the sweet sake of variety.—Well, we must all sin, and we must all repent, and there's an end on't" (3.1.413–16). Seeing through his lies, Florimell is surprised to find herself angry rather than amused, and the game turns serious:

> See what constant metal you men are made of! He begins to vex me in good earnest. Hang him, let him go and take enough of 'em: and yet methinks I can't endure he should neither. Lord, that such a Mad-Cap as I should ever live to be jealous! I must after him.
>> Some Ladies would discard him now, but I
>> A fitter way for my revenge will find,
>> I'le marry him, and serve him in his kind.
>>   (3.1.426–33)

This scene marks the climax or turning point in the action, the characters' mutual peripeteias. Having faced her own feelings, Florimell is free to "tame" Celadon by beating him at his own courtship game. Having faced his, Celadon is ready to be tamed. In the last scene, before the Queen, they enact their ritual of mutual capitulation, making provisos about each other's rights, freedoms, and restrictions after marriage, curbing their "natural" freedom to achieve a greater goal: a marriage based on mutual satisfaction and individual achievement rather than the subjugation of one partner by the other. The rewards of self-denial for them are patently worth more than the drawbacks, despite Celadon's last faint slap at marriage versus bachelorhood: "[It] is very good, but not so good, *Florimell.*"

While the individual plot lines of *Secret Love* have their own sources and analogues, it is the conjunction of the two that makes the play work as a coherent, multileveled instrument to satisfy the sophisticated theatergoer. The techniques that bind the two plots together include physical and familial connections; parallels of action, character, and language; and thematic resemblances. Physical conjunctions, such as the characters' relationships, make such characters seem complex as they engage in different actions. Philocles and Celadon are cousins; Florimell and Flavia are cousins and Maids of Honor to the Queen; Celadon and Asteria are brother and sister. Characters from both plots inhabit the same stage at the same time, and often operate in a limited way in the other plot: Flavia is Florimell's comrade and Lysimantes's spy; Asteria chides her brother before getting involved in the Queen's problems; Celadon rescues Philocles, helps him take the citadel, and then takes it back in the Queen's name.

Parallel actions exist in the two plots beyond the overall similarity of the two courtship situations. The Queen's and Florimell's jealousy provokes them into openly criticizing their rivals and punishing their suitors. Both contrive to test their lovers without revealing their own feelings, and achieve their goals with their secrets relatively intact. The objects of their love are inverted admixtures of constancy and fickleness— if Celadon has a certain amount of truth beneath his gaiety, Philocles wavers in his devotion to Candiope and his duty to the Queen. Again, the principal analogies in the play are between the two heroines—Florimell and the Queen—who are willful, single-minded, and relatively unscrupulous, thoroughly "masculine" in their desires and their methods. Both are the prime movers of their plots and the most fully realized characters in them, and this parallelism reinforces the complementary relationship between them that leads to the play's assertions about natural and social behavior.

The language of each plot distinguishes it from the other: the heroic verse of the high plot and the courtly prose of the humorous. Dryden also uses similar image patterns to connect and contrast the two plots, the most apparent being the light/dark image cluster endemic to heroic and romantic drama. In each plot, the imagery begins, conventionally, with the lovers speaking of their mistresses as "fair" ones, whose beauty casts "light" upon them. But in each of the two plots, the figure is then expanded to illustrate the object, the user, and the questions being raised.

Because of her royalty, the Queen's "light" is compared to that of the Sun, the giver of life. Lysimantes combines compliment with obeisance: "when those fair eyes / Cast their commanding beams" (1.3.98–99). The Queen uses it herself in "Sometimes I struggle like the Sun in Clouds" (2.1.279). Philocles refers to the Queen's capture as "but a short Ecclipse, / Which past, a glorious day will soon ensue" (4.2.74–75). Heroic plays from *The Siege of Rhodes* to *The Indian Emperor* customarily rendered the male heroic hero in terms of the sun, to isolate him from other characters, imply qualities of passion and courage, and suggest the responsibility the hero has to society, which reaps beneficial effects from him. In *Secret Love*, the addition of the "light" qualities associated with heroic heroines—beauty, chastity, compassion—adds to the light-as-power configuration, both by expanding it and by setting up unusual tensions, for example, between passion and chastity or power and compassion. With its correlate "glory," the Queen's light is dimmed by her love for Philocles.

Meanwhile, the light/dark imagery of the comic plot begins also with compliment, the courtier's art that Celadon has mastered, as he shows Melissa's daughters: "Found you! Half this brightness betwixt you was enough to have lighted me; I could never miss my way: Here's fair *Olinda* has beauty enough for one Family" (4.1.54–56). A more pertinent comparison is Celadon as the Sun:

> FLA.:   You are as unconstant as the Moon.
>
> FLO.:   You wrong him, he's as constant as the Sun; he would see all the world round in 24 hours.
>
> CEL.:   'Tis very true, Madam, but, like him, I would visit and away.
>
> (1.2.18–22)

This comparison fits Florimell also:

> FLOR.:   *Florimell*'s not handsome: besides she's unconstant; and only loves for some few days.
>
> CEL.:   If she loves for shorter time then I, she must love by Winter daies and Summer nights i'faith.
>
> (1.2.86–89)

The intermingled references to day/time/constancy are humorously exaggerated when Celadon invokes carpe diem in response to Florimell's love test:

> FLOR.:   [Y]ou will grant it is but decent you should be pale, and lean, and melancholick to shew you are in love: and that I shall require of you when I see you next.
>
> CEL.:   When you see me next? why you do not make a Rabbet of me, to be lean at 24 hours warning? in the mean while we burn daylight, loose time and love.
>
> (2.1.78–83)

Amusing as these comparisons are, they also suggest a somewhat more complex relationship between this "gay couple" and their environment than seen in previous comedies. Inhabiting a world where love is artificialized into elegant postures of eternal devotion and constancy, both Celadon and Florimell persist in making equally elegant (and extravagant) claims for their capriciousness. At first, it is a simply a game of conflicting poses, but eventually both lovers are forced to confront their attraction to the other:

> One basis for comparison of the two plots is the "secret love" of the title: . . . we must recognize that the language of Celadon and Florimell, when they are together, is calculated to mean something other than what it says. They have a secret love, which, because of their humours, they dare not express seriously, so they adopt the mask of persiflage. Or, more accurately, they begin with mockery and end in earnest. . . .
>
> The romantic action has proceeded upon similar lines; for the queen's secret love is a tyrant, an irrational inclination, a passion that threatens to destroy her practical judgment. The heroic plot represents, therefore, the fundamental dilemmas of love, writ large. If the virgin is all-powerful, as Florimell has shown herself to be, supreme imperial in her beauty, virtue, and control over her servant, then how can she perpetuate her power after marriage? The virgin queen, like Christiana of Sweden and Elizabeth of England, postpones as long as possible her decision to marry, just as the Millamants, Angelicas, and Florimells maneuver and delay an open declaration of love and betrothal.[22]

Although the virgin's position—as manipulator, aggressor, and so forth—is alike in Queen and Maid, these similarities work to make the women's relationship complementary rather than consonant. While the serious plot considers the conflicting demands of individual passion and public responsibility, the humorous plot shows a similar conflict between private and social expectations. Whereas the Queen feels she must sacrifice the former for the latter, Florimell makes the opposite choice.

To some extent, this has to do with generic conventions already established for heroic drama and social comedy. The conflicts in heroic drama are between love and honor or duty; the hero's greatness is a function both of his or her birth and position and of his or her character. In comedy, private and social expectations may offer similar conflicts, and the hero's ability to reconcile the two is a function of his or her wit, charisma, and social skill.

In *Secret Love*, insofar as the Queen is an exemplary heroic figure, her self-sacrifice is necessary and predictable. She cannot marry Philocles, not so much because he is low-born, but because doing so would reduce her "glory" to his level. Concession is not part of the heroic character; control is. And on these grounds, the Queen, like Montezuma or Guyomar, can only follow her highest nature. At the same time, in the Queen, Dryden depicts much more fully than in such other heroes the complexities of the necessary choice, showing the heroic ideal in a way that includes, perhaps unconsciously, some suggestion of its limitations. For this, the humorous plot is at least partly responsible, for in Florimell, Dryden provides a contrast to the Queen, albeit a humorous one, and the juxtaposition of the two plots and characters provides an extra dimension that may be thematic. Like the Queen, Florimell initially practices self-deception and holds her principles and her exalted position inviolate. Like the Queen, she sets out to remake her lover in her own image. Yet faced with the same final choice of principles and absolute control versus love, Florimell makes the opposite choice. Taking Celadon with all his flaws necessitates reducing her standards of the ideal lover to accord with his capabilities.

When we look for an interpretation that incorporates the entire play, we reach an impasse, or, rather, a multiplicity of possible choices. One choice is that the dedication to "glory" and high principles is more important than the dedication to courtly or social standards, and that one heroine must bear the weight of the former while the other can sacrifice the latter with little compunction. This hierarchical interpretation says that personal, physical gratification may be denied the heroic character (although in other heroic plays, it fell neatly into place), while lesser mortals can take their pleasure where they may, since both women make the choice that is "natural" to them. Another interpretation is that the magnetism of Celadon and Florimell and the satisfactory conclusion of their love affair, juxtaposed with the Queen's sterile rededication to ideal glory, tends to undermine her choice and, by extension, the heroic ideal itself.[23] A third possibility is that the two actions exist separately and can be judged in their own terms: the rightness of each ending apt for each genre and heroine, while perhaps suggesting some important questions about women and patriarchal authority.

I would argue for the validity of all three (or even more) possibilities and suggest, further, that different members of the contemporary audience might well see the play differently according to their own values and circumstances. That each interpretation is textually supportable and consistent, although at odds with each other interpretation, attributes a level of capability to Dryden along with a finely tuned awareness of his heterogeneous audience. It also suggests a level of tolerance on the part of that audience for consensus without unity, a radical concept for any large group. But Dryden's own practice in later plays like *Marriage A-la-Mode* (1671?), as well as the kind of comedy that appeared in the 1670s, substantiates the claim of multiplicity for *Secret Love*, whose success may well have ensured its succession.

The role of *Secret Love* in the evolution of serious and comic drama during the Carolean period is significant. It advanced the level of psychological realism by focusing on character more exclusively than its predecessors, by eliminating blocking figures and actions, and by using language to particularize and probe characters to reveal hidden desires and emotions. In their need for social freedom, their sexual frankness, their ambition to win contests for ascendency, and their readiness to display their superior intellect and power, the Queen, Celadon, and Florimell epitomize the working out on stage of certain appealing ideals of Hobbesian liberty and libertinism which would be seen throughout much of the 1670s in popular plays by Etherege, Wycherley, Behn, and Dryden himself. Not until the early 1680s would the cracks in these elegant facades be shown, as in the monarchy itself, by playwrights like Otway who pushed them beyond their limits, to demonstrate the unbridled lust and real revolution which underlay the gamesmanship.

Comedy: The Rover

Oh for my Arms full of soft, white, kind—Woman!
(The Rover, 2.1.27)[24]

About a decade after the premiere of *Secret Love*, in March 1677, the London theater audiences saw another premiere, this time of a new comedy by Aphra Behn (1640?–1689) called *The Rover; or, the Banish't Cavaliers*. It was revived fairly regularly during the rest of the seventeenth century and into the eighteenth century,[25] and this, along with the fact that Behn produced a sequel four years later, suggests its popularity during its own time despite the lack of production records. If Dryden's Celadon represents a kind of adolescent effervescence, Behn's Willmore represents adult male sexuality in full-bodied form, with all its potential danger to a well-ordered society. Like some other comic heroes who resist the taming effects of marriage, he also maintains a rather egalitarian camaraderie with certain women at certain times, and this presents us with a curious anomaly about male-female relationships in those comedies of the 1670s which has taxed generations of critics and readers.

Like all successful Carolean comedies, *The Rover* is a mixture of tones and techniques ultimately derived from the Jonsonian and Fletcherian comedies that formed the solid core of the late seventeenth- and early eighteenth-century repertory. Jonson's *Epicoene; or, the Silent Woman* (1609), for example, and Fletcher's *The Scornful Lady* had long lives on the London stage.[26] At the same time, experiments and combinations by new playwrights in the first decade after the Restoration produced comedies in which farce, satire, witty dialogue, sexual innuendo, and other elements were combined so satisfactorily that, for example, Dryden's *Feign'd Innocence; or, Sir Martin Mar-all* and Sir Robert Howard's *The Committee* also became staples of the theater long after their authors and original audiences had disappeared.[27] Unlike heroic tragedy, whose critical defenses advertised its authors' serious intentions, comedy developed without much constraint, and its authors, whether aristocratic or professional, seemed almost apologetic about writing it well. Dryden, for instance, commented in 1668 in the preface to *An Evening's Love*, "Neither, indeed, do I value a reputation gained from comedy so far as to concern myself about it any more than I needs must in my own defense: for I think it, in its own nature, inferior to all sorts of dramatic writing" (CD, 10:202). Like heroic drama, however, Carolean comedy underwent rapid changes in a relatively short time.

Inferior genre it might be, but Carolean audiences loved comedies, going to the theater two or three times as often to see them as to see tragedies. In comedy, they could see images of themselves performed by stellar actors, perhaps even see their desires and fantasies acted out on stage. In the first decade after the Restoration, popular new comedies presented male and female "heroes" who were lively and playful, but essentially moral. Even rakish types like Celadon and Florimell in *Secret Love* or Careless and Ruth in *The Committee* did their rakish deeds in the past or only verbally. A turning point of sorts came with Etherege's *She Would if She Could* (1668), often referred to as the first comedy of manners, yet even Courtall, that play's witty hero, shows some fastidiousness in refusing Lady Cockwood's amorous advances and appears to reform at the end of the play.[28]

Successful comedies of the 1660s were morally and structurally coherent even though they combined Jonsonian satire and Fletcherian romance, which had very different worldviews and structures. Early comic dramatists creating their own idiom found they had to do more than add a Fletcherian love interest to a Jonsonian cozening plot or vice versa; they had to create a setting in which love and cozening, romance and wit, were plausibly different capabilities of the same "heroic" characters. These settings ranged from Spain and Italy to London, with the more exotic Continental settings tending to house the more romantic plots. Typical of this subgenre is Sir Samuel Tuke's *The Adventures of Five Hours* (1662), a translation of Coello's *Los Empeños de seis horas*, which launched a number of imitations, including Dryden's *An Evening's Love* (1668). Tuke used his Spanish setting to create a moral universe wherein extravangances of love and honor, threatening guardians, distressed heroines, and sword fights were common currency. In other words, he produced a comic setting that could accommodate many of the effects of heroic tragedy. The tone was lightened with farcical humor provided by servant characters, and decorum was maintained because such servants existed outside the moral boundaries the other characters subscribed to.

Meanwhile, popular new comedies of the 1660s set in London achieved a unified sensibility by elevating efficiency or wit as a standard of judgment and giving it moral connotations. A good example is Howard's *The Committee*, an incredibly durable comedy[29] that puts its witty lovers in a Commonwealth setting that aggrandizes their loyalty to the absent king. The stock obstructive guardians of Fletcherian romance are also given a moral dimension by being made Puritans (Mr. Day is chairman of the hated Committee of Sequestration),[30] social climbers, and outright thieves and rascals. Like *The Adventures of Five Hours*, *The Committee* locates much of its farcical action in servant characters: here Teague, the "Faithful Irishman."[31] Indeed, Teague as brought to life by John Lacy may have been as responsible for the success of *The Committee* as James Nokes was for the somewhat later success of *Sir Martin Marall*, playing the part of Sir Martin that Dryden had written for him.

By the late 1660s, then, comedy had passed through its formative stage to become precisely what its authors and audiences wanted it to be. This is not to say that it was in any sense monochromatic or sterile; on the contrary, more than any other genre, comedy was fluid and diversified, responding quickly to changing tastes and fashions, to the need to create roles for popular actors and show off scenery, and to trendy foreign influences.[32] In the latter category, the amount of influence varied. The "Spanish plot" vogue introduced by Tuke's *The Adventures of Five Hours* was relatively short-lived and quickly Anglicized, but the French influence of Molière that occurred in the late 1660s and early 1670s was much more pervasive and far-reaching. The different impact of these two foreign influences was caused by a number of factors, but the two most important were timing and affinity. The Spanish plots were used earlier and were "naturally" absorbed because of their resemblance to Fletcherian comedy.[33] The French influence occurred a few years later and tied in more neatly with the movement away from a consensual moral framework, a movement already happening in popular new domestic comedies of the 1666–68 seasons, such as Dryden's *An Evening's Love*, *The Tempest*, and *Secret Love*, Sir Charles Sedley's *Mulberry Garden*, and Etherege's *She Would if She Could*.

One can hear the first salvos of the French invasion in these same two seasons, with the premieres of Dryden's *Sir Martin Mar-all* (1667) and Shadwell's *Sullen Lovers; or, the Impertinents* (1668). These comedies have major borrowings, respectively, from Molière's *L'Étourdi* (1658) and *Les Fâcheux* (1661). As Molière's popularity increased in France, so it did in England, and by the late 1660s and early 1670s, some 10 Molière-based plays were seen on the English stage.[34] Several reasons account for the success of this invasion, among them the structural congeniality of the Fletcherian mode with Molière's comedy and the importance of farce and other actors' business on both stages. But in some respects, the difference between the two comic modes was the more important factor. Molière's comedy provided a new focus and direction for Carolean comedy at a point in its development when its audiences and playwrights were looking for them.

Specifically, French comedy introduced a kind of satire not strictly based on cozening, like Jonson's, or courtship, like Fletcher's, though it was not antithetical to either. Following his own and his audience's interests, Molière exposed religious and social hypocrisy, foppery, and other "vices" by means of a series of protagonists—Tartuffe, Don Juan, Alceste, Jupiter, Arnolphe—who are complex, arresting figures and not easily defined or pigeonholed into stereotypes.[35] The English plays derived from Molière's comedies are therefore decentered in terms of more traditional Fletcherian or Jonsonian actions, and the counterparts of Molière's protagonists—whether an abused fool like George Dandin (Barnaby Brit-

tle in *The Amorous Widow*, 1670?), an inept bungler like Lélie (Sir
Martin in *Sir Martin Mar-all*), or a clever blocking parental figure like
Arnolphe (Sir Salomon in *Sir Salomon*, 1670)—are the progenitors of a
whole new movement in Carolean comedy. Specifically, this involves
shifting characters closer together into the same moral (or immoral) universe, so that all seek the same kinds of gratifications, albeit with different
results. The enhanced satiric level of Molière's characters helps make
distinctions between characters who share the same motivations and between situations that are remarkably similar. Furthermore, the wedding
of Fletcherian courtship actions to Molière's more open-ended satiric
plots creates endings, as in *Sir Salomon* or *The Amorous Widow*, that
are ambiguous and subject to audience interpretation. In *Sir Salomon*,
two radically different ideologies coexist uneasily; in *The Amorous Widow*,
the resolution can be interpreted as either real or ironic by various members of the audience.

The final component that accompanied Molière's plays to England was a particular kind of wittiness called *moraliste*, after the maxims
of French writers like La Rochefoucauld, pithy statements about human
nature based on observation of social habits or mores (see Rothstein and
Kavenik, 28–37). The use of such *moraliste* wit separated characters from
each other, first, on the basis of the quality of their perception about
themselves and the world, and second, on the basis of their ability to
articulate such perceptions in a concise way. Although witty characters
existed in earlier plays, such as *Secret Love* and *The Committee*, the sharp
satiric edge that generations of readers and playgoers have associated with
Carolean comedy (and that flourished especially in the 1670s) is bound
up with certain characters' ability to perceive others' motivations and
actions clearly, to separate form from content, and to make orderly the
disorder of passion, rivalry, and rampant desire. The fact that such characters are themselves "tainted" by sharing at least some of these same
motives and drives with their inferiors seems not to matter so much if
they can, at times, distance themselves from it linguistically.

All of these forces go into the making of *The Rover* and other
popular comedies of the 1670s up to the Exclusion Crisis of 1678. This
was a period in which, for a time, audiences may have been more flexible
about morality and more tolerant of others' views than before or after.
While some audience members would have seen these plays in simple
terms, others in the same audience could see their desires acted out on
stage so long as a pattern one might call "compromise formation" allowed
them to "sin" with safety of conscience. In Freudian terms, a compromise
formation is a kind of behavior that both gratifies an illicit desire and

also represses or punishes it. A rakish comedy in the 1670s mode would permit those spectators who were so inclined to imagine themselves rakes guiltlessly, usually either with an ending that seems moral (e.g., a marriage in the offing) or with a separate action that counterpoints the rakish one. As in the humorous plot of *Secret Love*, social expectations and freedom can coexist for characters onstage, and the audience can participate vicariously in that approval and freedom (see Rothstein and Kavenik, 8–9). At base, this meant that 1670s comedies could be sexier, more licentious than their predecessors, as long as they adopted some pattern that offered a moral alternative. In practice, this meant that such comedies created in counterpoint other characters, like Harcourt and Alithea in William Wycherley's *The Country-Wife* (1675), or an ambiguous ending, like Dorimant's proposed marriage to Harriet in Sir George Etherege's *The Man of Mode* (1676), that seemed to identify a conventional moral ending but could also be interpreted ironically.

The unorthodoxy of these comedies went well beyond sex into other realms of traditional social authority; the hegemony of parents over children, men over women, is significantly weakened, as are the controls of concepts like honor and friendship, and social compacts like marriage (see Rothstein and Kavenik, 167).[36] In this sense, the critics who have decried and been repelled by these plays for centuries are correct in adjudging them radical. But the hero(ine)s of these plays are radical in a special way; their concern is entirely for self-gratification rather than social transformation, and indeed part of the gratification comes from attaining their goals with maximum skill and ingenuity. All of which, of course, implicates the audience. Plays as different on the surface as Wycherley's *The Country-Wife* and *The Plain-Dealer* (1676), Dryden's *Marriage A-la-Mode*, Edward Ravenscroft's *The Citizen Turn'd Gentleman* (1672), Thomas Shadwell's *The Virtuoso* (1676) and *Epsom Wells* (1672), and Etherege's *The Man of Mode*, among others, subscribe to this pattern; so does *The Rover*.

The plot lines of *The Rover* are as varied and as entangled as any in Carolean comedy, and in true Fletcherian fashion, Behn moves between them or shifts direction in any of them unpredictably. Set in "Naples in Carnival-time," the play begins with a discussion between two sisters, Florinda and Hellena, that reveals their different natures: Florinda with her "secret love" for the exiled Englishman Belvile, Hellena with her "mad" humor to taste the delights of love during the carnival, "tho I ask first" (1.1.11). Both are designed, of course, for better things by their Spanish-style brother, Don Pedro—Florinda for his friend Don Antonio, Hellena for a career as a nun—and their thwarting of his designs establishes the intrigue level of the action. Indeed, the Belvile/Florinda plot follows pretty closely the kind of activity associated with Spanish-plot plays. It also provides a safe and comfortable resolution for those in the audience inclined to the romantic or moral.

The case is otherwise with Hellena and her choice of Willmore, the Rover of the title. Willmore is a member of the special class of Carolean rakes that includes Horner, Dorimant, and others; in both deed and word, he is a free spirit whose sexual conquests are legion. His achievements in this area distinguish him in this play both from tamer heroes like Belvile and from inept would-be rakes like Blunt, and though he is not as witty as Wycherley's Horner or Etherege's Dorimant, he can turn a phrase at need. To complicate the usual situation, Hellena's task is not only to render Willmore fit for marriage but to outvie her rival, the exquisite courtesan Angellica Bianca, with whom Willmore enjoys a passionate interlude. This plot and Angellica Bianca herself in fact constitute the only truly original action in a plot so clearly derivative in its other parts.[37]

On the one hand, Angellica Bianca's is a spirit as free as Will-more's, free to take and discard lovers at will. Our first encounter is not with the courtesan herself but with her picture, hung as advertisement outside her lodgings, which has all the men of Naples panting and checking their pocketbooks. In modern terms a "sex object," Angellica both uses and controls the status given her by men's lusts, and thus mirrors and reflects the attractiveness of Willmore, the rake-hero for all women. When such superior beings meet, sparks fly, but there is a also a sense of fellowship, which appears initially in act 2, scene 2 as verbal aggression that ultimately leads to the bedroom, but later turns into a frank and open exchange between equals. The arguments and sex are common comic fare by this time, but the aftermath is rare—another instance is between Horner and the "Virtuous Gang" of *The Country-Wife*. Such scenes suggest that when male and female characters openly admit their natural sexual instincts, they can at times meet and converse honestly, leaving aside for a time the gamesmanship and persiflage of most gendered discourse. Quite often, as in this scene of *The Rover*, these honest exchanges zero in on the typical behaviors society decrees for the love game:

ANG.:   —Pray, tell me, Sir, are not you guilty of the same merce-
          nary Crime? When a Lady is proposed to you for a Wife,

> you never ask, how fair, discreet, or virtuous she is; but
> what's her Fortune—which if but small, you cry—She
> will not do my business—and basely leave her, tho she
> languish for you. . . .

WIL.: It is a barbarous Custom, which I will scorn to defend
in our Sex, and do despise in yours.

(2.2.40)

Such frankness between men and women will not occur again in English drama before Shaw.

In terms of compromise formation, then, both Willmore and Angellica Bianca, like other rakish heroes, need to be contaminated or contained lest they threaten those in the audience who find them all too attractive, or too stiff a competition. Usually this is done by humiliating the hero, by degrading his or her power in one of several conventional ways. One is to have the hero experience failure, either a verbal put-down or a failed scheme. In *The Man of Mode*, Dorimant, like Courtall in Etherege's *She Would if She Could*, is confronted by a cast-off lover who refuses to be polite about it, and who makes a fool of him in front of the woman he is courting. In *The Man of Mode*, this gives Harriet a weapon, and she doesn't fail to use it. In *The Rover*, Willmore is similarly disconcerted in encounters with Hellena (3.1), Angellica (4.1), and then both together (4.1). Although he bounces back to play the game again, his power is shown to be less than absolute.

Another technique is to stress the parallels between the hero and the play's fools. The latter characters perform a distinct function in 1670s comedy beyond the simply satiric or humorous. Practically no comedy is complete without its fops and other "would-be's," its cuck-olded or outwitted husbands, its outmaneuvered guardians and parents, its unsuccessful suitor or jealous, cast-off lover. In a world where performance is the key to character, these standard figures all read "empty" or "inadequate"; they are figures of fun rather than of sympathy both inside and outside the play (Harriet laughs at Loveit, everyone mocks the husbands of *The London Cuckolds*). Indeed, it is the apparent cruelty evidenced toward these antagonistic characters, along with the sexuality, that later ages found so offensive about Carolean comedy. What later critics often did not notice, however, was how often these characters were used to contaminate the heroes by analogy. In *The Country-Wife*, for example, Pinchwife's motives for marriage, to keep a whore to himself, are not so different from Horner's wish to maximize his sexual activity by passing himself off as "no man," rendered impotent by an inept surgeon. Both wish to ensure their pleasure without consequence and with scant regard for their partners. By such means dramatists assured the audience that rakish heroes, however attractive, were not better than they.

In *The Rover*, Willmore is humiliated several times in the course of the play outside of his verbal battles with the women. He plays the fool or "dog" by upsetting his friend Belvile's love intrigue more than once with his drunken carousing and rapaciousness. Moreover, his resemblance to Blunt, the play's fool, is at times marked. Blunt's love intrigue ends in total humiliation when he is stripped of all his valuables and forced to escape through a sewer; not only are his desires unsatisfied, but he is left with nothing to show for it.

Angellica presents a slightly different case. She herself recognizes that she becomes vulnerable once she succumbs to loving Willmore. In their final confrontation in act 5 she rages and rails and threatens him with a pistol—in short, behaves like a romantic heroine or a cast-off mistress, thus degrading herself. Her humiliation is so much greater than Willmore's that one cannot help but suspect that sexual freedom is perceived as more of a social threat in the female than in the male of the species.[38] But the scene does not end here; she chooses not to shoot Willmore, "to show my utmost of contempt" (5.98) and thus regains some of her lost identity and ascendancy.

Hellena is a different story. Like most female heroes, she does not undergo contamination, perhaps because she remains safely female even in her "boy's clothes." A much more conventional figure than Angellica, she is ideally suited to take control of Willmore in ways that her rival cannot. Her youth, beauty, and sexual innocence (not to mention her substantial dowry) render her a worthy prize, a desirable object. Moreover, she is a fit match temperamentally for Willmore. In act 4, scene 2, reminiscent of Florimell, she dresses as a male, and encounters Willmore and Angellica as the latter is railing at him for inconstancy. Hellena's reaction: "my mad Captain's with her too, for all his swearing [fidelity to me]—how this inconstant Humour makes me love him" (4.2.71). Though Willmore succeeds in turning the tables on her later in that same scene, Hellena recovers in act 5, offering to "find out all your Haunts, to rail at you to all that love you, till I have made you love only me in your own Defence" (5.100). Taken as much by her aggressive behavior (Hellena is again in boy's clothes) as by her aforementioned qualities of wealth and beauty, the Rover succumbs: "Egad, I was never claw'd away with Broad-Sides from any Female before, thou hast one Virtue I adore, good-Nature; I hate a coy demure Mistres, she's a troublesom as a Colt, I'll break none; no, give me a mad Mistress when mew'd, and in flying on[e] I dare trust upon the Wing, that whilst she's kind will come to the Lure" (5.100). Although he quails still at the threat of "*Hymen* and Priest," the play ends with marriage in the offing.

In *The Rover*, some thematic weight can be given to the discussions of and references to nature versus social expectations, whether it be the rights of young women to ignore their brother's authority over them or the rights of sexually active young people of both sexes to seek gratification where they may. One can even see some substantive underpinnings in the fact that Willmore "roves" because he is an exiled royalist cut off from his homeland, that a man without a country is cut off from his moorings and therefore values only the momentary and ephemeral. That *The Rover* lends itself to such shadings of interpretation is part of its charm, and the reason that it, along with its fellow comedies, has provided food for thought for generations of critics. But as with *Secret Love*, we need to be cautious in assigning any interpretation to a play that, by its very nature, is flexible and meant to appeal to a heterogeneous audience.

The Rover represents one kind of 1670s comedy: lively and attractive protagonists, a setting that is a feast for the senses, enough intrigue to keep the audience guessing, and a happy ending for everyone who deserves it. There were certainly comedies that are more disruptive and offensive, Wycherley's *The Country-Wife* and *The Plain-Dealer*, Ravenscroft's *The London Cuckolds* and *The Cit Turn'd Gentleman*, Caryll's *Sir Salomon*, and Otway's *The Souldiers Fortune*, to name a few of the best known. Some of the unpleasant realities that are glossed over in *The Rover*, such as the betrayal of friendship and the "contract" between men and women, both in Willmore's infidelity to Angellica and Hellena and in his near rape of Florinda, reach fuller expression in other plays. Etherege's Dorimant is a social sadist, who enjoys humiliating those he considers inferior; Wycherley's Manly is brutal and animalistic, rejecting true friendship and loyalty; and Pinchwife in *The Country-Wife* displays a potential for violence only faintly controlled by his social mask. Most of these plays portray heroes who are more dishonorable and cynical than Willmore, who recognize no boundaries to their lusts and other freedoms. Honor, piety, friendship, vows, are mere words to these rakes, artificial barriers to be surmounted, challenges to their ingenuity.

Tragedy: Venice Preserved

The public stock's a beggar; one Venetian
Trusts not another.
(Venice Preserved, 2.3.69–70)[39]

With the Exclusion Crisis, which began in 1678, the temper of the London populace, and hence of the London theater audience, no longer maintained the tolerance for heterodoxy that had existed in the 1670s. The threat of another civil war acted as a damper on the libertine ethos that had been so appealing a year or so before. In other ways as well, "the tension and excitement of the anti-Catholic atmosphere adversely affected the theaters. The Epilogue to *The Feign'd Curtizans* (March 1679) emphasized the thinness of the town and the severity of the times. . . . That the parlous times affected players in other ways is suggested by the problem of Michael Mohun, who inquired of the King whether Mohun, a 'Popish recusant,' should obey the proclamation banning all Catholics from London" (*LS*, 1.271). During this period, Drury Lane was closed for a time entirely,[40] and even when the theaters were open, more plays were refused licenses or banned after a few performances than ever before, attesting to the "state of emergency" in the body politic.[41]

The efficient cause of the Exclusion Crisis was the Popish Plot of 1678, a confidence trick hatched by Titus Oates, a renegade Anglican cleric, and his cohort Israel Tonge, an impoverished clergyman and D.D. from Oxford.[42] Oates's story was that he had uncovered a plot against the king's life by Jesuits who wished to place Charles's brother, James, Duke of York, on the throne. Other accusers came forward, and the climate worsened: "Round Oates there surged a broth, all the ingredients of which had the same characteristic flavour. Incriminating letters were found behind wainscots or at the bottom of tubs; concocted papers were 'planted' on victims and then searched for; accused persons turned informers, and victimized others; the families of arch-informers took up the prosperous trade of papist-hunting, or made money by informing against their own relatives; confessions were recanted and again sworn-to; both truth and honour were completely dissolved in this boiling mass."[43] When the dust settled in 1681, about 35 persons in England had fallen direct victim to the justice system's witch-hunts and the public hysteria, whipped up by the Whig opposition in Parliament led by Anthony Ashley Cooper, the Earl of Shaftsbury. Their purpose was the exclusion of Catholic James from the succession and the advancement of their own political power over the king's. In a series of maneuvers over the next few years, Charles II jockeyed with a series of Parliaments, finally having Shaftsbury arrested and sent to the Tower in 1681. In the four years remaining before his own death, Charles recouped much of his power while the Whigs lost theirs.[44]

The theater responded to these troubled times in several ways. The most obvious response was the predominance of tragedies among the new plays during the years right after the Popish Plot and the deluge of political plays in general during the years 1679–82 (see Hume 1976, 340–60). Political comedies, as Hume points out, did not begin to appear until 1681, by which time the real political crisis had all but ended. Only one of these plays, Shadwell's *Lancashire Witches* (1681), was not unabashedly Tory or royalist in sentiment and design, and Shadwell's play, as might be expected, was substantially cut by the censors before being acted. On the royalist side were a number of efforts: Behn's *The Roundheads* (1681) and *The City Heiress* (1682), D'Urfey's *Sir Barnaby Whigg* (1681) and *The Royalist* (1682), Crowne's *The City Politiques* (1683). All these plays were moderately popular, though most did not remain so beyond their own time.

Political tragedies, appearing somewhat earlier, were popular not only in their own time but, in some cases, much longer. Hume points out that almost half of the new serious plays in the early 1680s were political in nature (1976, 342), and includes in this number Dryden's *The Spanish Fryar* (1680), Southerne's *The Loyal Brother* (1682), Lee's *Lucius Junius Brutus* (1680), Tate's *The Ingratitude of a Common-Wealth* (1681) and *The History of King Richard the Second* (1680), Crowne's *The Misery of Civil-War* (1680), *Henry the Sixth* (1681), Settle's *The Female Prelate* (1680), and Whitaker's *The Conspiracy* (1680). Their titles alone indicate the topicality of many of these efforts, and while many of these plays display anti-Catholic sentiments, Hume points out that during the late 1670s and early 1680s, this should be interpreted less as pro-Whig than as pandering to public fears in general.[45]

One of the best if not *the* best of these political tragedies is Thomas Otway's *Venice Preserved; or, a Plot Discovered* (1682), whose production history indicates its lasting appeal.[46] Written and produced just after Shaftsbury's bid for power had ended in defeat, this tragedy shows that the kind of oligarchy Shaftsbury represented is just as corrupt as the government it seeks to depose. Superimposing a political struggle between two equally vile alternatives on the personal, romantic tragedy of a pair

of innocent lovers caught in the middle, Otway questions the viability
of any system in a state so rife with egoistic and rotten politicians. Mal-
volio's "A plague on both your houses" might be the theme of *Venice
Preserved*.

The play begins with Jaffeir, a young Venetian who has married
a well-bred young woman, Belvidera, against her father's wishes. Not
content with cutting off his daughter's inheritance, the father, Priuli, has
been hounding the young couple ever since, and as the play begins,
Jaffeir has finally sunk his pride to plead with his father-in-law for the
sustenance of his family, which has hit bottom financially after several
years of scraping by. Priuli refuses, gloating over their distress, and the
desperate Jaffeir encounters his friend Pierre, who lends him money and
convinces him that Priuli, a senator, is a microcosm of the corruption
in Venetian politics. Enlisted to support the cause of justice and freedom,
Jaffeir finds that the conspirators, especially Renault, are as venal and
power mad as the senators, and turns on his newfound compatriots.
Multiple betrayals and "turns" ensue, and the play ends in the dramatically staged deaths of Pierre, Jaffeir, and Belvidera, all succumbing to
the double weight of systemic violence and personal guilt.

Although various critics have commented on the play's political
satire—namely, that the parallel portraits of Antonio the corrupt senator
and Renault the corrupt conspirator are both of the recently deposed
Shaftsbury[47]—one needs no program notes to understand its dynamics
or feel its power. Otway's immediate source was l'abbé de Saint-Réal's
La Conjuration des Espagnols contre la République de Venise (1674;
English translation 1675), to which he added the character of Belvidera
and the action surrounding her, with appropriate changes in the ending
of the play (see Kelsall, xv–xvi) to bring it fully into line with developments in Carolean tragedy to this time. These changes also, not inciden-
tally, provided a magnificent vehicle for the acting talents of Elizabeth
Barry and her successors.

Carolean tragedy had altered significantly since the mid-1660s
when *Secret Love* and other heroic plays gained the ascendancy they held
throughout most of the 1670s. When heroic drama disappeared rather
abruptly in the 1680s, unrhymed, blank verse tragedy was ready to take
over again, leaving the extravagant scenery and effects to opera and
reforming the heroic love-honor conflicts and the emotional affectivity to
suit its own ends. Gone forever was the rhymed couplet as an appropriate
medium for tragic drama, as part of the more general movement away
from the audience's admiration for exaggerated heroics on stage. When

late Carolean playwrights looked for models of true tragedy, they needed to go no further than their own repertory, where works by Fletcher and, to a lesser extent, Shakespeare had sustained a solid following even during the heyday of heroic drama.[48] As Rothstein puts it, "When rhyme, encumbered and artful, was forced to yield its place to simple language, passion, and nature, the tragedians discovered that the existing repertory of Renaissance blank-verse tragedy could serve them as a warehouse of models. They wanted to do what they thought Shakespeare and Fletcher had done" (1967b, 54), and he points to prefaces and to numerous adaptations (e.g., Dryden's *All for Love*, 1677) and borrowings (e.g., Otway's *Caius Marius*, 1679).

Before and even during the years of heroic drama's popularity, there were also new Carolean tragedies whose authors chose to imitate Fletcher, Shakespeare, or both, such as Porter's *The Villain* (1663), Falkland's *The Marriage Night* (1664), Wilson's *Andronicus Comenius* (1664), Edward Howard's *The Usurper* (1668), and Payne's *The Fatal Jealousie* (1672) and *The Siege of Constantinople* (1675). And when the heroic play itself began to respond to changing tastes by introducing more pathetic effects, unrhymed tragedy was not far behind. The difference between the heroic heroes of Dryden's *Aureng-Zebe* (1675) and his earlier *Secret Love* or *The Indian Emperor* is that *Aureng-Zebe* contains those qualities which Rothstein finds endemic to the late heroic play: the diminuition and sentimentalizing of the hero, conflict resolution without a clear removal of the blocking figure or heroic death, conflict between love and honor/glory, and the private life given predominance over the public (1967b, 88). These qualities are also present in *Venice Preserved*.

Other tragic dramatists besides Otway were also helping to chart new directions for tragedy: John Banks and Nathaniel Lee and, to a lesser extent, Nahum Tate, Elkanah Settle, John Crowne, and Thomas Southerne. As early as the mid-1670s but certainly into the early 1680s, plays like Dryden and Lee's *Oedipus* (1679), Lee's *Lucius Junius Brutus*, and Banks's *The Destruction of Troy* (1679), *The Unhappy Favorite* (1682), *Virtue Betray'd* (1682), and *The Island Queens* (1684) rang changes on both the form and the sensibility of tragic drama. Although these playwrights worked with different structures and subjects, each tended to denigrate the heroic character and ideology in return for enhanced sentiment and effects. Banks, for example, collapses male/female distinctions in order to elevate the personal and pathetic: "honor as an ideal, as a motive, as *the* motive, cannot be taken seriously. Love and friendship are taken seriously, and what honor there is must be construed in terms of these personal ideals. Personal relations had always been, and continued to be, women's province: dwelling upon them gives us Banks' she-tragedies, in which women are the principals and the men are womanish" (Rothstein 1967b, 97). The contrast between such tragedies and *Secret Love*, where the Queen is forced to renounce her "womanish" qualities for the public good and some abstract heroic ideal, shows the distance tragedy had traveled in a little more than a decade.

Otway mediates between the near heroics of Lee and the determined pathetics of Banks with tragedies that artfully balance the best qualities of both. Following his *Orphan* and *The Souldiers Fortune*, both produced in 1680, *Venice Preserved* shares with them a profound cynicism about both human society and human nature. In *The Orphan*, a tragedy, "nature becomes vicious because the characters, like those in Restoration comedy, assume it was vicious to begin with. . . . [E]ach of the protagonists comes to disaster because he fails to trust the others" (Rothstein 1967b, 101). In *The Souldiers Fortune*, a comedy, Otway presents a world in which natural urges and energies are relatively uncontrolled by society, where rules of behavior are manipulated for private ends, and where only a few basic ideals remain—loyalty to one's friend and to one's country. In the world of the play, the former is tainted by sexual rivalry, the latter by ingratitude and poverty, as Courtine's first speech indicates:

BEAUG.: [C]ome times may mend, and an honest Souldier be in fashion again—

COUR.: These greasie fat unwieldy wheezing Rogues that live at home and brood over their bags, when a fit of fear's upon 'em, then if one of us pass but by, all the Family is ready at the door to cry, Heaven's bless you, Sir, the Laird go along with you. . . . But when the bus'ness is over, then every Parish Bawd that goes but to a Conventicle twice a Week, and pays but scot and lot to the Parish, shall roar out fogh, ye Lowsy Red-coat rake hells! hout ye Caterpillars, ye Locusts of the Nation, you are the Dogs that would enslave us all, plunder our Shops, and ravish our Daughters, ye Scoundrels.

(1.1.196–211)[49]

The connections between these characters and Pierre, the returned soldier turned revolutionary in *Venice Preserved*, are clear, but in *Venice Pre-*

served it is Jaffeir rather than Pierre who is the center of the play, and it is Jaffeir's and Belvidera's emotions that control and manage the audience's reactions. Thus, in V*enice Preserved*, Otway's manipulations of plot and secondary characters are all directed toward the same end, showing the "heroic" character under stress.

From the beginning of the play, Jaffeir is a character deeply divided between conflicting pulls: love, loyalty, friendship, honor—all of which scan differently in different contexts. Honor, for example, which is presented as an absolute value in the heroic play, is here seen as situational and fuzzy. Jaffeir is first shown as a father and husband trying desperately to provide for his family, and subsuming his masculine pride to do so. When his sacrifice is rejected and mocked by Priuli, he is ripe for salvaging that masculine honor by avenging himself on Priuli and, by extension, the whole corrupt system, and Pierre offers him a means of doing both. When the suspicious conspirators demand a hostage from him, he offers Belvidera, his most precious possession, as surety. Again, his honor is forfeit when Renault attempts to rape Belvidera, and the angry and humiliated Jaffeir finds himself listening to her pleas to "save Venice." Despite his attempts to save Pierre and the rest of the conspirators, the Senate forces him to betray them, and in turn he nearly stabs Belvidera to regain his lost honor. Finally, he decides the only way to regain the honor he has staked and lost so many times is to kill Pierre at his friend's request, and then himself. Bereft, Belvidera goes mad and dies.

Minimally, in V*enice Preserved*, honor is no longer an absolute but a contingent value. Because our sympathies are with Jaffeir from the outset, we are willing to accept at each juncture that circumstances alter cases, and that his 180-degree turns are necessary and appropriate choices. A certain amount of psychological realism, even, is gained by Otway because of his setting, a mad world wherein the old order of paternal care is debased and the new order of youthful hope is crushed or perverted.

In its overall configuration, the play's handling of the generational conflicts that in some form are present in most Carolean drama demonstrates important changes since the 1660s and 1670s, when authors tended to resolve these conflicts wholly in favor of the younger generation, with its monopoly on sexual prowess, wit, and good judgment. These earlier plays showed the elder generation, stripped of the facade of custom and authority, as deficient both morally and physically, unable to stem the tide of change and deposition. Otway seems to be more ambivalent about the validity of this message: if the Senate represents deep-seated malaise in society, the conspirators are equally disreputable, and Jaffeir's dismay at Renault's "Shed blood enough, spare neither sex nor age / Name nor condition" (3.2.333–34) is shared by the audience. The senators and Renault, of course, represent the older generation. But within the younger generation, the best characters, Jaffeir and Belvidera, are weak and ineffectual, while Pierre's noble sentiments are undercut by his base motives—sexual pique and revenge. In this sense, Jaffeir—and to a lesser extent Belvidera—are true Fletcherian heroic types, trapped in a universe where "the highest virtue . . . very often consists in doing nothing. To act, as often as not, is to open the way to sinning."[50]

Venice Preserved also follows the Fletcherian pattern of climactic moments punctuated by extravagant rhetoric. Indeed, the power of language is attested to in speeches by Renault (esp. 3.2), Antonio (4.2, 5.2), and to a lesser extent, Pierre. But because it is a quality possessed by men who are self-deluded, base, and Machiavellian, eloquence is suspect, and Pierre's, Jaffeir's, or Belvidera's less finished emotional outpourings are ultimately more attractive. The most heightened scenes—Jaffeir and Pierre at the scaffold, Belvidera's mad ravings—are choppy and disjunct rather than rounded and periodic. It is this emotional level in both action and language that distinguishes *Venice Preserved* most from its predecessors and analogues in the repertory, even from works of Fletcher like *The Maid's Tragedy*. Because its structure is designed to convey the complexity of characters under stress, the language of *Venice Preserved*, though powerful, purports to be unrhetorical.

As many critics have noted, one means that Otway uses to deepen the effects in *Venice Preserved* is to link debased sexuality and political corruption (see Weber, 27–35). Nature or antinature plays a part in this confluence, as humans are consistently reduced to animals, identified by name and deed, and the most important of these relationships is between the senator Antonio and the courtesan Aquilina. In the scenes where Antonio plays "nicky-nacky" with her, chasing her around the bedroom barking like a dog and begging to be whipped,[51] we see not only Otway's skill in presenting the farcical mixed with the sardonic, but the dark underside of the libertine ethos extolled in Carolean comedy. Perverse but also powerful, Antonio possesses the means to effect his predatory aims on Aquilina and to outmaneuver Pierre or anyone else who bars his way, and is a sinister figure precisely because he shows there are not limits to what can be condoned and covered up in the state of Venice. He remains alive at the play's end, free to continue his depraved course unchecked.

Shaftsbury's other "self" in the play, Renault, is equally licentious, though less omnipotent. His attempted rape of Belvidera on the eve of the revolution he is leading forces Jaffeir's turnabout and shows the audience how little difference there is between the two sides vying for ascendancy. Even the noble Pierre is principally motivated by jealousy over Antonio's acquisition of *his* whore; for Pierre, sexual honor supersedes public honor: "A soldier's mistress, Jaffeir, 's his religion" (1.199). In contrast to these figures are Jaffeir and Belvidera, who are so far from embracing the libertine ethos that their idea of heaven is conjugal marital relations. "I have known / The luscious sweets of plenty, every night / Have slept with soft content about my head, / And never waked but to a joyful morning" (1.98–100), Jaffeir tells his father-in-law, presenting an eloquent counterpoint to everyone else's rampant sexuality and greed. Their love is like that of "turtle doves," not the dogs, kites, and toads that appear elsewhere in the play to refer to Antonio, Aquilina, or Renault, and like harmless doves, Jaffeir and Belvidera are fodder and prey for the powerful natural forces that surround them.

Wit, then, and sexual freedom—the *données* of 1670s comedy—are attacked in *Venice Preserved* on what appear to be moral grounds. The values that seem to be advanced by the playwright—goodness over capability—also posit a somewhat different audience relationship from that of previous comedies and tragedies. Jaffeir and Belvidera are not acting out the audience's desires on stage, rather their worst nightmares, yet the affective level is heightened—perhaps to "pity and fear." What we may have here is a new variation of the compromise formation, one that shows up in the comedies at around the turn of the century, like *Love's Last Shift* (1696). Jaffeir and Belvidera represent "safe sex," that is, a happily married couple whose extravagances of language and action are sanctified and therefore can be enjoyed by the audience without prurient guilt, whereas the Antonio/Aquilina action could not, and was suppressed in eighteenth-century productions.

The tone and setting of the play work to convey tension and horror. Despite its ranging through the streets and byways of Venice, *Venice Preserved* conveys an almost Ibsen-like feeling of entrapment. Jaffeir and Belvidera are caught in a maze, where every potential escape ends in a cul de sac. That the play is contained within a brief time span enhances the tension—Jaffeir must decide *now* to join the conspirators, decide *now* to betray them, decide *now* to kill Belvidera or Pierre. As inexorable as a drumbeat, the pressure mounts, and the audience is drawn in. Other plot elements are designed to elicit maximum sympathy.

A husband and father unable to provide for his wife and child, Jaffeir is a man at the mercy of powerful forces he cannot control, a man whose wife is nearly raped by someone he trusted, a man who betrays his dearest friend to death and suffers a blow and curses by that friend: who could help but feel sympathy? Belvidera is even more innocent and more pitiable: rejected by a doting father, forced to cope with bailiffs and a distraught husband, nearly raped by a stranger who brandishes the dagger her husband gave him, told that her husband means to fill the streets of Venice with blood, threatened with death by that beloved husband. Is it any wonder that she runs mad at the end of the play?

It is because the play is so vested in its hero and heroine as pitiable figures that the personal is commingled and counterpointed with the public. The scenes of "smuggling" (snuggling) that struck some later critics as oversentimentalized are as necessary to the emotional form as the conspiracy is to the plot. And the play's stage history as a vehicle for premiere actors in every theatrical generation attests to its life as an acting piece: Jaffeir and Belvidera made choice fare for stars from Thomas Betterton and Elizabeth Barry to David Garrick and Susannah Cibber. Nor is it impossible for a modern audience in the post-Vietnam era to appreciate the dilemma posed in *Venice Preserved*. Moral dilemmas, the intersection of public and private values, decisions which strain friendship and obligation—these seem particularly modern problems, no more soluble now than then.

Venice Preserved thus stands at the crossroads between the heroic extravagance of the 1660s and 1670s and the increasingly domestic sensibilities of the 1680s and 1690s. Recognizing the pulls of both sets of values, it could have, like Jaffeir, been torn apart by them; instead, it offers a mediated resolution of the conflict. In England too the conflict was resolved, for a time, by reestablishing Charles's monarchical rights over a stable state, at some cost to the public weal. But circumstances decreed that neither resolution would last very long.

3

The Last of the Stuarts

1685–1714

S everal factors directly affected the drama during the late seventeenth and early eighteenth centuries: the political tensions surrounding the succession, England's Continental wars, the altered social and cultural makeup of the city of London, and the realignments and adjustments that followed the splitting of the United Company in 1695. The theater became a risky venture at times, its financial health precarious as it faced a generation of theatergoers with different needs and expectations from those of its predecessors. In such a climate, theatrical competition around the turn of the century, instead of stimulating creativity, was almost suicidal, yet without such competition, dramatic development had nearly stagnated during the 1680s.

Politics affected the stage in primarily negative ways: the turbulence of the brief reign of James II (1685–88), despite James's support of the drama, meant darkened theaters during the worst of the crises. The accession of William and Mary (1688–1702) brought a continental war against the French and their allies that lasted, in various stages, for 25 years. Besides being consumed with other matters, neither William nor his successor, Anne (1702–1714), had much taste for the theater, and both Mary and Anne were sympathetic to the attempts of the Societies for the Reformation of Manners to subject the theater to moral scrutiny and control. Other social and economic changes that occurred during the reign of the last Stuarts, while positive in the long run, shook the financial foundations of the theater and made it experiment almost frantically in the hope of attracting new audiences.

The founding of the Bank of England in 1694 and other public finance measures, such as the South Sea Company formed in 1711, began to have substantial impact on the distribution of wealth and power in England. More generally, despite some hard times from 1704 to 1708, the war enriched England's merchant classes, which in turn affected London society and culture, and ultimately its theater: "By Anne's reign it was becoming apparent that money was gaining importance over birth or station in conferring power and influence. The blurring of lines dividing castes, the proliferation of intermediate social groups, growing geographical mobility at least of those in official positions and the professions from one region to another, and their concentration in London, meant that persons with pretensions or presumption could easily pass for gentlemen."[1] Accompanying cultural and intellectual changes played their part in "corroding traditional values" (Jones, 79). During the 1690s, the major works of John Locke, with their emphasis on the social contract, "became looked upon as the expression of the new age, as the modernization of beliefs and practices in science, theology, education, and politics."[2] Ideologies of all sorts were being challenged during the age of William and Mary, especially at institutions such as Leiden University in the Netherlands,[3] while in the streets of London after the lapsing of the Licensing Act in 1695, booksellers and publishers were producing pamphlets, newspapers, and books on a variety of controversial subjects for people to read, ponder, and debate in the London coffeehouses and clubs where men of diverse backgrounds and interests could mingle and exchange ideas: "London . . . provided the one mass market, of journalism and more scholarly literary activities. Political pamphlets, works of literature and criticism, religious works (especially sermons by popular preachers), almanacs, pornography—anything and everything that would sell—poured from the presses" (Jones, 78).[4]

Soon after the turn of the century came the era of the periodical. In 1702 the *Daily Courant*, the first daily newspaper, began publication, and in 1709 Sir Richard Steele's *The Tatler* appeared with its "mixture of news, gossip, and criticism," followed in 1711 by Steele and Joseph

Addison's *The Spectator*, which "did much to educate taste in every sphere" (Clark, 256–57). Clark goes on to suggest the importance of these periodicals as a cultural phenomenon: "In the *Spectator* commercial men and their affairs were treated with a respect which they had never before received from the public literature of Stuart England. This is one sign among many that by the later years of Queen Anne literature was coming to be more the common possession of the nation, or of the better-educated classes, than it had been before" (357). Perhaps most threatening to the traditionalists was the incorporation of science into the public realm during the early eighteenth century:

> Much of the interest shown in science by educated Englishmen was undiscriminating and naive, but a whole generation of scientists knew, and were not afraid to know, that they were exploring entirely new regions of knowledge and thought. The widespread interest in science represented a conscious turning away from the largely theological concerns of the previous generation of thinkers. . . . Furthermore, the acceptance of new ideas and theories by the educated, the virtual absence of widespread and popular prejudice and bigotry, was a sign of a capacity to adapt to change, to see in changes what was to emerge as a theory of progress. This was of vital importance to a society like England's in 1714, on the eve of a transformation of a kind that had never happened before in Europe.
>
> (Jones, 358)

It was in this environment that playwrights like William Congreve, Sir John Vanbrugh, and Thomas Southerne were writing:

> To the Tories, William III remained Hogen Mogen, the Dutch usurper; but to Whigs like Congreve, he was a hero, an opponent of French tyranny and the living representative of opposition to France and Louis XIV. The Whig theory of the Revolution as the final triumph of the rule of law and property was accepted even by men as inherently conservative as Swift; and, though some historians have argued that the Glorious Revolution brought with it a triumph of mediocrity and middle-class values, it also gave the nation a new stability. Congreve remained a Whig at heart, even when he was employed by the Tories; and one explanation for his startling and brilliant early career may be found in a milieu

favorable to a young romantic talent—a milieu full of new hope, excitement, and change.[5]

Such events and ideas were perceived not as progress but as retrograde by a particular subset of Anglican clergymen of the time, who stood against the tide of change that seemed to be sweeping over England, leaving tradition and religious and moral values in its wake. One of these was the Reverend Dr. Sacheverell, who "had a gift for inflammatory preaching, . . . denouncing whigs, dissenters, latitudinarians, and low churchmen" (Clark, 226). In 1709, in response to a "violent sermon" he gave before the Lord Mayor and aldermen of London, the government decided to impeach him. The results—a flood of pamphlets, riots in the streets, and destruction of dissenting meetinghouses—indicate how volatile these questions of religion and morality were for much of the populace. Inevitably, all these factors also affected the relatively small group of people who constituted the London theater audiences.[6] Bearing in mind Harold Love's caveat, that "there is no hard evidence whatsoever for any current view of the composition of the . . . audience,"[7] we can nonetheless make educated guesses about some of the alterations in this constituency.

First, late Stuart audiences were becoming different in makeup from their Carolean predecessors and perceiving themselves differently. Although heterogeneous, Carolean audiences had followed court tastes and values; Samuel Pepys is the classic case of one who attended plays regularly and changed his mind about them to agree with what his "betters" thought. But this top-down system gradually eroded after James's abdication. Even when he was at home, William was of the sober breed of Protestant that took no delight in plays and players, while Mary, who had acted at court in her youth, seems to have had a more complex relationship with the theater.[8] While she enjoyed and supported several plays, such as Behn's *The Rover*, that were flamboyantly immoral, her own reading leaned heavily toward scriptures; she "offered by her example a model of personal piety," and she publicly supported figures like Thomas Bray, the founder of the Society for Promoting Christian Knowledge.[9] Loss of strong monarchical support left a social vacuum quickly filled by antitheater groups like the Societies for the Reformation of Manners, founded in 1692 and increasingly active through the remainder of the century. The appearance of Jeremy Collier's *The Immorality and Profaneness of the Stage* in April 1698 was, as we shall see, part of this larger reform movement.

If not courtiers and those who shared their tastes, who were these new audiences? One theory, based on the number of prologues that address and seem to placate "the ladies" and the fact that theater managers in the 1690s and after the turn of the century actively courted new women playwrights, is that they were middle-class women. But David Roberts offers another interpretation of this evidence: "If there is no reason to doubt that comedy changed its style to suit the modesty of the ladies, there is every reason to be sceptical about the ladies' part in bringing the change about" (127), arguing that the "ladies" referred to in prologues were symbols of the bourgeoisie, not actual women. John Loftis suggests a general shift in social strata, that the same groups patronized the theaters—the gentlefolk, merchants, citizens—but their makeup was different. The "citizens," for example, were no longer exporters and financiers but petty traders and merchants, lower on the social and educational scale, while merchants and financiers were considered, or were actually, members of the gentry.[10] The tastes of these audience members had been formed in a different crucible from those of their predecessors; 35 years and more after the Restoration, London's population had become larger, more diverse, and more interested in business and politics. It was more sophisticated in some ways, less in others.

The relationship between audiences and the stage also changed, and audiences of the 1690s could exert box-office pressure more forcefully because they seemed willing to eschew the theater entirely, seeking entertainment elsewhere or nowhere. Especially after the splitting of the United Company in 1695, managers found themselves forced to cajole, seduce, and entice as never before to keep their theaters running in the black. If the union of the two theater companies from 1682 to 1695 had suggested that London simply could not support two fully operational theaters, the financial problems of theaters during the late 1690s seemed to confirm that premise.

From the standpoint of dramatic development, however, the end of competition in the 1680s had brought unhealthy conservatism. After the union, fewer new plays were produced, and those, "safe" repeats of previous formulas.[11] As long as audiences seemed satisfied, the United Company's nominal managers, Charles Davenant and Charles Killigrew, and its actual managers, actors Thomas Betterton and William Smith, grew complacent: "In the mid-seventies the Duke's Company had often mounted a dozen new plays each season, and together with the King's Company usually put on a total of eighteen to twenty-four new shows. In the five years after 1682 the United Company never mounted more than three or four new plays in any season. Why risk time and money?" (Milhous 1979, 42). A series of managerial changes after 1687 resulted in the ascension to power in 1693 of Christopher Rich as principal shareholder. Rich almost immediately engaged in, and won, a power struggle with Betterton, and began to operate the United Company in such a way as to maximize his own profits, at whatever expense to the players:[12] "[Rich] represents an ugly variation on the Killigrew approach to management: He was concerned with the company solely as an investment. He set about bilking and mistreating the actors, confident that the monopoly provision, a well-established precedent by 1695, would be enforced. The actors rebelled, and to Rich's chagrin, legal opinion held that the patents did not preclude a later monarch's granting licenses for other companies."[13] Via the Lord Chamberlain, William III gave the rebels a license in March 1695 to form a separate company. It was granted to a group of actor-sharers for no fixed period, at the pleasure of the monarch, enabling them to provide a real alternative to Rich's patent company.

Each company had competitive advantages and disadvantages. The patentees had exclusive rights to the theaters operating at the time of dissolution, Dorset Garden and Drury Lane, and retained all sets, costumes, and other properties, but they lost almost all their veteran actors and the managerial expertise Betterton had gained over 30 years. The company at Lincoln's Inn Fields started with all the premiere players—Thomas Betterton, Elizabeth Barry, Anne Bracegirdle, Cave Underhill, Edward Kynaston—and the goodwill of the king and a large proportion of the theatergoing public, but it had a small converted tennis court for a theater and lacked the means to build anew, especially when costumes, props, and scenery had to be provided from gate receipts.[14] For both companies, the problem of playscripts and rights reared its head almost immediately, much as it had for Killigrew and Davenant in the early 1660s. Unlike their predecessors, however, the two companies in 1695 chose not to engage each other directly on the issue of legal rights; instead, each simply put on the plays it chose from the repertory, often in direct competition with the rival house. Also, since each company realized its survival would depend on its ability to gauge the temper and attract the notice of fickle theatergoers, each began to encourage new playwrights: "for the first time in many years the recreational efforts of gentlemen amateurs and women had a real chance of production" (Milhous 1979, 98). Delayed by the death of Queen Mary in December, Betterton's company opened its doors at Lincoln's Inn Fields in April

1695 with the production of a new comedy, *Love for Love*, whose 25-year-old author, William Congreve, was already being hailed as Dryden's natural successor, and who would soon become a full sharer in Betterton's company.

Comedy: Love for Love

SCANDAL: *I was an Infidel to your Sex; and you have converted me—For now I am convinc'd that all Women are not like Fortune, blind in bestowing Favours, either on those who do not merit, or who do not want 'em.*

ANGELICA: *'Tis an unreasonable Accusation, that you lay upon our Sex: You tax us with Injustice, only to cover your own want of Merit. You would all have the Reward of Love; but few have the Constancy to stay till it becomes your due. Men are generally Hypocrites and Infidels, they pretend to Worship, but have neither Zeal nor Faith: How few, like* Valentine, *would persevere even unto Martyrdom, and sacrifice their Interest to their Constancy! In admiring me, you misplace the Novelty.*

*The Miracle to Day is, that we find
A Lover true: Not that a Woman's Kind.*
(Love for Love, 5.1.622–37)[15]

Though continuing to be more popular than tragedy, comedy seemed to be the genre most sensitive to what was happening in late Stuart England. It was more likely than serious drama to be banned or censored, its dramatists forced to compete vigorously with each other in a climate affected by hostile forces and disapprobation. Successful new comic dramatists like William Congreve, Colley Cibber, John Vanbrugh, and George Farquhar not only had to compete with the best of the old comedies—*The Committee, Epicoene, The Rover, The Tempest*—which remained popular in the repertory, but also needed to please tempermental audiences not entirely sure what they wanted to see. Dramatists also

MOST POPULAR PLAYS: 1685–1714
(Plays with 19 or More Performances
with Performance Numbers in Parentheses)

COMEDY
The Alchemist (19)
The Amorous Widow (33)
*Amphitryon** (22)
Bartholomew Fair (19)
*The [Beaux] Strategem** (40)
*The Busie Body** (25)
*The Careless Husband** (42)
The Chances (21)
*The Comical Rivals** (22)
The Committee (52)
*The Confederacy** (24)
*The Constant Couple** (32)
*The Emperour of the Moon** (36)
Epicoene (30)
Epsom Wells (19)
*The Fair Quaker of Deal** (31)
*The Funeral** (20)
The Island Princess† (31)
A Jovial Crew (23)
The Lancashire Witches (34)
The London Cuckolds (25)
*Love for Love** (59)
*Love Makes a Man** (43)
*Love's Last Shift** (20)
The Man of Mode (27)
The Northern Lass (36)
*The Old Batchelor** (31)
The Pilgrim† (39)
*The Recruiting Officer** (69)
The Rehearsal (22)
*The Relapse** (32)
The Rover (36)
The Royal Merchant† (23)
Rule a Wife and Have a Wife (32)
The Scornful Lady (22)
She Would if She Could (25)
Sir Courtly Nice (34)
*The Squire of Alsatia** (43)

The Tempest (52)
*The Tender Husband** (29)
*Tunbridge Walks** (26)
Volpone (24)

TRAGEDY
*Abra Mule** (19)
Aureng-Zebe (20)
*Cato** (32)
Don John [the Libertine] (31)
Hamlet (49)
The History of King Lear (25)
The Indian Emperour (30)
*Jane Shore** (19)
Julius Caesar (24)
Macbeth (50)
The Moore of Venice (31)
*The Mourning Bride** (21)
Oedipus (23)
*Oroonoko**(37)
The Orphan (19)
The Rival Queens (28)
Timon of Athens (32)
The Unhappy Favourite (44)
Venice Preserved (25)

TRAGICOMEDY
The Comical Revenge (22)
*The Fatal Marriage** (19)
The Humorous Lieutenant (20)
The Spanish Fryar (46)

HISTORY
Henry IV, I (20)

OPERA
*Almahide** (25)
*Arsinoe** (36)

Camilla* (65)
Hydaspes* (40)
Pyrrhus and Demetrius* (46)
Rinaldo* (27)
Thomyris* (29)

AFTERPIECE
The Country-Wake* (36)
The Stage-Coach* (32)
The Walking Statue* (38)

NOTES
*New play
†Revision

had to contend with critics who were outsiders, and sometimes seemed to make unrealistic and inappropriate demands upon the theater. That any new playwrights were successful under such adverse conditions is amazing, but the best of them sensed the need to shift the focus of comedy from showing pure competition among witty, licentious characters to depicting characters whose expertise also incorporated other values— feelings and virtues. In successful new comedies, merit was no longer solely a function of ingenuity and physical prowess; it could also be moral and could benefit society. Further, these comedies, unlike the compromise formation comedies of the 1670s, assumed a consensual framework for themselves and their audiences, and therefore treated issues of authority and sexuality differently from their predecessors.

The shift to incorporate feeling and emotion had occurred somewhat earlier in serious dramas that were now part of the popular repertory, but it was not until the 1690s that new comedies—often those which focused on marriage as well as courtship—began to show these changes. Marital plots were not entirely new—plays like *Marriage A-la-Mode*, *She Would If She Could*, *The Amorous Widow*, *The Country-Wife*, and *The London Cuckolds* had devoted a significant amount of space and satiric attention to the problem marriages among secondary or blocking figures. But new comedies like Cibber's *Love's Last Shift* (1696) and Vanbrugh's *The Relapse* (1696), by moving married couples to center stage, seemed deliberately to ask certain questions about conjugal relationships that courtship comedies, by definition, beg or leave ambiguous: Can libertines reform? Is there a double moral standard for men and women? Is monogamy "natural"? Who wields power in a marriage, and what does "liberty" mean in that context? Sometimes the conclusions of these comedies were deliberately ambiguous, but a skilled playwright could make this new emphasis into provocative drama. In another sense, the darkly satiric work of Southerne and Vanbrugh both feeds upon and makes normative the satiric, nihlistic visions of Wycherley and Otway.

Even in the more benign courtship comedies of Congreve and Farquhar there were substantial changes. As we have seen, Fletcherian and Carolean courtship comedies measured success in terms of payoffs and prizes; the desire for money, power, and sex motivated many if not all characters, and skill, wit, and insouciance won the day. The new courtship comedies gave similar rewards for less tangible heroic qualities—a good heart, the willingness to sacrifice oneself—that usually but not always were accompanied by the qualities admired in Caroline hero[-in]es—physical attractiveness, wealth, wit, the ability to manipulate others, courage, combativeness. Sometimes this new mixture seemed at war with itself unless handled by someone like William Congreve (1670–1729), whose plays nicely illustrate one aspect of the shift in 1690s comedies.

Congreve's third play, and comedy, produced within a two-year span,[16] *Love for Love* (1695), was also his most popular play, and justly so.[17] Of his two previous plays, *The Old Batchelor* (1693), for all its lively characters and witty dialogue, was basically a frenetically plotted rehashing of formulaic material: the cuckolded old cit-Puritan, the reluctant-to-commit-themselves young lovers, the "humourous" rake who enjoys the chase more than the capture, clever servants who ape their betters. *The Double-Dealer* (1693), on the other hand, dealt in stronger stuff and was censured as a result.[18] Eschewing the multiple plot lines of *The Old Batchelor*, it is much more focused and intense, with a genuine villain, Maskall, and sensible lovers who seem to exist in a world different from that inhabited by the hypocrites and fools of their social environment. The audiences' relatively cool reception of this comedy and *The Way of the World* in 1700 suggests they had different expectations from what Congreve was providing in these comedies, although both of these plays found considerable favor in the eighteenth century (see Avery 1951).

Although Congreve is sometimes considered out of synch with the developments in late seventeenth-century comedy, a comic playwright who would have been more at home with Wycherley, Behn, and Etherege than Steele, Centlivre, and Cibber, he is in fact one of those responsible for adding sensibility to the familiar evaluation mechanisms of wit comedy. These changes are evident even in *The Double-Dealer*, his most satiric comedy. The lovers Mellefont and Cynthia, although satisfactorily witty and intelligent, are sentimentally attached to one another with an openness that is alien to previous comic hero[in]es, who masked whatever feelings they had under a patina of sophistication. At the beginning of act 4, Mellefont and Cynthia acknowledge that their mutual attraction enables them to withstand their enemies, Maskwell and Lady Touchwood. Mellefont even suggests that they elope, thus relinquishing all hopes of inheritance from his uncle or her father: "Pox o'Fortune, Portion, Settlements and Joyntures" (4.1.30). This is extraordinary stuff. In the configuration of 1670s comedy, where money, power, and sex seemed the ultimate motivators of the comic hero[in]e's behavior, Dorimant would no more elope with a penniless Harriet than he would be castrated, and the Rover viewed Hellena's dowry as a major part of her attraction. Moreover, these love relationships were spiced by conflict *between* the gay-couple lovers, during which each asserted his or her self-directed ego and rakish temper. In *The Double-Dealer*, except for Mellefont's friend Careless, such attitudes and behaviors are entirely located in the fools and in villains like Maskall and Lady Touchwood. One reason for the play's failure to please may have been that its hero is *too* genteel.[19] More likely, however, is that the immorality of the other characters was unpleasantly highlighted by the relative purity of Mellefont and Cynthia, who introduce moral criteria that the audience might have found at odds with the rest of the characters and actions.[20]

In any event, *Love for Love* does a better job of creating a hero who is both perceptive and sensible, and its success was substantial and long-lived.[21] Valentine retains all the characteristics of the rake hero: he has wasted his fortune on "Love and Pleasurable Expense"; he has an illegitimate child and is hiding indoors from the duns; he reads Epictetus to learn how to become a stoic, to no avail, and thinks he might turn poet; he has no illusions about the town. Yet despite these vestigial libertine characteristics, he is also rather pitiable. He suffers the pains of unrequited love for Angelica, while his father, Sir Sampson, is determined to exert his "Arbitrary Power" to disinherit Valentine in favor of his younger brother Ben. As the play opens, Valentine is a virtual recluse, hiding indoors from his creditors and abandoned by most of his fashionable friends. The final straw is the arrival of his father's steward with a fool's bargain—that Valentine should sell his birthright for £4000.

Throughout the play, Valentine twists and turns in the web he and others have woven: Angelica's feelings are a mystery to him and to the audience until quite late in the play; his father's plans seem assured of success; his environment is entirely peopled with fools and dubious

characters except for his friend Scandal. Congreve, however, chooses not
to milk the audience's sympathy overmuch, presenting Valentine's plight
as mostly humorous. Moreover, Valentine, unlike Mellefont in *The
Double-Dealer*, has the wherewithal to extricate himself and sees clearly
who his adversaries are; he also has a charming resilience to the worst
blows befalling him. At the end of act 4, for example, wherein he has
played the madman to put off signing his father's document and to
extract a declaration from Angelica, he receives from her only a riddle:
"Uncertainty and Expectation are the Joys of Life. Security is an insipid
thing, and the overtaking and possessing of a Wish, discovers the Folly
of the Chase. Never let us know one another better; for the Pleasure of
a Masquerade is done, when we come to shew Faces; But I'll tell you
two things before I leave you; I am not the Fool you take me for; and
you are Mad and don't know it" (4.1.786–93). Instead of despairing, he
acknowledges temporary defeat, frustration, and a new resolve: "She is
harder to be understood than a Piece of *Egyptian* Antiquity, or an *Irish*
Manuscript; you may pore till you spoil your Eyes, and not improve your
Knowledge. . . . [S]he is a Medal without a Reverse or Inscription; for
Indifference has both sides alike. Yet while she does not seem to hate me,
I will pursue her, and know her if it be possible" (4.1.801–4, 810–13). His
resolution and romantic steadfastness, as much as his wit and energy,
finally award Valentine all the prizes; this is the main difference between
Love for Love and Carolean comedy.

The "world" represented in the play is somewhat broader than
those presented by Dryden or Behn, although it contains characters besides Valentine, his father, and Angelica whose analogues appeared in
earlier comedies: Foresight, a fool whose "superstition dominates his
entire life, whether as an astrologer or a cuckold" (Novak, 114); Tattle,
who simultaneously conceals and boasts of his sexual conquests; Mrs.
Foresight, who cannot "remember" a sexual encounter the morning after;
Mrs. Frail, who uses her ingenuity to enhance her fortune; and Scandal,
the critic of all he surveys. But two figures besides Valentine and Angelica
disturb the familiar pattern of comic antagonism these conventional characters delineate. Ben and Prue bring into the play, respectively, the air
of the sea and the country. Although both have analogues in previous
comedies—seamen like Manly and Freeman in *The Plain Dealer* or
country girls like Margery in *The Country-Wife* or Betty in *Sir Salomon*—
Congreve uses these two characters differently. Under Prue's conventional
garb of innocent lustfulness and Ben's vulgarity, both exhibit a native
shrewdness that throws into relief the social hypocrisy of the town.

Though Ben and Prue are mocked by Mrs. Frail—"if he be but as great a Sea-Beast, as she is a Land-Monster, we shall have a most Amphibious Breed—The Progeny will be all Otters" (1.1.570–72)—her analysis proves to be prejudiced, limited, and, ultimately, false. Prue, the ignorant country girl, begins to learn town ways rather quickly under Tattle's tutelage, and Ben, from his entrance in act 3, makes it clear that his values, like his language, are sea-bred: "it's but a folly to lie: For to speak one thing, and to think just the contrary way; is as it were, to look one way, and to row another. Now, for my part d'ee see, I'm for carrying things above Board, I'm not for keeping any thing under Hatches" (3.1.385–89). Part of the humor of these two characters is Ben's and Prue's antipathy toward each other, despite parental machinations. She finds him crude and "ugly," a veritable "sea-calf"; he considers her impertinent and unattractive, a "dirty dowdy." Each prefers the sophisticated charms, respectively, of Tattle and Mrs. Frail. Nonetheless, Ben and Prue together constitute a kind of "natural" counterweight to the artificiality of the town; because Congreve treats them gently, he implies that their views and manners are to be amalgamated into the world of the play.

Poised between the crude naturalism of Ben and Prue and the slick falsity of Tattle and Mrs. Frail are Scandal, Jeremy, Valentine, and Angelica. Valentine's friend Scandal is the complete cynic, the unreconstructed Carolean rake, and his determined seduction of Mrs. Foresight is as typical as his comments on human, especially female, behavior: "I believe some Women are Vertuous too; but 'tis as I believe some Men are Valiant, thro' fear—For why shou'd a Man court Danger, or a Woman shun Pleasure? . . . Honour is a publick Enemy; and Conscience a Domestick Thief; and he that wou'd secure his Pleasure, must pay a Tribute to one, and go halves with t'other. As for Honour, that you have secur'd, for you have purchas'd a perpetual opportunity for Pleasure . . . your Husband" (3.1.669–72, 675–79, 681). Jeremy, Valentine's pragmatic servant, is also prone to satiric commentary, and, like Scandal, finds Valentine a bit too romantic for his taste. Yet it is Valentine, not they, who is vindicated at the last and rewarded with Angelica and his inheritance.

Except for Mirabell, Valentine is the most self-aware and town-wise of Congreve's comic heroes, despite his poverty and lovesickness. Again and again he displays these qualities, particularly in conversing with Jeremy and Scandal in act 1 when, to their horror, he announces that he intends to become a playwright, and in his mad scenes in act 4. But wit is only one standard of judgment in the play; the other, good nature and depth of feeling, distinguishes Valentine even from Scandal and Jeremy, and shows up in both his courtship and his confrontations with his irascible father, first seen in act 2:

SIR SAMPSON:	How came you here, Sir? Here, to stand here, upon those two Leggs, and look erect with that audacious face, hah? Answer me that? Did you come a Voluntier into the World? Or did I beat up for you with the lawful Authority of a Parent, and press you to the service? . . .
VALENTINE:	I know no more why I came, than you do why you call'd me. But here I am, and if you don't mean to provide for me, I desire you wou'd leave me as you found me.
SIR SAMPSON:	With all my heart: Come, Uncase, Strip, and go naked out of the World as you came into't.
VALENTINE:	My Cloaths are soon put off:—But you must also deprive me of Reason, Thought, Passions, Inclinations, Affections, Appetites, Senses, and the huge Train of Attendants that you begot along with me. . . . I am of my self, a plain easie simple Creature; and to be kept at small expence; but the Retinue that you gave me are craving and invincible; they are so many Devils that you have rais'd, and will have employment.

(2.1.323–42, 345–48)

Although he calls up the libertine's creed—that nature demands recompense for its appetites and desires—Valentine's good humor in the face of extreme provocation argues that he is a "creature" of more depth and sensibility than he describes.

Weber places these qualities under the heading of the "philosophical libertine," who, unlike the earlier version epitomized by the real Lord Rochester (1647–80), and the fictional Dorimant in *The Man of Mode* or Willmore of *The Rover*, attempts to mitigate his appetite to attain a greater if quieter pleasure, thus redefining the rake-hero's "predilection for disorder and misrule" (Weber, 97). In *Love for Love*, the qualities for which Valentine is most admired, by Angelica and by the audience, are symbolized by his "madness" in act 4. When Angelica tells Tattle, "I never lov'd him till he was Mad" (4.1.572), and rejects Tattle's courtship with "when you are as Mad as *Valentine*, I'll believe you love me, and the maddest shall take me" (4.1.586–88), she is defining madness as generosity and passion that supersede self-interest and pragmatism. This explains her enigmatic words to Valentine a bit later: "you are Mad and don't know it" (4.1.792–93). As this exchange and the title suggest, it is Angelica and Valentine together who define the center of value in *Love for Love*.

Like Valentine, Angelica is a nice blend of wit and softer qualities more suited to the 1690s than the 1670s. She retains the toughness and purposefulness of Carolean female heroes like Florimell and Hellena, but lacks their dedication to the libertine ethos. We first see her (2.1) holding her own with her uncle, insisting on her right to freedom, and taunting him with his fears of cuckolding. Her elusiveness with Valentine is partly to assert her autonomy and wit; her independence gives her the security to make her own choices and shape her own life, and she is adroit at manipulating others. In the last act, she dupes Sir Sampson, Tattle, and Frail into restoring Valentine's inheritance. At the same time, she tests and teases Valentine, forcing him to confront her without disguise or arrogance, as he finally does: "Nay faith, now let us understand one another, Hypocrisie apart,—The Comedy draws toward an end, and let us think of leaving acting, and be our selves; and since you have lov'd me, you must own I have at length deserv'd you shou'd confess it" (4.1.706–10). His final test is passed when he believes she means to marry his father and offers finally to concede the battle: "I have been disappointed of my only Hope; and he that loses hope may part with any thing. I never valu'd Fortune, but as it was subservient to my Pleasure; and my only Pleasure was to please this Lady: I have made many vain Attempts, and find at last, that nothing but my Ruine can effect it: Which, for that Reason, I will sign to—Give me the Paper" (5.1.543–49). Angelica, in her turn, also unmasks: "Had I the World to give you, it cou'd not make me worthy of so generous and faithful a Passion: Here's my Hand, my Heart was always yours, and struggl'd very hard to make this utmost Tryal of your Virtue" (5.1.560–64).

What is most unusual about *Love for Love*, finally, is that it is woman-centered in this way, that "what starts as Valentine's play ends as Angelica's" (Milhous and Hume, 286). At least some of this shift was owing to the increased importance and popularity of female actors like Anne Bracegirdle and Elizabeth Barry, who played, respectively, Angelica and Mrs. Frail. For whatever reason, *Love for Love* significantly changes the male-centered rakish courtships of Carolean comedies wherein female

heroes joined their male partners, in language if not in deed, in subscrib-
ing to a libertine ethos. Desire in *Love for Love* has a dimension in which
feelings are, if not the only criterion for judgment, an important part of
the total picture. If the simplicity of the value structure in Carolean
comedy could be maintained only because it was liable to multiple interpretations, Congreve and later comic dramatists had to produce a more
complex value structure, accommodating more range under a single
edifice. Audiences no longer comfortable with their own heterogeneity
or heterodoxy needed to find consensus that was more broadly based,
like that provided in characters like Valentine and Angelica. In this
respect, *Love for Love* lays the foundation for other popular courtship
comedies of the time, from Farquhar's *The Constant Couple* (1699) to
Centlivre's *The Busie Body* (1709), wherein sensibility would be as important as wit in defining value and apportioning rewards, and ultimately
for eighteenth-century comedies, in which it would become more important.

Comedy: The Provoked Wife

> *What cloying meat is love, when matrimony's the sauce to it.*
> *Two years' marriage has debauched my five senses. Everything I*
> *see, everything I hear, everything I feel, everything I smell, and*
> *everything I taste—methinks has wife in't. No boy was ever so*
> *weary of his tutor, no girl of her bib, no nun of doing penance,*
> *nor old maid of being chaste, as I am of being married. Sure*
> *there's a secret curse entailed upon the very name of wife.*
>
> (The Provoked Wife, *1.1.1–8*)[22]

    Congreve was not the only writer attempting to find a comic mode
suitable to the 1690s. Two other playwrights who managed to make a
name for themselves during these unpredictable times were Colley Cibber
(1671–1751) and Sir John Vanbrugh (1666–1726), both of whom expanded the horizon of popular comedy to include marriage as well as
courtship. Cibber's *Love's Last Shift* (1696), followed by *The Careless
Husband* (1704), and Vanbrugh's *The Relapse* (1696) and *The Provoked
Wife* (1697)[23] create a comic mode that can provide a harsher perspective
on some of the same value shifts identified in *Love for Love*. In these

comedies, incorporating feelings and sensibility meant showing dimensions of human behavior within marriage that included the consequences of libertinism and selfishness: the married rake was not a pretty sight.

Cibber's *Love's Last Shift; or, the Fool in Fashion* premiered in January 1696 and has often been credited with revolutionizing the form of eighteenth-century comedy. In 1783–84, for example, Thomas Davies called *Love's Last Shift* "the first comedy, acted since the Restoration, in which were proffered purity of manners and decency of language, with a due respect for the marriage bed"[24] thus exaggerating a change that started somewhat earlier and was less radical. Indeed, if Congreve is sometimes given less credit than he deserves for creating new comic patterns, Cibber is given more. Basically, *Love's Last Shift* is indebted to a number of previous comedies, like Fletcher's *The Scornful Lady*, a repertory favorite since the 1660s for most of its multiple plot lines: four intertwined love relationships—two courtships and two affairs— that incorporate a wide range of compatibility and sensibility. The most conventional involve Young Worthy, a lively young wastrel who is trying to repair his fortune by marrying an heiress; his elder brother, whose courtship is rocky because he can't stop lecturing his intended about her social life; and Sir Novelty Fashion, a fool who interferes with their courtships and has trouble with his jealous and temperamental mistress. All three actions end conventionally: the lovers are rewarded, the elder generation outwitted, the fool punished.

The most original action in the play involves Loveless, the thoroughgoing rake who eight years before the time of the play left his wife, Amanda, to devote himself to wine, women, gambling, and travel. Mistakenly believing his wife dead, he has returned to England, destitute but unrepentant, only to find her patiently waiting still. Two key sequences in this plot occur in act 4, scene 3 and act 5, scene 2. In the first, Loveless has been brought to Amanda's townhouse apparently by mistake, and is allowed to "enjoy" this unknown woman illicitly, while she basks in the delights of conjugal love. The scene, which begins with Amanda entering "loosely dressed," is deliberately titillating, though technically moral, much as the love scenes in *Venice Preserved* between Jaffeir and Belvidera offered salacious delights in the guise of marital felicity. In act 5, Cibber delivers the payoff—Amanda reveals her identity to her husband, fainting from excess emotion, and Loveless, overcome with remorse and renewed sexual attraction, vows to reform. He even gets to speak the moral tag at the end: "And sure the nearest to the Joys above, / Is the chaste Rapture of a virtuous Love" (5.4.51–52).[25] In context, however, the Amanda-Loveless action is simply another manipulation from the hands of Young Worthy and young Cibber, a satisfactory ending for one of the play's multiple actions. The play's epilogue rather clearly states Cibber's purpose—to please everyone in a diverse audience, from "City-gentlemen" to rakes to ladies:[26]

> Kind City-Gentlemen o'th'middle Row;
> He hopes you nothing to his Charge can lay,
> There's not a Cuckold made in all his Play. . . .
>   Now, Sirs, To you whose sole Religion's Drinking,
> Whoring, Roaring, without the Pain of Thinking,
> He fears he's made a Fault you'll ne'er forgive, . . .
> An honest Rake forego the Joys of Life!
> His Whores, and Wine! t'Embrace a dull chaste Wife. . . .
>   But then again,
> He's lew'd for above four Acts, Gentlemen! . . .
> Four Acts for your course Palates were design'd,
> But then the Ladies Taste is more refin'd,
> They, for *Amanda's* Sake, will sure be kind.
>   (Epilogue, 2–4, 9–11, 13–16, 20–22)

Unlike Congreve's hierarchy of values, Cibber's parallels offer variant fare for various "palates," as many Carolean comedies do. *Love's Last Shift* also inspired a better and more revolutionary comedy from John Vanbrugh, *The Relapse; or, Virtue in Danger*, in which Loveless succumbs to his old life and habits and Amanda barely restrains herself from having a compensatory adulterous affair.

As this sequence suggests, what Cibber treated somewhat flippantly as a catchy plot device—incompatible marriage—Vanbrugh saw as a serious social problem, one he treated again in his second comedy, *The Provoked Wife*. From its opening scene, we find ourselves in the midst of a "modern" marriage: Sir John Brute has married to satisfy his lust; Lady Brute, to satisfy her desire for money and position. In matching soliloquies in act 1, scene 1, husband and wife bemoan their fate, permanently trapped in marriage with a hated spouse. Of the two, Sir John is the more despicable, and the rest of the play shows his cowardice, his debauchery, his verbal and physical abuse of his wife, and his gutter habits in all their glory. When Lady Brute half-decides to cuckold her husband with her faithful but unrequited lover Constant, we sympathize because we share her disgust for such a husband and admire the kind of frankness with which she ends her first soliloquy: "Lord, what fine notions of virtue do we women take up upon the credit of old foolish philosophers. Virtue's its own reward, virtue's this, virtue's that. Virtue's an ass, and a gallant's worth forty on't" (1.1.75–78). Unlike Cibber's or even Vanbrugh's Amanda, Lady Brute is aware of her own sexual and emotional needs and can fulfill them only illicitly. As she explains to her niece and confidante, Bellinda, "I'm in danger. Merit and wit assault me from without, nature and love solicit me within, my husband's barbarous usage piques me to revenge, and Satan catching at the fair occasion throws in my way that vengeance which of all vengeance pleases women best" (1.1.155–60). Lady Brute thus becomes the thinking person's hedonist; if ever a wife since Margery Pinchwife is justified in seeking solace outside marriage, she is. Yet Vanbrugh evades the final adultery, deliberately leaving the ending of this plot open and allowing the audience to create their own resolution.

A second plot presents an updated version of the gay couple in Bellinda and Heartfree, witty, satiric, and reluctant to give up their autonomy. Heartfree begins the play as a misogynist, but drops the pose rather abruptly when he encounters Bellinda. In turn, Bellinda is put off by Heartfree's relative poverty, but manages finally to choose the man over the estate. She explains to Lady Brute, "I like him and have fortune enough to keep above extremity. I can't say I would live with him in a cell upon love and bread and butter; but I had rather have the man I love, and a middle state of life, than that gentleman in the chair there and twice your ladyship's splendor" (5.2.120–24). As this speech suggests, Vanbrugh choreographs the parallels and analogues between plot lines and characters to underscore their commentary on one another. Articulate and aware characters reinforce these parallels in dialogue:

HEARTFREE: [I]n as plain terms as I can find to express myself: I could love you even to—matrimony itself a'most, egad.

BELLINDA: Just as Sir John did her ladyship there. What think you? Don't you believe one month's time might bring you down to the same indifference, only clad in a little better manners perhaps. Well, you men are unaccountable things, mad till you have your mistresses, and then stark mad till you are rid of 'em again. Tell me honestly, is not your patience

HEARTFREE:	put to a much severer trial after possession than before?
HEARTFREE:	With a great many, I must confess, it is, to our eternal scandal. But I—dear creature, do but try me.
BELLINDA:	That's the surest way indeed, to know, but not the safest.

(4.4.122–33)

Though this plot ends with marriage in the offing, then, it too has an open-endedness that is more starkly knowing than the ambiguity that often occurs at the end of Carolean courtship comedy.

Along with Sir John Brute, the lovers' principal antagonist is Lady Fancyfull, a vain and affected coquette who is piqued by Heartfree's rejection because she needs to be "adored by all the men and envied by all the women" (1.2.89–91). When Heartfree gravitates to Bellinda, Lady Fancyfull vows revenge, nearly succeeding in splitting them apart with lies about each other's fidelity. Only a fairly implausible deux ex machina ending reconciles the disenchanted lovers to one another. Lady Fancyfull is interesting because her worst qualities are shadowed in Lady Brute and Bellinda, as Sir John's are in Constant and Heartfree. Because Lady Fancyfull and Sir John are not just inadequate but vicious and malignant, these similarities taint the heroic characters more seriously than fops and fools do Carolean comic heroes, and the play's hopeful denouement is decidedly muted as a result.

Vanbrugh also employs familiar comic scenes, such as the closet "discovery" scene and the masked assignation in the park, with new twists that push the limits of these comic conventions. Sir John is not just a drunken would-be cuckold but a violent and disgusting animal; his wife's shudders of horror at the prospect of sharing a bed with him are not mere affectation but real revulsion. At the same time, Constant's veiled threat to kill his rival stretches the boundaries of comedy in another direction. As the street fighting that Sir John so enjoys exposes the violent underside of previous heroes' drunken ramblings, these acts expose the real malice and viciousness underlying behaviors that previous comedies glossed over or laughed away.

The Provoked Wife is bound together by a satiric tone and commentary that are Vanbrugh's trademark and that establish his contribution to comic development. The play focuses on tensions between and within characters responding to several contradictory forces: natural urges, whether emotions like attraction and antipathy or appetites like drunkenness and sex; social urges, like competition and reputation; and moral urges, like reason and honor. In the conflicts Vanbrugh sets up, morality tends to be the least powerful determinant, consistently overborne by emotion or appetite, with social constraint a weak enforcer of the higher values. As in Otway's plays, wit is often counterproductive. Wit allows characters to construct rationalizations for behavior they know is dishonorable, and while it enables them to strip the facades from themselves and each other, it offers no solace or solution to what they see. At various times, Heartfree, Bellinda, Lady Brute, Constant, and even Lady Fancyfull and Sir John act as satiric voices for the author, becoming a mouthpiece for Vanbrugh's "plain English" indictment of his age. This gives a peculiar ambiguity to some characters, such as Sir John, who otherwise is cloddish and repulsive, and to the ending, which is so abrupt and inconclusive that it leaves a bitter aftertaste. Unlike Carolean comedies, in which wit and competence could imply, if one wished, reformation and a happy ending, and unlike Congreve's careful blending of sense and sensitivity in *Love for Love*, *The Provoked Wife* shows that wit produces only unease and discomfort. Vanbrugh presents a modern setting in which characters openly discuss "divorce," that is, separate maintenance (1.1.53–54; 3.1.101–4), as a civilized solution to marriages where there is no respect or affection. The convention of happy cuckolds and serial lovers, so often presented as natural and free in Carolean comedy, has been stripped to show its ugly foundations.

What we see in comedies even before the outside influence of Jeremy Collier, then, is a readiness to grapple with certain conventions and presuppositions of Carolean comic form and character, much as Otway had done in *Venice Preserved*. Flouting authority and marriage, aggrandizing youth and sexual freedom, and dismissing emotions and unsophisticated characters are seen in the comedies of Congreve and Vanbrugh to have repercussions damaging to individuals and society. In the kind of comedy that depends on broad-based consensus among its audience members about what is acceptable and what is not, dramatists had less latitude in presenting acceptable behaviors onstage, even though they could, if they were able, imply more complex psychological motivation than their predecessors had. If they lost the hard edge of competition between some audience members and stage heroes, along with the laughter bought at the expense of inferior types, they gained the appeal of sympathy and enhanced realism. The impact of the Collierites on comic form, then, merely hastened the process already begun a few years before.

Comedy: The Beaux Strategem

SIL.:   *What care I for his Thoughts? I shou'd not like a Man*
with confin'd Thoughts, it shows a Narrowness of
Soul. Constancy is but a dull, sleepy Quality at best;
they will hardly admit it among the Manly Vertues,
nor do I think it deserves a Place with Bravery,
Knowledge Policy, Justice, and some other Qualities
that are proper to that noble Sex.
                        (The Recruiting Officer, *1.2.50, 1.2.53)*[27]

As skilled as Congreve and Vanbrugh were at producing a comic
style that suited the 1690s, their plays were matched and sometimes
eclipsed in popularity in the following decades by those of George Farquhar (1678–1707), who instinctively seemed to understand what audiences of the late seventeenth and early eighteenth centuries wanted. If
his comedies lack the bite of some of Congreve's and Vanbrugh's best
satiric thrusts, they also possess a comprehension of the best in human
nature that makes his predecessors' vision sometimes seem confined and
narrow. Undoubtedly, some of the change evident in Farquhar's comedies comes from the public debate about morality and the theater that
exploded in the late 1690s in what is now called the Collier Controversy.
Most of Congreve's and Vanbrugh's work predates Collier; most of Farquhar's is after.

Just a few years after the premiere of *Love for Love* and one
year after that of *The Provoked Wife* came an event that had serious
consequences for dramatic development: the publication of Jeremy Collier's *A Short View of the Immorality and Profaneness of the English Stage*
(April 1698). In this work, Collier, a fanatic high-Anglican nonjuring
clergyman, identified Congreve and Vanbrugh, among others, as modern
playwrights responsible for the stage's betrayal of morality and religion.
What Collier introduced, or reintroduced, was the notion outlined most
elaborately by Sir Philip Sidney in his *Defense of Poesy* (1595) that literature's primary function was didactic; in Collier's words, "The business
of *Plays* is to recommend Virtue, and discountenance Vice; to shew the
Uncertainty of Humane greatness, the suddain Turns of Fate, and the
Unhappy Conclusions of Violence and Injustice: 'Tis to expose the Singu-
larities of Pride and Fancy, to make Folly and Falsehood contemptible,
and to bring every Thing that is Ill Under Infamy, and Neglect."[28] On

these grounds, Collier said, late seventeenth-century drama in general, and comedy in particular, is a miserable failure—teaching "immorality and profaneness" and contempt for marriage, the church, and God. In rebutting Collier, Congreve conceded his opponent's premises but claimed that the comedies remediated the follies and vices they displayed by shaming those in the audience who needed it and warning others; the audience's laughter was the effective agent. John Dennis expanded Congreve's argument to include the beneficial effects of catharsis on Englishmen's "gloomy and sullen Temper" (Harwood, 23–26). Despite the ingenuity of Congreve, Dennis, and other respondents, Collier was, of course, quite correct: if one accepts the didactic function of comedy, most Carolean comedies do make vice attractive; that is why they require a compromise formation.

There is little doubt that Collier was speaking for a substantial segment of the general if not perhaps the theatergoing public.[29] Indeed, the Collier Controversy was part of the much larger religious and moral disputation which began in the 1690s and penetrated into the eighteenth century, in which the Anglican clergy felt itself besieged on all sides and fought back. It began with William III's introduction of tolerance for dissenting ministers, allowing rival clergy to compete within the same parish; at the same time, "the rise of religious indifference was at least as alarming as the appearance of nonconformists."[30] Moreover, with the lapsing of the Licensing Act in 1695, "works critical of Anglicanism, and even of revealed religion, poured from the press where previously they would have been stifled by ecclesiastical censors" (Speck, 53). One off-shoot of this ferment, previously mentioned, was Queen Mary's sponsor-ship of the Societies for the Reformation of Manners, founded in 1692, which sought reform in both society and literature and gained substantial membership throughout the 1690s and afterward.

This fertile ground first produced Sir Richard Blackmore, with his preface to *King Arthur* in 1695, and then Collier, whose accusations touched a chord in the public's consciousness. Over the next five years or so, until managers and playwrights reached some accommodation with that public, the theaters were often censured and plays withdrawn by court order, not so much for political reasons, as previously, but for "immorality and profaneness."[31] Milhous describes in detail a situation where reformers used the full weight of the law to censure plays (1979, 125–28). Informers attended performances, taking notes that would later form the basis of their testimony against individual players, under an old statute passed in the time of James I that called for a £10 fine for "any Person or Persons . . . in any Stage play . . . [who] jestingly or Prophanely speake or use the holy Name of God or Christ Jesus, or of the Holy Ghoste or of the Trinitie" (quoted in Milhous 1979, 126). Some "straitlaced merchants" tried to get playbills advertising the day's entertainment banned entirely as a public nuisance (playbills, at this time, being the theaters' sole advertising medium). The Lord Chamberlain's censuring powers, often indifferently applied, were now extended to prologues and revived plays as well as the texts of new plays. The sensible playwright or manager could scarcely ignore the signs that the public's acceptance of licentious behavior and religious satire onstage had declined.

Yet new moral comedies, whether with "tacked on" endings or entirely devoted to "conscious" themes, weren't doing much better. If we look at the few hit comedies of the most harrowed years, 1695–1702, we find only Vanbrugh's *The Relapse* and perhaps *The Provoked Wife*, Cibber's *Love's Last Shift*, Farquhar's *The Constant Couple*, and Steele's *The Funeral*, all mixtures of satire and sensibility, while more uniformly moral comedies had a very high infant mortality rate. The fact that at this time the two companies not only engaged in cutthroat competition with the same or similar plays and operas but also introduced entr'acte entertainments ranging from foreign singers and dancers to strongmen and performing animals paints a picture of frenetic, Quixote-like encounters with a whimsical, perhaps mythical, enemy: the audience. It is entirely possible that potential London theatergoers either stayed home or filled their leisure time in other ways during these years; at any rate, they were anything but a predictable mate for the wooing.

The frenzied competition ended on 31 December 1707, when the Lord Chamberlain ordered the companies formally united, with operas to be performed at the Haymarket, comedies and tragedies at Drury Lane. In other ways too 1708 marked the end of an era, with most of the original Lincoln's Inn Fields actors at or nearing the end of their careers: Bracegirdle retired in February 1707, Barry in 1709, Verbruggen died in 1708 and Betterton in 1710; Underhill, Doggett, and Powell played only occasionally thereafter (Milhous 1979, 275 n. 65). With Farquhar dead and Vanbrugh and Congreve only peripherally involved with the theater, it was the effective end of a tempestuous era.

Farquhar, however, belongs to that time, perhaps more fully than any other dramatist; his first play, *Love and a Bottle*, probably produced in December 1698; his last, *The Beaux Stratagem*, in the year of his death, 1707.[32] In less than a decade, he managed to produce eight plays, four of which—*The Constant Couple* (1699), *The Stage-Coach* (1704), *The Recruiting Officer* (1706), and *The Beaux Stratagem* (1707)—remained popular in the repertory for nearly a century. More than any other dramatist of his time, Farquhar managed to create a tone and sensibility that genuinely rectified Carolean comedy for the eighteenth century, in essence capturing the high good humor of Behn's Rover while refitting Willmore for later tastes. If the Rover's "conversion" from rake to gallant to husband was meant to be highly ambiguous, the similar transformations of Farquhar's Sir Harry Wildair, Plume, Aimwell, and Archer were thoroughly convincing as part of a generous ethos that admitted reform as a possibility of character. One looks to the testimony of Justice Balance in *The Recruiting Officer* on Plume: "I was much such another Fellow at his Age; I never set my Heart upon any Woman so much as to make me uneasie at the Disappointment, but what was very surprising both to my self and Friends, I chang'd o'th' sudden from the most fickle Lover to be the most constant Husband in the World" (3.1.68–69).

More fully than Cibber, Vanbrugh, or even Congreve, Farquhar created in his heroes what Weber calls the "philosophical libertine" (91–97), and John K. Sheriff calls the "Good-Natured Man":[33] "By the end of the century, libertinism had become a gentleman's creed. Moderate pleasure, retirement, love of art and gardens; skepticism, and refinement of manners then became the new libertine ethos."[34] Farquhar's version is less contemplative and mannered, more active and playful, but unlike the Carolean hero he is never mean-spirited or vengeful or seriously competitive, even over women. Accosted by Standard over their courtship of Lurewell, Sir Harry Wildair in *The Constant Couple* would rather relinquish the prize than fight:

> WILD.: [Y]ou're a Soldier, Colonel, and Fighting's your Trade; And I think it down-right Madness to contend with any Man in his Profession.
>
> STAND.: Come, Sir, no more Dallying: I shall take very unseemly Methods if you don't show your self a Gentleman.
>
> WILD.: A Gentleman! Why there agen now. A Gentleman! I tell you once more, Colonel, that I am a Baronet, and have eight thousand Pounds a Year. I can dance, sing, ride, fence, understand the Languages. Now, I can't conceive how running you through the Body shou'd

>| | contribute one Jot more to my Gentility. But, pray Colonel, I had forgot to ask you: What's the Quarrel? |
>| STAND.: | A Woman, Sir. |
>| WILD.: | Then I put up my Sword. Take her. |

$$(4.1.129)^{35}$$

Farquhar's heroes are also distinguished from the true libertine in their sexual practices, as Plume explains to the disguised Silvia: "I am not that Rake that the World imagines; I have got an Air of Freedom, which People mistake for Lewdness in me, as they mistake Formality in others for Religion; the World is all a Cheat, only I take mine which is undesign'd to be more excusable than theirs, which is hypocritical; I hurt no body but my self, and they abuse all Mankind—" (4.1.82). For Plume, Sir Harry, and other Farquhar heroes, women are but one expression of their joie de vivre; drinking, male companionship, and even war are also part of life's rich banquet.

Friendship, indeed, is one of the highest values for Farquhar's male and female heroes, and he often uses female characters to show how friendship has more value than sexual conquest. Silvia, in *The Recruiting Officer*, firmly ensconces herself in Plume's favor while dressed as a man, confirming his judgment that she is a rarity. He declares: "I love *Silvia*, I admire her frank, generous Disposition; there's something in that Girl more than Woman, her Sex is but a foil to her—The Ingratitude, Dissimulation, Envy, Pride, Avarice, and Vanity of her Sister Females, do but set off their Contraries in her—In short, were I once a General, I wou'd marry her" (1.2.50). Silvia herself prefers to be androgynous: "troubled with neither Spleen, Cholick, nor Vapours, I need no Salts for my Stomach, no Hart's-horn for my Head, nor Wash for my Complexion; I can gallop all the Morning after the Hunting Horn, and all the Evening after a Fiddle: in short, I can do every thing with my Father but drink and shoot flying; and I'm sure I can do every thing my Mother cou'd, were I put to the Tryal" (1.3.52). Thus Silvia represents the Natural woman, sharply contrasted to Melinda, Lurewell, and other affected ladies created by Farquhar, and a real advance on his rather passive and unformed heroine of *The Constant Couple*, Angelica. Silvia's analogues and antecedents include "breeches part" roles like Fidelia in *The Plain-Dealer* and Florimell in *Secret Love*, women who assume male guise to follow, and sometimes humiliate, their chosen mates. But Silvia's is more than a convenient or necessary disguise; like Hellena in *The*

Rover, she seeks the freedom of action and word that males enjoy, and she wants to interact with Plume as friend and partner, to amalgamate the companionship of male bonding with sexual intimacy. When her brother's death abruptly changes her status, turning her father into a benevolent tyrant as she becomes his sole heir, she takes her brother's role, along with his clothes, and becomes a "recruit" for her Recruiting Officer.

As this variation suggests, although Farquhar writes primarily courtship comedies, he frequently offers new perspectives on its stock characters and relationships. Lurewell in *The Constant Couple*, though modeled on the vengeful losers at the love game, such as Lady Fancyfull in *The Provoked Wife*, is treated sympathetically by Farquhar. A woman debauched and abandoned in her youth, she now derives satisfaction from teasing and abandoning men, but the author sets up two scenes that allow Lurewell to tell her own story in her own words. Similarly, Farquhar makes Serjeant Kite's polygamy in *The Recruiting Officer* humorous rather than immoral, a character quirk that seemingly harms no one. What a satirist like Vanbrugh or a serious moralist like Steele would consider social ills—seduction, phony marriage, and forced enlistment—Farquhar shows as flaws to be rectified or absorbed into a society that he makes inclusive rather than exclusive. His comedies seem to allow human nature the latitude to reach its happier, rather than bleaker, accommodation with social institutions. This breadth of vision shows up most clearly in his treatment of the English countryside and its inhabitants.

For Carolean comic dramatists, the "country" was a place of exile or reparation, inhabited by "clowns" and fools who lacked wit or sense. Following this tradition, Vanbrugh's *The Relapse* shows the country as the home of the awful Squire Sir Tunbelly Clumsey and his even more awful daughter Hoyden, even though for Loveless and Amanda the country also represents moral sanctuary. For Vanbrugh's characters, most of life's pleasures and stimulations, as well as agreeable society, inhabit the town, and Congreve modifies that picture only slightly in *Love for Love*. Not so in Farquhar. In his comedies, the country—whether the Shrewsbury of *The Recruiting Officer* or the Lichfield of *The Beaux Stratagem*—is simply a variation of the city, with intelligent, sensible people like Justice Balance and Lady Bountiful cohabiting with boobies like Sullen and Costar Pearmain. [36] It is possible that Farquhar's own youthful experiences in Ireland, along with his recruiting excursions in Lichfield and Shrewsbury, enabled him to see the virtues in both town and country; whatever the reason, his comic vision was more inclusive and democratic than that of most of his predecessors and fellow playwrights, and laid the groundwork for his successors.

The differences between Farquhar's idea of comedy and that of his contemporaries can be seen most clearly in his last play, *The Beaux Stratagem*, in which, like Cibber and Vanbrugh, he balances a marital and courtship action. Having spent their fortunes of £10,000 on pleasure, Aimwell and Archer are knights-errant in search of reparation in the form of an heiress or two. Their sojourn in Lichfield is the first in a series of planned stopovers, at Nottingham, Lincoln, and Norwich, before they "bid adieu to *Venus*, and welcome *Mars*" (1.1.130), in other words, join the army. At each stop alternately, one will play the master, the other the man, the better to coordinate their assault; at Lichfield, Archer attends Aimwell in a saucy style reminiscent of the mouthiest Spanish and Italian manservants of Carolean comedies. Though allied in status and spirit as well as friendship, the two men are distinct characters; Archer (played by actor Robert Wilks, Farquhar's friend) is more of a rogue, Aimwell more of a gentleman. Thus, while Archer merrily hobnobs with Cherry, the Landlord's daughter, and plays games with various highwaymen, servants, and a French-Irish priest, Aimwell trolls in church and falls seriously in love with Dorinda, a country heiress and daughter to Lady Bountiful.

Aimwell's seriousness bothers Archer: "you're such an amorous Puppy, that I'm afraid you'll spoil our Sport: you can't counterfeit the Passion without feeling it" (1.1.130). And indeed, Aimwell is several times apparently handicapped by his scruples, most critically at the eleventh hour when, on the point of marrying Dorinda, he responds in kind to her generous confession of doubts and inadequacies:

> AIM.:   Such Goodness who cou'd injure; I find my self un-
>   equal to the Task of Villain; she has gain'd my Soul,
>   and made it honest like her own;—I cannot, cannot
>   hurt her. [*Aside*] . . . Madam, behold your Lover and
>   your Proselite, and judge of my Passion by my Conver-
>   sion.—I'm all a Lie, nor dare I give a Fiction to your
>   Arms; I'm all a Counterfeit except my Passion.
>   (5.4.184–85)

When it appears that Dorinda has rejected him, he confesses to Archer, who in turn casts him off as unworthy to be friend or complotter:

AIM.:   O, *Archer*, my Honesty, I fear, has ruin'd me.

ARCH.:   How!

AIM.:   I have discover'd my self.

ARCH.:   Discover'd! and without my Consent? what! have I
         embark'd my small Remains in the same bottom with
         yours, and you dispose of all without my Partnership?

AIM.:   O, *Archer*, I own my Fault.

ARCH.:   After Conviction—'Tis then too late for Pardon.—You
         may remember, Mr. *Aimwell*, that you propos'd this
         Folly—As you begun, so end it.—Henceforth I'll hunt
         my Fortune single.—So farewel.

                                                    (5.4.185)

Like Valentine's in *Love for Love*, however, Aimwell's generosity receives
its proper reward, and when Dorinda returns to announce she will marry
him, the men's friendship is resurrected as well.

Archer is not only the more witty and rakish of the two beaux,
but also the more pragmatic. While Aimwell is rapturing on pastorally
about Dorinda's attributes—"she look'd like *Ceres* in her Harvest, Corn,
Wine and Oil, Milk and Honey, Gardens, Groves and Purling Streams
play'd on her plenteous Face"—Archer's response is earthy—"Her Face!
her Pocket, you mean; the Corn, Wine and Oil lies there. In short,
she has ten thousand Pound, that's the English on't" (3.2.146). This
pragmatism has him declare his fascination with Mrs. Sullen sight unseen:

ARCH.:   You say there's another Lady very handsome there.

AIM.:   Yes, faith.

ARCH.:   I'm in love with her already.

                                                    (3.2.146)

Upon meeting the two women, he reveals another kind of earthiness:
"Corn, Wine, and Oil, indeed—But, I think, the Wife has the greatest
plenty of Flesh and Blood; she should be my Choice" (3.3.152).

As is his character, Archer's match is more complicated than
Aimwell's. His "choice" is already married, unhappily, to Lady Bountiful's son Sullen. Like Archer and Aimwell, the two women are also

distinguished by their attitudes and their preferences. While Dorinda is a witty, virginal country girl, Mrs. Sullen finds enjoyment only in town: "Country Pleasures! Racks and Torments! dost think, Child, that my Limbs were made for leaping of Ditches, and clambring over Stiles; or that my Parents wisely foreseeing my future Happiness in Country-pleasures, had early instructed me in the rural Accomplishments of drinking fat Ale, playing at Whisk, and smoaking Tobacco with my Husband; or of spreading of Plaisters, brewing of Diet-drinks, and stilling Rosemary-Water with the good old Gentlewoman, my Mother-in-Law" (2.1.134). Her discontent and need for diversion bring her to the brink of adultery with Archer, but as she has earlier promised Dorinda, "while I trust my Honour in your Hands, you may trust your Brother's in mine" (2.1.137), even though Sullen tells her that "if you can contrive any way of being a Whore without making me a Cuckold, do it and welcome" (3.3.158). Assured of her husband's utter indifference, Mrs. Sullen resolves to cast off the shackles of "slavery."

If Sullen lacks the "easy" sophistication and sexual appetite of the unreformed Loveless or Sir Charles Easy, neither is he quite as crude or callous as Sir John Brute.[37] But then, Lady Sullen is no Amanda, to suffer in silence. She complains loudly and eloquently to Dorinda about the horrors of the conjugal bed:

> O Sister, Sister! if ever you marry, beware of a sullen, silent Sot, one that's always musing, but never thinks:—There's some Diversion in a talking Blockhead; and since a Woman must wear Chains, I wou'd have the Pleasure of hearing 'em rattle a little—Now you shall see, but take this by the way;—He came home this Morning at his usual Hour of Four, waken'd me out a sweet Dream of something else, by tumbling over the Tea-table, which he broke all to pieces, after his Man and he had rowl'd about the Room like sick Passengers in a Storm, he comes flounce into Bed, dead as a Salmon into a Fishmonger's Basket; his Feet cold as Ice, his Breath hot as a Furnace, and his Hands and his Face as greasy as his Flanel Night-cap.—Oh Matrimony!—He tosses up the Clothes with a barbarous swing over his Shoulders, disorders the whole Oeconomy of my Bed, leaves me half naked, and my whole Night's Comfort is the tuneable Serenade of that wakeful Nightingale, his Nose.—O the Pleasure of counting the melancholly Clock by a snoring Husband!
>
> (2.1.135)

On the other side of this matrimonial mismatch, Sullen's best scene occurs when he encounters his wife's (unknown) brother at the inn; to keep his new "friend" by his side, he drunkenly tells his woes:

> SULL.: [U]nless you have pitty upon me, and smoke one Pipe with me, I must e'en go home to my Wife, and I had rather go to the Devil by half.
>
> SIR CH.: But, I presume, Sir, you won't see your Wife to Night, she'll be gone to Bed—you don't use to lye with your Wife in that Pickle?
>
> SULL.: What! not lye with my Wife! why, Sir, do you take me for an Atheist or a Rake?
>
> (5.1.175)

Unlike Vanbrugh's bitter portraits, Farquhar's depiction of the Sullen marriage is humorous and relatively evenhanded. Neither party is fault-less—if Sullen is brutish adolescence, Mrs. Sullen is shrill affectation; it is the utter incompatibility of these self-centered people that makes their marriage hellish.

Farquhar teases the audience—will she? won't she?—over Mrs. Sullen's potential adultery. Flirtatious by nature, feeling abused and trapped, she certainly toys with the idea and confesses her ambivalence and her needs to Dorinda: "It happens with us, as among the Men, the greatest Talkers are the greatest Cowards; and there's a Reason for it; those Spirits evaporate in prattle, which might do more Mischief if they took another Course;—Tho' to confess the Truth, I do love that Fellow [Archer];—And if I met him drest as he shou'd be, and I undrest as I shou'd be—Look'ye, Sister, I have no supernatural Gifts; I can't swear I cou'd resist the Tempta-tion,—tho' I can safely promise to avoid it; and that's as much as the best of us can do" (4.1.170). The critical decision occurs in act 5, scene 2, and, as has often been noted, bears a striking resemblance to Loveless's "rape" of Berinthia in *The Relapse* (4.3), a play familiar to both Farquhar and his audiences, where Berinthia is carried off crying "*very softly,*" "Help, help, I'm ravished." In contrast, Mrs. Sullen "*shreeks*" and is prepared to fend Archer off in earnest, despite her temptation:

> MRS. SULL.: What! approach me with the Freedoms of a Keeper: I'm glad on't, your Impudence has cur'd me.

ARCH.:   If this be Impudence [*Kneels*] I leave to your partial
              self; no panting Pilgrim after a tedious, painful
              Voyage, e'er bow'd before his Saint with more
              Devotion.

MRS. SULL.:   Now, now, I'm ruin'd, if he kneels! [*Aside*] rise
              thou prostrate Ingineer, not all thy undermining
              Skill shall reach my Heart—Rise, and know, I am
              a Woman without my Sex, I can love to all the
              Tenderness of Wishes, Sighs and Tears—But go
              no farther—Still to convince you that I'm more
              than Woman, I can speak my Frailty, confess my
              Weakness even for you—But—

ARCH.:   For me! [*Going to lay hold on her.*]

MRS. SULL.:   Hold, Sir, build not upon that—For my most mor-
              tal hatred follows if you disobey what I command
              you now—leave me this Minute—If he denies,
              I'm lost. [*Aside.*]

                                                        (5.2.178)

The scene turns comical when Scrub, the butler, mistakes Archer for
another of the robbers who have invaded the house, and Archer, taking
instant advantage, offers Mrs. Sullen his protection in exchange for her
person: "You see now, Madam, you must use Men one way or other;
but take this by the way, good Madam, that none but a Fool will give
you the benefit of his Courage, unless you'll take his Love along with
it" (5.2.179–80). After they best the villains, working together, Archer
resumes his seduction:

ARCH.:   [H]ow can you after what is past, have the Confi-
              dence to deny me?—Was not this Blood shed in
              your Defence, and my Life expos'd for your Protec-
              tion?—Look'ye, Madam, I'm none of your *Roman-
              tick* Fools, that fight Gyants and Monsters for
              nothing; my Valour is downright *Swiss*; I'm a Sol-
              dier of Fortune and must be paid.

MRS. SULL.:   'Tis ungenerous in you, Sir, to upbraid me with
              your Services.

ARCH.:   'Tis ungenerous in you, Madam, not to reward
              'em.

                                                        (5.3.183–84)

Before Mrs. Sullen can respond, they are interrupted by her brother's arrival.

The final few scenes are a farrago of authorial sleight of hand. To resolve the courtship plot, Farquhar kills off Aimwell's elder brother, making Aimwell the Viscount he has been pretending to be so he can honorably marry Dorinda. Further, with a stroke of the pen, Farquhar liberalizes England's divorce laws and stages a no-fault separation between the irreconcilable Sullens,[38] with a rhythmic and lively antiproviso scene between the couple, in which Lady Sullen's brother Sir Charles and Archer play judge and attorney, and the Count offers comic interpolations. Farquhar's wit is much in evidence here, as he plays on the audience's expectations about proviso scenes and their knowledge of the law and marriage, as well as their suspense about the outcome of this unholy match:

SIR CH.:	What are the Bars to your mutual Contentment.
MRS. SULL.:	In the first Place I can't drink Ale with him.
SULL.:	Nor can I drink Tea with her.
MRS. SULL.:	I can't hunt with you.
SULL.:	Nor can I dance with you.
MRS. SULL.:	I hate Cocking and Racing.
SULL.:	I abhor Ombre and Piquet.
MRS. SULL.:	Your Silence is intollerable.
SULL.:	Your Prating is worse.
MRS. SULL.:	Have we not been a perpetual Offense to each other—A gnawing Vulture at the Heart?
SULL.:	A frightful Goblin to the Sight.
MRS. SULL.:	A Porcupine to the Feeling.
SULL.:	Perpetual Wormwood to the Taste.
MRS. SULL.:	Is there on Earth a thing we cou'd agree in?
SULL.:	Yes—To part.
MRS. SULL.:	With all my Heart.
SULL.:	Your Hand.
MRS. SULL.:	Here.
SULL.:	These Hands join'd us, these shall part us—away—

MRS. SULL.:   North.

SULL.:   South.

MRS. SULL.:   East.

SULL.:   West—far as the Poles asunder.

COUNT.:   Begar the Ceremony be vera pretty.

(5.4.189–90)

From Archer comes the final summation of the play's complicated relationships:

> 'Twou'd be hard to guess which of these Parties is the better pleas'd, the Couple Join'd, or the Couple Parted? the one rejoycing in hopes of an untasted Happiness, and the other in their Deliverance from an experienc'd Misery.
>> *Both happy in their several States we find,*
>> *Those parted by consent, and those conjoin'd.*
>> *Consent, if mutual, saves the Lawyer's Fee,*
>> *Consent is Law enough to set you free.*
>
> (5.4.191)

Of course it is not, in Farquhar's England at least. But this fantasy of mutual relinquishment of a bad marriage acknowledges that there is more to wedlock than mutual self-interest. In that respect, though vastly different in tone and sensibility from late Stuart comedies by Congreve, Cibber, Vanbrugh, and others who dissect modern marriage, *The Beaux Stratagem* shares their recognition of its travails and assumption that something better can and should exist.[39]

Thus, the playful air and delightful construction of *The Beaux Stratagem* comfortably makes that shift in the design of comedy that also exists in plays by Congreve, Cibber, and Vanbrugh. To an even greater degree than Farquhar's other comedies, his last play supplants the individual, self-serving ethos of Carolean comedy with a vision of human nature and human society in which community and a generous spirit take precedence. Farquhar's comic world is a moral universe in which the final test of any action is whether it reflects well on the actor and does well by the recipient. In this scheme, Lady Bountiful, otherwise a relatively minor character in *The Beaux Stratagem*, becomes a powerful image of what Lichfield has to offer: "Lady Bountiful is a constant cornucopia:

she gives freely and unaffectedly whatever she has" (Rothstein 1967b, 153). Although she has little direct contact with Aimwell and Archer, her presence acts as a touchstone for their conversions; she symbolizes that they can gain entry to Lichfield only by deserving its hospitality, not by assault and subterfuge.[40] Thus, it is irrelevant whether Dorinda and Aimwell move to London, as long as they take the air of Lichfield with them, whereas Loveless in *The Relapse* could not withstand the siren enticements of the town. While not thoroughly reformed, Archer and Mrs. Sullen have changed as well. They each get their heart's desire— not each other, but freedom and independence (with money to sustain it). Having played, respectively, the roles of servant and wife/slave, they are ready to taste the delights of freedom from such bondage. I am aware that this interpretation contradicts those which focus on Mrs. Sullen's being left in "limbo," that is, without a satisfying marriage, at the end of the play. But I would suggest that whatever problems her "divorce" might create in the long term, her short-term goals are quite clearly achieved: liberation from an awful marriage and the country, and the substitution of a benevolent brother for an uncaring father and spouse. Within the world defined by this comedy, such a substitution, though open-ended, is more hopeful than any alternative.

Although critics have had some problems with Farquhar's come-dies, audiences of his own and succeeding times have not. Unlike the heroic characters of Carolean comedy, his can be enjoyed without guilt, without a "compromise formation" to bring them into line with the audience's values and expectations. At the same time, their real moral core is so unaffected and palatable, that it neither strains credulity nor sours the disposition. One finds pleasing self-images in abundance in Farquhar's plays, along with a version of society that mirrors one's own without overt flattery or cynical degradation. What Rothstein calls a "system of external norms . . . which joins the moral and the natural through the idea of law" (1967b, 167) and which depends more on relationships between characters than on individual characters in isolation is the foundation of Farquhar's comedies. Such comedy is entirely conge-nial with the values of later eras, including our own.

Comedies by Congreve, Vanbrugh, and Farquhar dealt differently with overall questions about freedom and authority, society and nature, than their predecessors had. Parental control, anathema to the younger generation in Carolean comedies such as Behn's *The Rover,* is seen as ineffectual in *Love for Love* and relatively benign in *The Recruiting Officer,* whereas members of the older generation such as Lady Bountiful provide a solid foundation of value in *The Beaux Strategem*. Gender roles are seen to be in congruence rather than in conflict with one another, so that the cross-dressing of Silvia, unlike that of Florimell and Hellena, indicates fellowship between the sexes rather than conquest. In fact, it is men who become gentler and less libertine, rather than women who become more hard-edged, in these new comedies. The other side of the picture appears in Vanbrugh, where the love games become earnest, where license is ugly, and where the marital double standard is exposed in all its cruelty and violence. Following the pattern if not the values of Carolean comedy, Congreve and Vanbrugh exposed to satire what Farquhar chose to laugh out of existence.

Tragicomedy and Tragedy: Oroonoko *and* Jane Shore

> *Hard fare and whips and chains may overpow'r*
> *The frailer flesh and bow my body down.*
> *But there's another, nobler part of me,*
> *Out of your reach, which you can never tame.*
> (Oroonoko, 1.2.252–55)[41]

> *Can that delicate frame*
> *Endure the beating of a storm so rude? . . .*
> *Now sad and shelterless, perhaps, she lies*
> *Where piercing winds blow sharp, and the chill rain*
> *Drops from some penthouse on her wretched head,*
> *Drenches her locks, and kills her with the cold.*
> *It is too much—Hence with her past offenses;*
> *They are atoned at full.*
> (Jane Shore, 5.111–12, 125–30)[42]

In *The Development of English Drama* (448), Robert D. Hume identifies a number of kinds of tragedy vying for public favor during the late seventeenth and early eighteenth centuries, showing the rich variety of serious drama during this period. While comedies still represented two-thirds of the most popular plays in the repertory, the vigor and longevity of the few very well-received tragedies and tragicomedies suggests that audiences found considerable appeal in both older and new serious plays that articulated their own questions about politics, nature, and ethical behavior, and perhaps reassured them about the prospects for stability and order in a time when both were somewhat shaky. Like *Venice Preserved*, these serious plays contained both heroic and pathetic elements, although some, like *The Rival Queens* (1677) and *Cato* (1713), leaned more toward the heroic, while others, like *The Orphan* (1680) and *Jane Shore* (1714), leaned more toward the pathetic. Pure heroic drama had, as Rothstein, Kirsch, and others have pointed out, lost any claim to ascendency long before,[43] but the heroic impulse was alive and well, subsumed in more complicated formats. The purest heroic, of course, was reserved for opera, which distilled off the essence—spectacle, song, magnificent rant and posturing—of the audience appeal of the older heroic drama. But a new version of heroicism—intermixed with pathetic or stoic acceptance—was working to reform the outlines and emphases of serious drama, particularly the central protagonist(s). If the heroic hero acted out of self-interest and society benefited, newer heroes were often in conflict with a world that was sick, disordered, or base, and that destroyed the hero but not his or her honor. Two new plays that seem to incorporate most of the shifts in serious drama during this time are Thomas Southerne's *Oroonoko* (1695) and Nicholas Rowe's *Jane Shore* (1714). Each blends heroic, pathetic, comic, and serious elements in ways that produce a tragic environment different from that which underlay most serious drama before 1685.

In *Oroonoko* (1695), derived from Aphra Behn's novel *Oroonoko; or, the Royal Slave* (1688), Thomas Southerne (1659–1746) renews the split-plot tragicomic form of plays like *The Comical Revenge, The Humorous Lieutenant*, and *Secret Love* by adding a comic action to Behn's story. But whereas the high heroics and high comedy of *Secret Love*'s two plots maintained a kind of tonal unity and *The Comical Revenge* mediated its highest and lowest actions with a third, midlevel plot, the comic and tragic plots of *Oroonoko* seem far apart.[44] The comic plot begins the play on a lively note: two sisters, Charlotte and Lucy Welldon, have come to Surinam from London in search of security in the form of a pair of husbands. Charlotte, the elder, goes Florimell and Hellena one better by dressing as a man through much of the play, in that guise courting and marrying a rich widow to secure her foolish son for Lucy. By the time Charlotte is ready to unveil, she has also chosen her own mate from among the available gentlemen, testing his honesty by putting her fortune in his trust. The second scene of the first act introduces the

tragic plot, with Oroonoko, an African prince treacherously betrayed into
slavery by Captain Driver, being paraded before the citizens of Surinam
like a captive lion.[45] As this plot evolves, Oroonoko is unexpectedly
reunited with his wife, attempts to escape, is recaptured, and kills his
wife and himself rather than live to see his family enslaved.

Within the popular repertory, Oronooko resembles figures like
Aureng-Zebe of *Aureng-Zebe* (1675) and Montezuma of *The Indian Emperour* in that he is meant to attract both admiration and pity. His egoism
is expressed at his first entrance; at the end of a line of slaves, he speaks
his contempt and defiance to the dishonorable Captain:

> Live still in fear; it is the villain's curse
> And will revenge my chains. Fear even me
> Who have no pow'r to hurt thee. Nature abhors
> And drives thee out from the society
> And commerce of mankind for breach of faith.
> Men live and prosper but in mutual trust,
> A confidence of one another's truth.
> That thou hast violated. I have done.
> I know my fortune and submit to it.
> (1.2.212–20)

His fortunes at their lowest ebb, he declares himself inviolate, subject to
no one's authority in his most essential being:

> Hard fare and whips and chains may overpow'r
> The frailer flesh and bow my body down.
> But there's another, nobler part of me,
> Out of your reach, which you can never tame.
> (1.2.252–55)

When Blanford, the Governor's agent, offers to succor him and renames
him Caesar, Oroonoko responds, "I am myself, but call me what you
please" (1.2.262), recalling Almanzor's "But know that I alone am King
of Me" in Dryden's *The Conquest of Granada* (1670).

Once set, Oroonoko's heroic character does not change essentially in the course of the play, but his circumstances alter. When he
is responsible only for himself, he is content to await the Governor's
decision to restore him to his homeland. Reunited with Imoinda, his
lost wife, he becomes concerned that she is at the mercy of the Lieuten-

ant Governor's lust, an instigating factor added by Southerne. Oronooko
is still, however, reluctant to take the final step toward freedom. When
Aboan, his friend and faithful lieutenant, argues that they ought to "cut
our oppressors' throats" and that "'tis justified by self-defense and natural
liberty" (3.2.84, 87–88), Oroonoko argues for the "innocence" of the
slaveholders:

> If we are slaves, they did not make us slaves,
> But bought us in an honest way of trade
> As we have done before 'em, bought and sold
> Many a wretch and never thought it wrong.
> They paid our price for us and we are now
> Their property, a part of their estate,
> To manage as they please.
>
> (3.2.107–13)

It is a remarkable defense of property rights, and because it was added
to Behn's story by Southerne, suggests the play was aimed at an audience
of gentry, merchants, and citizens who might consider a slave rebellion
an offense against their interests. The factor that ultimately ensures Oroonoko's rebellion is Imoinda's pregnancy: neither husband nor wife can
bear to have their child born into slavery. Oroonoko reluctantly agrees
to lead the other slaves to freedom, but nobly insists that "the means
that lead us to our liberty must not be bloody" (3.2.232–33).

    One of the peculiarities of *Oroonoko* to a modern reader is the
hero's reluctance to rebel, to meet violence with violence, and to assert
wholeheartedly his "natural" right to freedom. In the context of the
changes in the heroic hero, however, it does make sense. Oroonoko is
foremost an African prince, perhaps analogous to Othello in the popular
The Moore of Venice, who represents the nearly perfect balance between
natural and civilized qualities.[46] His prowess in battle, love for his family,
and leadership qualities are joined to eloquence, rationality, and a sense
of honor superior to that of almost every other character in the play, white
or black, but particularly to its "libertines," the Captain and Lieutenant
Governor. His closest competitor for this superiority, Blanford, while
much more advantageously placed than Oronooko, fails time and again
to rescue the slaves from the Lieutenant Governor and the mob of plant-
ers. Thus, while Oroonoko's actions result only in further misery and
degradation, there is no sense that inaction would have served him better.
Like Jaffeir, he is caught in a web of entanglements that allow no room

for maneuvering, compromise, or virtue's reward. He also resembles Jaffeir in that his suicide is the best available means of escape from an intolerable life.

What has the comic plot of *Oroonoko* to do with any of this? The editors of the Nebraska edition suggest one possibility: "there is a clear parallel between the institution of slavery and the institution of marriage. . . . The parallel with Oroonoko's situation is not merely that the Well-dons are victims of a type of social injustice, but that women, like slaves, are treated as commodities, without regard for their humanity, their needs, or their desires" (Novak and Rodes, xxii–xxiii). They point to Charlotte's long speech on the double sexual standard in act 4, scene 1, with its financial metaphors: "[Men's] is a trading estate that lives upon credit and increases by removing it out of one bank into another. Now poor women have not these opportunities. We must keep our stocks dead by us at home to be ready for a purchase when it comes, a husband, let him be never so dear, and be glad of him; or venture our fortunes abroad on such rotten security that the principal and interest, nay, very often our persons, are in danger" (4.1.57–65). And they conclude that "the Welldons are ultimately on the side of natural law in matters of love and marriage" (Novak and Rodes, xxv).

But "nature," as we have seen, is constructed differently in *Oroonoko* than in Carolean dramatic forms. Thus, libertinism is no more recommended in the comic plot than in the tragic, and the analogues to the Captain and the Lieutenant Governor are not Charlotte and Lucy, but the widow and her booby son. The exemplary characters in the comic action, the two sisters and the Stanford brothers, are coolheaded and self-aware, but their self-interest is not necessarily at the expense of others. Charlotte's "wit" consists of contriving an advantageous marriage for her sister, helping Jack Stanmore to a somewhat reluctant bride, and allying herself both materially and emotionally with the elder Stanmore. The "bed trick" with the Widow, a variation of the ancient comic device, satisfies everyone in both the short and the long term, as even the widow acknowledges when all the plots are discovered. What is new about the comic action is partly, as the Nebraska editors note, that the women are in the rake, that is, controlling, position, and partly that there is little punishment or upheaval involved in any of their contrivances. Insofar as Lucy and Charlotte appear to sink comfortably back into their woman's role at the end of the play, *Oroonoko* no more contains serious criticism of society's treatment of women than it does of the institution of slavery. Both critiques are carefully modulated.

What we have in both plots of *Oroonoko*, I think, is a delicate balance between poles of feeling and pragmatism or sensibility and sense. Those who respond almost entirely to the dictates of their animal "nature"—most of the slaves, the Lieutenant Governor, Daniel Lackitt—are counterweighted by the extreme pragmatists, or materialists—the Captain and the Widow, Hottman the treacherous slave. Neither extreme is lauded in the play; each is found wanting. Characters like Oroonoko and Charlotte, and to a lesser extent Blanford, Stanmore, Lucy, and Imoinda, find a middle ground between the demands of nature and pragmatism. Thus Oroonoko's defense of property-holding slaveowners is like Charlotte's defense of her own activities to Stanmore: "I might have married you in the person of my English cousin, but could not consent to cheat you even in the thing I had a mind to. . . . Can you forgive me for pimping for your family?" (5.1.67–69, 85). Both characters acknowledge and to some degree respect the enlightened self-interest theory of social intercourse.

Again, one might speculate that in the London of the 1690s, where banking and mercantilism were powerful agents of change and where audiences were increasingly composed of those who derived sustenance in such arenas, it was merely practical politics for Southerne to include their values in his play. Moreover, the public discussions about individual responsibility to the state and to the tenets of religion and morality were likely to be somewhat altered under a system that actively supported capitalism, materialism, and controlled progress. If such debates were in the air during the late seventeenth century, popular drama might be likely to reflect them, as *Oroonoko* seems to, or to incorporate them, as *Jane Shore* does, into a tragic structure that amalgamates political and private concerns in its comprehensive worldview.

Along with his *Fair Penitent* (1703), *The Tragedy of Jane Shore* (1714), by Nicholas Rowe (1674–1718), is generally considered archetypal "she-tragedy," the term Rowe himself coined to describe female-centered serious drama that elevated suffering to high art.[47] But *Jane Shore* is as different from *The Fair Penitent* as Jane is from Calista. The heroine of *The Fair Penitent*, like Oroonoko, is an equal mix of heroic and pathetic elements; Jane is all suffering and despair. *Jane Shore* begins at the point in the saga of Richard III when he is Lord Protector of the realm and has decided to take the next step to the kingship by declaring Edward IV's sons illegitimate and himself the true heir (Shakespeare's act 3).[48] The political environment is therefore hostile to Jane, Edward's former mistress, and to Hastings, her advocate and would-be lover, who is one of the nobles prepared to oppose Richard's ambitions. Early on, in act 1, scene 2, we learn that Jane has already been brought low and is living in virtual poverty, a social outcast. Her only friends are her neighbor Bellmour, her friend Alicia, and Hastings. As the plot develops, the alliances change: Hastings, whom she considered her disinterested friend, turns out to be interested in bedding her; Alicia, Hastings's former mistress, turns vengeful and treacherous when she learns of his new "love" for Jane; Bellmour introduces a servant to Jane's household, Dumont, who is actually her discarded husband Shore. After a brief, hopeful interlude, Hastings is executed and, partly owing to Alicia's contrivance, Jane is made a pariah by Richard's order, forced to wander barefoot and starving through the London streets until she dies in the arms of her forgiving husband.

From this précis, *Jane Shore* might seem diametrically opposed to *Oroonoko*, but although its tone is more grim throughout, *Jane Shore* also displays a mixed heritage of comic and tragic devices and structures. Despite its political background, it deals with private rather than public morality; its domestic concerns, such as spousal rights and woman's role, are in counterpoint to and mostly dominate the issues of subject rights and responsibilities or the issue of usurpation. The play ends before Richard's coronation or the murders of the princes in the Tower, its political action largely discarded after Hastings's death. Within the domestic plot, devices such as the disguised husband, the rakish lover, and the jealous rival all have comic origins, and their tragic consequences in *Jane Shore* would not entirely have obliterated their comic connotations for an eighteenth-century audience.

The mixed mode is particularly evident in the person of Hastings, who simultaneously plays two very different roles. He is the stalwart patriot, so loyal to the legacy of legitimate kingship embodied in the dead King Edward and his son that he is blind to Richard's overreaching. Called in to counsel with Richard on the issue of urban unrest (3.106–245), Hastings unknowingly signs his own death warrant by his intransigent loyalty, which Rowe presents with full ironic effect:

> The duke is surely noble; but he touched me
> Ev'n on the tend'rest point, the master-string
> That makes most harmony or discord to me.
> I own the glorious subject fires my breast,
> And my soul's darling passion stands confessed.
> Beyond or love's or friendship's sacred band,

Beyond myself I prize my native land.
On this foundation would I build my fame.
And emulate the Greek and Roman name;
Think England's peace bought cheaply with my blood,
And die with pleasure for my country's good.
(3.237–47)

Yet this same Hastings ignobly discards Alicia, his old mistress, without much compunction, and refuses to accept Jane's rejection of him. In his pursuit of Jane, he acts the thoroughgoing libertine, and when Dumont, playing the loyal servant, prevents him from outright rape, Hastings has him imprisoned:

This foolish woman hangs about my heart,
Lingers and wanders in my fancy still;
This coyness is put on, 'tis art and cunning,
And worn to urge desire. I must possess her.
The groom who lift his saucy hand against me
Ere this is humbled and repents his daring.
Perhaps ev'n she may profit by th'example,
And teach her beauty not to scorn my pow'r.
(3.98–105)

In such a thoroughly mixed character, Hastings's best qualities are compromised by his worst. Yet despite his inadequacy as a hero, Hastings's confessions and pleas for forgiveness on the way to his beheading are as moving as any in the play, and his sacrifice offers a foretaste of Jane's to come.

For the play's third mixed character, Alicia, personality shifts are sequential rather than simultaneous. Through act 1, scene 2, she is a model of female friendship to the friendless Jane, offering advice and comfort, and making a promise that, like Hastings's declaration or Anne's curse in Shakespeare's *Richard III*, returns to haunt her later on:

To my other self I vow.
If I not hold her nearer to my soul
Than ev'ry other joy the world can give,
Let poverty, deformity and shame,
Distraction and despair seize me on earth;

> Let not my faithless ghost have peace hereafter,
> Nor taste the bliss of your celestial fellowship.
> (1.2.148–54)

Jane entrusts to Alicia the last of her fortune, a casket of jewels, and responds, "thou art true, and only thou art true" (1.2.155). All this amity is destroyed almost immediately in the confrontation between Hastings and Alicia, where he rejects her and she (correctly) divines that he has set his sights on Jane. Alicia's passionate nature, like that of the jealous females of heroic drama and Carolean comedy, demands redress, and she contrives to destroy both Hastings and Jane by sending a letter of warning to Richard about their nonexistent "plot" against him.[49] From this point, she and Jane (played by stellar actresses Mary Porter and Anne Oldfield) become the centers of a range of oppositional qualities: selfishness and selflessness, courtly corruption and domestic honor, madness and sanity.

Although we are not meant to sympathize entirely with Hastings or Alicia, their sufferings are made real and compelling. Hastings falls from favor and is beheaded, and Alicia, after a final meeting with him, goes mad. In keeping with the play's domestic focus, hers is the more poignant case, and her final confrontation with Jane (5.186–253) is punctuated with horrible and violent images that her disordered brain has contrived to torment her. Far from detracting from Jane's suffering, the analogous fates of Hastings and Alicia tend to highlight and build anticipation for it, emphasizing her innocence compared with their relative guilt. If we pity them, how much more should we not pity her? And pity her we do. Her original adultery is so far in the background and Jane is so penitent about it that we see her as essentially an innocent victim throughout the play. Her rejection of Hastings, her tears over her "dead" husband, her acceptance of pain and poverty—all point toward a character who has cleansed herself of sin. Dumont/Shore is, of course, the audience's agent here, and his ability to forgive her adultery and succor her distress paves the way for our pity and "catharsis." Early in act 5, he says, "Hence with her past offenses; / They are atoned at full" (129–30), and his presence makes her death easier:

> SHORE: Be witness for me, ye celestial host,
>   Such mercy and such pardon as my soul
>   Accords to thee, and begs of heav'n to show thee,

> May such befall me at my latest hour,
> And make my portion blest or curst forever.

JANE SHORE: Then all is well, and I shall sleep in peace.

(5.415–20)

Even more than *Venice Preserved* and *Oroonoko*, *Jane Shore* shows the erosion of libertinism and the privatization of the heroic ethos. Except for Hastings's loyalty to his boy king, no values that might be termed "aristocratic" are exalted in the play, while a host of aristocratic vices are shown as contemptible. Edward IV, however good a ruler in some respects, is remembered as a libertine who willfully destroyed the marriage of Jane and Shore.[50] Richard himself is seen as the worst kind of political manipulator, not even blanching at murder to advance his own interest, with no regard for his country's health and well-being, and with outright contempt for the citizenry:

> The state is out of tune; distracting fears
> And jealous doubts jar in our public councils:
> Amidst the wealthy cit murmurs rise,
> Lewd railings and reproach on those that rule,
> With open scorn of government; hence credit
> And public trust 'twixt man and man are broke.
> The golden streams of commerce are withheld,
> Which fed the wants of needy hinds and artisans,
> Who therefore curse the great and threat rebellion.
>
> (3.119–27)[51]

Alicia, apparently of gentle birth, is licentious, jealous, and vengeful— debasing the unwritten laws of friendship and womanliness, as well as the religious sacrament of marriage. Not one character who might be termed "noble" is presented in a kindly light by Rowe, in contrast to the manifest virtues of the presumably middle-class Bellmour, Dumont/ Shore, and Jane.

Usurpation exists at all the different levels of *Jane Shore*, and the play therefore reasserts the value of traditional kinds of authority. By undermining the social control of marriage, Edward IV set the stage for Richard III to usurp his sons' proper inheritance of the throne. In confirming his shaky title, Richard must destroy those, like Hastings, who will not countenance his actions, though Hastings is perfectly ready to subvert other kinds of social bonds—friendship or fidelity. And women who step out of their role, like Jane and Alicia, pay a terrible price for their freedom. The only alternative to this topsy-turvy world gone mad is a world where nature reigns supreme. One of the most poignant moments of the play comes at the end of act 2, when Dumont tells Jane of the retreat he and Bellmour have found for her in the country:

> Leave this fatal place,
> Fly from the court's pernicious neighborhood,
> Where innocence is shamed, and blushing modesty
> Is made the scorner's jest; where hate, deceit,
> And deadly ruin wear the mask of beauty,
> And draw deluded fools with shows of pleasure. . . .
> Bellmour, whose friendly care still wakes to serve you,
> Has found you out a little peaceful refuge.
> Far from the court and the tumultuous city,
> Within an ancient forest's ample verge,
> There stands a lonely but a healthful dwelling,
> Built for convenience and the use of life.
> Around it fallows, meads, and pastures fair,
> A little garden, and a limpid brook,
> By nature's own contrivance, seem disposed;
> No neighbors but a few poor simple clowns,
> Honest and true, with a well-meaning priest.
> No faction, or domestic fury's rage,
> Did e'er disturb the quiet of that place. . .
> Your virtue, there, may find a safe retreat
> From the insulting pow'rs of wicked greatness.
> (2.297–302, 305–17, 319–20)

Like Castilio's speech in Otway's *The Orphan* (1680), this pastoral evocation is meant to highlight the corruption and misery of the world represented in the play. But in Otway, because the play is already set in a relatively pastoral environment, human nature was the culprit, not the temptations of wealth and ambition. In *Jane Shore*, the corruption seems vested entirely in the nobility, who control court and town, while the common people, the bourgeoisie, maintain clear ideas of right and wrong, loyalty, and Christian forgiveness. For such people, the pastoral can be a real possibility rather than an evocative dream, and its unattainability for Jane heightens rather than diminishes the play's affective appeal.

Like comedy, tragedy was using older dramatic conventions in new ways during the years 1685–1714. Not quite willing to let go of the energy and egocentrism of the older heroic ideal, it managed to introduce substantial pathetic effects by the judicious use of setting and structure, while retaining the hero[in]es' stature and distinction. Neither Oroonoko nor Jane Shore is an Every[wo]man, but an extraordinary figure, elevated above his or her fellows by peculiar circumstances that create the tragic environment, and by internal qualities that enable him or her to reach some sort of apotheosis. An audience is able to identify with these characters in a positive way because their specialness flatters us; even while we pity them, that pity does not degrade them. As spectators, we are awed while our emotions are touched, neither sensibility canceling out the other. This delicate balance, of course, does not exist in all the popular tragedies of the late seventeenth and early eighteenth centuries, but it seems to be present in a number of them, not just *Jane Shore* and *Oroonoko*, but *Cato*, *Aureng-Zebe*, *The Mourning Bride*, *Venice Preserved*, and perhaps even the versions of *Othello*, *Hamlet*, and *King Lear* currently being staged.

I have spent some time noting the comic structural devices, character configurations, and incidents and the mixed characters in late seventeenth- and early eighteenth-century tragedy for a reason. In both *Jane Shore* and *Oroonoko*, as well as *Cato*, *The Orphan*, *The Mourning Bride*, and other serious drama popular at that time, there is more than just "pandering" to popular or authorial whimsy. Perhaps unconsciously, both authors and audiences were groping for a way to incorporate sensibility and admiration into the same package, not to reduce tragedy but to enhance its ability to speak to a restored faith in social and political order, hardly won. The seriocomic ending of *Oronooko* and the redemptive ending of *Jane Shore* both assert the value of human capabilities even when the systems surrounding them are corrupt or perverted. We are a long way from Hobbes's war of human animals, or even from the poetic justice of Rymer; we are in a world where character rendered with a certain psychological verisimilitude seems to be taking over from the deliberately unrealistic heroic characters that were so popular through the 1660s and 1670s.[52] "Psychological realism" is, of course, a term that has little intrinsic meaning separated from its time and place. What was psychologically real in a Fletcher play to an Elizabethan might seem otherwise to those who first watched Shaw or Ibsen, and theirs, in turn, unreal to audiences who nowadays favor Churchill, Shepard, and Mamet. In the late seventeenth and early eighteenth centuries, the term seemed to invoke a certain complexity of tone and ambiguity of character: heroes are not uniformly heroic, nor villains villainous, and circumstances batter characters into positions that make them choose unwisely, closer to Aristotle's tragic error than a tragic flaw. In a world where external forces—war, political turmoil, social dislocation—made absolute decisions less viable, audiences might welcome characters whose motives and actions, like their own, were less clear-cut and absolute. So the mixed tragic mode, in all its various manifestations, flourished.

Conclusion

One cannot deal with the period in English drama between 1685 and 1714 without confronting several questions about the changes that occurred. One is the question of its "feminization." The standard argument goes something like this: as interest in the theater declined among the court and the upper classes, managers and playwrights were forced to appease audiences who were increasingly bourgeois and dominated by "feminine" ideals of moral propriety and religious values. Accompanying this shift were numbers of new women playwrights and male playwrights, like Southerne, Rowe, and Steele, who wrote "she-tragedies" or espoused womanish virtues in comedy.[53] Even Congreve, otherwise considered a victim of the shift in audience interest from libertinism and "hard comedy," can be accused, in *The Mourning Bride*, of pandering "to the feminine audience": "By chaining the hero to the earth in a circle of death created by the two women who love him, Congreve allowed little scope for Ozmyn to act until the very end, and the play lacks a certain masculine force" (Novak, 136).

Although I have occasionally used the terms *masculine* and *feminine*, along with *libertine* and *moral*, in charting the course of the changes in comedy and serious drama between 1685 and 1714, it seems more useful to me, and even more accurate, to continue looking at how the drama deals with questions about authority. At the same time, we need to acknowledge that this drama shifted from the mimetic forms of comedy and serious drama present in the Carolean period to more didactic forms.

We have seen that Carolean drama tended to question traditional authority in various ways: by denegrating fathers in the family and older people in the sex game, by overthrowing or questioning the legitimacy of inherited rulers and church spokesmen, by offering women more voice and choice in their own destiny. To do this, dramatists constructed plays such that audience members could, in effect, choose among variant "readings" of the play before them: from the most revolutionary to the most conservative interpretation. Under scrutiny by critics determined to take them at face value, such plays could not ultimately pretend to fit any of the usual definitions of didacticism, and began to be superseded by plays better able to make such claims, either by showing the ill effects of license and usurpation or by offering an extremely mild form of revolt. Thus, in the late seventeenth and early eighteenth centuries, while many Carolean plays continued to be popular and a few new ones, like Southerne's *Sir Anthony Love* (1690), were written along the same lines, most of the new plays showed social and political order to be a function of traditional values, and reestablished parental authority, male dominance, role specialization, legitimate kingship, and the church, sometimes with tacked-on moral epithets at the conclusion of these plays:

> Seest thou, how just the Hand of Heav'n has been?
> Let us that thro' our Innocence survive,
> Still in the Paths of Honour persevere;
> And not from past or present Ills Despair:
> For Blessings ever wait on vertuous Deeds;
> And tho' a late, a sure Reward succeeds.
> (*The Mourning Bride*, 5.2.317–22)

> By such Examples are we taught to prove,
> The Sorrows that attend unlawful Love;
> Death, or some worse Misfortunes, soon divide
> The injur'd Bridegroom from his guilty Bride:
> If you wou'd have the Nuptial Union last,
> Let Virtue be the Bond that ties it fast.
> (*The Fair Penitent*, 5.1.302–7)

> I hope there is a place of happiness
> In the next world for such exalted virtue.
> Pagan or unbeliever, yet he lived
> To all he knew; and if he went astray,
> There's mercy still above to set him right.
> But Christians guided by the heavenly ray
> Have no excuse if we mistake our way.
> (*Oroonoko*, 5.5.305–11)

> Let those who view this sad example know
> What fate attends the broken marriage vow;
> And teach their children in succeeding times,
> No common vengeance waits upon these crimes,
> When such severe repentance could not save,
> From want, from shame, and an untimely grave.
> *   (Jane Shore,* 5.1.435–40)

But "virtue" is more than a simple pandering in these plays; it is a systematic denial of both accident and willful self-aggrandizement as determiners of individual fate. Following the rules pays off, at least sometimes, and breaking the rules, as seen in *Jane Shore* or *The Provoked Wife*, brings unpleasant or tragic consequences.

At the same time, the rules themselves have changed. What Congreve and Farquhar, Southerne and Rowe, promote in different ways is a system of values relying on internal verities that are at one with the best interests of the community; morality and social regulation promote the general welfare even at the expense of the individual, but they are also "natural," reflecting the inherent goodness of humankind. Where the alternative to the hero[in]es' freedom and natural authority in Carolean comedies and heroic drama seemed to be blind obedience to a debased parental or political authority, the obedience of Valentine, Aimwell, Oroonoko, and Jane Shore is to a higher authority, one at war with neither their own honor and fulfillment nor the unstated rules of the society they inhabit. Such plays are both exemplary and consensual in a broad way to incorporate the values of an audience that chooses to subsume its differences.

If these plays substitute feminine for masculine ideals, then, it is because the feminine is exalted as natural and sensitive. Males and females subscribe to the same values: generosity, benevolence, honor, friendship. Women "know their place" but are not subservient; fully aware of the higher self-interest of community, they embrace the rewards of limited freedom. These lessons male heroes continue to learn from their female counterparts in drama throughout the eighteenth century.

4

The Hanoverian Accession to Garrick's

1714–1747

Overall, the London theater between 1714 and 1747 was prosperous, diverse, and innovative. Just before the Licensing Act of 1737 worked its depredations, London audiences had as many as five different theaters, with two or more different kinds of performances in each, to choose from on a given evening.[1] These performances ranged from Italian opera, ballad opera, tragedy, and comedy to the farcical afterpieces, short musical interludes, and pantomimes that regularly accompanied them. While purists deplored these latter "entertainments"— particularly pantomimes, which were made up mostly of dancing, singing, and acrobatics—audiences loved them, and certain afterpieces were staple fare at a given company, playing repeatedly season after season. Competition stimulated creativity, especially during the eight-year period from 1729 to 1737,[2] when new plays represented more than one-fifth of all recorded performances again, and, except in the case of opera, brought prosperity to the companies. During these years, the very form of drama was subject to experimentation, its most notable products John Gay's ballad operas and Henry Fielding's satires.

Avery indicates (LS, vol. 2) that Drury Lane, in particular, had hugely profitable seasons in the 1710s and 1720s, clearing between £3,000 and £4,000 annually. Although probably less profitable, Rich's company at Lincoln's Inn Fields and then Covent Garden also did well, while the lesser theaters at Goodman's Fields, the New Haymarket, and elsewhere also remained viable. But competition was not always healthy. Because financing for the opera houses was primarily by subscription and patronage rather than from box-office receipts, these companies were more extravagant, spending "enormous sums on salaries, costumes, music, and decor, incurring large deficits" (LS, 2:53), and the "opera wars" of the 1730s and 1740s damaged both companies by splitting what was probably always a relatively select audience. As Scouten puts it, "Since London in the 1720s had found it difficult to support a single opera company in high style, it seemed doubly certain that in the 1730's and 1740's one, if not both, of the competing companies would have difficulty in sustaining a solvent enterprise. That proved to the be the case" (LS, 3:70–71).[3]

The process that had begun at the turn of the century—diversity of offerings on the evening bill—became the norm during the first two decades of the century and afterward. As described by Avery, the repertory

> came to include, more often than not, a play and afterpiece, prologue and epilogue, music, dance, singing, and specialties. In fact, a cursory glance at a lengthy bill might suggest a submersion of the play in song and dance; nevertheless, the play remained the center of the program. Except under extraordinary circumstances, the managers built the evening's offerings around it, without, however, any genuine intent to create a single mood, for the manager might schedule a Scotch Dance between Acts I and II of *Othello*, an Italian song at the next interval, a sonata by Corelli between Acts III and IV. Instead, the producer's aim gradually came to be a fully rounded program of drama, music, dance, and specialties that would attract and please the whole range of taste in London.
>
> (LS, 2:112)

Although there had been experimentation before—with double bills, afterpieces, farces, singing and dancing, entr'actes, and even horses, dogs, and rope tricks—after the opening of the new Lincoln's Inn Fields by

John Rich in 1714, both theaters began using afterpieces with increasing frequency, with Rich's company leading the way. The huge success of two pantomimes, *Harlequin Doctor Faustus* at Drury Lane and *The Necromancer* at Lincoln's Inn Fields, in 1723–24 "established the afterpiece as a common, though not obligatory, part of the program" (*LS*, 2:118); it was still regularly eliminated, for example, during the initial run of a new play or new revival.

This renewal of theatrical energy took place in a salubrious political and social climate. After the relative lack of interest of the last Stuarts, the first Hanoverians were again enthusiastic supporters of the theater, and much of the public seemed to follow their example: "From 1714 onwards some of the playhouses could depend upon payments from royalty and their retinue. Royal attendance from the court of George I first favored Drury Lane, but Lincoln's Inn Fields later gained recognition, and George I's difficulties with the English language led him to patronize the performances by foreign comedians, especially the French, at the Haymarket. He also liberally supported opera, not only with a yearly grant of £1,000 for a considerable period but also with frequent attendance" (*LS*, 2:55). And what George I began, George II continued. More broadly, companies that had been groping for an audience, any audience, at the turn of the century were managing to fill substantially larger theaters 30 years later; they had seemingly found what their audiences wanted.

But all these signs of well-being belong to the late 1720s and 1730s; there was little indication at the beginning of the 1714–15 season that this new era of prosperity was dawning. With the ascension of George I, Christopher Rich petitioned to have his "silencing" removed and his patent restored; although he died in November, his restored patent went to his son John, who operated under it at the renovated Lincoln's Inn Fields and, after 1732, the new theater at Covent Garden until his death in 1761. By all accounts, John Rich was a better owner-manager than his father, giving both actors and writers due respect for their talents; he also had an acute sense of audience appeal and was responsible, during the 1720s, not only for the increase in pantomime entertainments as afterpieces but also for the first wave of Shakespearean revivals and for producing Gay's *The Beggar's Opera* after its rejection by the Drury Lane company.

Drury Lane was run by a series of actor-managers from 1710 onward, when Colley Cibber, Robert Wilks, and Thomas Doggett received a license to play there. Barton Booth replaced Doggett in 1713–14;

the following year, Sir Richard Steele received a patent from the new king and became the fourth shareholder until his death in 1729.[4] These actor-managers were particularly sensitive to the needs and capabilities of writers and actors. A member of the company since 1690, Colley Cibber was himself both actor and playwright, although his responsibilities as manager soon eclipsed his writing. As veterans of the chaos of the first decade of the eighteenth century, these men also understood, close up, the perils of bad management practices, and soon developed a system that served them well for nearly two decades. In 1714 their company started with the enormous advantage of veteran actors Robert Wilks, Anne Oldfield, Colley Cibber, and Thomas Doggett, and with a repertory of popular plays by Farquhar, Centlivre, Rowe, and others; they were soon enjoying the status of premiere company, which lasted until the crisis of the 1732–33 season.

In addition to the two patent companies, numerous theaters during the 1714–47 period also operated under licenses like that given to Betterton in 1695 and the Drury Lane group in 1710; others operated with neither patent nor license,[5] particularly after 1730, when the huge success of the *The Beggar's Opera* made theatrical entrepreneurship look like a paying proposition. Theaters in the New Haymarket and Goodman's Fields "took off" during the early 1730s, providing competition for and stimulating creative activity at the patent theaters,[6] and there were occasional performances at the Great Room in York Buildings, in Richmond, and at the Tennis Court on James Street. Comparing this period with the heyday of the Elizabethan/Jacobean theater, Scouten points out that these alternative theaters performed substantially more new plays than either Covent Garden or Drury Lane during the period of maximum competition, and that this competition provided "genuine outlets . . . for authors who had written new plays, whether these plays were bizarre or conventional," and "stimulated an interest of authors in the drama," bringing writers to London "with a play in their hip pocket" (*LS*, 3:146). Audiences responded enthusiastically, and during Easter Week of 1733, a mere decade after Rich's company had suffered from low attendance, London theaters were playing to some 2,500 spectators a night (*LS*, 3:147). Although their structure continued to be along the lines established during the early Carolean period, the size of these theaters varied considerably, between 600 and 700 at the Haymarket and Goodman's Fields to perhaps 1,400 at Rich's new Covent Garden, which opened in 1732.

Most Popular Plays: 1714–1747
(Plays with Fifty or More Performances
with Performance Numbers in Parentheses)

COMEDY

Aesop (61)
The Alchemist (64)
The Amorous Widow (111)
Amphitryon (56)
As You Like It† (127)
The Beaux Strategem (305)
A Bold Stroke for a Wife* (74)
The Busie Body (210)
The Careless Husband (176)
The Committee (243)
The Confederacy (99)
The Conscious Lovers* (190)
The Constant Couple (220)
The Country-Wife (140)
The Double Dealer (103)
The Double Gallant (129)
The Drummer* (75)
Epicoene (54)
The Fair Quaker of Deal (83)
The Funeral (98)
The Gamester (56)
The London Cuckolds (80)
Love for Love (234)
Love Makes a Man (225)
Love's Last Shift (167)
The Man of Mode (76)
Measure for Measure (60)
The Merchant of Venice† (65)
The Merry Wives of Windsor (182)
The Miser* (144)
The Mistake (67)
The Nonjuror* (54)
The Old Batchelor (226)
Pasquin* (70)
The Pilgrim (84)
The Plain-Dealer (57)
The Provoked Husband* (262)

The Provoked Wife (182)
The Recruiting Officer (274)
The Rehearsal (176)
The Relapse (170)
The Rover (111)
The Royal Merchant (123)
Rule a Wife and Have a Wife
    (171)
The Scornful Lady (53)
She Would and She Would Not
    (83)
Sir Courtly Nice (77)
The Squire of Alsatia (82)
The Tempest (123)
The Tender Husband (107)
The Tragedy of Tragedies* (66)
The Twin Rivals (83)
Volpone (73)
The Way of the World (126)
Wit without Money (60)
A Woman's Revenge* (70)

TRAGEDY

All for Love (69)
Cato (174)
The Distrest Mother (94)
The Fair Penitent (133)
The False Friend (50)
Hamlet (284)
The History of King Lear
    (149)
Jane Shore (97)
Julius Caesar (133)
The London Merchant* (98)
Macbeth (219)
The Moore of Venice (223)
The Mourning Bride (96)
Oedipus (50)
Oroonoko (171)

The Orphan (173)
Richard III (170)
The Rival Queens (64)
The Siege of Damascus* (53)
Tamerlane (196)
Theodosius (63)
Timon of Athens (63)
The Unhappy Favourite (110)
Venice Preserved (131)

TRAGICOMEDY
The Fatal Marriage (60)
The Island Princess (91)
The Spanish Fryar (219)

AFTERPIECE
Acis and Galatea (50)
The Anatomist (131)
Apollo and Daphne/The
    Burgomaster* (244)
Britannia/The Royal Lovers* (74)
Cephalus and Procrus* (168)
The Cheats/The Tavern Bilkers*
    (73)
The Cheats of Scapin (59)
The Chymical Counterfeits* (61)
The Cobler of Preston* (86)
The Colombine Courtezan* (101)
The Comical Rivals/The School Boy
    (113)
The Contrivances* (85)
The Country House (82)
The Country Wake/Hob (125)
Damon and Phillida* (187)
The Dragon of Wantley* (147)
A Duke and No Duke* (58)
The Emperour of the Moon (96)
The Fall of Phaeton* (90)
The Fortune Tellers* (53)
Harlequin a Sorcerer* (79)
Harlequin Doctor Faustus* (156)
Harlequin Restor'd* (110)
Harlequin Shipwreck'd* (129)
The Harlot's Progress* (111)

The Imprisonment . . . of
    Harlequin* (70)
The Jealous Doctor* (63)
Jupiter and Io* (52)
The King and Miller of Mansfield*
    (158)
The Lying Valet* (184)
The Magician* (57)
The Necromancer* (291)
The Old Debauchees* (50)
Orpheus and Eurydice* (208)
Perseus and Andromeda/The Cheats
    of Harlequin* (162)
Perseus and Andromeda/The
    Spaniard Outwitted* (81)
Perseus and Andromeda/The Rape
    of Colombine* (58)
The Rape of Proserpine* (312)
Robin Goodfellow* (77)
The Royal Chace* (216)
The Stage-Coach (112)
Tom Thumb* (66)
The Toy-Shop* (52)
The What D'Ye Call It* (160)

MASQUE/OPERA
Comus* (64)
King Arthur* (51)
The Prophetess (91)

BALLAD OPERA‡
The Author's Farce* (65)
The Beggar's Opera* (491)
The Beggar's Wedding/Phebe* (130)
The Devil to Pay* (525)
Flora/Hob's Opera* (247)
The Honest Yorkshireman* (116)
The Intriguing Chambermaid* (83)
The Lottery* (138)
The Lover's Opera* (97)
The Mock Doctor* (316)
An Old Man Taught Wisdom*
    (261)

Notes
*New play
†New revival
‡Includes both mainpieces like *The Beggar's Opera* and afterpieces like *The Lottery*

Innovations in dramatic form during the period begin with the afterpiece. By the 1720s, the standard bill of any evening performance at any of the regular theaters included an afterpiece, whether a panto-mime, a one-act comedy like Farquhar's *The Stage-Coach*, or a short farce.[7] The popularity of these semiliterary pieces is undeniable; a high percentage of recorded plays and new plays performed between 1714 and 1747 were afterpieces, and some specific afterpieces had formidable performance records. The list of most popular plays shows 39 percent comedies, 31 percent afterpieces, and 21 percent serious drama, but the proportion of afterpieces among the new plays and revivals is much higher: of the 52 new plays on the list, 36 (69 percent) are afterpieces, while only 11 (21 percent) are comedies and 2 (4 percent) are tragedies. Nicoll says that both John Rich and John Weaver have been cited as originators of the pantomime just after the turn of the century, and identifes "four distinct strains" of origin: "the influence of classic myth, that of the Italian *commedia dell'arte*, that of previous English farce, and that of contemporary satire." He goes on to outline the common form: "The novelty of the eighteenth century pantomime consisted in the elabo-rating of the unspoken devices of Harlequin and Columbine into a regular story told by 'heel' instead of 'head,' but the pantomime has many points of relationship with opera and farce of the time. Most commonly, indeed, these silent antics of the pantomime characters were combined with dialogue recited or sung by other figures moving alongside of the dancers and acrobats."[8] Avery (*LS*, 2:117–20) identifies the four kinds of afterpieces as farcical pieces (one- or two-act), such as Gay's *What D'Ye Call It* (1715) and Charles Johnson's *The Cobler of Preston* (1716); musical entertainments, such as Motteux's *Acis and Galatea* (1702, revised in 1714 with music by Handel) and *The Beau Demolished* (1715); proces-sions, as from coronations or other court ceremonies presented as stand-alone pieces; and pantomimes, such as *Mars and Venus* (1717) or *The Cheats* (1717). Pantomimes, largely dependent on spectacle and dance, became the dominant mode of afterpiece in the 1720s, particularly at Lincoln's Inn Fields (see Hughes 1971, 97–98ff.). Some members of the audience, like Pope, felt these entertainments detracted from and de-graded the serious plays in the program, and playwright Charles Johnson agreed: "the Actors may design it as a Desert, but they generally find the Palates of their Guests so vitiated that they make a Meal of Whipt Cream, and neglect the most substantive Food which was design'd for their Nourishment" (quoted in *LS*, 2:120). Nicoll speaks even more strongly, lumping afterpieces together with other new forms as evidence of the degradation of the theater and audience taste in the early eighteenth century.[9]

These critics of pantomime in the eighteenth and twentieth centuries have a legitimate case. As pantomimes became popular and necessary, they did tend to pull money and talent away from the mainpiece; there were, for example, virtually no new mainpiece playwrights being fostered by the theaters during the first two decades of the eighteenth century, and relatively few thereafter. The most popular mainpiece plays are almost entirely revivals and rewritings of old favorites. At the same time, pantomimes were at least partly responsible for drawing new audiences into the theaters and making the stage profitable again. In the time before the Licensing Act, the theaters came alive once again, with authors and managers spurring each other on to test the limits of audience acceptance, and it was these theatrical conditions that produced the delights of *The Beggar's Opera* and Fielding's satires.

Nontraditional Forms

BALLAD OPERA: THE BEGGAR'S OPERA

> *Of all animals of prey, man is the only sociable one. Every one of us preys upon his neighbor, and yet we herd together.*
>
> (The Beggar's Opera, 3.2.5–7)

> *Through the whole piece you may observe such a similitude of manners in high and low life, that it is difficult to determine whether (in the fashionable vices) the fine gentlemen imitate the gentlemen of the road, or the gentlemen of the road the fine gentlemen.*
>
> (The Beggar's Opera, 3.16.16–20)[10]

As its name implies, *The Beggar's Opera* satirized, among other things, traditional operatic forms, particularly the Italian opera that was in vogue during the early eighteenth century. Although Italian opera on the London stage dates from January 1705, with the production of *Arsinoe* at Drury Lane and the opening of the Queen's theater in April of that year, English opera dates from the early seventeenth century, with the court masques of Ben Jonson and Inigo Jones, a joint venture of drama, music, and scene design wherein "the poet and the composer could collaborate on more nearly equal terms, although both were held in subjection by that far more important personage the scenic architect."[11] Jonson enhanced the textual level of the form and in his 1609 *Masque of Queens* added an antimasque performed by professional dancers that provided a dramatic counterpoint to the static panegyric. After Jones and Jonson parted company in 1631, Jones worked with James Shirley or William Davenant. Although Dent does not think highly of Davenant's talents as a writer, Davenant did transfer the operatic form to the public stage, though his plans to build a theater in the late 1630s devoted to "musical presentments, scenes, dancing, or any other the like" (quoted in Dent, 43) were not fulfilled. At the waning of the interregnum in 1656, Davenant produced two "entertainments" at Rutland House, the second of which was *The Siege of Rhodes*, discussed earlier in terms of its influence on heroic drama. Scored by five separate composers, *The Siege of Rhodes* was entirely sung in recitative to avoid Commonwealth strictures against drama, with musical accompaniment and instrumental interludes, and although Davenant himself did not follow up its operatic possibilities on the Carolean stage, others did.[12]

About a decade later, the episodic structure, multiple scene changes, and recitative of *The Siege of Rhodes* reappear in English opera, which featured spoken dialogue rather than recitative. Thomas Shadwell's *Psyche* (1673), with music by Matthew Locke, provoked a parody, *Psyche Debauched* (1674), by Thomas Duffett. Both were moderately successful, implying that seriousness was not an essential element of the operatic form. But not until Henry Purcell made his stage debut, writing the music for Nathaniel Lee's *Theodosius* (1680), did English operas become truly popular. Purcell followed with the music for Charles Davenant's *Circe* (1677) in 1685, Betterton's successful adaption of Fletcher's *The Prophetess; or, the History of Dioclesian* (1690), and Dryden's *King Arthur* (1691).[13] Despite these successes, few new English operas were produced during the 1690s,[14] leaving the field clear a decade later for Vanbrugh's and Rich's Italian imports, with each company trying to outdo the other. These operas—*Arsinoe* (1705), *Camilla* (1706), *Rosamond* (1707), *Almahide* (1710), and *Rinaldo* (1711)—were entirely sung, in English,

Italian, or both, and featured expensive sets and costumes, along with even more expensive and temperamental stars. Throughout the first decades of the eighteenth century, finances were a continual problem; opera "never succeeded in operating within the money paid by listeners, which was often high but rarely sufficient" (LS, 2:60). The subscription system began in 1707–8, and in 1719 the formation of the Royal Academy of Music offered some stability, but it ceased operations in 1728, to be replaced by the "Opera of the Nobility" in the 1730s. There were hiatus periods, with no operas produced in 1717–19, 1728–29, 1738–41, and 1744–45, but two opera companies operated from 1733 to 1737, with Handel's oratorios competing at Covent Garden.

Despite these difficulties, after 1705 opera was in London to stay, as much a part of the London theater world as the productions at Drury Lane, Lincoln's Inn Fields, and Covent Garden. Successive managers, entrepreneurs, and friends produced, season after season, brilliant and exciting Italian-style operas for fans and patrons to enjoy. Opera's main competition after 1728 came only from its bastard offspring, the ballad opera.

In January 1728, this new genre hit London in the form of the enormously successful *The Beggar's Opera*, which had 78 performances in its first season[15] and 413 more before 1747. It was the product of the imagination of John Gay, poet, friend of Swift and Pope, and member of the Scriblerus Club, who had published some poetry and produced a number of plays, only two of which—*The What D'Ye Call It* and *The Captives*—had been successful. Catapulted to fame and fortune with *The Beggar's Opera*, Gay received benefits on the third, sixth, ninth, and fifteenth nights and sold the printed version—in toto, getting about £800 for the play.[16]

Briefly, *The Beggar's Opera*, a tale told by the Beggar-author, is set in the underworld of contemporary London inhabited by tavernkeepers, whores, criminals, and other lowlife. Their affectations are similar to those of conventional comic characters, but the crimes they commit against society, though remarkably like those of their comic ancestors—sexual excess, greed, and self-serving—are punishable by death. The plot centers on Macheath, the highwayman-hero, a smooth-talking rake who charms the ladies while he plies his trade as a fairly competent robber who enjoys the comradeship of his male companions. He runs afoul of Peachum, their "fence," by marrying Peachum's daughter Polly, and is arrested and taken to Newgate to be hanged, only to be rescued by the jailer's daughter Lucy Lockit, Polly's rival for his affections. Meanwhile, their daughters' love rivalry over Macheath spreads to the heretofore partners-in-crime Lockit and Peachum. Recaptured, Macheath, fortified by wine, nobly takes leave of his two "wives" before being led off to his death. But the Beggar-author reappears as a deus ex machina and, bowing to generic conventions and the "taste of the town," reprieves his hero from the gallows, grumbling, "Had the play remained as I first intended, it would have carried a most excellent moral" (3.16.20–2).

This brief summary cannot do justice to the mad gaiety and provocative allure of *The Beggar's Opera*, elements that have long out-lasted its contemporary significance. Eighteenth-century audiences saw it again and again;[17] it was imitated to death; and it has provoked revivals and translations like Bertolt Brecht's *Threepenny Opera* (1928) and the 1960s hit song "Mack the Knife." Yet despite its freshness and topicality, it was also deeply indebted to the comic and serious repertory of its time. Stripped of its contemporary references and its music, the plot is basically Fletcherian—a young man juggling mistresses and money problems and locked in conflict with his elders. In the comic repertory of the 1720s and 1730s, Macheath was comfortably ensconced among similar types, like Fletcher's Valentine in *Wit without Money* or the Younger Loveless in *The Scornful Lady*, Behn's Rover, Congreve's Valentine in *Love for Love*, and Farquhar's Archer and Plume. The episodic plot movement, with its abundant climaxes and reversals and the deus ex machina ending, is also Fletcherian, while the underworld setting is seen in repertory comedies like Brome's *The Jovial Crew*, Bullock's *The Woman's Revenge*, and Henry Norris's *The Royal Merchant*, taken from Fletcher's *The Beggar's Bush*.[18] More interesting, perhaps, are the resemblances between *The Beggar's Opera* and popular tragedies, such as Macheath's gallows scene and Pierre's in *Venice Preserved* or Hastings's in *Jane Shore*. An audience accustomed to such fare in the early eighteenth-century repertory would have found *The Beggar's Opera*, for all its newness, comfortably familiar. Yet it was the newness that made *The Beggar's Opera* so popular, and that provoked its imitation.[19]

Unlike most of these other comedies, however, *The Beggar's Opera* is enriched by multiple levels of parody, irony, and satire. Gay's brand of comical satire was admirably suited to the stage. His musical format enabled him to use irony along with parody to create a kind of theater where nothing is fixed, everything is fluid. While offending some moralists of his own time, Gay produced in the play's elaborate network of satiric reference and comic innuendo a kind of humor that blended topicality with typicality.

The Beggar's Opera was both a parody of and in competition with Italian opera, "ridiculing the affectation and ornamentation of Italian music and its usual libretto."[20] Yet Schultz overstates the case when he suggests that it "severely crippled" serious opera of its time (139); the opera's financial woes were responsible for its closing in 1729, and it was healthy from midcentury onward. Indeed, the very popularity of Italian opera ensured that the central conceit of *The Beggar's Opera*, its burlesque of the well-worn conventions of Italian opera, found a knowledgeable and ready audience. Gay "lowered" his opera by using ballad tunes instead of grand arias, sung by beggars and criminals instead of kings and nobles, but he maintained grand opera's stop-action for arias and solos, the conflict between competing divas (Polly and Lucy for Cuzzoni and Faustina), and the "Prison Scene which the Ladies always reckon charmingly pathetic" (intro., 19–20). These burlesque techniques were copied, though usually less successfully, in the host of ballad operas that followed.[21]

The play offers social satire at several levels. Macheath, it is widely agreed, was based on a real character, "Jack Sheppard, whose spectacular escapes from Newgate were unprecedented," while Peachum was based on Jonathan Wild, "whose organizational genius in the dual capacity of receiver of stolen goods and thief-catcher was never matched" (Roberts and Smith, xxiii). Both had been recently executed, and both were the subjects of popular pamphlets and periodicals. Obviously intended to pique the interest of Gay's audiences, these contemporary references also provoked those who condemned the play on moral grounds:

> Must not a play whose hero was a highwayman, all of whose characters came from the criminal classes, contribute by this very fact to public immorality; would it not encourage young men to imitate Macheath? The Reverend Thomas Herring, later to become Archbishop of York and of Canterbury, preached against the opera "as a Thing of every evil Tendency." Newspapers and journals recorded the arrests of men disastrously influenced by Macheath and his friends: a stroller named Hutchinson was committed to jail as a forger, seized as he was about to act the part of Captain Macheath; antagonistic commentators recorded many similar instances of corruption supposedly caused directly or indirectly by the play.
>
> (Spacks, 122–23)

Yet the beggar's "world" is also a mirror for the middle-class audience's own world, with its rampant ambition, hierarchies of power, and self-serving ethos. Like the beasts in Gay's *Fables* (1727), the criminals talk and act like merchants and tradesmen, citizens and gentlemen, rather than like the real inhabitants of St. Giles's and Newgate.

At this level, *The Beggar's Opera* comments on the ambiguities within the human condition, with music and other authorial devices controlling the audience reaction. The ballads themselves contained substantial ironies for contemporary audiences: "A large majority of the tunes he chose were associated with amorous words, and not infrequently Gay kept phrases, refrain lines or half lines, or followed the earlier verbal patterns, for his new lyrics" (Bronson, 301). Among the play's many targets are the manners of the aristocracy, the conflicting demands of friendship and avarice, and one's obligations to family, society, and the state; like comedies of its own and earlier eras, *The Beggar's Opera* focuses much of this satire on questions of power and authority. For the elder Peachums, materialists to the bone, their daughter's marriage to Macheath is an unmitigated disaster, since it has given Macheath power to "hang his father and mother-in-law in hope to get into their daughter's fortune" (1.8.59–60). Though Polly has earlier assured her father, "A woman knows how to be mercenary, though she hath never been in a court or at an assembly. We have it in our natures, Papa" (1.7.2–4), she now admits, "I did not marry him (as 'tis the fashion) coolly and deliberately for honor or money. But I love him" (1.8.61–62). Polly is, of course, a romantic, who later in the play sings about turtledoves and swallows who mate until death, but who would also prefer Macheath dead rather than unfaithful. At about the same time, Macheath is indulging in some deathbed heroics of his own:

> Then farewell, my love—dear charmers, adieu.
> Contented I die. 'Tis the better for you.
> Here ends all dispute the rest of our lives,
> For this way at once I please all my wives.
>   (3.11.72–75)

Gay contrives that these humorously exaggerated sentiments with their pragmatic underlayer lighten the play's tone at the very point when it might turn serious. They also show Macheath and Polly, as "gentleman" and "lady," as well matched as the play's other marriage of true minds, Lockit and Peachum.

Sex is both a commodity and an appetite in *The Beggar's Opera*.

Filch helps "ladies to a pregnancy against their being called down to sentence" (3.3.6–7), that is, to escape hanging by pleading their "bellies," while Jenny Diver, Diana Trapes, and the rest will "shop" a man as readily as sell themselves to him. Interestingly, the elder generation, unlike their counterparts in earlier comedies, are not in sexual competition with Macheath and his cohorts. Sex has little place in the competitive world of Peachum and Lockit, where power and conquest are measured by gold: "In the world of Peachum there is no longer any tension between pleasure and business, for pleasure exists only in business, in the ability to translate all emotion, all relations, all life, into financial terms" (Weber, 205). In contrast, Macheath and his friends consider drinking and sex as careless indulgences of the flesh they are heir to, and sex can be seen as at least marginally life-affirming in Macheath, Polly, and Lucy (particularly the very pregnant Lucy). Sex, therefore, is linguistically associated with the terms of commodity and barter or with animals following their natural bent. The abundant animal imagery is often used for comic effect, as when Macheath is analogized as a "cock," but Lockit uses the connection to show that humans are inferior to animals: "Lions, wolves, and vultures don't live together in herds, droves, or flocks. Of all animals of prey, man is the only sociable one. Every one of us preys upon his neighbor, and yet we herd together" (3.2.ii.4–7). It is within the context of this human-eat-human world that Macheath and Polly can seem "the only saving grace in a society utterly corrupt and degraded" (Weber, 206).

Macheath is difficult to dislike. He inherits some of his appeal from similar "gentlemen of the sword," rake-heroes in the repertory like Careless of *The Committee*, Horner of *The Country-Wife*, and Dorimant of *The Man of Mode*. His "I love the sex [i.e., woman]. And a man who loves money might as well be contented with one guinea as I with one woman. . . . I must have women. There is nothing unbends the mind like them" (2.3.2–3, 19–20), bears strong resemblance to Willmore's "Oh for my Arms full of soft, white, kind—Woman!" (2.1.27). Macheath's rampant sexuality is more severely controlled than that of other comic rakes, however, because he inhabits a world where other characters are more powerful than he, where youth, intelligence, and sexual attractiveness are not enough to establish control. In a society dedicated to mercenary values, he loses authority by "spending" himself and his money freely: "His sexual generosity . . . corresponds to his later largess in offering assistance to his gang when the road proves 'so barren of money' [3.4.1]" (Weber, 209). In this sense, he is a post-

Carolean rake, closer in spirit to Valentine of *Love for Love* and Aimwell of *The Beaux Stratagem* than to Dorimant or Horner. He is also, as Yvonne Noble points out, contrasted sharply with his heroic counterpart in Italian opera, the *castrato*: "in Macheath—vigorous, English, generous, and manly—*The Beggar's Opera* implicitly appeals to its audiences to reaffirm their allegiance to what is native, natural, life-giving, and good—in short, to the values that in literature we generally call comic."[22]

Yet another layer of *The Beggar's Opera* is its political satire, directed primarily at Sir Robert Walpole, who came to power as First Minister just after the collapse of the South Sea Company in 1721 had severely weakened the people's confidence in the government and who reigned supreme for the next 20 years. He was heartily detested by many prominent Londoners, among them Swift, Pope, and Gay, who saw in Walpole not only a shift in the balance of power from Tory to Whig but a shift in the very nature of politics. Under Walpole, they perceived their country turning into "a base marketplace where shysters and hacks and grotesque foreigners swarmed" (Noble, 4), and where corruption and misuse of power were standard political coin. Gay, who had had hopes for a court preferment and had once again been disappointed with Walpole's reinstatement at the ascension of George II, was ideally placed to satirize him in *The Beggar's Opera*.

References to Walpole show up in various characters, incidents, and songs. Peachum represents not only Jonathan Wild, but also Walpole:

> Gay's wit lies in bringing out the more submerged likenesses between Wild and Walpole—their success at attaining and retaining command over their societies; their brazenness; their duplicity; their bland materialism ("All these men have their price," we remember Walpole saying; Wild notes in his accounts, "One man, hanged, £40"); and, alas, their manipulation and corruption of a willing public. . . . The political force of Gay's comparison, carried out to such length, lies in its clear indictment of the leader who cares for nothing but the material, the commercial, and the expedient, both by showing us such a man in the figure of Peachum and by reminding us over and over that the Peachums flourish in the example of, and in the moral climate set by, the Court, the aristocracy, the First Minister—leaders of the society at large.
>
> (Noble, 6–7)

Macheath's womanizing is also analogous to Walpole's (see Schultz, 195–96), and numerous incidental references in the play were interpreted by contemporary audiences as directed at the Prime Minister: "the audience's attention is drawn to the comedy's satiric relevance by Peachum's list of aliases for Walpole, applied to a member of Peachum's gang *Robin of Bagshot*, alias *Gorgon*, alias *Bluff Bob*, alias *Carbuncle*, alias *Bob Booty*" (Spacks, 127). An eyewitness relates Walpole's reaction during the first-night performance:

> In the scene where Peachum and Lockit are described settling their accounts, Lockit sings the song, "When you censure the age, &c."[23] which had such an effect on the audience, that, as if by instinct, the greater part of them threw their eyes on the stage-box, where the Minister was sitting, and loudly *encored* it. Sir Robert saw this stroke instantly, and saw it with good humor and discretion; for no sooner was the song finished, than he encored it a second time himself, joined in the general applause, and by this means brought the audience into so much good humor with him, that they gave him a general huzza from all parts of the house.
>
> (Quoted in Schultz, 186)

What else could a smart politician do? But in time-honored fashion, Walpole didn't get mad, he got even. Unable to stop the already licensed production of *The Beggar's Opera*, he used the Lord Chamberlain's office to ban the milder *Polly*, and began his preventive campaign to control the theaters.

Thus, the success of Gay's "opera" as satire had both short- and long-term consequences for the London theater. Its popularity opened the eyes of current and potential theater managers to unseen possibilities, "that London had a large, hitherto almost untapped audience. The play pulled into the theater not only a multitude of repeat attenders but also a large group of potential and occasional theater-goers who could perhaps be induced to attend regularly" (Hume 1988, 36). In the short term, it provoked an outbreak of satiric plays, ballad operas, and other types at all the London theaters, and this in turn led to the Licensing Act of 1737, which in effect muzzled the drama for a long time to come. Though he died in 1732, Gay had inadvertently started a rebellion wherein popular culture, for a time, seemed at the vanguard of popular taste.

Comedy: The Author's Farce

*Hang his Play, and all Plays; the Dancers are the only People
that support the House; if it were not for us they might Act their
Shakespeare to empty Benches.*

(Pasquin, *3.32)*

But sure the Gods will side with Common-Sense.

(Pasquin, *4.36)*[24]

Much of what happened between 1728 and 1737 was unpredictable; certainly no one attending *The Beggar's Opera* in its first season
would have anticipated the proliferation of new plays, actors, and theaters
that appeared over the next eight years. But in August 1729, when Henry
Fielding returned to London after a brief stint at the University of Leyden
in the Netherlands, *The Beggar's Opera* was still riding high, playing at
both patent houses to "great applause." Within months, Fielding had a
play—*The Temple Beau*—successfully produced by Henry Giffard at
Goodman's Fields, beginning a dramatic career in which he wrote three
to four plays a year, 26 in all, over the next seven years.[25] Of this
output, 10 had 50 or more performances before 1747: three comedies,
two afterpieces, and five ballad operas.

Between March 1730 and December 1735, Fielding had his plays
produced at the New Theater in the Haymarket and Lincoln's Inn Fields
but primarily at Drury Lane after 1732, up to and during the major
actors' defection under Theophilus Cibber in fall 1733, when Fielding
supported Highmore, the owner-manager.[26] When Cibber and the others
returned in March 1734, Fielding began producing plays at other theaters.
Pat Rogers sees this as a kind of "fortunate fall":

> This troubled phase of theatrical history had the effect of impeding
> Fielding as a dramatist, but to no unfortunate end. If the Drury
> Lane management had gone on its accustomed way, he would
> very likely have continued to produce the mixture as before, with
> a special emphasis on the orthodox five-act comedies in which
> he obviously wished to excel. As things turned out, he found
> himself thrust willynilly into the live action; and he was best as
> a playwright when dealing with the events and personalities of
> contemporary England. In a quieter theatrical climate, he might

have been pushed into academic modes and conventional themes.[27]

In the short run, however, as Hume points out, Fielding's situation was not happy; he was "probably both short of money and acutely aware that his relations with the new Drury Lane management were strained or worse" (1988, 185). His revised *The Author's Farce* had undoubtedly alienated Theophilus Cibber, who was, under Fleetwood, the stage manager of the theater; Drury Lane also had little interest in producing new plays, except for afterpieces (Hume 1988, 186–87). After the failure of *The Universal Gallant* in February 1735, Fielding retired to the country, returning in December 1735 as manager and premiere author of "The Great Mogul's Company of Comedians" at the New Haymarket. Thus, he entered into direct competition with the more conventional offerings at the patent theaters. The new company hit its stride around February 1736, and produced no fewer than 11 new plays before the end of the season: "The company was from its inception an exponent of the theater of commitment; it promised new forms and stretched the frontiers of drama, but it drew primarily on an underlying vein of political fervour" (Rogers, 86).[28] Fielding's own *Pasquin*, which premiered on 5 March, set the tone for what was to follow. Various other satires and burlesques culminated in *The Historical Register for the Year 1736* and *Eurydice Hiss'd*, both satires on politicians in general and Walpole in particular. It is to these plays that most commentators attribute the passage of the Licensing Act of 1737,[29] which in turn precipitated Fielding into his new careers, at age 30, as lawyer and then novelist.[30] Hume, however, disagrees, pointing to the Barnard bill of 1735, virtually identical to the Licensing Act, which failed to pass Parliament only by a fluke (1988, 198, 249). In effect, when Walpole began to move in spring 1737, he had a solid base of support in the House and the City to capitalize upon. Confident of the bill's passage, he shut down the Haymarket on 25 May, and the act took effect one month later (Hume 1988, 244).

Yet their topicality is only one part of the modern reader's interest in Fielding's plays, which experiment with the nature of theater itself. An author whose least popular plays were his most conventional—the five-act comedies like *The Modern Husband* or the *The Universal Gallant*,[31]—Fielding was best at stretching the limits of the eighteenth-century audiences' expectations about theatrical form and content: *The Author's Farce* or *The Tragedy of Tragedies* (especially in its heavily annotated published version), *Pasquin*, and *The Historical Register*. These latter plays seem to be composed of frenetic energy, attacking the conventions of traditional theater by destroying the boundaries between audience and artifact, reality and fantasy, actor and role. They often seem to be asking for a new kind of relationship with the audience, an intimacy bound up with cognitive distance. Fielding might have transformed the theater of his time had he remained an active playwright, but he did not, perhaps to the detriment of both.[32]

One of his best experimental plays is *The Author's Farce*, which predates his reign as the "Grand Mogul." In both its 1730 original and its 1734 revised forms,[33] it begins conventionally with the unpublished author Luckless arguing with his landlady, Moneywood, over nonpayment of his rent—we are reminded of Valentine in *Love for Love* and other impecunious gentlemen of comic misfortune. Luckless's love for the landlady's daughter Harriot and the mother's opposition to the match are also comic clichés, along with the friend, Witmore, who bails him out. But unlike Congreve's Valentine, Luckless is a genuine, though unproduced, playwright, and the 1734 version enhances the role of two characters to satirize the policies of the London establishment toward unfledged authors: Bookweight and Marplay Jr., understood to represent publisher Edmund Curll and Theophilus Cibber, respectively.[34] Bookweight refuses to publish the play before it is accepted by the theaters, adding, "This . . . is a plentiful year of plays, and they are like nuts: in a plentiful year they are commonly very bad" (1.6.9–11). He goes on to lecture Luckless on the difference between "your acting plays and your reading plays," those which are only theatrically viable and those which have "wit and meaning" enough to support publication (1.6.21–22, 28). Lest we think Bookweight's response that of a sensible, albeit particularly mercenary, tradesman, Fielding produces in the next act an elaborate parody of the bookseller's practices of plagiarism and hackwork.

The second character present only in the second version is Marplay Jr., who struts around Luckless's apartment in act 1, scene 6, explaining how he and his father alter plays, even Shakespeare, to suit the public taste: "Alackaday! Was you to see the plays when they are brought to us, a parcel of crude, undigested stuff. We are the persons, sir, who lick them into form, that mould them into shape. The poet make the play, indeed!" (1.6.22–25). At the same time, he defends his own failed plays by reviling the audience's "prejudice." These clear hits at Theophilus Cibber and, in the original, his father, Colley, suggest Fielding's attitude toward the arrogant managers at Drury Lane and, undoubtedly, toward John Rich as well.

The second act shifts scene to the places of judgment themselves—the playhouse and the bookseller's shop. The playhouse is more fully exposed as a place where ignorance and pomposity reign. Luckless reads his play to the managers (Marplay/Cibber and Sparkish/Wilks in version 1, Marplay and Marplay Jr. in version 2), who proceed to "rewrite" it, substituting absurdities for his tragic lines. The simile "look lovely as the smiling infant spring" is to be changed, for example, to "look green as Covent Garden in the spring" (2.1.5, 19), Marplay patiently explaining that Covent Garden Market sells "greens" (2.1.21). After all their attempts to "rescue" it, the managers still refuse the play; when Luckless leaves, Marplay explains to his partner that he has no sound reason for his decision—"It may be a very good [play] for aught I know" (2.2.3)—but is swayed by other factors. In version 1, it is the author's lack of influence, or "interest": "Interest sways as much in the theater as at court, and you know it is anot always the companion of merit in either" (2.2.6–8). In the second version, it is personal pique: "I am resolved, since the town will not receive any [plays] of mine, they shall have none from any other. I'll keep them to their old diet" (2.2.3–6). In both versions, Marplay/ Cibber expresses his contempt for his audiences and his determination to "cram down their throats" what he will have them swallow.

Rivero feels that Fielding uses Luckless's tragedy "both as example and as caveat to contemporary advocates of traditional forms. It also serves as Fielding's dispassionate evaluation of certain potentially disastrous tendencies in his own writing" (37), but I suspect Fielding's motives were less clear-cut. At the time he was writing *The Author's Farce*, he was also writing traditional comedies like *The Modern Husband*. Objecting to the Cibbers' high-handed methods, he undoubtedly still admired their success, and if Luckless represents Fielding the playwright, he is a burlesque version, especially in act 3.

Later, in act 2, the satire shifts from the playhouse to the publishing business, where Bookweight and his "scribblers"—Dash, Quibble, and Blotpage—are contriving rhymes and similes, conducting near-libelous pamphlet wars, and producing title pages complete with "ghosts and murders." Business is so good that Bookweight takes on another clerk, Scarecrow, who is, like Luckless, a failed author, and when Luckless comes to tell Bookweight that his new play, a puppet show, has been accepted at the Haymarket, Bookweight is suddenly eager to buy it, since it is no longer financially risky. The remainder of act 2 reintroduces the framing action, with Moneywood and Harriot arguing about love and self-interest, and Harriot's immortal lines "give me the man who, thrown naked upon the world like my dear Luckless, can make his way through it by his merit and virtuous industry" (2.10.14–17). Had the play ended here, it would have been a tidy two-act comedy, a mixture of satire and sentiment quite within the usual mode of its time.

But act 3 is something else. It layers its fictions one upon the other in a dizzying display of invention, out-Gaying Gay with its metamorphoses and multiple topical references. The act begins in the playhouse, with Luckless as "Master of the Show," combining the roles of director and prompter for the performance of his play *The Pleasures of the Town,* the satiric farce he has written to suit the low taste of the town. As he explains to the player who wants to pull the performance because "It is beneath the dignity of the stage" (3.5), "That may be; so is all farce, and yet you see a farce brings more company to a house than the best play that ever was writ, for this age would allow Tom Durfey a better poet than Congreve or Wycherley. Who would not then rather eat by his nonsense than starve by his wit?" (3.6–10).

Having convinced the player, Luckless proceeds to direct the play, set in the underworld and acted by "puppets" (actors representing puppets), including the most ancient of puppets, Punch and Joan (i.e., Judy). At first, the satiric butts in the play-within-the-play are generic— a poet, a sexton, Punch and Joan as the modern married couple—but the next boatload for Charon's ferry includes primarily theatrical figures like Sir Farcical Comick, Signior Opera, Monsieur Pantomime, and Mrs. Novel, characters associated, respectively, with Colley Cibber, Francesco Senesino, John Rich, and Eliza Haywood.[35] They also represent more general flaws, from plagiarism to pandering. Once in the Court of Nonsense, Fielding introduces more contemporary satire with a bookseller (the Prime Minister) and a card game between four women that erupts into a brawl, a song and dance between Somebody and Nobody, and a scene where the Goddess of Nonsense falls madly in love with Monsieur Opera. He, unfortunately, is already married to Mrs. Novel.[36] With this opening, the others pay suit to the Goddess, to no avail; she is placated finally by being declared Goddess of Wit on earth, acknowledging the final conquest of the theater by nonsense.

At this point, (3.684), the play-within-the-play is interrupted by one Murdertext, a "Presbyterian parson," who brings a Constable to stop the play by arresting Luckless "for abusing Nonsense. . . . People of quality are not to have their diversions libeled at this rate" (3.693–95). Novel, however, persuades him to join the dance, and one's expectation is that Fielding will return us to the play-within-the-play. Instead, he gives us a deus ex machina ending for the framing action, the first level of the fiction: Luckless is identified (by his pawned hat) as the lost heir to the King of Bantam,[37] who conveniently dies between one messenger and the next, making Luckless the new king. He immediately proposes to Harriot, whose mother turns out to be the exiled Queen of Brentford[38] as well as Punch's mother. In his new role, Luckless offers everybody a job: the Constable "shall be chief constable of Bantam. You, Mr. Murdertext, shall be my chaplain; you, sir, my orator; you my poet laureate; you my bookseller; you, Don Tragedio, Sir Farcical, and Signior Opera, shall entertain the city of Bantam with your performances; Mrs. Novel, you shall be a romance writer, and to show my generosity, Marplay and Sparkish shall superintend my theaters" (3.853–60).

In terms of straightforward dramaturgy, much less the Three Unities, this denouement is a nightmare. Woods calls Fielding's method "emblematical": "[L]ikely to give characters and plot an allegorical significance, [it] often does not pretend to represent surface appearances of life as we know it. At times, however, what may be called non-realistic elements are juxtaposed or mingled with realistic elements in such a way that a peculiar satiric effect is gained, as in the hilarious ending of *The Author's Farce* when the symbolic or allegorical figures and the flesh-and-blood characters are shown to have family ties" (Woods and Zimansky, xvi). Remarking the multiple levels of fiction in act 3 and suggesting that the play-within-the-play enhances the actuality of the framing action, Rivero calls Fielding's technique "double satire, . . . the twofold censuring or ridiculing of an individual or subject matter, first in the frame, then in the puppet show" (43). He points to a number of parallel actions in the first and third acts, such as Charon's demanding his fare and Moneywood's demanding her rent, but these devices are each so commonplace that his reasoning here is less convincing than the other kinds of doubling he identifies: Marplay–Sir Farcical Comic–Cibber and Bookweight–Curry–Edmund Curll. Only these two characters, besides Fielding himself (as Luckless, Scarecrow, the poet in the underworld), exist on multiple fictional levels, thus reinforcing the play's satiric focus on the theater itself and the playwriting business.

All of these devices force the audience to maintain separate fictive dimensions simultaneously, but this is easier for an audience than a reader, and perhaps easier in a well-lit, noisy eighteenth-century theater than, say, a dark, quiet modern one. Fielding's audience might even, if they chose, involve themselves in the fantasy; Fielding produced no "extra" audience for *The Pleasures of the Town*, but used the one already in place at the Haymarket. If so, Fielding's audiences might also be

prepared to accept their own implicit guilt for the ascendancy of Nonsense, at the core of the foolery and authorial legerdemain in *The Author's
Farce*. They might also, of course, see themselves as the alternatives,
like Fielding himself, to the degradation of taste going on in the patent
theaters.

The success of *The Author's Farce* no doubt encouraged Fielding
to use similar techniques again in *Pasquin* and *Euridyce Hiss'd*, where
the satiric targets include politics along with the stage, entertaining his
audiences with portraits of and references to Walpole and his cohorts.
But however ready his audience might have been to be amused by hard-
hitting satire, those in power were unprepared for the stage to become a
vehicle for political criticism. The combined efforts of moralists, traditionalists, and the managers at Drury Lane and Covent Garden, all of
whom for different reasons saw these alternative theaters and their offerings as a threat, served to curb the excesses of the unlicensed playhouses
and personnel. By granting exclusive contracts to the two "legitimate"
theaters and the opera house and reasserting the authority of the Lord
Chamberlain over them, the Licensing Act of 1737 effectively brought
the London theaters under state as well as popular control for the rest of
the eighteenth century. Fielding and Gay, by stretching the limits of
what drama could say and do, succeeding only in defining those limits
more narrowly for the playwrights, managers, and audiences who followed them on the London stage.

Traditional Forms

Slightly earlier than the innovations of Gay and Fielding, changes were
also taking place in more traditional forms of comedy and tragedy. As
usual, only a few of the new comedies and tragedies were popular enough
to join the repertory of old plays with which they were competing, but
those which did marked developments in those genres in the directions
already established: the incorporation of feelings and community values in
comedy, the enhancement of emotional "catharsis" in tragedy. Looking at
shifts in popular culture, including the novel, Scouten points to the
increasing taste for morality and sentiment, especially during the 1730s
and 1740s: "The reading public for whom Swift and Pope wrote and the
theater-goers who applauded the plays of Congreve and Gay were yielding
to a new audience affected by a recrudescence of English Puritanism.

Outside the theater, Richardson's *Pamela* and Young's *Night Thoughts* were being provided for this new middle class audience: within, the 'weeping comedies' and the *drame* from France were supplanting the comedy of manners" (*LS*, 3:169). And critics like John Loftis and Ernest Bernbaum see a shift occurring in drama after the turn of the century, from plays seemingly based on "ethical theories assuming human depravity to those assuming human benevolence."[39] John K. Sheriff refines the influences even further, to the rational and emotional sentimentalists represented by philosophers like John Locke and David Hume, each defining a slightly different path by which humans could recover their "natural" goodness (chap. 1).

The list of popular comedies of the 1714–47 period shows only 11 new mainpiece comedies (20 percent) and two of these—Shakespeare's *As You Like It* and *The Merchant of Venice*—are new revivals, while Cibber's *The Provoked Husband* and Bullock's *The Woman's Revenge* are rewrites of other authors' works.[40] The changes in traditional comedy are most likely to be coming from Susanna Centlivre (1667/69–1723) and Sir Richard Steele (1672–1729), two playwrights who produced popular comedies before and after 1714 and who died before the hectic 1730s, and who each have three comedies on the list. In representative plays like Centlivre's *A Bold Stroke for a Wife* (1718) and Steele's *The Conscious Lovers* (1722), these authors produced comedies that were popular through the eighteenth century, incorporated important changes occurring in post-Stuart England, and offer exemplary heroes who blend intellect and sensibility.

The two dramatists were political allies and, in the small literary world of early eighteenth-century London, friends.[41] One significant change in their comedies is that, unlike their predecessors—Congreve, Vanbrugh, and Farquhar—both Steele and Centlivre often feature admirable merchants in their plays: "Even before 1710, several writers—Burnaby, Baker, Steele, and Mrs. Centlivre, among others—wrote plays in which there is a perceptible modification of social judgment: not a decisive shift of sympathy from the gentry to the merchants (as there was in certain plays of a decade or so later), but still a departure from the unyielding assumption that in the antagonism between merchants and gentry the merchants were in an indefensible position" (Loftis 1959, 44).[42] Centlivre and Steele, however, extend this benevolence in their plays mostly to very wealthy men of business, veritable merchant princes, not to ordinary shopkeepers and traders. They also reserve the right to mock some members of the breed. In Centlivre's *The Busie Body* (1709), Sir Jealous Traffick has gotten his absurd notions about childrearing from his years in Spain plying his trade, while in A *Bold Stroke for a Wife,* a decade later, the admirable merchant Freeman is counterbalanced with the stockjobber Tradelove, "a fellow that will outlie the devil for the advantage of stocks and cheat his father that got him in a bargain, . . . a great stickler for trade and hates everything that wears a sword" (1.1.108–11).[43] Moreover, Centlivre reserves the position of hero for a gentleman-soldier, Colonel Fainwell, and shows Freeman doubting his friend's ability to outwit the various guardians who bar his way to a match with Mrs. Lovely: "If it depended on knight-errantry, I should not doubt your setting free the damsel; but to have avarice, impertinence, hypocrisy, and pride at once to deal with requires more cunning than generally attends a man of honor" (1.1.132–35). There is still, then, a sense that the businessman and the gentleman, though they inhabit the same world and complement each other, subscribe to somewhat different value systems.

Even more than Centlivre, Steele was sustained by and contributed to the changed theatrical and social conditions after 1714. Steele was given the Drury Lane patent shortly after George I's arrival in England, apparently as a reward for political services and for his attempts as critic and author to make the stage a moral agent in society. The decision was widely praised by those who wished to see such reform, rather than the elimination of the theater promoted by Collier, and who saw in Steele "at once a reformer and a devoted friend of the theater" (Loftis 1952, 14):

> Steele's many essays praising actors, plays, and the theater as an institution can be fully understood only in the context of the puritanical opposition he faced from such men as Collier, Blackmore, Defoe, and, a little later, William Law. Steele employed his persuasive gifts in the *Tatler,* the *Spectator,* the *Guardian,* the *Town Talk,* and the *Theater* to convince his readers, many of whom belonged to social groups that had only recently begun to take an interest in literature, that the theater, in so far as it was not morally offensive, deserved support. Committed politically to the merchants, Steele tried in his essays and by the example of *The Conscious Lovers* to make the theater more hospitable to them.
>
> (Loftis 1959, 32–33)

Though Steele may have brought new audiences to the theater and the theater to new audiences, ultimately his success as a manager was less important than as an essayist and playwright, an advocate for didactic comedy whose lasting legacy was *The Conscious Lovers*.

His best-known and most popular play, *The Conscious Lovers* can be seen as a deliberate attempt to incorporate his ideas about reforming the stage and his social politics with traditional comic patterns. It was begun at least a decade or so earlier than its first production, during the heyday of the political debates at the end of Queen Anne's reign, and during Steele's own "vigorous years when he was writing the essays on which his fame rests (Loftis 1952, 193, see also Loftis 1959, 83), and shows the moralist and the sentimentalist coming together to produce a comic hero worthy of emulation, a new hero for a new age.

Comedy: The Conscious Lovers

> How engaging is Modesty in a Man, when one knows there is a
> great Mind within—So tender a Confusion! and yet, in other
> Respects, so much himself, so collected, so dauntless, so
> determin'd!
>   (The Conscious Lovers, 2.3.187–90)[44]

Despite its familiar London setting, the environment of *The Conscious Lovers* is substantially different from those of Carolean and late Stuart comedies. It is a London inhabited by characters who define merit very differently from those of Dryden and Behn, and somewhat differently from those of Congreve and Farquhar. Despite resemblances of plot and character types between Steele's comedies and his predecessors', Steele's characters often speak sententiously rather than wittily, there is no smut or double entendre, and the conventions of romance intrude on the conventions of satire. Because his principal characters are stylistically and substantively altered from their comic predecessors, the relationships between fathers and sons, friends, and lovers are also changed, such that patterns of authority are reinstated, along with conventions of behavior and language that chafed earlier comic hero[in]es.

This new order is most immediately evident in the father-son relationship between Sir John Bevil and Bevil Jr. In contrast to previous comic heroes who yearned for their independence, Bevil Jr. gracefully relinquishes his:

SIR JOHN BEVIL:	But what charms me above all Expression is, that my Son has never in the least Action, the most distant Hint or Word, valued himself upon that great Estate of his Mother's, which, according to our Marriage Settlement, he has had ever since he came to Age.
HUMPHREY:	No, Sir; on the contrary, he seems afraid of appearing to enjoy it, before you or any belonging to you—He is as dependant and resign'd to your Will, as if he had not a Farthing but what must come from your immediate Bounty—You have ever acted like a good and generous Father, and he like an obedient and grateful Son.

(1.1.33–43)

Where Carolean heroes spoke longingly of their fathers' demise, Bevil Jr. has no wish for an early inheritance; at the masquerade, he leaps to his father's defense, and he strives to protect his father from the faintest hint of discomfort. This creates a different set of comic problems, based not on antagonism but on misunderstanding; the old family servant, Humphrey, comments, "[T]ho' this Father and Son live as well together as possible, yet their fear of giving each other Pain, is attended with constant mutual Uneasiness" (1.1.116–18). The staple comic device, parental obstruction to marriage, takes a new turn in this play as a result. Sir John has contrived his son's betrothal to Mr. Sealand's daughter Lucinda, but when he accidentally discovers his son loves another woman (Indiana), he works hard to discover Bevil Jr.'s true inclinations. A scene ensues where Sir John and his son maneuver carefully around each other's feelings, and where Bevil Jr. reveals an unexpected, and rare, sense of humor:

BEVIL, JR.:	As I am ever prepar'd to marry if you bid me, so I am ready to let it alone if you will have me.
SIR JOHN BEVIL:	Look you there now! why what am I to think of this so absolute and so indifferent a Resignation?
BEVIL, JR.:	Think? that I am still your Son, Sir,—Sir—you have been married, and I have not. And you

have, Sir, found the Inconvenience there is,
when a Man weds with too much Love in his
Head. I have been told, Sir, that at the Time
you married, you made a mighty Bustle on the
Occasion. There was challenging and fighting,
scaling Walls—locking up the Lady—and the
Gallant under an Arrest for fear of killing all
his Rivals—Now, Sir, I suppose you having
found the ill Consequences of these strong Passions and Prejudices, in preference of one
Woman to another, in Case of a Man's becoming a Widower— . . . I say Sir, Experience has
made you wiser in your Care of me—for, Sir,
since you lost my dear Mother, your time has
been so heavy, so lonely, and so tasteless, that
you are so good as to guard me against the like
Unhappiness, by marrying me prudentially by
way of Bargain and Sale. For, as you well judge,
a Woman that is espous'd for a Fortune, is yet
a better Bargain, if she dies; for then a Man
still enjoys what he did marry, the Money; and
is disencumber'd of what he did not marry, the
Woman.

(1.2.47–69)

This father-son exchange directly contradicts the usual relationships in
Carolean comedy, wherein older and younger men were generally in
competition, sometimes for the same women, and this essential change
permeates all the relationships in *The Conscious Lovers*.

One is male friendship. Although friendly alliances between men
were common in Carolean comedy—such as between Dorimant and
Medley in *The Man of Mode* or Willmore and Belvile in *The Rover*—
often these friendships ran aground when the men found themselves
competing over money or women, or when their "honor" was engaged,
particularly in Spanish-plot comedies, with their dueling climaxes. In
The Conscious Lovers, Steele deliberately invokes this tradition to degrade
it, making Bevil Jr.'s friend Myrtle a jealous and unsuccessful lover who
misconstrues Bevil Jr.'s intentions about Lucinda and challenges his
friend to a duel. Bevil Jr.'s reaction demonstrates his rationality as he
controls, with some difficulty, his automatic reaction: "I have never been
more thoroughly disturb'd; This hot Man! to write me a Challenge, on

supposed artificial Dealing, when I profess'd my self his Friend! I can live contented without Glory; but I cannot suffer Shame. What's to be done?" (4.1.46–49). Bevil Jr., as Steele's spokesman, repudiates the ridiculous custom of dueling as a test of honor: "this Duelling, which Custom has impos'd upon every Man, who would live with Reputation and Honour in the World:—How must I preserve my self from Imputations there? He'll, forsooth, call it, or think it Fear, if I explain without Fighting—" (4.1.73–77). In the ensuing scene, he indeed tries to calm his "hot" friend, without much success, and finds his own temper aroused at last:

BEVIL JR.: Sir, shew me but the least Glimpse of Argument, that I am authoriz'd, by my own Hand, to vindicate any lawless Insult of this nature, and I will shew thee— to chastize thee—hardly deserves the Name of Courage—slight, inconsiderate Man!—There is, Mr. *Myrtle*, no such Terror in quick Anger; and you shall, you know not why, be cool, as you have, you know not why, been warm.

MYRTLE: Is the Woman one loves, so little an Occasion of Anger? You perhaps, who know not what it is to love, who have your Ready, your Commodious, your Foreign Trinket, for your loose Hours; and from your Fortune, your specious outward Carriage, and other lucky Circumstances, as easie a Way to the Possession of a Woman of Honour; you know nothing of what it is to be alarm'd, to be distracted, with Anxiety and Terror of losing more than Life: Your Marriage, happy Man! goes on like common Business, and in the interim, you have your Rambling Captive, your *Indian* Princess, for your soft Moments of Dalliance, your Convenient, your Ready *Indiana*.

BEVIL JR.: You have touch'd me beyond the Patience of a Man; and I'm excusable, in the Guard of Innocence (or from the Infirmity of Human Nature, which can bear no more) to accept your Invitation, and observe your Letter—Sir, I'll attend you.

(4.1.134–55)

Of course, they do not duel; Bevil Jr. controls his anger and shows Myrtle Lucinda's letter, which reveals that their engagement is a sham and that she is wary of Myrtle's jealousy. During the rest of the play, the friends remain friends. If especially on the page, there is a sense of authorial contrivance about this scene; it serves Steele's multiple purposes in the same way as the father-son confrontation in act 1, scene 2 does. While showing the exemplary hero in his best, most rational self, both scenes display other dimensions of the almost-too-perfect Bevil Jr., a touch of humor and temper beneath the smooth facade of the consummate genteel hero.

The other important relationships are between the young couples, Bevil Jr. and Indiana, Myrtle and Lucinda. The first of these, between Bevil Jr. and Indiana, is highly romanticized—he has rescued her from an evil stepbrother—but also decorous; because of his engagement to Lucinda and Indiana's dependence on him, he never declares his feelings. He explains to Humphrey, "For tho' I doat on her to death, and have no little Reason to believe she has the same Thoughts for me; yet in all my Acquaintance, and utmost Privacies with her, I never once directly told her, that I loved. . . . My tender Obligations to my Father have laid so inviolable a Restraint upon my Conduct, that 'till I have his Consent to speak, I am determin'd, on that Subject to be dumb for ever—" (1.2.227–36). Humphrey responds, perhaps with some irony, "[Y]ou are certainly the most unfashionable Lover in *Great-Britain*" (1.2.237–38). In contrast to the sexually aware and verbally direct hero [in]es of Carolean comedy, these lovers are attracted to the other's inner qualities, not beauty, money, or sex appeal. Bevil Jr. describes Indiana as "a virtuous Woman, that is the pure Delight of my Eyes, and the guiltless Joy of my Heart" (2.1.125–26), while she refers to him as a man of sincerity, honor, and intelligence, who "has Sense enough to make even Virtue fashionable" (2.2.84–85).

What their relationship epitomizes for Steele and his audience is the higher calling of "esteem," and the "conscious [i.e., conscientious] lovers" discuss its value at some length:

BEVIL JR.:   If I might be vain of any thing, in my Power, Madam,
              'tis that my Understanding, from all your Sex, has
              mark'd you out, as the most deserving Object of my
              Esteem.

INDIANA: Should I think I deserve this, 'twere enough to make
              my Vanity forfeit the very Esteem you offer me.

BEVIL JR.:   How so, Madam?

INDIANA:	Because Esteem is the Result of Reason, and to deserve it from good Sense, the Height of Human Glory: Nay, I had rather a Man of Honour should pay me that, than all the Homage of a sincere and humble Love.
BEVIL JR.:	You certainly distinguish right, Madam; Love often kindles from external Merit only—
INDIANA:	But Esteem arises from a higher Source, the Merit of the Soul—
BEVIL JR.:	True—And great Souls only can deserve it. [*Bowing respectfully.*]

(2.3.24–39)

The contrast between this heightened sensibility and the frank sexuality of Carolean lovers is instructive; clearly, Steele is attempting to substitute for love based on appearances and self-satisfaction a higher love based on the refined spiritual and intellectual qualities that attract the "esteem" of honorable men and women.

When love based on sex and money does appear in the play, it is seen in "low" characters like servants and satiric butts, such as Lucinda's suitor Cimberton and Mrs. Sealand. Thus, Steele presents a kind of hierarchy of what passes for love: Bevil Jr. and Indiana inhabit the heights, Myrtle and Lucinda the middle ground, while the depths are peopled by servants, fools, and fops, all of whom exhibit mixtures of practicality, avarice, and carnal desires. However much they feign the high-flown passions and rhetoric of their betters, the servants, Phillis and Tom, define a love that acknowledges basic human instincts. Phillis explains this kind of love to her mistress:

LUCINDA:	Who was that you was hurrying away?
PHILLIS:	One that I had no mind to part with.
LUCINDA:	Why did you turn him away then?
PHILLIS:	For your Ladyship's Service, to carry your Ladyship's Letter to his Master: I could hardly get the Rogue away.
LUCINDA:	Why, has he so little Love for his Master?
PHILLIS:	No; but he has so much Love for his Mistress.

LUCINDA: But, I thought, I heard him kiss you. Why do you
             suffer that?

PHILLIS: Why, Madam, we Vulgar take it to be a Sign of Love;
             we Servants, we poor People, that have nothing but
             our Persons to bestow, or treat for, are forc'd to deal,
             and bargain by way of Sample; and therefore, as
             we have no Parchments, or Wax necessary in our
             Agreements, we squeeze with our Hands, and seal
             with our Lips, to ratifie Vows and Promises.

                                                        (3.117–32)

Lucinda is puzzled, not surprisingly, since she is being indoctrinated with
her mother's very different interpretation of love, a kind of ultrarefined
nonsense that is the veneer over lust for status and gain:

LUCINDA: [M]y Mother says, it's indecent for me to let my
             Thoughts stray about the Person of my Husband:
             nay, she says, a Maid, rigidly Virtuous, tho' she may
             have been where her Lover was a thousand times,
             should not have made Observations enough, to
             know him from another Man, when she sees him in
             a third Place.

PHILLIS: That is more than the Severity of a Nun, for not to
             see, when one may, is hardly possible; not to see
             when one can't, is very easy: at this rate, Madam,
             there are a great many whom you have not seen
             who—

LUCINDA: Mamma says, the first time you see your Husband
             should be at that Instant he is made so; when your
             Father, with the help of the Minister, gives you to
             him; then you are to see him, then you are to Ob-
             serve and take Notice of him, because then you are
             to Obey him.

PHILLIS: But does not my Lady remember, you are to Love,
             as well as Obey?

LUCINDA: To Love is a Passion, 'tis a Desire, and we must have
             no Desires. Oh! I cannot endure the Reflection! With
             what Insensibility on my Part, with what more than
             Patience, have I been expos'd, and offer'd to some

> awkward Booby or other, in every County of *Great
> Britain*.
>
> (3.155–76)

Lucinda's plight, as the final lines imply, is to be sold at auction by her mother, whose false gentility hides the mercenary bawd.

Lady Sealand's choice has fixed upon Cimberton, her own kinsman; vulgar and avaricious, he is one of Steele's best satiric portraits. Like Lady Sealand, Cimberton masks these qualities behind a surface gentility: "the young Women of this Age are treated with Discourses of such a Tendency, and their Imaginations so bewilder'd in Flesh and Blood, that a Man of Reason can't talk to be understood: They have no Ideas of Happiness, but what are more gross than the Gratification of Hunger and Thirst" (3.217–21). He goes on, much to his kinswoman's gratification, to laud ancient customs whereby "the whole Female World was pregnant, but none, but the Mothers themselves, knew by whom; their Meetings were secret, and the Amorous Congress always by Stealth" (3.238–40), but his diction soon degenerates as he praises Lucinda's physique as if she were a horse: "the Vermilion of her Lips . . . Pant of her Bosom . . . Her forward Chest . . . High Health . . . Proud Heart . . . her Arms—her Neck—what a Spring in her Step!" (3.266–78). To appease mother and daughter, he explains, "I am considering her, on this Occasion, but as one that is to be pregnant. . . . And pregnant undoubtedly she will be yearly. I fear, I shan't, for many Years, have Discretion enough to give her one fallow Season." One can only echo Lucinda's horror: "The familiar, learned, unseasonable Puppy!" (3.287–92). Puppy he is, but also a parody of the genteel hero, and thus Bevil Jr.'s analogue and antagonist as much as Myrtle's. Lady Sealand and Cimberton together show the degradation of love to its meanest form, barter and exchange. In this respect, they are also contrasted with the humane parents, Sealand and Sir John, who only want the best for their children.

In its own time and after, critics have praised *The Conscious Lovers* for its exemplary hero, formulated according to the highest principles of gentlemanly conduct, intended for emulation.[45] But Loftis also points out that Steele established his exemplary comedy at the expense of comic humor: "Curious as it appears from a writer of his unquestioned gift for humor, he persistently expressed a distrust of laughter itself (while creating several delightfully comic characters), insisting, in theory at least, on the superiority of the more severe pleasures. His indictment of laughter in

the epilogue to *The Lying Lover* links it, as Collier had done, to insanity.
. . . As late as the preface to *The Conscious Lovers*, in justifying the
inclusion of a pathetic event in comedy, he wrote of 'a joy too exquisite
for laughter' " (Loftis 1952, 20; see also 197–201). Bevil Jr., as we have
seen, is quirky enough to be amusing at times, but mostly *The Conscious
Lovers* locates humor in servant characters and their antics, as Spanish-
plot comedy did, and for the same reason, to preserve decorum. Steele
also provides near-pathetic heroines, shadow figures who inhabit the
peripheries of his comic landscape, in sharp contrast to the active female
heroes of Dryden, Behn, Vanbrugh, Congreve, and Farquhar. Lucinda
and Indiana wait patently to be rescued, their only capability, like that
of Centlivre's Mrs. Lovely, passive resistance to the control exerted over
them by parents, society, and fate. Though they exhibit some intelligence
and discernment, making them fit mates for the genteel hero, they have
lost whatever freedom of language and action their predessors enjoyed,
and they no longer demand it, content to pass into the hands of their
male rescuer to fulfill their role in a paternal, patriarchal society.

The huge success of *The Conscious Lovers*[46] in its own time and
beyond ensured its imitation, and comedies written afterward tended to
pattern themselves after Steele rather than Gay or Fielding. One good
example is Benjamin Hoadly's *The Suspicious Husband* (1747), one of
the most successful comedies in the late eighteenth century, with 212
performances from its premiere to 1779. Though it offers a more complicated plot than *The Conscious Lovers*, Hoadly's play also showcases its
genteel heroes, Frankly and Bellamy, who are contrasted with both
Ranger, their rakish counterpart, and Strickland, the suspicious husband,
as models of male virtue and appropriate behavior. In that *The Conscious
Lovers* was so widely imitated, it was a more powerful agent of change
than occurred in tragedy as a result of *The London Merchant*.

Tragedy: The London Merchant

> *What have I done! Were my resolutions founded on reason and
> sincerely made? Why, then, has Heaven suffered me to fall? I
> sought not the occasion and, if my heart deceives me not,
> compassion and generosity were my motives. Is virtue inconsistent
> with itself? Or are vice and virtue only empty names? Or do they
> depend on accidents beyond our power to produce or to prevent,*

> *wherein we have no part and yet must be determined by the*
> *event?—But why should I attempt to reason? All is confusion,*
> *horror, and remorse. I find I am lost, cast down from all my*
> *late-erected hopes, and plunged again in guilt, yet scarce know*
> *how or why.*
>
> (The London Merchant, *2.14.1–11*)[47]

In his preface to *Tom Thumb* in April 1730, Henry Fielding humorously "congratulate[d] . . . Cotemporary [sic] Writers, for their having enlarged the Sphere of Tragedy."[48] In fact, his congratulations were only slightly premature; it was another year before George Lillo's *The London Merchant* (1731) hit the boards to make true in a different way what Fielding had ironically predicted. Lillo's prologue begins by delineating the role of the Tragic Muse in ages past, "princes distrest, and scenes of royal woe" (1.1.2), but soon moves on to the subjects of the present, firmly allying himself with Otway, Southerne, and Rowe in the process:

> In ev'ry former age, and foreign tongue,
> With native grandeur thus the goddess sung.
> Upon our stage, indeed, with wish'd success,
> You've sometimes seen her in a humbler dress,
> Great only in distress. When she complains
> In Southerne's, Rowe's, or Otway's moving strains,
> The brilliant drops that fall from each bright eye
> The absent pomp, with brighter gems, supply.
> Forgive us then, if we attempt to show,
> In artless strains, a tale of private woe.
> A London 'prentice ruin'd is our theme,
> Drawn from the fam'd old song that bears his name.
>
> (1.1.11–22)

As this last line suggests, *The London Merchant*, like *Jane Shore*, is based on a popular ballad, "The Ballad of George Barnwell," which Childe dates from the middle of the seventeenth century (see McBurney, Appendix C), in turn based on a true Elizabethan case. The story of George Barnwell was thus well known to eighteenth-century London audiences, who, according to Theophilus Cibber, came the first night, ballad in hand, "intending to make their pleasant remarks (as some afterwards

owned) and ludicrous comparisons between the ancient ditty and the
modern play." Instead, they soon "drop[ped] their ballads, and pull[ed]
out their handkerchiefs" (quoted in McBurney, xii). Using domestic
settings and themes, Lillo thus complemented Steele by producing a
didactic model for tragedy.

The success of *The London Merchant* in 1731 and afterward
startled its author and the managers of Drury Lane, who had given it a
premiere during the summer season, expecting a limited engagement.
Critics have since puzzled over its appeal, especially since it had few
imitators, none of which were particularly successful, thus presenting an
apparent anomaly in repertory development. Partly this is owing to the
overwhelming competition from older tragedies by Rowe, Otway, Shakespeare, and others that limited any "experiments" in tragedy, especially
after 1737. Also, those new tragedies which succeeded in the last half of
the century except for *The Gamester* in 1753, subsumed Lillo's domestic
values in a more traditional heroic format, creating a mixed mode that
appealed to contemporary audiences. *The London Merchant* is more
blatant in its aims and ideology.

From the first words of *The London Merchant*, the audience is
introduced into a tragic world ruled by prose rather than poetry. Instead
of the courts of kings or the fields of combat, they are in a merchant's
house, although Lillo shows us immediately how Thorowgood's business
is connected with the interests of the state with the "packet from Genoa":
"Heaven be praised! The storm that threatened our royal mistress, pure
religion, liberty, and laws, is for a time diverted. The haughty and re-
vengeful Spaniard, disappointed of the loan on which he depended from
Genoa, must now attend the slow return of wealth from his New World
to supply his empty coffers ere he can execute his purposed invasion of our
happy island; by which means time is gained to make such preparations on
our part as may, Heaven concurring, prevent his malice or turn the
meditated mischief on himself" (1.1.2–11). Later Lillo drives the point
home, again through Thorowgood, "how honest merchants, as such may
sometimes contribute to the safety of their country as they do at all times
to its happiness" (1.1.16–18). Thus Thorowgood, and by extension the
merchants of Elizabethan England, are seen as true patriots, activists in
the defense of the realm. The connection of this higher calling with
moral rectitude is also introduced early, as Thorowgood instructs his
apprentice, Trueman: "if hereafter you should be tempted to any action
that has the appearance of vice or meanness in it, upon reflecting on the
dignity of our profession, you may with honest scorn reject whatever is

unworthy of it" (1.1.19–22). Lillo does not pretend that this view of the heroic merchant is universal; in the next scene, Thorowgood and his daughter Maria allude to the nobility's prejudice against baseborn merchants, but both are also convinced that merit will eventually prevail.

This father-daughter scene demonstrates how benevolence penetrates to the domestic level. Unlike the fathers of Fletcherian and Carolean drama who act as obstructors of their children's happiness, Thorowgood is a benign and sensitive patriarch. He inquires about Maria's preference among her many suitors so that he can follow, rather than challenge, her inclination: "as I know love to be essential to happiness in the marriage state, I had rather my approbation should confirm your choice than direct it" (1.2.42–45). The contrast with *Romeo and Juliet* and resemblance to *The Conscious Lovers* is instructive, as Maria and her father go on to show how delicately they both tread around the notion of filial "obedience," he carefully not introducing his "bias" into her decision:

> MARIA: [H]ad you asserted your authority and insisted on a parent's right to be obeyed, I had submitted and to my duty sacrificed my peace.
>
> THOROWGOOD: From your perfect obedience in every other instance I feared as much, and therefore would leave you without a bias in an affair wherein your happiness is so immediately concerned.
>   . . .
>
> MARIA: I cannot answer for my inclinations, but they shall ever be submitted to your wisdom and authority; and, as you will not compel me to marry where I cannot love, so love shall never make me act contrary to my duty.
>   (1.2.51–58, 68–70)

Like Steele's, this vision of perfect parental-filial relations is a wishful projection of what Lillo finds exemplary in the British national character: citizens and merchants working in perfect harmony with rulers and nobles for the good of the state.

The concept of obedience arises again in the next few scenes between Millwood, the evil temptress, and George Barnwell, Thorowgood's other apprentice. Lured to her apartment, the innocent 18-year-old has to leave if he is to complete his duty to his master: "I never yet neglected his service. He is so gentle and so good a master that should I wrong him, though he might forgive me, I never should forgive myself" (1.5.65–68). The speech proves portentous when a few tears from Millwood induce him to stay; the maid Lucy comments on the significance of this relatively minor defection from duty: "So! She has wheedled him out of his virtue of obedience already and will strip him of all the rest, one after another, till she has left him as few as her ladyship or myself" (1.5.84–86). Indeed, the transformation is rapid. By the next morning, when George has returned to Thorowgood's house, having given his master's money to Millwood, the rot has begun to set in. Overcome with guilt and fear, George responds sharply to his friend Trueman's solicitude, in'words and sentiments that echo Millwood's: "Friendship and all engagements cease as circumstances and occasions vary, and, since you once may hate me, perhaps it might be better for us both that now you loved me less" (2.2.36–39). The speed of his transformation may seem puzzling, yet it serves Lillo's purpose—showing how moral corruption can act quickly to undo the foundation of virtue. Once George's weak defenses are breached, his fall is swift and sure. He is brought back to heel by Millwood in the last scenes of act 2, and wavers only once again.

   This push-me-pull-you occurs again in act 3, as related by Lucy, when Millwood adds the last nail to George's coffin by persuading him to rob and kill his uncle and benefactor. After George does the deed, her anger that he has not stolen the money and her fear of implication cause her to have him arrested (4.13). If George's nadir was the killing of his uncle, this scene is Millwood's peripeteia. Shortly afterward, she finds that her servants have turned against her, and in her confrontation with Thorowgood, that her arts and deceptions avail her nothing.[49] Trapped and disarmed at the end of act 4, Millwood verbally counterat-tacks—asserting that her sins were learned from the men who "spoiled" her and from the society that condones venality and hypocrisy for a price. This scene is highly theatrical, providing a great acting role for Elizabeth Butler and her successors on the eighteenth-century stage.

   After Millwood's impassioned outbursts, act 5 seems a prolonged denouement. What it is, of course, is a ritual purification of George that enables him to die heroically, reinstated as the "much loved and much lamented youth" (5.2.56–57) of legend and ballad. Millwood is, in fact, not permitted onstage at all, lest she elicit either sympathy or admiration; we hear only secondhand that she remains "proud, impatient, wrathful, and unforgiving" (5.1.30).[50] Instead, George's friends and loved ones parade through his cell, by ones and twos, generously offering balm and forgiveness, reasserting their love and pity, and mingling their tears with his. The last to arrive is Maria, who finally confesses her love for George, thereby heightening his distress but also convincing him of the possibility of heavenly peace and forgiveness. His final speech announces his recognition that his story will become a cautionary tale for future generations:

> Justice and mercy are in Heaven the same; its utmost severity is mercy to the whole, thereby to cure man's folly and presumption which else would render even infinite mercy vain and ineffectual. Thus justice, in compassion to mankind, cuts off a wretch like me, by one such example to secure thousands from future ruin.
>   If any youth, like you, in future times
>   Shall mourn my fate, though he abhors my crimes,
>   Or tender maid, like you, my tale shall hear
>   And to my sorrows give a pitying tear,
>   To each such melting eye and throbbing heart,
>   Would gracious Heaven this benefit impart:
>   Never to know my guilt, nor feel my pain.
>   Then must you own you ought not to complain,
>   Since you nor weep, nor shall I die in vain.
>
>   (5.10.16–31)

Thus ends the tragic history of George Barnwell.

Throughout the play, Lillo focuses on certain key words, which have completely opposite meanings in the two environments presided over by Thorowgood and Millwood. *Love, obedience, friendship, interest*, and other similar concepts gloss differently in the worlds dedicated to good and evil. The most interesting terms, perhaps, are the cluster including *master/servant, obedience*, and *slave*, which relate to the major themes of love and natural behavior. In the world ruled by Thorowgood, a natural hierarchy exists, with God and the monarch at the top and an appropriately graded set of relationships on down, in a sort of feudal hierarchy or eighteenth-century version of the Great Chain of Being. Masters such as Thorowgood are kind and generous to their "servants," whose "obedience" acknowledges both superior status and merit. A master, who in turn owes service to God and country, treats his servants well and uses his power judiciously, giving trust and forgiveness freely where it is deserved. The good servant, like Trueman, does not abuse that trust, any more than the master betrays his country or the daughter abuses the liberty her father gives her. Lest anyone miss the point, this also is patriarchy at its best, airbrushed to perfection.

In almost every way, the world of Millwood, like Millwood herself, questions and reverses every "rule" in this carefully constructed paradise-on-earth. She, a woman, knows no master, but in fact takes over the reins of power by means of her wit and beauty. Again, the setting reinforces the dichotomy, with Thorowgood's house the seat of right reason and appropriate authority, and Millwood's house their perversion, ruled by passion and a woman.[51] Like George himself, Thorowgood's house is not impervious to invasion, and in act 2 Millwood seduces George under his own master's roof after he has resolved to follow the straight and narrow forevermore. In a parallel scene, act 4, scene 16, Thorowgood invades *her* house and demonstrates his power there. These two "invasions" demonstrate Millwood's earlier ability and later inability to overcome the power Thorowgood represents.

The strong antifeminism of *The London Merchant* makes it strikingly different from other plays in the repertory, even those it superficially resembles. The fallen woman/seductress is treated rather sympathetically in Farquhar's *The Constant Couple* and Behn's *The Rover;* the repentant fallen woman is the sympathetic protagonist/hero even in tragedies like Rowe's *Jane Shore* and *The Fair Penitent,* Dryden's *All for Love,* and Otway's *The Orphan,* while Congreve's *The Mourning Bride* and Lee's *The Rival Queens* take pains to elicit some sympathy for their "dark ladies" in the paired dark-and-light females vying over the hero. Harold Weber quite properly points to Millwood's inheritance from these tragic villainesses (186); he also notes her resemblance to Congreve's Maskwell in *The Double-Dealer,* "the first rake we considered whose sexual powers serve only his passion for destruction" (190). Yet Weber acknowledges that Lillo's Millwood is potentially more disruptive than any of these figures, and goes all the way back to the drama of Jacobean England for an appropriate analogue:

> We probably have to return to Webster's Vittoria Corombona to find a woman at once so evil and destructive, and yet so dramatically vibrant. Both Vittoria and Millwood dominate the men who oppose their desires, Vittoria's triumph over Monticelso in his judicial ritual paralleled by Millwood's defense of herself to Thorowgood that leads him to admit, "Truth is truth, though from an enemy and spoke in malice. You bloody, blind, and superstitious bigots, how will you answer this?" Both women possess a

> dramatic power that allows them a measure of triumph even in defeat; the male world succeeds in destroying these women, but not before Vittoria and Millwood suggest the fragility and insignificance of the assumptions and sureties that buttress the masculine order.
>
> (185)

Thus Millwood, like Thorowgood, Barnwell, Maria, and Trueman, constitutes a statement on the new economic order and the need to rectify and make orderly the disruptions of the past. For this reason, the substitution of Maria for Millwood in act 5 and thematically throughout the play is more than just a simple trade of goodness for evil. Like the reassertion of passive womanly virtue and genteel male dominance in *The Conscious Lovers*, it rings the death knell for the male and female rake heroes. Where consensual community values take precedence over individual satisfaction, the community is best served by those who "know their place" and respect the boundaries of position and role. There is, of course, room for meritorious advancement, in accord with the increased social flexibility of eighteenth-century London, but even that is circumscribed by social rules and approval. And women, by custom and law, find their aspirations and freedoms more narrowly defined in that arena.

Conclusion: After the Licensing Act

The proliferation of theaters, companies, and performances that characterized the early to middle 1730s was curtailed by the Licensing Act of 1737, reinforced by legislation in 1752 and 1755,[52] the culmination of years of wrangling between the theater managers and the Lord Chamberlain's office over precisely what jurisdiction each had over stage performances. Plays had been banned or censored before 1737 for political or moral reasons, and technically each theater's license or patent said that each new play, prologue, and epilogue was to be submitted to the Lord Chancellor, along with a fee, before it was performed. Also, there were only two or three legitimate patents or licenses out at any given time—generally for Drury Lane, the other company, and an opera company. Yet performances were being given at Goodman's Fields, the Haymarket, James Street, and various other places during the 1730s, and in May 1733, the first bill "to regulate the Playhouses" was introduced and debated in

Parliament. Another bill, introduced by Sir John Barnard in April 1735, was only marginally defeated, and two years later Walpole introduced an amendment to a vagrancy statute that passed both houses and was signed by the King, in effect regulating the theaters, both the number of theaters (two, plus opera) and all performances, to control by the Lord Chamberlain.

There were only sporadic performances outside the two main theaters for the next three years, but in the fall of 1740 Giffard reopened Goodman's Fields, technically evading the law by advertising paid concerts with a "free" play in between; he operated for a full season under this "concert formula," and soon other theaters had reopened under the same conditions, or using other ingenious evasions[53] that obeyed the letter but not the spirit of the law; others just openly defied the act. Some were shut down by the authorities, but others, inexplicably, were not, and it was not until 1752 that Parliament finally passsed legislation that in effect shut down the smaller theaters and performances at the summer fairs.

Despite these rebellions, the years from 1737 to 1747 show clearly that the energy of the 1730s had been brought under state control. During the entire decade, only 159 new plays were performed, and many of these were farcical afterpieces and pantomimes. In terms of the repertory evidence, Hume seems entirely justified in his conclusions:

> The calamitous effects of the Licensing Act on British drama follow from the limitation to patent theaters, not from censorship. Political plays became virtually impossible, but the drama turned stodgy not because of censorship, or sentimentalism, or bourgeois audiences, but because without competition the theater managers saw no reason to risk money on new plays, and certainly not on experimental ones. Fielding had to leave the theater in 1737 not because he could no longer write political satires but because Drury Lane and Covent Garden reverted to the monopolistic ways of the mid-1720s. . . . As in the 1720s, earning a living as a professional playwright became impossible, and it was to remain impossible for twenty years.
>
> (1988, 249)

In certain obvious ways, what was possible or likely before 1737—the excesses and experiments of a Gay or a Fielding—became impossible and unlikely afterward.

At the same time, the real changes that occurred in comedy and to a lesser extent in tragedy during 1714–47 were permanent contributions to the development of a drama that spoke to and for its audiences. If we see two separate directions for dramatic development during this era— the one set by the alternative theater defined by Gay, Fielding, and other satirists, and the other set by Steele, Centlivre, Lillo, and other traditionalists—we ignore the similarities between them. Both kinds of plays were didactic in their intent to reform the taste and behavior of audience members. If the Licensing Act of 1737 cut off the promise of plays like *The Author's Farce* and *The Historical Register* as it cut off the theatrical career of Henry Fielding, *The Beggar's Opera* and many of Fielding's plays survived during the later eighteenth century and were imitated in countless afterpieces, short satiric comedies, and musicals. Meanwhile, the exemplary form of tragedy and comedy seen in *The London Merchant* and *The Conscious Lovers* survived along with these plays, in tragedies that ranged from heroic to pathetic and in comedies that mixed their sentimental and satiric components variously but always provided models for appropriate conduct in society.

5

The Age of Garrick

1747–1779

The Garrick years of the London theater and British drama, dating from his assumption of managerial responsibilities at Drury Lane in 1747 to his death in 1779 three years after his retirement, are remarkable for more than the presence of what some have called the greatest actor who ever lived. These years saw the flowering of the London theater as popular culture, fully integrated with the lives of contemporary Britons. At midcentury in a city of some 676,000 inhabitants, Pedicord and others speculate, perhaps 12,000 attended the theater in a given week, and as the population of London rose to nearly 1 million at the end of the century, so did attendance figures.[1] Looking back on those years, Garrick's contemporary, playwright and critic Arthur Murphy, said, "In his time, the theater engrossed the minds of men to such a degree, that it may now be said, that there existed in England a *fourth estate*, King, Lords, and Commons, and *Drury-Lane play-house*."[2] Unlike the fits and starts it experienced in previous eras, the theater as a business enterprise went from strength to strength during these three decades, making substantial profits for managers, investors, and personnel. In the season of 1760–61, for example, John Rich made a profit of £2,900 at Covent Garden, and Garrick's profits in the seasons for which details are available ranged between £3,000 and £6,000 (Hume 1980, 11).

In other ways as well, the theatrical environment was relatively more stable than during any previous era.[3] Drury Lane was under the management of Garrick and James Lacy until Lacy's death in 1774, when his son Willoughby Lacy took over his role; in 1776, Garrick sold his share of the patent for £35,000 to Richard Brinsley Sheridan and others, who became partners with Willoughby Lacy; in May 1778, Lacy sold his share to Sheridan for about £31,000 and a lifetime annuity of £1,000. Covent Garden had a secure management for a time, but this disintegrated during the late 1760s and early 1770s. John Rich ruled until his death in 1761; his son-in-law John Beard succeeded him as manager until July 1767, when he sold his patent for £60,000 to a coalition that included Thomas Harris and the elder George Colman,[4] a coalition that soon erupted into open warfare, lockouts, and lawsuits. The Harris-Colman case was openly aired in the periodical press long before it was heard in court, but the July 1770 decision supported Colman and left him primarily in charge of operations until he sold his share of the patent in April 1774 to Thomas Hull, who reigned thereafter under Harris as premiere manager. Meanwhile, the opera, despite its continued high production costs and a hiatus between May 1750 and winter 1753 after its manager absconded with the funds, apparently operated in the black by means of a combination of subscriptions and gate receipts. And finally, despite the successful efforts of the licensing authorities to throttle theatrical productions other than these three, there was Samuel Foote at the Haymarket.

Actor, playwright, entrepreneur—Foote (1720–77) came as close as any in this conservative era to producing the alternative theater of Fielding and Gay.[5] His theatrical career was entirely devoted to fighting the stranglehold of the patentees, and his biographer suggests that it represents the darker side of the relative stability enjoyed by the companies at Drury Lane and Covent Garden:

> The monopolistic control of the London stage gave an enormous power to the patentees that was not necessarily seen or intended by the originators of the [Licensing] Act. After 1737 any patentee, whether an actor-hating pantomimist like Rich, a profligate amateur like Fleetwood, or a theatrical genius like Garrick, had call on the law to stifle any dramatic venture that might threaten their

investment. As a consequence of that control, actors were unable
to negotiate terms on an equitable basis; if they refused the terms
of their articles, they would be forced to perform out of London.
Playwrights were even more vulnerable than actors, who at least
were necessary. Under these circumstances there was little pressure on the patentees to produce new plays. Indeed it was far
more profitable to revive an old one and not pay for new sets,
costumes, and third-night benefits for the author.[6]

He concludes that during this period, "the theater was nearly impotent
and ultimately self-destructive" (Trefman, xi). Although Foote's career
as actor and playwright bridged the two worlds, in a sense his choices as
manager and playwright at the Haymarket were made in the context of
and in opposition to the patterns established at Drury Lane and Covent
Garden. We might also note that his career, which began as an actor in
1744 and playwright in 1747 and ended with his death in 1777, almost
exactly conforms in time to Garrick's.

     Like Betterton, John Rich, and Garrick, Foote came into his
managerial role after serving his term as an actor, and, like them, he
continued to act as well as manage and write plays thereafter. Throughout
the 1750s, he divided his time between acting at Drury Lane or Covent
Garden, or in Dublin or Edinburgh, while sometimes managing and
acting in his own plays at the Haymarket during the summer after the
patent theaters had closed. After a successful summer at Drury Lane in
1761, wherein he and his friend Arthur Murphy wrote and staged their
own plays, he began using the Haymarket during the summer on a
regular basis and discontinued acting at the London patent theaters.
Foote continually attempted to obtain a regular patent for the Haymarket,
but was unsuccessful until the winter of 1766, when he fell off a horse
and broke his leg, which had to be amputated. His friend the Duke of
York offered Foote the consolation of a patent for the Haymarket, but it
permitted only summer performances (15 May –15 September) and was
only for Foote's lifetime. By that summer, Foote had resumed his acting
career, using his wooden leg to advantage in roles like the rheumatic
Mother Cole in *The Minor* (1760) and the limping Peter Paragraph in
The Orators (1762).[7] Though short, the season was profitable enough to
encourage Foote to purchase the Haymarket and refurbish it, adding an
upper gallery and a new facade. Although he continued to petition George
III to allow the Haymarket to operate year-round, he was unsuccessful.
Late in 1776, he leased the patent to Colman for £800 semiannually,

with £500 for his unpublished plays; less than a year later, Foote was dead.

Afterpieces and Comic Operas:
Polly Honeycombe, The Duenna,
The Jubilee

A novel is the only thing to teach a girl life, and the way of the world, and elegant fancies, and love to the end of the chapter.
(Polly Honeycombe, *1.60–61*)[8]

LOUISA: *I do not doubt your sincerity, Antonio: But there is a chilling air around poverty that often kills affection, that was not nurs'd in it—If we would make love our household god, we had best secure him a comfortable roof.*
(The Duenna, *3.3.24–28*)[9]

I hanno' been abed, not I, nor canno' rest since this racket begun. . . . I verily think, neighbor, this Jubillo will be death o' me.
(The Jubilee, *1.1.9–12*)[10]

Foote's long and profitable career is partly attributable to his mastery of the short comedy/afterpiece so popular at the time. The *London Stage* editors note that during Garrick's reign, Drury Lane produced 63 new mainpieces and 107 new afterpieces, while during the same time Covent Garden produced 51 new mainpieces and 47 new afterpieces (*LS*, 4:169). Our list of most popular plays shows even more startling figures: 13 new comedies (22 percent), 12 new tragedies (28 percent of serious plays), 23 new operas and other musical pieces (70 percent), and 80 new afterpieces and other short forms (76 percent). Although some critics and purists continued to grumble about them, audiences came to expect these "entertainments" as part of the evening bill, such that somewhere around 1767–68 the practice of presenting new plays alone, without afterpieces, was dropped. Some authors, like Foote, wrote nothing but short plays, while others, like Colman, Garrick, and Richard B. Sheridan, wrote both long and short pieces. Occasionally, a play like Murphy's *The Way to Keep Him* (1760) was expanded from three to five acts, but usually the two kinds of plays were distinct in nature and intent. Especially as sentimentalism made greater inroads into the five-act comic form, short comic pieces seemed to offer the last bastion of the kind of satire found in earlier plays; witness the dialogue between Sir Christopher Cripple and Major Rachett in Foote's *The Maid of Bath* (1771):

> SIR CHR.:   [T]o be buried alive—to be married.
>
> RACH.:   Pho! Is that all? The ceremony was, indeed, formerly looked upon as a kind of metaphorical grave; but the system is changed, and marriage is now considered as an entrance to a new and better kind of life.
>
> SIR CHR.:   Indeed!
>
> RACH.:   Pshaw! who talks now of the drudgery of domestic duties, of nuptial claims, and of bonds? mere obsolete words! They did well enough in the dull days of queen Bess but a modern lass puts on fetters to enjoy the more freedom, and pledges her faith to one, that she may be at liberty to bestow her favours on all.[11]

Although the Major is not the hero of the play, and is rejected by Kitty Linnet, who prefers to earn her own living as a singer, the expression of such attitudes by a nonvillainous character is rare in the latter eighteenth century.[12] Short comedies, then, increasingly acted as a kind of alternative to the emotionalism on display in the new comic mainpieces, retaining some of the sharp focus and hard edge of older social comedy.

At the same time, they resembled the longer comedies of their own time in their inclusion of characters like bankers and businessmen, mercers and city wives and their interests, while tending to punish rather than reform the grinning fops and "macaronis," social climbers, and other familiar satiric butts. Short comedies also contained almost all the personal satire of late eighteenth-century comedy, and Foote the author wrote Foote the actor a number of roles based on people and incidents familiar to Londoners; even Garrick was not immune.[13] Skirting the line of acceptability, Foote was sued by a Welshman named Apreece for his parody of him in *The Author* (1757), and the Duchess of Kingston was

MOST POPULAR PLAYS: 1747–1779
(Plays with Thirty or More Performances
with Performance Numbers in Parentheses.
When two or more versions of a play exist in the repertory,
author's name is included.)

COMEDY
The Alchemist (75)
All in the Wrong* (57)
Amphitryon (37)
The Anatomist (165)
As You Like It (90)
The Beaux Strategem (208)
A Bold Stroke for a Wife (92)
The Brothers* (42)
The Busie Body (186)
The Careless Husband (74)
The Chances (39)
The Clandestine Marriage* (117)
The Committee (71)
The Confederacy (56)
The Conscious Lovers (174)
The Constant Couple (62)
The Country Lasses (54)
The Double Dealer (41)
The Double Gallant (43)
The Drummer (38)
The English Merchant* (34)
Every Man in His Humour (163)
The Fair Quaker of Deal (55)
The Funeral (58)
The Hypocrite* (32)
The Inconstant (56)
The Jealous Wife* (116)
Love for Love (101)
Love Makes a Man (75)
Love's Last Shift (45)
Measure for Measure (43)
The Merchant of Venice (152)
The Merry Wives of Windsor (92)
The Miser (109)
Much Ado about Nothing (119)
The Old Batchelor (47)

The Plain Dealer (41)
The Provoked Husband (211)
The Provoked Wife (145)
The Recruiting Officer (122)
The Refusal (45)
The Rehearsal (88)
The Relapse (49)
The Rivals* (33)
The School for Lovers* (32)
The School for Scandal* (96)
She Stoops to Conquer* (57)
She Would and She Would Not
    (74)
The Suicide* (30)
The Suspicious Husband (194)
The Tempest (117)
Twelfth Night (59)
The Twin Rivals (33)
The Way of the World (110)
The Way to Keep Him* (83)
The West Indian* (95)
The Winter's Tale (30)
The Wonder (130)

TRAGEDY
All for Love (40)
Barbarossa* (47)
Cato (34)
Coriolanus* (35)
Cymbeline,* Colm (39)
Cymbeline,* Garr (102)
Cyrus* (40)
The Distrest Mother (99)
Douglas* (50)
The Earl of Essex,* Jones (78)
The Fair Penitent (143)
The Gamester* (43)

The Grecian Daughter* (51)
Hamlet (233)
The History of King Lear, Tate (63)
Jane Shore (187)
King John (55)
King Lear,* Garr (63)
The London Merchant (99)
Macbeth (155)
Merope* (66)
The Moore of Venice (141)
The Mourning Bride (107)
Oroonoko (83)
The Orphan (141)
The Revenge (45)
Richard III (241)
The Rival Queens (111)
The Roman Father* (43)
Romeo and Juliet (350)
The Siege of Damascus (50)
Tamerlane (88)
Tancred and Sigismunda (60)
Theodosius (57)
Venice Preserved (129)
Zara (94)

TRAGICOMEDY
The Fatal Marriage (38)
Rule a Wife (107)
The Spanish Fryar (52)

HISTORY
Henry IV, I (102)
Henry IV, II (70)
Henry V (82)
Henry VIII (93)

OPERA
Alessandro Nell'Indie* (31)
Artaserse* (42)
Artaxerxes* (87)
La Buona Figliuola* (90)
Demetrio* (30)
Il Demofoonte* (41)

The Feast of Alexander (43)
Love in a Village* (233)
L'Olimpiade* (30)

ORATORIO
Judas Macchabaeus (87)
The Messiah (121)
Samson (67)

COMIC OPERA
The Duenna* (138)
Il Filosofo di Campagna* (39)
The Jovial Crew (91)
The Maid of the Mill* (124)
The Maid of the Oaks* (41)
La Schiava* (38)
The Spanish Barber* (38)
I Viaggiatori Ridicoli* (42)

BALLAD OPERA
The Beggar's Opera (455)

DRAMATIC OPERA
Cymon* (73)

BURLETTA
La Cicisbea alla Moda* (40)
The Golden Pippin* (49)
Midas* (190)
La Strattaggemma* (72)

MASQUE
Comus (170)
The Druids* (62)

DRAMATIC POEM
Elfrida* (44)

PASTORAL
The Gentle Shepherd (68)

INTERLUDE
Acis and Galatea (58)

ENTERTAINMENT
*A Christmas Tale** (59)
The Old Woman's Oratory (114)

AFTERPIECES, FARCES, SHORT
COMEDIES
*The Animal Pantomime** (49)
Apollo and Daphne (165)
*The Apprentice** (145)
*Auction of Pictures** (61)
*The Author** (136)
*The Bankrupt** (38)
*Bon Ton** (53)
*The Camp** (57)
*Catherine and Petruchio** (142)
*The Chaplet** (161)
The Cheats of Scapin (78)
*The Citizen** (192)
The Comical Rivals (42)
*The Commissary** (114)
*The Contrivances** (130)
*The Coronation** (136)
*The Cozeners** (42)
*Cross Purposes** (64)
Damon and Phillida (95)
*Daphne and Amintor** (69)
*The Deserter** (61)
*The Deuce Is in Him** (102)
The Devil to Pay (284)
*The Devil upon Two Sticks** (98)
The Double Disappointment (83)
The Dragon of Wantley (48)
A Duke and No Duke (163)
*The Elopement** (110)
*The Englishman in Paris** (150)
*The Englishman Return'd from
    Paris** (70)
*The Fair** (126)
*The Fairy Prince** (36)
*A Fairy Tale** (50)
*The Flitch of Bacon** (39)
Flora (68)
*Fortunatus** (157)
*The Genii** (207)

*The Guardian** (51)
Harlequin a Sorcerer (335)
Harlequin Doctor Faustus (125)
*Harlequin Ranger** (95)
*Harlequin's Frolic** (37)
*Harlequin's Invasion** (212)
*Harlequin's Jubilee** (35)
*The Hermit** (47)
*High Life below Stairs** (153)
*The Institution of the Garter** (35)
The Intriguing Chambermaid (118)
*The Irish Widow** (84)
*The Jubilee** (168)
The King and Miller of Mansfield
    (128)
*The Knights** (88)
Lethe (238)
The Lottery (99)
*Love a-la-Mode** (108)
*The Lyar** (127)
The Lying Valet (216)
*The Maid of Bath** (50)
*The Male Coquette** (34)
*Man and Wife** (48)
*The Mayor of Garratt** (195)
*Mercury Harlequin** (51)
*The Minor** (169)
Miss in Her Teens (265)
The Mock Doctor (113)
*Mother Shipton** (117)
*The Musical Lady** (78)
*The Nabob** (55)
*The Norwood Gypsies** (51)
*The Old Maid** (105)
*An Old Man Taught Wisdom**
    (110)
*The Oracle** (31)
*The Orators** (80)
Orpheus and Eurydice (138)
*The Oxonian in Town** (39)
*The Padlock** (406)
*A Peep behind the Curtain** (70)
Perseus and Andromeda (200)

The Pigmy Revels* (44)   The Sylphs* (48)
Polly Honeycomb* (122)   Taste* (57)
The Portrait* (30)   Thomas and Sally* (165)
Prometheus* (35)   The Touchstone* (42)
Proteus* (33)   A Trip to Scotland* (54)
The Quaker* (43)   True Blue* (47)
Queen Mab* (283)   The Two Misers* (34)
The Rape of Proserpine (127)   The Upholsterer* (144)
The Register Office* (64)   The Waterman* (76)
The Rites of Hecate* (51)   The What D'Ye Call It (52)
The Rival Candidates* (39)   What We Must All Come To* (36)
The Royal Chace (301)   The Witches* (103)
Selima and Azor* (35)   The Wonders of Derbyshire* (34)
La Serva Padrona* (209)

NOTE
*New play

so offended by his portrayal of her "double marriage" in A Trip to Calais (1775) that she had it permanently suppressed by the Lord Chamberlain.

Although Foote was unique in his willingness to burlesque individuals, more generalized satire occurs in other afterpieces and short comedies written during this time. Colman's Polly Honeycombe (1760), with 122 performances during this period, is a case in point. Colman's first produced play manages to satirize, in a perfectly good-humored way, a number of types familiar to contemporary Londoners. Polly herself is a young lady who has read too many romantic novels and, like her successor Lydia Languish, insists that her own courtship conform to the ones she has read about. Therefore, she summarily rejects her parents' choice, a businessman named Ledger, for a young lawyer's clerk, Scribble, and is overjoyed rather than dismayed when her father locks her in her room to compel her obedience. Indeed, whenever anyone does something that fulfills literary precedent, she glosses the behavior. "I am now, for all the world, just in the situation of poor Clarissa,—and the wretch is ten times uglier than Soames himself"(2.59–60), she comments when her father forces her to entertain Ledger. Calling him a "vile book of arithmetic," she sends her suitor off and congratulates herself: "Ha! ha! ha!—There he goes!—Ha! ha! ha!—I have out-topped them all— Miss Howe, Narcissa, Clarinda, Polly Barnes, Sophy Willis, and all of them. None of them ever treated an odious fellow with half so much spirit.—This would make an excellent chapter in a new Novel.—But here comes Papa—In a violent passion, no doubt.—No matter—It will only furnish materials for the next chapter" (2.135–40). Supporting Polly is a cast filled with equally intriguing types: her blustering father; her fluttery, hypochondriac mother; her mercenary merchant suitor and his romantic but probably equally mercenary rival. Mocking all its characters, the play ends with a standoff—Polly refuses to marry her father's choice; the two suitors have left; Polly's mother chases after her, and Old Honeycombe is left alone to lament to the audience, "[W]hat a situation I am in!—Instead of happiness and jollity,—my friends and family about me,—a wedding and a dance,—and everything as it should be,—here am I, left by myself. . . . This comes of cordials and novels,—Zouns, your stomachicks are the devil—and a man might as well turn his daughter loose in Covent Garden, as trust the cultivation of her mind to A CIRCULATING LIBRARY" (4.189–96). But it is Polly who gets the last lines in the epilogue, demanding a New World Order for herself and others:

> Too long has human nature gone astray,
> Daughters should govern, Parents should obey;
> Man shou'd submit, the moment that he weds,
> And hearts of oak shou'd yield to wiser heads:
> I see you smile bold Britons!—But tis true—
> Beat You the French;—But let your Wives beat You.—
>
> (epilogue, 33–38)

A charming trifle, *Polly Honeycombe* represents the last stronghold of Carolean comedy's iconoclasm in the latter eighteenth century. Polly is certainly in a line of generation that would include Margery of *The Country-Wife* and Behn's Hellena, but she is also asexual and thus no longer poses a threat to authority or conformity. Tamed and confined, she is a running jest, and like the kind of comedy that she inhabits, her bold words mount no real challenge to social order.

Another mongrel form increasingly popular during the last half of the eighteenth century combined music, spectacle, and narrative. Prominent among the most popular plays are new operas, comic operas, dramatic operas, masques, and burlettas,[14] with the musical numbers composed by great and near-great contemporary composers like Dr. Thomas Arne. *The Duenna* (1775), by Richard Brinsley Sheridan

(1751–1816), presents a typical example of these achievements in sight and sound. One of the most popular plays of the late eighteenth century,[15] it seems to have been a rather haphazard collaboration between Sheridan, his very pregnant wife, and his father-in-law, Thomas Linley,[16] with frenzied changes in the text and the songs being made in the month before production. Despite these problems, audiences and critics liked it, noting its resemblance to *The Beggar's Opera* and praising Sheridan "for having revived the honour of the drama, by boldly rescuing the stage from that state of lethargy, and melancholy madness, into which Cumberland and his sentimental compeers had lulled it" (20–22 November 1775; quoted in *Dramatic Works*, 1:207). Most of the adverse criticism was leveled, surprisingly, at the music; one critic suggesting the play "would deserve more approbation, if it was freed from its musical appendage, and performed as a comedy" (17 November 1775; quoted in *Dramatic Works*, 1:209). A few others were displeased with the play's double entendres and the "bacchanal vespers" at the convent; others criticized its lack of originality.

The public, however, loved it. Pirated versions were performed in Dublin; pirated copies of the songs were sold on the street. Sheridan made £200 on the music copyright alone, and *The Duenna* played 75 nights in its first season, comparable to 78 for *The Beggar's Opera* in its first season. While the action is a pretty standard Spanish-plot format of two sets of lovers eluding their parents and reforming their own slight inadequacies, Sheridan adds some distinctive touches, particularly in characters like Isaac Mendoza, the Jewish Portuguese suitor; Father Paul, the sottish friar; and Margaret, the clever Duenna whose age and ugliness are a continuing sight gag. The plot lacks the danger or the tension of a play like *The Adventures of Five Hours*, its tone mostly high-spirited and amiable, with music and songs interpolated freely throughout the text to provide a second layer of meaning: "Sheridan's songs, too often overlooked, reveal versatility in theme and tone as well as dramatic appropriateness in interpretations of emotional nuances. . . . The grotesquerie of Isaac's lines, conveyed not in the words themselves but in the incongruity between his lyrical tone and his ego, appearance, and motive, appears among the heart-felt love songs of the young lovers. Sheridan moved easily from comic irony in some of the songs to a passionate but nearly always witty expression of emotion. And he could turn a drinking song of good fellowship as adroitly as a love song" (Loftis 1977, 64). Loftis goes on to suggest that the overall plan and writing of *The Duenna* is far superior to many contemporary "musicals" and mentions Charles Dibdin's *The Wedding Ring* (1773); it is certainly better than Kane O'Hara's

The Golden Pippin (1773) or Colman's *The Spanish Barber* (1777), also popular at the time.

One play in the category of afterpiece/entertainment is genuinely difficult to define: Garrick's *The Jubilee*, which was both a celebration of and a substitute for an event of unsurpassed theatricality. Although Garrick's interest in Shakespeare predates it, Garrick's Shakespeare Jubilee of 1769 epitomizes the influence of the actor-manager on the playwright's reception in a climate of public approbation. In her book on the Jubilee, Martha England suggests that Garrick was a true mirror of his age,[17] and that the Jubilee represented some important changes occurring in the later eighteenth century: "Fueled by growing literacy and the expanding market for the printed word, literary production in the later eighteenth century grew exponentially. Shakespeare and his words were an important part of this industry; the eighteenth century witnessed not only the remarkable proliferation of new editions of Shakespeare but a phenomenal growth in the number of books and essays written about him."[18]

The three-day Jubilee was actually the culmination of a series of events initiated by the people of Stratford to honor their most famous resident. In 1767, while a new town hall was being built, some prominent citizens had the idea of requesting that Garrick donate a statue of Shakespeare to be placed in the hall; by the following year, they also wanted a portrait of Garrick as well, "that the memory of both may be perpetuated together" (quoted in England, 11). The notion of a Jubilee, however, was Garrick's own—planned, financed, and executed by him with minimal involvement from the town. The idea had apparently been percolating in his mind for almost two years, but was publicly announced only in May 1769, along with his official title as Steward of Shakespeare's Jubilee. While Londoners were accustomed to attending jubilees filled with dancing, music, and fireworks at the public gardens to celebrate a military victory or a public hero, a jubilee in the countryside was unprecedented. Immediately, some critics objected to the idea that the Bard should be used as a publicity gambit and made the property of Garrick the actor instead of, say, Samuel Johnson the scholar, whose *Works* of Shakespeare had appeared in 1765. Anti-Jubilee sentiment appeared most often throughout the summer in the *Public Advertiser*, a prominent London newspaper, in the form of satires, letters, and essays.

Nonetheless, Garrick's plans moved forward. An army of builders, designers, composers, costumers, and lighting and stage technicians was mobilized in London and set to work on transforming the small town of Stratford into a huge outdoor theater. The portraits of Garrick and Shakespeare were painted, and a statue of the Bard commissioned. Garrick wrote an *Ode upon Dedicating a Building and Erecting a Statue to Shakespeare*, set to music by Dr. Thomas Arne. When 5 September came, thousands of Londoners descended on Stratford, many in costume, for the festivities. The first day went off without a hitch, with processionals, splendid entertainments, and good weather, but the second day's events were flooded out by torrential rains except for the performance at the newly erected Rotunda of the *Ode to Shakespeare*. By Friday, the Rotunda was clearly unsafe and further festivities were carried on at the inns around town. By Saturday, most of the visitors had had enough, and were bargaining for any available transportation back to town. The deficit for the Jubilee was reckoned at £2000, which Garrick eventually paid out of his own pocket. Yet the following year and for 60 years thereafter, Stratford retained the Jubilee, sans Garrick, on a much smaller scale. "So strangely did life imitate art that the Jubilee became in very truth what it should have been—by romantic standards—in the first place" (England, 68)—a local festival.

The event at Stratford produced numerous poems and parodies, but its principal offshoots were two short plays for the London stage— George Colman's *Man and Wife*, which opened at Covent Garden on 7 October, and Garrick's *The Jubilee*, which opened a week later at Drury Lane. Of the two, Colman's play is more ordinary—a farcical concatenation of a quarreling husband and wife, each of whom wants their daughter to marry a different suitor, and the daughter's successful efforts to choose her own mate. The Jubilee setting is used mainly in the prologue and at the beginning of the play, set in a busy Stratford innyard, and in the procession scene in act 2. Otherwise, *Man and Wife* is a conventional short farce and soon lost the competition against Garrick's *The Jubilee*.

Garrick's play is quite different: a "short view" of the Jubilee, capturing some of the excitement, confusion, and thrills of the actual event. *The Jubilee* is a series of short vignettes, some featuring the townspeople of Stratford, some the Londoners come to the celebration, with the only linkage besides the setting an Irishman (ably played by John Moody) who complains and cavorts throughout the play. Offsetting this humorous business are serious excerpts from the Jubilee ceremonies and pageants, with the music and dancing highlights reprised for the London audience. Like Covent Garden, Drury Lane went all out in reproducing the spectacular pageantry, but Garrick's version, for once, was the more splendid, and he used the actual street outside Drury Lane for part of the procession, which then came up to the stage through the audience.[19] The audience was also invited to sing along with the chorus, and as

England puts it, "In *The Jubilee* the boundary-line between art and life was made almost to disappear" (102).

Together, the Jubilee and *The Jubilee* tapped into the rich lode of popular interest in Shakespeare, what England calls the "Grass Roots of Bardolatry" (chap. 6), that had grown gradually since the 1730s.[20] In turn, they helped cause a revolution in the theaters, which took the form of an increased use of historically accurate costume for Shakespeare's plays and, more broadly, "the concept of historical relativism" in play production (England, 172). Such costuming, begun by Garrick in his productions of both parts of *Henry IV* during the season of 1770–71, soon caught hold at Covent Garden as well. But even more important than the visual effects of historical costume were the verbal effects of the new respect for Shakespeare's language:

> It was in the study of Shakespeare's language that the major change came and the major gains were made. Here the genuine historical approach manifested itself in its most permanently valuable aspect, and it is to the credit of the periodicals that they led the way in the movement toward a better gloss and urged the work upon the scholars. . . . That language was of rational origin and poetry and criticism ought at least in theory to be governed by the consequent ideas of clarity and the related concepts of metaphor and metrics, that common sense was all one needed to understand "good" language—these neoclassical concepts were being replaced by ideals of emotion, music, and ambiguity as positive values. . . . No longer was one to regularize and improve Shakespeare, for his words had emotional connotations, his metrics had emotional bases, and his vocabulary had historical overtones that were to be heard and understood.
>
> (England, 177; see also Marsden, 62–80)

It is this legacy that had the most lasting effect on Shakespearean production well beyond the time of the eighteenth-century stage.

Tragedy: The Gamester

Ye slaves of passion, and ye dupes of chance,
Wake all your pow'rs from this destructive trance!
Shake off the shackles of this tyrant vice:

Hear other calls than those of cards and dice:
Be learn'd in nobler arts, than arts of play,
And other debts, than those of honour *pay:*
No longer live insensible to shame,
Lost to your country, families and fame.
                              (The Gamester, *prologue*)[21]

As in the earlier eighteenth century, a mixed tradition of tragedy existed between 1747 and 1779, when proportionally more of the popular repertory than ever before was devoted to tragic drama. Looking at the most popular comedies and serious dramas (tragedies, tragicomedies, histories), we find that between 1714 and 1747 the ratio was about 2:1 overall, with 11 new or newly revived comedies versus only two new tragedies on the list. Between 1747 and 1779, the ratio was about 3:2, with almost as many new and newly revived or revived tragedies (12) as comedies (14). Much of this enhanced popularity is owed to Garrick's continuation of the Shakespearean revival of the 1730s, to which he contributed his own "restored" texts and his power as an actor. Garrick was not the only playwright who exploited the taste for Shakespeare in one form or another—among the most popular tragedies are also versions of *Cymbeline* (1767) by George Colman and *Coriolanus* (1749) by James Thomson—but it is Garrick's contributions that are remembered and revered.

Garrick worked on revisions of 12 Shakespearean plays during his long theatrical career (see Dircks, 48–52, 79–99). Of these, *The Fairies* of 1755 (from *Midsummer Night's Dream*) and *The Tempest* of 1756 were musicals with only peripheral relationship to their original texts and not particularly popular. The other 10—from *Macbeth* in 1744 to *Hamlet* in 1772—were attempts to restore Shakespearean texts that had undergone numerous adaptations and emendations during the late seventeenth and early eighteenth centuries. Garrick produced versions of the plays that effectively superseded Davenant's *Macbeth* (1671), James Howard's *Romeo and Juliet* (1662?), Tate's *History of King Lear and His Three Daughters* (1681), the Dryden/Davenant/Shadwell *The Tempest* (1674), and the Hughes-Wilks *Hamlet* (1718).[22]

Garrick did not, to be sure, completely restore Shakespeare's originals. His versions are generally a combination: original Shakespearean texts with emendations and substitutions (e.g., *heaven* for *God*) and cuts to make the action move more quickly, retention of some parts of earlier stage versions such as Tate's *King Lear* (including the happy ending), and added or enhanced scenes to suit the eighteenth-century audience's, and Garrick's own, taste for elaborate death speeches and spectacle. In Garrick's version, Macbeth's dying, for example, takes eight more lines than in Shakespeare's, and the last act of Garrick's *Romeo and Juliet* has an elaborate funeral for Juliet and an added scene in the tomb. Closest to Shakespeare's texts were Garrick's 1757 *The Tempest* (with only 432 lines cut) and his 1761 *Cymbeline*, with some scenes shifted and lines cut. A purist might feel that Garrick did not go far enough in his "restorations," but as Dircks comments about his *Lear*, "his version of the play was much closer to Shakespeare's work in spirit, vitality, and scope than what the Restoration and eighteenth-century audiences had seen for almost a century" (88).

Probably also either inspired by or riding on the coattails of these Shakespeare revivals are those new tragedies which offer admixtures of heroic, pathetic, and quasi-Elizabethan elements in a classical setting, like John Brown's *Barbarossa* (1754), Arthur Murphy's *The Grecian Daughter* (1772), William Whitehead's *The Roman Father* (1750), and John Hoole's *Cyrus* (1768). Except for *The Roman Father*, these plays share common elements: villainous usurpers or tyrants who need to be overthrown by a coalition of loyalists to the "true" ruler, sometimes a female, who has been stoic and heroic for many years (and for a couple of hours onstage). These tragedies show abrupt turns of fortune based on multiple disguises and misunderstandings, scenes of weeping, kneeling, and clinging, but all except *The Roman Father* end happily, with the usurper killed and harmony restored to the kingdom. *The Roman Father*, presumably derived from Corneille's *Horace*, is different in that its focus is primarily on the suffering of Horatia, secretly married to a warrior of Alba, which at present is at war with Rome. Torn between fear for the lives of her husband and brothers, and fear that they will not behave nobly, she weeps and rages through five acts until she contrives to have her remaining brother end her misery. Almost a distillation of the love-honor conflicts of heroic drama, *The Roman Father* also has analogues in Rowe's she-tragedies, *Jane Shore* and *The Fair Penitent*, which continued in the popular repertory. Indeed, all these tragedies are woman-centered, focusing on the distresses and joys of female characters, and demoting male characters to pawns moved about by circumstances and often left offstage. Plot has been reduced to a series of highly charged scenes and confrontations, often among good characters who are misinformed or ignorant and thus act wrongly out of the best motives. The kind of poignancy based on dramatic irony that Otway and Rowe used so skillfully has become formula, and it is perhaps not surprising that the older plays like V*enice Preser'd* and *The Orphan* were still considerably more popular onstage than their successors.

Paralleling the classical tradition in new tragedies of the late eighteenth century were plays that derived their themes and characters from British history and may be seen as part of the grassroots interest not only in Shakespeare but in Chaucer, Spenser, Bunyan, and Milton occurring at this time (see England, chap. 6). *The Earl of Essex* (1753) by Henry Jones was one of three plays with that title existing during that time. The other new play, by Henry Brooke, premiered in the season of 1760–61 and was moderately popular as well, with 22 performances before 1779. Both plays ultimately took over the popularity enjoyed by John Banks's *Unhappy Favourite* (1681), which had only 13 performances after 1747 but more than 150 between 1685 and 1747. The structure and other details are very similar in Jones's and Banks's tragedies, but Jones attempts to restore more of the public dimension to events during the brief last period of Essex's fall and execution, and makes Essex more an innocent victim than a self-immolated hero. The other new historical tragedy is *Douglas* (1757), by John Home, which resembles *Cyrus* in its merging of romantic and political elements, and also in its focusing of attention not on the "stranger" as warrior-hero and long-lost heir but on his mother and her fluctuating emotions. Analogues in the repertory would include the versions of *Cymbeline* produced by Garrick in 1761 and Colman in 1767, with the Garrick version the more popular.

With the enhanced interest in Shakespeare's tragedies and stiff competition from old favorites like Otway's and Rowe's best plays, it is not surprising that the bulk of the new tragedies followed, as far as they were able, these models. At the same time, even in these political plays we sense a divorcement from any linkage with contemporary political issues, making it irrelevant whether their settings are classical Rome or Saxon Britain. And while it was always true, for example, that the Spanish conquest of Mexico was chosen more for its exotic locale than its political analogies, heroic and other serious drama of the late seventeenth century drew some of their life from discussions of kingship or commonweal that had contemporary relevance. By the last half of the eighteenth century, political backgrounds in serious plays were largely cardboard cutouts; the real action was between characters on the forestage or within characters themselves, with the audience invited to watch their agonies and ecstasies, to weep or sigh along with them. It was the individual character's merit and suffering that were the attraction, not his or her representative weight.

Under this system, all tragedies were in some sense "domestic," and the stage was ripe for another genuinely domestic tragedy.

The Gamester (1753), by Edward Moore (1712–57), is often cited as one of the few successful tragedies modeled on Lillo's *The London Merchant*,[23] though I would include Otway's *Venice Preserved* as a possible influence. More important, perhaps, is *The Gamester*'s resemblance to the tone and structure of Vanbrugh's *The Provoked Wife* and *The Relapse*, and to the style of Steele's *The Conscious Lovers*. All five of these older plays were still popular in the repertory during the latter part of the eighteenth century, and may have laid the groundwork for Moore's unusual blending of tragic and comic conventions

Like *Venice Preserved*, *The Gamester* begins in medias res, with the protagonist Beverley deeply enmeshed in the toils of his "friend" Stuckely and his criminal cohorts. The setting is contemporary London, with characters both typical and commonplace: Beverley himself is an Everyman figure, his wife, friends, and activities familiar to the middle-class audience. We soon learn that, like Jaffeir, Beverley is a victim of outside forces as well as his own bad judgment. His sin is the "gaming" that has already lost him his own estate and that of his long-suffering wife; as the play evolves, he also loses her jewels and his sister Charlotte's inheritance, and he mortgages the inheritance he anticipates from his dying uncle. Near the end of the play, imprisoned for debt and filled with guilt, in a final act of despair he drinks a vial of poison, to discover, too late, that his family has been rescued and Stuckely unmasked by Lewson, Charlotte's suitor. This bare plot outline would suggest a thesis play on the evils of gaming; what it doesn't reveal is the depth of ambivalence and affinity *The Gamester* evokes in its audience.

Domestic or sentimental tragedy works its wiles by means of the basic Fletcherian model of a passive, ineffectual protagonist—whether male or female—trapped in circumstances beyond his or her control. In *The Gamester*, Beverley is not even onstage during the first act; instead, we see the rest of his household—Mrs. Beverley and Charlotte—arguing over whether he has sunk to a new low by gaming all night long. To Charlotte's justified criticisms, Mrs. Beverley responds with forbearance, wifely concern, and forgiveness. She refuses to blame her husband, and insists that the poverty to which his gaming has reduced them is merely an inconvenience: "give me but a bare subsistence, and my husband's smiles, and I'll be the happiest of the poor" (1.1.421–22). Even when Charlotte reminds her that her son is also destitute, Mrs. Beverley remains calm:

Why, want shall teach him industry. From his father's mistakes he
shall learn prudence, and from his mother's resignation, patience.
Poverty has no such terrors in it as you imagine. There's no condition of life, sickness and pain excepted, where happiness is ex-
cluded. The needy peasant, who rises early to his labour, enjoys
more welcome rest at night for't. His bread is sweeter to him; his
home happier; his family dearer; his enjoyments surer. The sun
that rouses him in the morning, sets in the evening to release him.
All situations have their comforts, if sweet contentment dwell in
the heart. But my poor Beverley has none. The thought of having
ruined those he loves, is misery for ever to him. Would I could
ease his mind of That!

(1.1.422)

The pastoral, romantic quality of this speech is reminiscent of similar
speeches in *The Orphan* or *Jane Shore*, other tragedies in which the
tensions of city and society created an environment that made rural
solitude seem a blissful escape. Mood is an important component of this
kind of tragedy, and Moore, like Otway and Rowe before him, constructs
within these initial scenes a tension that will be carried throughout the
play, wherein the domesticity of Beverley's home is in constant conflict
with the outside environment controlled by Stuckely and his kind.

This initial scene also establishes Mrs. Beverley as the moral
center of the play, far removed from the vanity and avarice of the normal,
fashionable world outside. Despite a weak moment at the end of act 3
that humanizes rather than diminishes her, she remains the epitome of
wifely virtue, propriety, and goodness, keeper of hearth and home and
protector of her husband's reputation, throughout the play. Moore uses
her to focus sympathy for Beverley, not just in her eloquent defense of
him to others, but because she reminds us that Beverley once appreciated
and deserved her love and loyalty. She is also, to some extent, his mirror;
naive like him, she trusts Stuckely until forced to recognize his true
character.

At the opposite end of the moral universe from Mrs. Beverley is
Stuckely, whom we first see ingratiating himself with her, but who soon
reveals his true colors to the audience:

Yet why should [Lewson] suspect me? I appear the friend of Beverley as well as he. But I am rich it seems: and so I am; thanks
to another's folly and my own wisdom. To what use is wisdom,

but to take advantage of the weak? This Beverley's my fool: I
cheat him, and he calls me friend. But more business must be
done yet. His wife's jewels are unsold; so is the reversion of
his uncle's estate. I must have these too. And then there's a
treasure above all. I love his wife. Before she knew this Beverley,
I loved her; but like a cringing fool, bowed at a distance, while
He stept in and won her. Never, never will I forgive him for it.
My pride, as well as love, is wounded by this conquest. I must
have vengeance.

(1.8.433–34)

This revelatory speech does more than supply information to the audience; Moore gives Stuckely the rambling discourse and choppy sentence
patterns of a mind not quite in balance, while other soliloquies suggest
Stuckely's fertile and malicious intellect and a personality that feeds on
its own guilt and is never sated. If Mrs. Beverley represents one side of
her husband's character, the loving family man, Stuckely represents the
other side, the man consumed with gaming fever and a restless, uncertain
temper. Stuckely is the dynamic center of the play, an actor's actor who,
like Iago, plays his victim like a well-tuned instrument. And as with
Iago and Othello, Stuckely's determination to destroy Beverley serves the
dramatic function of elevating his victim and removing from him some
of the responsibility for his downfall.

Stuckely's only fit opponent is Lewson, who, with Charlotte,
defines the rational center of the play. These very sensible lovers actively
work to uncover Stuckely's plot and rescue the family from ruin. Like
Bevil Jr. in *The Conscious Lovers*, Lewson seems to be a gentleman of
the town with no taste for fashionable pursuits; both he and Charlotte
work in their own ways to succor Beverley's family. Charlotte tries to get
her inheritance back from her brother so that she can support his dependents with it, and postpones her marriage to Lewson to take care of her
sister-in-law and nephew. Lewson combines small acts of kindness—
buying personal household items to restore to Mrs. Beverley when their
house is sold—with more extensive attempts to rescue Beverley from
Stuckely's clutches. For his efforts, he is publicly abused by Beverley and
nearly becomes Stuckely's murder victim.

Lewson and Charlotte reveal themselves most fully in act 3, scene
4, where they engage in a genteel version of the wit game and discover
their compatibility. Lewson delicately asks Charlotte if her sentiments
for him have changed over the year of their engagement:

LEW.:   Time, and a near acquaintance with my faults, may
          have brought change: if it be so; or, for a moment, if
          you have wished this promise were unmade, here I
          acquit you of it. This is my question then; and with
          such plainness as I ask it, I shall entreat an answer.
          Have you repented of this promise?

CHAR.:   Stay, Sir. The man that can *suspect* me, shall *find* me
          changed. Why am I doubted?

LEW.:   My doubts are of myself. I have my faults, and You
          have observation. If from my temper, my words or ac-
          tions, you have conceived a thought against me, or
          even a wish for separation, all that has passed is noth-
          ing.

CHAR.:   You startle me—But tell me—I must be answered first.
          Is it from honour you speak this? or do you wish me
          changed?

LEW.:   Heaven knows I do not. Life and my Charlotte are so
          connected, that to lose one, were loss of both. Yet for
          a promise, though given in love, and meant for binding;
          if time, or accident, or reason should change opinion,
          with Me that promise has no force.

CHAR.:   Why, now I'll answer you. Your doubts are prophe-
          cies—I am really changed.

LEW.:   Indeed!

CHAR.:   I could torment You now, as You have Me; but 'tis not
          in my nature. That I am changed I own; for what at
          first was inclination, is now grown reason in me, and
          from that reason, had I the world—nay, were I poorer
          than the poorest, and You too wanting bread; with but
          a hovel to invite me to—I would be yours, and happy.

LEW.:   My kindest Charlotte!

                                                         (3.4.458)

The scene is reminiscent of lovers' confrontations in both *Love for Love*
and *The Conscious Lovers*, with its careful blending of reason and sentiment, faith and temperament. Lewson and Charlotte represent the play's
ideal of potential conjugal felicity, contrasted not only with the dysfunc-
tional marriage of the Beverleys but also with the illicit passion of Stuckely. Appropriately, it is Lewson who utters the moral over Beverley's
remains:

Thou, poor breathless corps, may thy departed soul have found the rest it prayed for! Save but one error, and this last fatal deed, thy life was lovely. Let frailer minds take warning; and from example learn, that want of prudence is want of virtue.

Follies, if uncontroul'd, of every kind,
Grow into passions, and subdue the mind;
With sense and reason hold superior strife,
And conquer honour, nature, fame and life.

(5.12.501–2)

Lewson thus demonstrates in word and deed the contrast between the late eighteenth-century hero, who is master of his irrational passions, and the heroes of heroic drama and Carolean comedy, who allowed their passions to define their interests.

As moral drama, one of the major questions of *The Gamester* is, 'What is a man?'[24] In his first appearance, Beverley asks his faithful steward Jarvis how the world speaks of him; the response is "as of a good man dead" (2.3.439).[25] Shortly thereafter, we see Stuckely induce his despondent "friend" to try the gaming tables just once more, with the exhortation, "Prithee be a man, and leave dying to disease and old age" (2.4.440). In attempting to resist, Beverley uses the same words but with unconsciously deeper meaning: "Prithee let me be a man" (2.4.442). It is, of course, Stuckely's aim to "unman" Beverley by reducing him to animal instincts and unreasoning behavior, and by the end of the play Beverley is "unmanned" in the other sense, reverting to hysteria and suicide. The play's version of a true man is not Beverley but Lewson, in whom sensitivity, good sense, active virtue, and strong moral principles combine into the ideal eighteenth-century gentleman.

In *The Gamester*, we see the stage serious drama has reached by the late eighteenth century. Stripped of classical or foreign setting, "high" characters and political background, it lays bare the essential elements tragedy had aggrandized in different ways since its earliest Carolean beginnings: pure affectivity, linking spectator and stage, the pathetic and heroic existing in the same universe to exert strong pulls on the audience's emotions. What is interesting in contemplating *The Gamester* is the close kinship between such a play and late eighteenth-century comedy. If *The Gamester* has no absolute necessity to produce a tragic finale for Beverley,[26] there is likewise no absolute happy ending to comedies produced at the same time. John Loftis comments on Richard Cumberland, "Cumberland was, and knew that he was, a leading writer of a form of comedy in which catastrophe rather than happy marriage would seem to be the logical result of the events depicted. His exploitation of pathos in his portrayal of passive and innocent characters . . . was excessive, and in order to save his heroines he was compelled to assume the existence of a benevolent providence controlling seeming accidents and the repentances of villains" (1977, 18). The line between tragedy and comedy, never absolute, has virtually disappeared.

Comedy: The West Indian

BEL.:   *Well, Mr. Stockwell, for the first time in my life,*
         here am I in England; at the fountain-head of
         pleasure, in the land of beauty, of arts, and
         elegancies. My happy stars have given me a good
         estate, and the conspiring winds have blown me
         hither to spend it.

STOCK.: *To use it, not to waste it, I should hope; to treat it,*
         Mr. Belcour, not as a vassal, over whom you have
         a wanton and a despotic power; but as a subject,
         which you are bound to govern with a temperate
         and restrained authority.

BEL.:   *True, Sir; most truly said; mine's a commission,*
         not a right: I am the offspring of distress, and every
         child of sorrow is my brother; while I have hands to
         hold, therefore, I will hold them open to mankind:
         but, Sir, my passions are my masters; they take me
         where they will; and oftentimes they leave to reason
         and to virtue nothing but my wishes and my sighs.
                                   (The West Indian, 1.5.7)[27]

         Unlimited wealth, a generous spirit, passion needing to be curbed by reason—Belcour in *The West Indian* (1771), by Richard Cumberland (1732–1811), epitomizes the hero in late eighteenth-century comedies that deliver a moral message without sacrificing liveliness, suspense, or laughter. *The West Indian* was significantly popular in its own time, with 95 performances before 1779, and continued to be popular well into the nineteenth century; it is often anthologized today as representing the best of the subgenre of "sentimental comedies" that supposedly reigned supreme from the late 1760s through the 1770s, with the exception of Goldsmith and Sheridan. In fact, *The West Indian* fits neatly into the varied stew of old and new comedies enjoyed by audiences between 1747 and 1779—most of these comedies were combinations of satire and sensibility without the sexual excess of Carolean comedy.

A look at the most popular comedies of those years acknowledges the range and variety rather than the constraint of the comic spirit. In the old plays with more than 100 performances, we find Ravenscroft's *The Anatomist* (165), Farquhar's *The Beaux Stratagem* (208) and *The Recruiting Officer* (122), Centlivre's *The Busie Body* (186) and *The Wonder* (130), Jonson's *Every Man in His Humour* (163), Congreve's *Love for Love* (101) and *The Way of the World* (110), Shakespeare's *The Merchant of Venice* (152), *Much Ado about Nothing* (119), and *The Tempest* (117), Hoadly's *The Suspicious Husband* (194), Steele's *The Conscious Lovers* (174), Vanbrugh and Cibber's *The Provoked Husband* (211), and Vanbrugh's *The Provoked Wife* (145). Among the 13 new plays, we find comedies by Cumberland, Garrick, Colman, Murphy, Sheridan, and Goldsmith that are substantially popular and almost equally varied in tone, topic, and degree of seriousness. All of these plays together indicate a stage set for the kind of comedy that, though more purposeful than its older analogues, had a great deal of flexibility and contained a range of effects.

Two plays from 1761, for example, show how different dramatists deal with the same theme—the destructive effects of jealousy. *All in the Wrong*, by Arthur Murphy (1727–1805), provides three pairs of lovers, one married, two courting, all of whom suffer to different degrees from the curse of unreasoning jealousy. The married couple, Sir John and Lady Restless, are particularly culpable and spend much of the play sneaking around spying on each other and drawing the wrong inferences from what they see. Eventually, the presumably younger couples catch the fever as well, and Murphy shifts all six of them around like puzzle pieces to create dizzying patterns of errors that provoke angry or weeping confrontations and renunciations.

While Murphy is a perfectly competent comic dramatist, he often carries dramatic irony beyond its usefulness as a structural device; his plays are a blend of farcical misunderstandings, often rendered in scenes where two people are talking at cross-purposes and misinterpreting each other, and carefully contrived plots with visual misunderstandings, near misses, and eavesdroppings that lead to erroneous conclusions. The redundancy level of the intersecting plot lines and characters is high, and the resolutions necessarily implausible and openly manipulative; Murphy also relies heavily on asides and middialogue interruptions. More pertinent is the possibility that Murphy's own theories about what comedy ought to be and do limited his talent. He rejected Foote's characters as implausible, wanting his own to be more "natural"; he deplored the license of Behn's *The Rover* and Farquhar's *The Constant Couple*, and sought to write "a comedy of manners qualified by moderate sentimentalism and moral didacticism" (Emery, 40–41, 62). Yet within those same parameters, for the same audiences, Colman and Cumberland wrote more complex and interesting comedies.

As its title suggests, Colman's *The Jealous Wife* covers some of the same ground as *All in the Wrong*—the damage jealousy can do to conjugal happiness.[28] But this is only one thread of Colman's play, where the fits and starts of Mrs. Oakly are shown not only as unwarranted but as a deliberate attempt to keep her husband "tied to [her] apron strings"[29] by manipulating him; meanwhile, another plot shows Oakly's brother rescuing a country girl who is at the mercy of her father's matchmaking and a pair of sophisticated town types. Colman arranges these familiar elements in a fresh way to produce a comedy that comfortably accommodates a surprising range of character types and situations drawn from the fashionable world, the country, and the comfortable middle classes who exude good sense and sound dealing.

Somewhat outside these boundaries lies Major Oakly, a self-proclaimed libertine who dispenses advice on women to his brother, married to the Jealous Wife, and his nephew, courting the country heiress: "They all love to give themselves airs, and to have power. Every woman is a tyrant at the bottom. But they could never make a fool of me" (1.1.61), insisting that "nobody knows how to manage a wife, but a bachelor" (4.1.93). While the play confirms the Major's reading of Mrs. Oakly, his influence almost causes Charles to lose his country wife. As much as Mrs. Oakly, the town fop, or the country bumpkin, then, Major Oakly is presented as an object of satire in *The Jealous Wife*; his advocacy of total freedom is easily bested by his brother's arguments in favor of a fuller, richer life, although elsewhere Mr. Oakly is ridiculed at his brother's expense:

> MAJ.:   Women are all alike in the main, brother; high or low, married or single, quality or no quality. I have found them so, from a duchess down to a milkmaid.

OAK.: Your savage notions are ridiculous. What do you know of a husband's feelings? You, who comprise all your qualities in your *honour*, as you call it! Dead to all sentiments of delicacy, and incapable of any but the grossest attachments to women! This is your boasted refinement, your thorough knowledge of the world! While, with regard to women, one poor train of thinking, one narrow set of ideas, like the uniform of the regiment, serves the whole corps.

(1.1.61)

In this way, *The Jealous Wife* carefully balances its satire and sentiment, shifting comic ground so as to center the forces of rational sensibility over the appeal of those controlled by their passions or appetites.

Cumberland's *The Brothers* (1769) was already popular in the repertory when he wrote *The West Indian*, and contained many of the same elements of the latter play in a more exaggerated form. From the opening scene—a tempest raging on the coast of Cornwall, with a ship foundering in the distance and a miserable hovel in the foreground—*The Brothers* transports its audience into a more romantic world than the drawing rooms and London streets of most comedies, more akin to the world of Shakespearean romance or, looking ahead, romantic melodrama. With its villainous usurpers, harpies, distressed damsels, and valiant young men, *The Brothers* found some favor with late eighteenth-century audiences, and Cumberland varies its somber tone with amusing scenes between Sir Benjamin Dove and his "termagant" wife, and those involving the bluff and hearty Captain Ironsides with his colorful language. But *The Brothers* lacks the finely tuned sureness of *The West Indian* in delivering its complicated blend of humor and sentiment.

In *The West Indian* (1771), Cumberland was conscious of writing a new kind of purposeful comedy that retained the vitality of old comedy and did not cross the line between sentiment and bathos. He writes in his *Memoirs*:

As the writer for the stage is a writer to the passions, I hold it matter of conscience and duty in the dramatic poet to reserve his brightest coloring for the best characters, to give no false attractions to vice and immorality, but to endeavor, as far as is consistent with that contrast, which is the very essence of his art, to turn the fairer side of human nature to the public, and, as much as in him

lies, to contrive so as to put men into good humour with one
another. Let him, therefore, in the first place, strive to make worthy
characters amiable, but take great care not to make them insipid;
if he does not put life and spirit into his man or woman of virtue,
and render them entertaining as well as good, their morality is not
a whit more attractive than the morality of a Greek chorus. He
had better have let them alone altogether.

(141)

He goes on to repeat, with variations, Collier's main argument against
comic writers of the late seventeenth and early eighteenth centuries:
"Congreve, Farquhar, and some others have made vice and villainy so
playful and amusing, that either they could not find in their hearts to
punish them, or not caring how wicked they were, so long as they were
witty, paid not attention to what became of them: Shadwell's comedy is
little better than a brothel" (141). By acknowledging the affective qualities
of characters he finds unsavory, Cumberland dedicates himself to finding
ways to make virtue equally compelling and delightful.

The West Indian's immediate and lasting appeal depends on Cumberland's ability to mix a substantial amount of spice into his recipe for
moral comedy. The spice comes primarily from the Indies, specifically
Belcour, the West Indian who has traces of Willmore the Rover in his
hot blood and high spirits, and traces of Oroonoko the noble savage in his
natural generosity; like both characters, he is outspoken and a "stranger" to
the world he inhabits. From the outset of the play, it is clear that strict
moral judgment will need to be tempered with some flexibility if we are
to deal with this phenomenon, and Stockwell, the father Belcour doesn't
know, acts as the audience's agent in this process. A figure of rigid
propriety and strong moral fiber, Stockwell has followed his son's progress
at a distance: "All the reports I ever received, give me favourable impres-
sions of his character, wild, perhaps, as the manner of his country is,
but, I trust, not frantic or unprincipled" (1.4.5), and Belcour's arrival
confirms that his father will need to cultivate some elasticity in testing
his offspring's worthiness.

Belcour proceeds to show the accuracy of his self-analysis as he
tries to adjust to the alien society of London. He swallows the lies of the
Fulmers about Louisa Dudley and ignores the "truth" of her—that she
is Charles's sister, not his mistress—but he does so because his passion
is aroused, and he wants to believe that Louisa's favors can be bought.
Otherwise, Belcour's judgment is sound, and his nature both spontaneous

and generous, as he helps Captain Dudley and Charlotte with no desire for thanks or recompense. More lively and unconventional than his English counterpart, Charles Dudley, Belcour is also more interesting. Whereas Charles maintains physical and emotional distance from Charlotte because of his poverty, Belcour happily succumbs to love, defending himself to Stockwell by the conventional justification—Nature:

> BEL.: A woman: one that can turn, and overturn me and my tottering resolutions every way she will. Oh, Sir, if this is folly in me, you must rail at Nature: you must chide the sun, that was vertical at my birth, and would not wink upon my nakedness, but swaddled me in the broadest, hottest glare of his meridian beams.[30]
>
> STOCK.: Mere rhapsody; mere childish rhapsody; the libertine's familiar plea—Nature made us, 'tis true, but we are the responsible creators of our own faults and follies.
> (3.1.33)

Despite his sternness, however, Stockwell is beguiled by this child of nature, even admitting a startling amount of fellowship: "Away goes he upon the wing for pleasure. What various passions he awakens in me! He pains, yet pleases me; affrights, offends, yet grows upon my heart. His very failings set him off—forever trespassing, forever atoning. I almost think he would not be so perfect, were he free from fault" (3.1.34). Later still, Stockwell describes Belcour to Charlotte: "I flatter myself you will not find him totally undeserving your good opinion; an education, not of the strictest kind, and strong animal spirits, are apt sometimes to betray him into youthful irregularities; but an high principle of honour, and an uncommon benevolence, in the eye of candour, will, I hope, atone for any faults, by which these good qualities are not impaired" (3.5.40). The number of such interpolations in the play suggests that Cumberland was worried that his hero might offend some audience members, and sought to co-opt their criticism by using Stockwell as a mediator. If so, he succeeded admirably. Stockwell's rather stuffy rectitude provides a useful counterweight to Belcour's borderline excesses, without unduly constraining or confining their comic effect.

In sharp contrast to the language describing Nature, principle, and honor in the play is the language accompanying the various business transactions that take place. From the opening scene in Stockwell's countinghouse, money plays an important role in *The West Indian*, acting as a kind of touchstone and reward for value. People with money can use it judiciously and act generously with it, like Stockwell, Charlotte, and Belcour, or they can hoard it and use it to wield power, like Lady Rusport. People without money can behave honorably, like the Dudleys and Major O'Flaherty, or they can be venal and malicious, like the Fulmers. At the same time as the playwright contrives that virtue brings concrete monetary rewards and that vice is punished with monetary losses, he is remarkably realistic in confronting the reality of poverty in the Dudleys. As in *The Gamester*, lack of money can cause real distress to the deserving and render them insecure and vulnerable; it also tests their character, and shows that true virtue surmounts worldly distress.

The diction of barter and exchange, the precision of exact sums of money lent or needed, serves to particularize how quantitative value is offset by qualitative value in *The West Indian*. The most crucial bargaining of this sort takes place when Belcour dickers with Mrs. Fulmer for Louisa's favors, thinking that Charles is courting Charlotte while "keeping" Louisa:

> BEL.: Dudley is an unconscionable young rogue to think of keeping one fine girl in pay, by raising contributions on another; he shall therefore give her up; she is a dear, bewitching, mischievous, little devil; and he shall positively give her up.
>
> MRS. FUL.: Ay, now the freak has taken you again; I say give her up; there's one way, indeed, and certain of success.
>
> BEL.: What's that?
>
> MRS. FUL.: Out-bid him, never dream of out-blustring him; buy out his lease of possession, and leave her to manage his ejectment.
>
> BEL.: Is she so venal? Never fear me then; when beauty is the purchase, I shan't think much of the price.
>
> (3.3.35–36)

When Louisa, soon after, questions the sincerity of his passion—"I must have better proofs of your generosity, than the mere divestment of a little superflous dross, before I can credit the sincerity of professions so abruptly delivered" (3.4.39)—he is encouraged by Mrs. Fulmer to think she's holding out for more money, rather than evidence that his feelings are genuine. The audience, of course, knows differently, and scarcely needs her explanation to her brother's "Has [Belcour] made any professions to you?" "He has, but altogether in a style so whimsical and capricious, that the best which can be said of them is to tell you, that they seem'd more the result of good spirits than good manners" (3.10.47). Belcour here makes the cardinal error of confusing one kind of value for another, and his later humiliation is punishment for that mistake.

At the same time, because of his status as an outsider in the normal London world, Belcour functions not just as a satiric butt but also as a satiric agent, cutting through the facade of gentility and good manners around him with his crude honesty. His indictments are directed primarily not at the world of fashion but at the world of commerce and middle-class society: "I think the town and the town's-folk are exactly suited; 'tis a great, rich, overgrown, noisy, tumultuous place: the whole morning is a bustle to get money, and the whole afternoon is a hurry to spend it" (3.7.42). He is superseded in this role, however, by an astute character who acts even more decisively in the Charlotte-Charles courtship: Major O'Flaherty.

Comparable to Stockwell in his functions as mediator, counselor, and moralist, Major O'Flaherty is an interesting and original creation, given the long tradition of the farcical stage Irishman from Teague in *The Committee* on down. Cumberland's *Memoirs* indicate he was quite deliberate in his choice:

> I fancied there was an opening for some originality, and an opportunity for showing at least my good-will to mankind, if I introduced the characters of persons who had been usually exhibited on the stage, as the butts for ridicule and abuse, and endeavored to present them in such lights as might tend to reconcile the world to them, and them to the world. I therefore looked into society for the purpose of discovering such as were the victims of its national, professional, or religious prejudices; in short, for those suffering characters which stood in need of an advocate, and out of these I meditated to select and form heroes for my future dramas, of which I would study to make such favorable and reconciliatory delineations, as might incline the spectators to look upon them with pity, and receive them into their good opinion and esteem.
>
> With this project in my mind, ... I took the characters of an Irishman and a West Indian for the heroes of my plot, and began to work it out into the shape of a comedy.
>
> (142)

Like Belcour, the Major is an "alien" with a good heart, but also with a useful knowledge of the town. He begins by courting Charlotte's avaricious and spiteful stepmother, Lady Rusport, but soon turns away from her in disgust when he learns how she has treated her impecunious nephew and brother-in-law. He then uses his access to the household to counteract her plots; learning of Lady Rusport's scheme to suppress her father's will reinheriting Charles and Louisa, the Major outmaneuvers her and brings the deserving lovers together. Unlike most of the other characters, the Major is a moral agent who rejects sentiment, yet his actions speak as loudly in its behalf as Stockwell's do. Although "Providence" is given credit for the happy ending, then, the accolades would better go to those two unlikely "angels," the Major and the merchant.

The West Indian is often identified, along with other new comedies in the late eighteenth-century repertory, like Hugh Kelly's *False Delicacy* (1768) and Whitehead's *School for Lovers* (1762), as an example of "sentimental comedy," the kind against which Oliver Goldsmith (1728–74) inveighed in "An Essay on the Theater; or, a Comparison between Laughing and Sentimental Comedy," which appeared in *Westminster Magazine* in December 1772, about two years after the premiere of *The West Indian*.[31] The question he raised has been argued ever since by successive generations of critics: did sentimental comedy drive laughing comedy off the stage? The basic argument is that beginning as far back as Cibber's *Love's Last Shift* (1696) and *The Careless Husband* (1704) and Steele's *The Conscious Lovers* (1722), "sentiment" in the form of goodness and virtue began to take precedence over older values of wit and sexual prowess as objects of admiration in comedy. In his description of this transformation, Ernest Bernbaum uses audience-based phrases like "aroused admiration for persons like themselves," "exhibited faith in the natural impulses of contemporary middle-class people," and "confidence in the goodness of average human nature" (1–2) to fix responsibility. He finds a falling off of this sentimental revolution during the 1730s, 1740s, and 1750s, but its restoration in the 1760s and 1770s, in the form of comedies featuring moral characters, armed with aphorisms, pious speeches, and tears, who prevail over their opponents in plots designed to show the workings of Providence in rewarding virtue. Bernbaum suggests further that writers of these comedies saw their primary role as teaching audiences by example rather than by satire (242). In his essay, Goldsmith had earlier distinguished the two comic modes: "[A] new species of Dramatic Composition has been introduced under the name of *Sentimental* Comedy, in which the virtues of Private Life are exhibited, rather than the Vices exposed; and the Distresses, rather than the Faults of Mankind, make our interest in the piece. . . . If [the characters] happen to have Faults or Foibles, the Spectator is taught not only to pardon, but to applaud them, in consideration of the goodness of their hearts; so that Folly, instead of being ridiculed, is commended, and the Comedy aims at touching our Passions without the power of being truly pathetic" (212). His conclusion is that attending the theater to watch sentimental comedy is "as gloomy as at the Tabernacle" (213) and that such comedies should be driven off the stage by "laughing" comedies.

In an essay entitled "Goldsmith and Sheridan and the Supposed Revolution of 'Laughing' against 'Sentimental' Comedy,"[32] Robert D. Hume asks some pertinent questions about sentimental comedy and the relationship of Goldsmith and Sheridan to it,[33] among them "what is sentimental?" and "what is Goldsmith saying in his essay and why?" Hume is by no means the first to note the slipperiness of the term *sentimental*:

> In considering the English plays of [the 1760s and 1770s] we should be careful not to confuse the general air of geniality, which all of them create, with the true-blue sentimentalism found in certain ones. The sentimental comedy which Goldsmith was derid-ing in his "Essay on the Theater" is easily recognized; it is highly sententious; it preaches at every opportunity; it harps on the innate nobility of human nature, a nobility to be awakened by any suffi-ciently emotional experience; it equates virtue with glowing senti-ment, and presents as characters to be admired genteel men and women who are veritable machines of delicate, benevolent feeling. By no means all Georgian comedies, however, embody this kind of sentimentalism.[34]

Seeking a definition, Hume examines the repertory to distinguish between "sentimental" and "exemplary" comedies, and concludes that "there is little necessary connection between ideal characters and the common features of what we generally think of as sentimental comedies" (1983, 320). He goes on to scrutinize Goldsmith's arguments in "Essay on the Theater" and finds that Goldsmith both overstates the takeover of sentimental comedy and exaggerates its importance in order to "puff" his own *She Stoops to Conquer*, which premiered three months later. Whereas Goldsmith deliberately produces no concrete examples to sup-port his case against sentimental comedy, Hume examines the new comedies of the 1760s, play by play, to determine the success of satiric and sentimental comedies, and concludes "that 'flood' is a rather exaggerated description of the flow of sentimental comedies and further, that with an occasional exception, they weren't doing well in the theater" (1983, 332). His final conclusion is that "whether he cared to admit it or not, Goldsmith was writing for a theater in which several distinguished popular writers of laughing comedy were active—Murphy, Macklin, Colman, Garrick, and Foote" (1983, 335).

Hume leaves Cumberland off his list, implicitly accepting a dichotomy between "sentimental" and "laughing" comedy that I think false. Based on the most popular plays in the repertory, I find the changes in comic form more gradual and the plays themselves more inclusive than Goldsmith or other critics have acknowledged. Looking back to the 1690s and the early decades of the eighteenth century, the new comedies that began to emerge to compete with those Carolean comedies still in the repertory started to mix satiric and moral characters and actions somewhat differently from their Carolean predecessors, where exemplary qualities show up primarily in secondary couples and lesser plots in plays like *The Country-Wife* or *The Rover*, allowing some audience members to interpret them as the play's dominant values. In the new comedies, exemplary attitudes and actions were shifted to the protagonists, who continued to be witty and satiric and often needed reforming, but who were no longer licentious or totally self-serving. *Love for Love* and *The Beaux Stratagem* fit this pattern, while *The Conscious Lovers*, a bit later, adds a layer of sensibility to the basic design, with romance elements and sententious speeches.[35] Different comic dramatists mixed the components of satire and sympathy differently, and very gradually over the course of the eighteenth century, some comedies dropped out of the repertory, while others stayed. By the last half of the century, the list of most popular comedies no longer contained *The Man of Mode, The Rover,* or *The Country-Wife*,[36] while *The Way of the World, The Beaux Stratagem,* and *The Provoked Husband* were still extremely popular. Congreve's *Love for Love,* along with *The Way of the World,* was much more popular than his *The Old Batchelor* or *The Double Dealer*,[37] and *The Provoked Wife* had twice as many performances as *The Careless Husband,* and nearly three times as many as *The Relapse.* The shift is clearly away from straight Carolean comedy, but scarcely away from satiric or "laughing" comedy.

The new comedies repeat this pattern, but given that audience expectations for new plays would be higher than for old favorites, we would expect to see sentiment and exemplary behavior more openly displayed in new plays. Yet those comedies generally seen as marking the changes in comic development into sentimentalism are either not among the most popular plays, like Hugh Kelly's *False Delicacy*, or only moderately popular, like William Whitehead's *The School for Lovers* and Colman's *The English Merchant*. Among the new plays that were very popular, *The Clandestine Marriage* offers a pair of pitiful lovers and the noble benignity of Lord Ogelby and Sir John Melvil, in conjunction with trenchant satire against social climbing, old people pretending to be young, and avaricious parents; *The Jealous Wife* satirizes "petticoat government," fashionable town behavior, and mercenary parents, while its hero needs only to curtail his drinking and fighting to be worthy of the heroine. *The West Indian* fits neatly into this mixed mode, but so do the comedies of Goldsmith and Sheridan, the archetypal "laughing comedies."

Comedy: The School for Scandal

SIR PETER:	*'[T]is edification to hear him converse—he professes the noblest—Sentiments.*
SIR OLIVER:	*Ah plague on his Sentiments—if He salutes me with a Scrap of morality in his mouth I shall be sick directly.*
	(The School for Scandal, *2.3.386.28–31*)[38]

Coming out within two years of one another, Goldsmith's *She Stoops to Conquer* (1773) and Sheridan's *The Rivals* (1775) are filled with amiable, goodhearted characters who still manage to provide barriers to their own and one another's happiness in true comic fashion. Those who are obstructive suffer from the kinds of self-delusions and humors that are amusing rather than offensive, and readily correctable by the playwright's master hand. Goldsmith's alternative title, *The Mistakes of a Night*, is apt for both plays, because what their authors offer us in place of hard-edged satire, real character flaws, or villains are misinterpretations and errors that fall somewhere between farce and the controlled, balletlike movement of pantomime. There is no apprehension that the heroes and heroines will not be properly rewarded, and no exclusion or serious punishment of deficient characters at the end of the play. Both dramatists create a limited comic environment, whether physically circumscribed by the Hardcastles' house and the nearby tavern or the environs of Bath, emotionally circumscribed by a controlled range of characters and temperaments, or linguistically circumscribed by dialogue that is not too witty, not too sententious, not too vulgar. In the world defined by Goldsmith and Sheridan in these two plays, conflict is choreography.

There are tensions, to be sure, modifications of those which existed in Carolean comedy: generational conflicts, town versus country values, avarice, and assertions of power. In both plays, the older generation—Mr. and Mrs. Hardcastle in *She Stoops to Conquer*, Sir Anthony Absolute and Mrs. Malaprop in *The Rivals*—use their authority somewhat tyrannically and not always wisely. But their children, like Steele's Bevil Jr., respect their parents even while they are trying to outmaneuver them. In *She Stoops to Conquer*, Kate never resents her father's arranging a match for her with his friend Marlow's son but also expects him to accept her own choice. Indeed, she forces her father to give Marlow a second chance when Hardcastle later becomes disgusted with his behavior: "I hope, sir, you have ever found that I considered your commands as my pride; for your kindness is such, that my duty as yet has been inclination."[39] Similarly, Jack Absolute in *The Rivals* is respectful of his father even though he is intent on choosing his own marriage partner.

The kinds of generational conflicts more customarily seen in older comedies here exist in the secondary, and female, "parents"—Mrs. Hardcastle and Mrs. Malaprop—although this kind of misogyny doesn't exist in the authors' other plays. Mrs. Hardcastle uses her position of authority to wield power over her niece Constance Neville and her son Tony Lumpkin, withholding Constance's jewels until she marries Tony and preventing Tony from getting his inheritance otherwise. Both her charges rebel, quite properly, against this high-handed treatment, and much of the humor in the play comes from watching Mrs. Hardcastle get her comeuppance at the hands of her brutish but clever son. In one of the funniest scenes in the play, after he has led his mother on a wild ride through every "pond or slough within five miles of the place," Tony offers her a home truth:

MRS. HARD.:	And is it to you, you graceless varlet, I owe all this? I'll teach you to abuse your mother, I will.
TONY:	Ecod, mother, all the parish says you have spoiled me, so you may take the fruits on't.

(5.2.208.5–9)

As Hardcastle comments, "There's morality . . . in his reply" (5.2.208.13). In *The Rivals*, Mrs. Malaprop is punished more publicly; exposed and rejected as O'Trigger's "Delia," she loses whatever limited authority she had over Lydia and is forced to bow to Sir Anthony's greater authority.

Even more than Goldsmith, Sheridan peoples his comedy with eccentrics, characters so idiosyncratic that they stretch the boundaries of the types they represent. Thus, the range of comic effects in *The Rivals* is considerably greater than in *She Stoops to Conquer*, with characters like Sir Anthony, Lydia, Faulkland, Mrs. Malaprop, Bob Acres, and Sir Lucius O'Trigger bordering on Jonsonian humours characters. Sheridan also offers a range of sensibility in *The Rivals*. While sentimentality and romanticism are set up for ridicule in Lydia and Mrs. Malaprop, Julia and Faulkland are clearly sentimental lovers. Looking backward, a critic of 1830 suggested that it was this juxtaposition that damned the play on its first appearance:[40]

> It must be remembered that this was the English "age of senti-
> ment," and that Hugh Kelly and Cumberland had flooded the
> Stage with moral poems under the title of Comedies, which took
> their views of life from the drawing-room exclusively, and coloured
> their characters with a nauseous French affectation. "The Rivals,"
> in my opinion, was a decided attempt to overthrow this taste, and
> to follow up the blow which Goldsmith had given in "She Stoops
> to Conquer." My recollection of the manner in which the former
> was received, bears me out in the supposition. The audience on
> this occasion were composed of two parties—those who supported
> the prevailing taste, and those who were indifferent to it and liked
> nature. On the first night of a new play, it was very natural that
> the former should predominate;—and what was the consequence?
> why that Faulkland and Julia (which Sheridan had obviously intro-
> duced to conciliate the sentimentalists, but which in the present
> day are considered heavy incumbrances), were the characters
> which were most favourably received; whilst Sir Anthony, Acres
> and Lydia, those faithful and diversified pictures of life, were barely
> tolerated; and Mrs. Malaprop (as she deserved to be) was singled
> out for particular vengeance.
>
>   (John Bernard, quoted in *Dramatic Works*, 1:54)

At the same time, *The Rivals* seems to achieve a kind of consistency in its very madness, which gave it strength as a repertory piece well beyond its own time. Sheridan's comedy seems to depend less on the particulars of time and place than on the idiosyncracies of its characters as self-contained portraits of foible and folly who overshadow the love plot.

The heroes of the two plays are also forced to undergo humiliations before they are rewarded with the ladies of their choice. Both suffer from arrogance, which in Marlow's case approaches snobbery. In order to reconcile the two sides of his personality—the bashful gentleman and the arrogant "puppy"—Goldsmith provides two Kates, the genteel lady and the barmaid, and enlightens the other characters one by one until Marlow stands alone in his ignorance. In devaluing his hero, Goldsmith humanizes him, and Marlow is never more attractive than when he is totally routed by Kate:

> MARL.: Zounds, there's no bearing this; it's worse than death!
>
> MISS HARD.: In which of your characters, sir, will you give us leave to address you? As the faltering gentleman, with looks on the ground, that speaks just to be heard, and hates hypocrisy; or the loud, confident creature, that keeps it up with Mrs. Mantrap, and old Miss Biddy Buckskin, till three in the morning? Ha! ha! ha!
>
> MARL.: O, curse on my noisy head! I never attempted to be impudent yet, that I was not taken down. I must be gone.
>
> HARD.: By the hand of my body, but you shall not. I see it was all a mistake, and I am rejoiced to find it. You shall not, sir, I tell you. I know she'll forgive you. Won't you forgive him, Kate? We'll all forgive you. Take courage, man.
> [*They retire, she tormenting him, to the back scene.*]
>
> (5.3.212.27,213.1–15)

Since we never questioned his good heart after he offered marriage to the "poor relation," it is only his manners that needed reformation.

Jack Absolute's humiliation has more thematic relevance, and demarks Sheridan's middle ground on sentiment and wit. Through the first three acts, Absolute has as much control over the action as any

Carolean rake: he has successfully courted Lydia in the guise of Ensign Beverley; he advises his friend Faulkland to treat Julia better lest he lose her; he maneuvers cleverly around his father's peremptory order to marry an heiress. If Jack at times seems contemptuous of those he is manipulating, this contempt seems justified when we see his flattery, lies, and chameleon personality overcoming all obstacles to his desired ends. Yet when the whole edifice comes tumbling down in act 4, scene 2 and Jack is exposed and rejected by Lydia, an interesting transformation takes place that is equally pleasurable to the audience. Up to the duel in act 5, scene 3, a different Jack emerges. Sullen and resentful that his schemes have failed, he is reduced to our level, and when the smooth manipulator reappears at the end of the play, we like him better for having seen the social mask discarded and the emotions underneath revealed.

That affection for the hero is what brings together Belcour, Marlow, and Jack Absolute under a comic pattern that discards the competitiveness and the omniscience of the Carolean rake, along with his sexual appetite, and that dates back to Congreve's Valentine and all of Farquhar's heroes. Assured of their own superiority, audiences were free to allow their emotions more latitude and to admire and laugh simultaneously. Even in a more openly satiric play like Sheridan's *The School for Scandal*, that bond held firm.

The School for Scandal (1777) was even more popular than *The Rivals* in its own time, both with critics and audiences, and helped to foster the body of critical opinion that dubbed Sheridan "the modern Congreve,"[41] seeing a return, albeit briefly, to the true spirit of wit comedy. Indeed, the tone and structure of *The School for Scandal* do bear some resemblance to the bite and thrust of late seventeenth-century comedy, especially Congreve's *Love for Love* and *The Double-Dealer*, where we also find, respectively, the financially distressed hero and the villain who assumes the guise of a friend. It also recalls the comedies of Molière, particularly *Tartuffe* (see Loftis 1977, 78–79). Yet *The School for Scandal* is a product of its time in that value is grounded not in verbal wit but in sensibility, generosity, and virtue. The characters who possess these qualities prosper, and those who do not, however clever or outwardly attractive, fail.

The most interesting structurally of Sheridan's comedies, *The School for Scandal* is a play without a hero. Though he is the subject of conversation, speculation, and gossip, Charles Surface, the ostensible protagonist, does not appear onstage until act 3, scene 3, and then only in two sequences, one at his own house, the second at his brother's, before the denouement. Maria, the object of his affections, is even less in evidence, showing up in a few brief scenes and often standing silent even while she is physically present.[42] Unlike the case with most social comedies, then, our attention is not so much on courtship as on the juxtaposition of personalities and behaviors displayed by the range of characters cohabiting the London world of the play. The prime movers of the plot, in fact, are not Charles or Maria but Sir Peter Teazle and Sir Oliver Surface, representing the older generation. Both have antecedents and analogues within the repertory in a long line of old husbands and wise merchants, but are given special status and treatment by Sheridan. Equally important are their principal female antagonists, Lady Teazle and Lady Sneerwell, the young country-bred wife and the doyenne of the "school for scandal," and Joseph Surface, the cold-blooded "man of sentiment."

In its displacement of the young lovers to secondary position in the plot, *The School for Scandal* is free to present a series of vignettes whose purpose is to satirize London social mores. The opening scene in Lady Sneerwell's salon is a classic of its kind, its fast pace and sharp dialogue among a stageful of characters who abut against and abet one another resembling key scenes in Carolean drawing rooms created by Wycherley, Etherege, or Congreve. Yet for all its contained brilliance, Lady Sneerwell's "school" is not the primary setting of *The School for Scandal*; nor are she and Joseph its principal players.[43] Physically, only one more scene is set there, as the focus shifts to settings in which Sir Peter Teazle and Sir Oliver Surface hold sway, even Joseph's own library. It is precisely because these mediative characters are onstage and in control of most of the action that *The School for Scandal* preserves the same balance of sentiment and satire as *The Rivals*, despite its sharper edge.

Sir Peter, like Lord Ogleby of *The Clandestine Marriage*, seems formed to be a dupe, but like Ogleby, he recovers his authority in the course of the play. He is that stereotypical product of Carolean comedy, the old man who marries a young wife and then reaps the whirlwind:

> When an Old Bachelor takes a young Wife—what is he to ex
> pect!—'Tis now Six Months since Lady Teazle made me the happi
> est of Men—and I have been the miserablest Dog ever since that
> ever committed wedlock:—we tift a little going to church—and
> came to a Quarrel before the Bells were done ringing—I was more
> than once nearly choak'd with gall during the Honeymoon—and

had lost all comfort in Life before my Friends had done wishing me Joy— . . . She dissipate[s] my Fortune, and contradicts all my Humours:—Yet the worst of it is I doubt I love her or I should never bear all this—However I'll never be weak enough to own it.

(1.2.371.4–10,17–19)

At the same time, he is entirely taken in by Joseph Surface and Lady Sneerwell, who plot to destroy Charles's reputation and have Maria marry Joseph. Sir Peter swallows Joseph's "man of Sentiment" pose and suspects Charles of seducing Lady Teazle. Yet even as he blusters and fumbles along, guided by unseen hands, he shows some good judgment and finer feelings. He finds the School members and their gossip odious, and he genuinely loves his wife—providing her with a generous settlement even though he suspects her fidelity. In this movement from dupe to exemplary figure, Sir Peter demonstrates the distance Sheridan has moved from Wycherley or Congreve, whose comedies would not have admitted such a transformation in such a character.

Sir Oliver is another indicator of change. Replete with wealth he has earned through colonial trade, he brings a fresh perspective to the London world and corrects its deficiencies. Reluctant to believe the worst of Charles or the best of Joseph without hard evidence, he proceeds to test his nephews by playing the role of Premium the moneylender and Mr. Stanley the impecunious relative, looking for the real men beneath the Surfaces. By rejecting the needs of his mother's relative with pious sentiments and lies, Joseph shows his selfishness; by retaining his absent uncle's portrait while cheerfully selling off the rest of his ancestors and by sending £100 of the bounty to "Mr. Stanley," Charles reveals his generous spirit. Sheridan makes Sir Oliver more than a mere functionary, of course: he has a lot of personality and a humorous distaste for moralizing—but he is, foremost, a figure of authority.

In this respect, *The School for Scandal*, like so many other comedies in the eighteenth century, reasserts traditional authority: of the state over its subjects, of parents over children, husbands over wives, of men over women. If the first act demonstrates how contemporary London has lost its bearings, such that mostly virtuous young people like Charles, Maria, and Lady Teazle are under siege and powerless, it is implicitly because the older generation has either abdicated its responsibilities (Sir Oliver) or been toppled from power (Sir Peter, Rowley). Sheridan rigs the game, of course, because the older generation still retains the power of wealth and can easily reassert its authority by its ability to give or withhold money. Sir Oliver, however, combines this material power with the perception and wisdom of his experience.

The authority of husbands over wives is tested in the Teazles. Here Sheridan plays with his audience, first showing Sir Peter as a domestic tyrant, although an amusing one:

ROWLEY:	Nay I'm sure your Lady Sir Peter can't be the cause of your uneasiness.
SIR PETER:	Why has anyone told you she was dead?
ROWLEY:	Come—come Sir Peter you love her notwithstanding your tempers do not exactly agree.
SIR PETER:	But the Fault is entirely hers Master Rowley—I am myself the sweetest temper'd Man alive and hate a teizing Temper—and so I tell her a hundred Times—a day—
ROWLEY:	Indeed!
SIR PETER:	Aye and what is very extraordinary in all our disputes she is always in the wrong! but Lady Sneerwell and the Set she meets at her House encourage the perverseness of her Disposition—then to complete my vex[a]tions—Maria—my Ward—whom I ought to have the Power of a Father over—is determined to turn Rebel too—.

(1.2.371.26–37,372.1–2)

But Lady Teazle reveals herself to be as bad as or worse than her husband, and he gains stature and sympathy by default:

SIR PETER:	Lady Teazle—Lady Teazle I'll not bear it.
LADY TEAZLE:	Sir Peter—Sir Peter you—may bear it or not as you please, but I ought to have my own way in every thing, and what's more I will too—what! tho' I was educated in the country I know very well that women of Fashion in London are accountable to nobody after they are married.
SIR PETER:	Very well!—Ma'am very well! so a husband is to have no influence, no authority?

LADY TEAZLE: Authority! no to be sure—if you wanted authority over me you should have adopted me and not married me I am sure you were Old enough.

(2.1.373.19–29)

Sir Peter's ultimate weapon, of course, is his good nature; when Lady Teazle overhears that he intends to settle an income on her, she is ashamed and melts into obedience and proper conduct. Maria's brief "rebellion" against her guardian is even less important.

Unlike Sir Peter, Sir Oliver possesses the authority of wit, bridging the gap between characters like Lady Sneerwell's scholars and the sympathetic Maria, who is neither witty nor inspires wit in others.[44] Sheridan provides Charles with some good lines of dialogue, such as his similitude on drink and wit: "now instead of the social spirit of Raillery that used to mantle over a glass of bright Burgundy their conversation is become just like the Spa water they drink which has all the Pertness and flatulence of Champaine without its Spirit or Flavour—" (3.3.397.3–7). Yet Charles is witty only in the narrow sense, as inept as Maria in rescuing himself from the situation he is in. In Sir Oliver, Sheridan questions the composition of wit as language, cleverness, and substance,[45] and shows most of the characters wanting in some area. By embracing "Dullness" and being incapable of managing her own affairs, Maria is no contestant, but the Candor, Backbite, Crabtree contingent suffers from the opposite disorder—more sound than sense—while the other characters, from Sneerwell to Charles, possess variable amounts of linguistic talent, cozening capabilities, and serious understanding. To make the contest more fair, Sheridan deliberately eschews uncommon heights in what Loftis calls "linguistic virtuosity":

It is in his dialogue that Sheridan most resembles the great comic dramatists of the late seventeenth century. . . . Sheridan's characters, like Congreve's, strain for epigram, and frequently they achieve it, in expressions so neatly turned that a remark which is appropriate dramatically articulates a thought that has occurred to many people at many times. . . . The characters achieve their effects, not by extravagance of conceit or unusual boldness of metaphor, but by common images used in unexpected ways; and they make judgements of unexpected acerbity. The dialogue resembles familiar conversation in its separate components, but it is syntactically much more carefully contrived than even the best conversation, and it scores its satirical points with more regularity than the cleverest wit ever did in unpremeditated repartee. The eighteenth-century fondness for elaboration of sentence structure, with frequent parallelism and antithesis, is apparent, and as we read the closely controlled prose we find it easy to understand why Samuel Johnson proposed Sheridan for membership in the Club.

(Loftis 1977, 90–91)

While making the dialogue in the play as attractive and lively as that in any late eighteenth-century comedy, Sheridan is careful to give such dialogue no more than its due. Wit that is harmful or meaningless (like Sir Benjamin Backbite's awful poem) is inferior to wit that shows real perception and produces good results like Sir Oliver's.

Conclusion

The last half of the eighteenth century is generally considered lacking in playwrights of genius, though abundantly supplied with ones who were competent and prolific. Of the works of the dramatists who produced a body of popular plays between 1747 and 1779—Arthur Murphy, the elder George Colman, Samuel Foote, William Cumberland, Richard B. Sheridan, and Garrick himself—Sheridan's plays are nearly the only ones remembered and regularly performed and anthologized today, along with those of the occasional playwrights Oliver Goldsmith (*She Stoops to Conquer*), Edward Moore (*The Gamester*), and John Home (*Douglas*). When we consider the number of plays from earlier eras of the seventeenth and eighteenth centuries that are still read and appreciated and sometimes produced today, from *The Country-Wife* to *The Beggar's Opera*, this fact seems curious.

Various explanations have been offered for this dearth of exciting playwrights, none of which seems quite adequate. The most common is that the restrictions of the Licensing Act sent talented writers into other media, particularly the novel, instead of the theater. What we know to be true of Fielding, and to a lesser extent perhaps, of Goldsmith becomes an explanation for the fact that authors like Samuel Richardson, Tobias Smollett, Laurence Sterne, Eliza Haywood, and Frances Burney chose to write for the novel-reading rather than the playgoing public. Yet we can see from the equally impressive list just cited that plenty of writers were still attracted to the theater, which had become, if anything, *more* profitable for authors than ever before, as well as more respectable. Another explanation is that the presence of stellar actors like Garrick, Peg Woffington, Susannah Cibber, and Charles Macklin meant that audiences went to see performers, not plays, little caring what vehicles their favorites were in. Underlying this thesis are unspoken assumptions about the taste of the increasingly middle-class audience, who might not be expected to appreciate or understand complex or sophisticated drama. Yet every previous age had its star actors and their followers, and an audience that demanded and supported so many Shakespearean revivals in their "original" text cannot summarily be dismissed as ignorant and vulgar.

Most convincing, perhaps, is John Loftis's discussion of what made late eighteenth-century comedy "bland." He contends that these comedies "take a genial and optimistic view of the human condition and . . . avoid disturbing issues" such as the economic problems surfacing with the industrial revolution, political controversy of any kind, the American Revolution, and sexuality (Loftis 1977, 31ff.). It is true that, compared with plays of the 1680s or the 1730s, plays between 1747 and 1779 did avoid topical subjects, but so did Sheridan's and Goldsmith's, and we readily forgive them for it. Further, Martha England invites us to look beyond these plays' placid surface for another kind of revolution: "Thomas Sheridan, William Kenrick, Francis Gentleman, and John Walker did not cause the French Revolution, but they lived in a time of great social change and deep unrest, and they were not unaware of the time. When a lot of people decide to rise in the world, some sort of Bastille looms on the horizon, even if the only question at stake is a rhetorical one. More and more people were in a mood to climb. More and more men and women were less and less content to remain in the estate to which they had been born" (202). She judges rightly that simply by expanding their range of characters, settings, and actions, late eighteenth-century plays participated in the process that would further democratize England and its social institutions.

Finally, the answer must lie in the different audience expectations in Garrick's time and our own. The process that began in the late seventeenth century with Fletcherian revivals had as its main goal the maximization of affective appeal by means of spectacle and text. The shift from heroic to pathetic effects occurred relatively quickly in tragedy, such that by the early eighteenth century, even a "classical" tragedy like *Cato* had pathetic qualities and was vying on the stage with *The Orphan* and *The Fair Penitent*. In comedy, the process took longer. Despite the success of moral comedies like Steele's *The Conscious Lovers* and Cibber's *The Careless Husband*, genuinely pathetic elements do not intrude on comedy until the Garrick era, wherein they found themselves compatible with the new modes of acting introduced by Macklin and Garrick: "Style changed from often exquisite presentation of universals (the passions of love, fear, hate, anger, jealousy, and the like, in abstract) to individualistic treatments of the passions aligned with the characters and situations that produced them—Macbeth's fear (after killing Duncan), different from the fear of Drugger (after dropping a urinal); Lear's anguish in contemplating filial ingratitude, different from that of Romeo's contemplating Juliet in the tomb" (Stone, 187). Stone points out that such acting was also responsible for bringing "freshness" to old texts, thus making "older plays new to mid-eighteenth-century audiences" (Stone, 187). What this meant for the eighteenth century was an expansion of the capability of plays, both old and new, to evoke emotional responses in their audiences, whether laughter or tears. And if twentieth-century audiences find these plays less affective, it is not because they are cold-blooded but because they have developed modes of popular culture more appealing to their own tastes.

6

Conclusion

The development of drama by means of an active repertory theater between 1660 and 1779 is, in a sense, a case study of how a popular-culture genre accommodates and influences popular taste and ideology to produce literature. We have seen how, at times, this drama responded quickly to outside events like political and social changes that expanded its horizons and made its themes relevant, and how, at other times, outside forces constricted its range of interests, thought, and language. But such dramatic development more usually responds to gentler influences, changing incrementally rather than radically, shifting emphasis and exploring new territory as audiences begin to perceive themselves differently and make different demands on the theater, or as certain forms of drama become exhausted and are replaced by other forms. Within the popular repertory, such shifts can be charted by observing the replacement of one set of popular plays by another and by identifying what in the new plays seems to speak more directly to contemporary audiences. Between 1660 and 1779, several alterations of this kind occurred, playing out the complex dance of conformity and change.

What did not change was that the primary if not the exclusive function of late seventeenth- and eighteenth-century drama was to affect its audiences, to move their emotions and appeal to their senses. From its earliest beginnings, some writers and critics, such as Dryden, openly acknowledged this purpose, while others knew it only instinctively. Yet the most successful dramatists of every generation exploited the mechanics of the living theater—whether spectacle and costume, female actors in female roles, or music and dance—incorporating these capabilities into their plays. Whether they belonged to the 1680s or the 1760s, such dramatists wrote plays to utilize the particular talents of an Elizabeth Barry or a Susannah Cibber, to show off the scenic delights of Drury Lane or Covent Garden, to tap the genius of Henry Purcell or Handel. At the same time, the kinds of emotions their plays were meant to elicit altered over time. In tragedy and other serious forms, the awe accorded to grandiose heroic hero[in]es of the 1660s and 1670s was combined with the pity elicited by trapped and distressed hero[in]es in the plays of the 1680s and 1690s. As the depiction of suffering onstage and on the page became an art in itself, that emotion became central in the "she-tragedies" of the late seventeenth and early eighteenth centuries, a form that remained popular in the repertory into the late eighteenth century. By the early to middle eighteenth century, playwrights began adding pathetic effects to comedies as well, creating a wider range of interest and appeal by balancing satiric and sentimental elements.

Thus, enhancing affectivity inevitably altered the traditional forms of comedy and tragedy inherited at the reopening of the theaters in 1660, a process set into motion when early managers and playwrights chose to produce and imitate "mongrel" Fletcherian tragicomedies more often than Shakespearean or Jonsonian forms. These Fletcherian plays formed the nucleus of new Carolean dramatic modes, such as heroic drama and Spanish-plot comedy, but also maintained their own popularity long after these offshoots had disappeared from the stage. The mixed mode changed somewhat in the 1680s and 1690s, as dramatists like Otway, Congreve, and Vanbrugh produced comedies with serious implications and consequences, while Rowe and Southerne incorporated comic patterns and character types into their tragedies and tragicomedies. Indeed, the mixing worked so well that by the middle of the eighteenth century, drama was being written and performed in which there was no formal inevitability of outcome. Neither Moore's *The Gamester*, Cumberland's *The Brothers*, nor many of the other new tragedies and comedies that appeared during this time have absolute endings in the Aristotelian sense;[1] all could be rewritten as their generic opposite. Even Shakespeare, whose plays became more popular over time, was subject to such alterations, as Tate's and Garrick's happy-ending versions of *King Lear* testify.

These formal changes were accelerated and given some direction by forces external to the theaters. At around the turn of the eighteenth century, outside pressure from moralists like Jeremy Collier induced an important shift in the ostensible basis for comic drama from mimetic, imitating reality, to didactic, teaching morality. Those defending earlier comedies called them mimetic to sanction their exploitation of satiric or humorous effects; those advocating didactic comedies demanded that these effects be curbed in the service of morality. While authors of many late seventeenth-century comedies expected audience members to make their own accommodations with the play's characters and behaviors, interpreting them as moral if they so wished, authors of didactic comedies had to make sure that vice was not rewarded and that a kind of "poetic justice" was served. Subjected to moral scrutiny, the earlier comedies could not withstand the charges of "immorality and profaneness" leveled at them; their inherent message was that human appetite and desire could be satisfied by those who played the game well for its own sake. Although the audiences who attended the theaters during the late seventeenth century had found this message palatable, their early eighteenth-century successors did not; instead, they wanted to think of themselves as moral and benign. Thus, comic dramatists around the turn of the century, like Congreve and Farquhar, had to rectify their heroes and actions to incorporate values that included generosity and benignity and accommodated moral reformation. Somewhat later, Centlivre and Steele made their heroes exemplary, no longer in need of reformation at all and capable of rectifying the world around them. While these plays still had a satiric dimension, their satire was directed primarily at secondary characters and blocking figures whose vices contrasted with the protagonists' virtues.

Didactic forms of drama established a somewhat different relationship between the audience and the stage from what had existed previously, although plays still essentially produced self-images that audiences wanted to accept. Both tragic and comic dramatists wishing to draw on the audience's sympathy updated their protagonists and changed their venues: merchants and other middle-class figures replaced princes and idle gentlemen, inhabiting the country and the countinghouse as often as the drawing rooms and parks of London. Even plays whose tragic settings and character types were still centered on war and politics domesticated those concerns, and tragedies like John Home's *Douglas* or Arthur Murphy's *The Grecian Daughter* are female- and family-centered, fully congruent with the merchant heroes and genteel gentlemen of contemporary comedies.

Overall, the movement from late seventeenth- to eighteenth-century dramatic forms incorporated and was based on a shift in values from the individual to the community; if the underlying assumption of heroic drama and Carolean comedy was that what was good for the hero benefited society, the assumption underlying eighteenth-century tragedy and comedy was that what was good for society was good for everyone in it. These later plays therefore privileged traditional values and patterns of authority that reached downward from the monarchy to the family, in contrast to the challenges to such authority prevalent in the drama of the Carolean period. Eighteenth-century dramatic forms also reinforced role and gender specialization, so that a character like Mrs. Beverley in *The Gamester* clearly prefigures the "angel of the hearth" often associated with the ideology of Victorian Britain.

Were eighteenth-century audiences therefore so different from their predecessors? I think not. The research of Pedicord, Loftis, and others seems to show that while these later audiences were somewhat differently constituted, with more merchants, soldiers, and sailors, their makeup was essentially the same as that of the audiences existing at the reopening of the theaters in 1660. They were still looking for diversion, for entertainment; they wanted to be flattered and feel good about themselves. Yet eighteenth-century audiences clearly felt better when they thought of themselves as moral, even righteous, rather than as rebels against the system that had served their parents; they wanted to think of themselves as members of a unified community rather than as individuals creating their own alternatives. They wanted to weep along with pathetic hero[in]es rather than feel godlike and omnipotent along with larger-than-life warriors and sexual athletes. And what they wanted, of course, they got.

Yet the lines of force are not entirely simple in popular culture, for the form also exerts a kind of pressure and gets to set the terms of the relationship. Theater audiences tend to accept what they are given, by and large, and to want more of the same until they are given something else. Thus, the great leaps forward in dramatic development are generally the result of a significant "technological" change, such as the addition of female actors or the exploitation of scenic capabilities, or the product of a creative mind, like Dryden's or Fielding's. The enormous popularity of pantomime and other short musical pieces, for instance, began with and was stimulated by the genius of John Rich and the unnamed scenic designers, composers, and performers who worked for him, not with the audiences enjoying them. These are only the most blatant instances of how the theaters made their mark on dramatic development; it is a small step to find their influence on less radical changes as well, particularly on the creation of images upon which successive generations of theatergoers modeled their behaviors and expectations.

What is finally most interesting about the plays written and performed between 1660 and 1779 is that the dramatic forms that attained independent life during those years still exist in the popular culture of today, altered over time to suit different audiences and incorporate different technologies. The films of Mel Brooks and the Zuckers or the television skits of *Saturday Night Live*'s Not Ready for Prime Time Players and the "Monty Python" group have their origins in the burlesque tradition which V. C. Clinton-Baddeley traces from the late seventeenth century.[2] From Samuel Butler's *Hudibras* (1663), the Duke of Buckingham's *The Rehearsal* (1671), and Thomas Duffett's parodies of opera, the burlesque evolved into the eighteenth century through Gay and Fielding to Sheridan's *The Critic* (1779). During the nineteenth century, melodrama and horror romances gave new life and subject matter to burlesque. As Clinton-Baddeley puts it, "It [was] difficult to select from all this richness . . . of burlesqueable material" (80), and playwrights like Thomas Dibdin and W. S. Gilbert, as well as novelists like Dickens and Thackeray, mocked melodramas in their works. And while burlesque was relegated to the music halls and vaudeville theaters in the early twentieth century, it resurfaced again in the "talkies" and on television, finding a voice and apt subject matter for parody in the later twentieth century.

If Gay contributed to the long line of burlesque with a play like *The What D'Ye Call It* (1715), *The Beggar's Opera* had even more impact on successive generations of dramatic entertainments. In the hands of Gay's imitators, the musical theater left the heights of opera for the verisimilitude of late eighteenth-century burletta, comic opera, and operetta. Whether in their native England or transported to America, these musical plays evolved during this time span to become singular art forms in which text and music were fully integrated with one another.[3] The nineteenth and early twentieth centuries witnessed the operettas of Gilbert and Sullivan competing with the works of Edward Rice and other lesser-known composers and writers in London and New York, the centers of musical theater. By the early twentieth century, George M. Cohan had graduated from vaudeville to writing and performing musical drama, paving the way for Irving Berlin, the Gershwins, Cole Porter, and others of the 1920s to 1940s. Late twentieth-century stage and film musicals continued the graceful merger of fanciful plots with whatever music form was popular at the time, from pop ballad to rock-and-roll.

Other dramatic forms have undergone similar transformations. One can see a line of domestic comedy from Farquhar and Sheridan to television sitcoms or *When Harry Met Sally*, or from the pathetic tragedies of Rowe and Lillo to today's soap operas or *Sleeping with the Enemy*. Less obvious, perhaps, is the way eighteenth-century drama altered expectations about form and content, erasing what had seemed to be absolute lines between comedy and tragedy, private and public, satiric and sentimental. *The Beggar's Opera*, with its complex merger of serious, comic, and musical forms, made possible the similar interweaving of disparate elements in a text like Laurents, Bernstein, and Sondheim's *West Side Story* or Rogers and Hammerstein's *The Sound of Music*. More than a contemporary translation of *Romeo and Juliet* or a concentrated rendering of the Trapp family's ordeals, these modern dramas use their music as a thematic component of the text, signifying freedom from the confining and degrading environment that, like Gay's St. Giles and Newgate, threatens the protagonists. Nor do these modern dramatists see any conflict between tragedy bordering on sentimentality and the song or dance that punctuates and enhances the climactic moments in their plays.

Similarly, the mixture of comic and serious that began with Vanbrugh, Steele, and Lillo and extended through Moore, Cumberland, and nineteenth-century melodrama focuses on middle-class subjects in ways we are accustomed to. From the time of Ibsen and Shaw, the idea that domestic settings and characters are appropriate environments and subjects for modern drama has had critical sanction and public acceptance. Plays like Miller's *Death of a Salesman*, Williams's *The Glass Menagerie*, or O'Neill's *Long Day's Journey into Night* presume that the important moral questions of contemporary times can be asked in domestic settings, while a play like Churchill's *Cloud Nine* extends and expands the "family" over time and space to break down the artifice of realism with a different kind of artifice. Our debt to the late seventeenth- and eighteenth-century drama is both formal and conceptual.

If the foregoing conclusions seem to ignore long-held assumptions about the difference between haute and popular culture, then it is because I believe that such distinctions are often artificially constructed by critics after the fact. Harriet Hawkins talks of "the continuing cross-fertilisation between 'high' literature and popular genres,"[4] and other recent studies focus on the ways popular culture shapes and is shaped by public ideology in modern times. In dealing with late seventeenth- and eighteenth-century drama, I have simply transported these assumptions into a time when the same audiences enjoyed Italian opera and ballad opera on different nights and when, for all practical purposes, the repertory theater was the main form of popular culture. That successive generations have succeeded in canonizing these plays, relegating them to the study rather than the stage, is their loss, and ours.

chronology

1660   Charles II restored to the throne of England. Samuel Pepys begins his
        diary. Theatrical patents granted to Thomas Killigrew and Sir William
        Davenant. First woman acts on the public stage.

1661   Davenant's *The Siege of Rhodes* performed in two parts. The Duke's
        Company begins acting at Lisle's Tennis Court in Lincoln's Inn
        Fields.

1662   Charter granted to the Royal Society by Charles II. Sir Robert
        Howard's *The Committee* produced. Molière's *L'Ecole des femmes*
        produced in France.

1663   Samuel Butler's *Hudibras* published. The King's Company moves to
        new Theater Royal in Bridges Street, Drury Lane. Sir Samuel Tuke's
        The Adventures of Five Hours produced.

1664   Nell Gwyn begins acting career. John Dryden and Sir Robert
        Howard's *The Indian Queen* and George Etherege's *The Comical
        Revenge* produced.

1665   The Second Dutch War begins. The Great Plague rages in London, closing the theaters for 16 months. Dryden's *The Indian Emperor* and Roger Boyle, Earl of Orrery's *Mustapha* produced.

1666   The Fire of London devastates much of the city; Christopher Wren commissioned to redesign the city, including St. Paul's Cathedral. Molière's *Le Misanthrope* produced in France.

1667   The Second Dutch War ends. Milton's *Paradise Lost* published. Dryden's *Secret Love*, Dryden and Davenant's *The Tempest*, Dryden and the Duke of Newcastle's *Sir Martin Mar-all* produced.

1668   Death of Davenant; actors Thomas Betterton and Henry Harris manage the Duke's Company. Dryden becomes Poet Laureate, publishes "An Essay of Dramatic Poesy." Etherege's *She Would if She Cou'd*, Thomas Shadwell's *The Sullen Lovers*, Dryden's *An Evening's Love* produced. Molière's *Tartuffe* produced in France.

1669   Pepys ends his diary.

1670   Betterton's *The Amorous Widow* and Dryden's *The Conquest of Granada, Part 1* produced.

1671   John Milton's *Paradise Regained* and *Samson Agonistes* published. The Duke's Company moves to new theater in Dorset Garden. The Duke of Buckingham's *The Rehearsal* and Dryden's *The Conquest of Granada, Part 2* produced.

1672   William of Orange marries Mary, eldest daughter of James, brother and heir to Charles II. Third Dutch War begins. John Bannister begins public concert series in London. Theater Royal burns; King's Company moves to Lincoln's Inn Fields. Dryden's *Marriage A-la-Mode*, Shadwell's *The Miser* and *Epsom Wells*, Edward Ravenscroft's *The Citizen Turn'd Gentleman* produced.

1673   Elkanah Settle's *The Empress of Morocco* produced. Molière's *Le Malade imaginaire* produced in France.

1674   Third Dutch War ends. King's Company moves to new Drury Lane theater designed by Christopher Wren. Elizabeth Barry begins acting career. Shadwell's musical *The Tempest* and Thomas Duffett's *The Mock Tempest* produced.

1675   William Wycherley's *The Country-Wife*, Dryden's *Aureng-Zebe*, Shadwell's *Psyche* produced.

1676   Etherege's *The Man of Mode*, Wycherley's *The Plain-Dealer*,

Shadwell's *The Virtuoso*, Thomas Otway's *The Cheats of Scapin* produced.

1677   Thomas Rymer's *Tragedies of the Last Age Considered* published. Charles Killigrew, son of Thomas, becomes manager of the King's Company. Aphra Behn's *The Rover*, Dryden's *All For Love*, Nathaniel Lee's *The Rival Queens* produced.

1678   The Popish Plot. Society for the Reformation of Manners founded. John Bunyan's *The Pilgrim's Progress, Part 1* published. Dryden and Lee's *Limberham* and Shadwell's *Timon of Athens* produced.

1679   The Earl of Shaftsbury introduces first Exclusion Bill in Parliament to prevent James from succeeding Charles II; it dies when Charles dissolves Parliament. Shadwell's *The Woman-Captain* produced.

1680   Dryden's *The Spanish Fryar*, Otway's *The Orphan* and *The Souldiers Fortune*, Lee's *Lucius Junius Brutus* produced.

1681   Charles II dissolves Parliament. Dryden's *Absalom and Achitophel* published. Nahum Tate's *King Lear*, Ravenscroft's *The London Cuckolds*, John Banks's *The Unhappy Favourite*, Shadwell's *The Lancashire Witches* produced.

1682   Dryden's *Macflecknoe* and *Religio Laici* published. The United Company formed from merger of King's and Duke's companies. Otway's *Venice Preserved* and Dryden and Lee's *The Duke of Guise* produced.

1683   The Rye House Plot. John Crowne's *City Politiques* and Otway's *The Atheist* produced.

1684   Tate's *A Duke and No Duke* produced.

1685   Charles II dies; James II succeeds him. The Duke of Monmouth, Charles's eldest illegitimate son, invades England and is defeated and executed. Crowne's *Sir Courtly Nice* and Dryden's *Albion and Albanius* produced.

1686   Dryden's *Spanish Fryar* ordered "no more to be played."

1687   Sir Isaac Newton's *Principia* and Dryden's *The Hind and the Panther* published. Behn's *The Emperour of the Moon* produced.

1688   The Glorious Revolution. William of Orange is invited to England by nobles and other leaders; James and family flee to France. Henry Purcell begins his connection with the theater. Anne Bracegirdle begins acting career. Shadwell's *The Squire of Alsatia* produced.

1689   William and Mary proclaimed King and Queen by Parliament,
        accepting a Bill of Rights acknowledging Parliament's supremacy over
        the monarchy. William forms Grand Alliance with Spain and Austria
        and begins war against Louis XIV. Shadwell becomes Poet Laureate.
        Tate and Purcell's *Dido and Aeneas*, Dryden's *Don Sebastian*,
        Shadwell's *Bury Fair* produced.

1690   John Locke's *Two Treatises of Government* and *An Essay concerning
        Human Understanding* published. Colley Cibber and Thomas
        Doggett begin acting careers. Dryden's *Amphitryon* and Betterton and
        Purcell's *The Prophetess* produced.

1691   Societies for the Reformation of Manners flourish. Dryden and
        Purcell's *King Arthur* produced.

1692   Tate becomes Poet Laureate. Shadwell's *The Volunteers* and Settle (?)
        and Purcell's *The Fairy-Queen* produced.

1693   Rymer's *A Short View of Tragedy* published. Alexander Davenant
        absconds to the Canary Islands, leaving Christopher Rich in charge of
        the United Company. William Congreve's *The Old Batchelor* and *The
        Double Dealer* produced.

1694   Death of Queen Mary. Bank of England founded. Actors led by
        Betterton leave United Company. Thomas Durfey's *Don Quixote*, in
        two parts, produced.

1695   The *Post Boy*, first successful daily newspaper, founded. Betterton's
        company licensed by William III to act at Lincoln's Inn Fields.
        Congreve's *Love for Love*, Thomas Southerne's *Oroonoko*, Purcell's
        operatic *Indian Queen* and *Bonduca* produced.

1696   Cibber's *Love's Last Shift*, Ravenscroft's *The Anatomist*, John
        Vanbrugh's *The Relapse* produced.

1697   Treaty of Ryswick ends the War of the League of Augsburg.
        Congreve's *The Mourning Bride* and Vanbrugh's *The Provoked Wife*
        produced.

1698   Jeremy Collier's *A Short View of the Immorality and Profaneness of
        the English Stage* published. Actor Robert Wilks joins Drury Lane
        Company. George Farquhar's *Love and a Bottle* and Catherine
        Trotter's *Fatal Friendship* produced.

1699   Farquhar's *The Constant Couple* and Peter Motteux's operatic *The
        Island Princess* produced.

1700   Whigs form the Kit-Cat Club. A number of indictments against players by reformers. Anne Oldfield and Barton Booth begin acting careers. Congreve's *The Way of the World* and Cibber's *Love Makes a Man* produced.

1701   Death of James II; his son becomes the Old Pretender/James III. Act of Settlement ensures Protestant succession in England. The War of the Spanish Succession begins. Richard Steele's *The Funeral* and Nicholas Rowe's *Tamerlane* produced.

1702   Death of William III; accession of Queen Anne. John Churchill, Duke of Marlborough, appointed commander of English forces. The *Daily Courant* begins publication. The Earl of Clarendon's *A History of the Rebellion and Civil Wars in England* and the anonymous *A Comparison between the Two Stages* published. Cibber's *She Would and She Would Not* and Farquhar's *The Inconstant* and *The Twin Rivals* produced.

1703   Vanbrugh begins construction of the Queen's theater in the Haymarket. Storm destroys Dorset Garden theater. Rowe's *The Fair Penitent* and Steele's *The Lying Lover* produced.

1704   Capture of Gibraltar, Battle of Blenheim. Daniel Defoe's *Review* begins publication. Newton's *Opticks* published. Jonathan Swift's *Tale of a Tub* and *The Battle of the Books* published. Cibber's *The Careless Husband* produced.

1705   The *Daily Courant* begins printing playbills. Queen's theater opens, with Vanbrugh and Congreve as owner-managers. Steele's *The Tender Husband*, Susannah Centlivre's *The Gamester*, Vanbrugh's *The Confederacy* produced.

1706   Vanbrugh appoints Owen Swiney manager of Queen's theater. Farquhar's *The Recruiting Officer* produced.

1707   Union of Scotland and England to form Great Britain. The Lord Chamberlain "silences" Christopher Rich. Farquhar's *The Beaux Stratagem* and Cibber's *The Double Gallant* and *The Lady's Last Stake* produced.

1708   The two theater companies united: serious plays offered at Drury Lane, operas at Queen's. John Downes's *Roscius Anglicanus* published.

1709   The Reverend Sacheverell prosecuted after an inflammatory sermon; becomes a martyr for the high church Tories. The *Tatler* begins publication. Rowe's edition of Shakespeare published. Rich expelled from Drury Lane and yearly licenses issued to Drury Lane actors under Aaron Hill as manager. Betterton and some actors begin performing at Queen's. Centlivre's *The Busie Body* produced.

1710   Whigs replaced by Tories in high government offices. Berkeley's *A Treatise concerning the Principles of Human Knowledge* published. George Frideric Handel arrives in England. Theater companies united again. Charles Shadwell's *The Fair Quaker of Deal* produced.

1711   Marlborough dismissed as Commander in Chief of allied forces. The *Spectator* begins publication. Alexander Pope's *An Essay on Criticism* published.

1712   Pope's *The Rape of the Lock* published. Ambrose Phillips's *The Distrest Mother* and Charles Johnson's *The Wife's Relief* produced.

1713   Treaty of Utrecht ends the War of the Spanish Succession. Scriblerus Club formed. Owen Swiney, manager of Queen's, absconds with funds; John James Heidegger takes over management. Joseph Addison's *Cato* produced.

1714   Death of Queen Anne; accession of George I. Whigs replace Tories in high government offices. Steele made governor of Drury Lane patent, sharing management with actors Robert Wilks, Colley Cibber, and Barton Booth. Christopher Rich dies; his son John Rich becomes owner-manager at Lincoln's Inn Fields. Centlivre's *The Wonder* and Rowe's *Jane Shore* produced.

1715   Jacobite Rebellion under James Edward, the Old Pretender, is crushed in Scotland. Rowe becomes Poet Laureate. Steele receives Drury Lane patent. John Gay's *The What D'Ye Call It* and Rowe's *Lady Jane Grey* produced.

1716   Addison's *The Drummer* and Johnson's *The Cobler of Preston* produced.

1717   Cibber's *The Non-Juror* produced.

1718   Quadruple Alliance declares war on Spain. Lady Mary Wortley Montagu introduces inoculation for smallpox. Centlivre's *A Bold Stroke for a Wife* produced.

1719   Peace with Spain. Daniel Defoe's *Robinson Crusoe* published. Steele's patent revoked.

1720   Little Theater in the Haymarket opens. Steele removed from Drury Lane management. John Hughes's *The Siege of Damascus* produced.

1721   The South Sea Bubble causes financial chaos. Robert Walpole becomes First Minister. Steele restored to Drury Lane. Cibber's *The Refusal* and Hill's *Fatal Extravagance* produced.

1722 Defoe's *Moll Flanders* and *Journal of the Plague Year* published. Steele's *The Conscious Lovers* produced.

1723 Elijah Fenton's *Mariamne* produced.

1724 Defoe's *Roxana* published.

1725 Pope's edition of Shakespeare published. Francis Hutcheson's *An Inquiry into the Original of Our Ideas of Beauty and Virtue* published. Allan Ramsay's *The Gentle Shepherd* produced.

1726 William Law's *The Unlawfulness of Stage Entertainments*, Swift's *Gulliver's Travels*, James Thomson's *Winter* published.

1727 Death of George I; accession of George II. Gay's *Fables* published.

1728 Pope's *The Dunciad* and Law's *A Serious Call to a Devout and Holy Life* published. Cibber and Vanbrugh's *The Provoked Husband* and Gay's *The Beggar's Opera* produced.

1729 Swift's *A Modest Proposal* published. Goodman's Fields theater opens. Kitty Clive joins Drury Lane company. Charles Johnson's *The Village Opera*, Cibber's *Love in a Riddle*, Samuel Johnson's *Hurlothrumbo* produced.

1730 Colley Cibber becomes Poet Laureate. Thomson's *The Seasons* published. Henry Fielding's *The Author's Farce* and *Tom Thumb* produced.

1731 Henry Giffard begins operating Goodman's Fields. The *Gentleman's Magazine* begins publication. George Lillo's *The London Merchant* and Fielding's *The Grub Street Opera* produced.

1732 Benjamin Franklin's *Poor Richard's Almanac* published. Drury Lane receives new patent. John Highmore buys half of Booth's patent share; Colley Cibber assigns his share for one year to his son Theophilus. Covent Garden Theater opens. Giffard opens new theater in Ayliffe Street. Charles Johnson's *Caelia* and Fielding's *The Mock Doctor*, *The Covent Garden Tragedy*, and *The Modern Husband* produced.

1733 Opposition to Walpole increases, supported by Frederick, Prince of Wales. Pope's *An Essay on Man* (Epistles 1–3) published. John Highmore becomes primary owner of Drury Lane, and actors under Theophilus Cibber defect and begin performing at the New Haymarket; Highmore files suit against them. John Rich buys dormant Killigrew patent. Fielding's *The Miser* produced.

1734   Pope's *An Essay on Man* (Epistle 4) published. Lewis Theobald's edition of Shakespeare published. Highmore sells his share of the Drury Lane patent to Charles Fleetwood; rebel actors return to Drury Lane. Fielding's *Don Quixote in England* produced.

1735   William Hogarth's "The Rake's Progress" series of engravings published. Henry Giffard buys a share in the Drury Lane patent. Hill's *Zara* and Fielding's *An Old Man Taught Wisdom* produced.

1736   Laws against witchcraft repealed. Fielding leads "Great Mogul's Company" at the Little Theater in the Haymarket. Fielding's *Pasquin* and Lillo's *Fatal Curiosity* produced.

1737   The Prince of Wales leads opposition to Walpole. The Licensing Act prohibits nonpatent theaters and performances and reinforces the authority of the Lord Chamberlain's office over the patent theaters. David Garrick and Dr. Samuel Johnson travel to London. Fielding's *The Historical Register for 1736* and *Eurydice* and Henry Carey's *The Dragon of Wantley* produced.

1738   Agitation for war with Spain increases. Anti-French riots at the Little Haymarket theater.

1739   Walpole reluctantly declares war against Spain. Famine in Ireland. John Wesley begins preaching. David Hume's *A Treatise of Human Nature* published. Thomson's *Edward and Eleanora* produced.

1740   Samuel Richardson's *Pamela* and Cibber's *An Apology for the Life of Colley Cibber* published. Giffard's company operating at Goodman's Fields. Peg Woffington begins acting career. Garrick's *Lethe* and Thomson and Arne's *Alfred* produced.

1741   Walpole resigns and is succeeded by Whigs led by Henry Pelham and the Duke of Newcastle. Spanish War develops into the War of the Austrian Succession. Garrick's London acting debut at Goodman's Fields. Garrick's *The Lying Valet* produced.

1742   Fielding's *Joseph Andrews* and Pope's *The Dunciad* published. Handel's *Messiah* first performed in Dublin. Goodman's Fields closed; Giffard's company moves to Lincoln's Inn Fields.

1743   English victory over French at the Battle of Dettingen. Fielding's *Jonathan Wild* published. Drury Lane actors, including Garrick and Charles Macklin, secede from company in the fall, protesting Fleetwood's management; Garrick and others except Macklin return in December.

1744   War with France. Lincoln's Inn Fields theater abandoned. Audiences riot at Drury Lane in response to rise in ticket prices. Fleetwood sells patent to bankers Richard Green and Morton Amber; they appoint James Lacy as manager.

1745   Invasion of Scotland by Charles Edward, the Young Pretender; defeated by the Duke of Cumberland at the Battle of Culloden. Thomson's *Tancred and Sigismunda* and Fielding's *The Debauchees* produced.

1746   Garrick acting at Covent Garden. Macklin's *A Will and No Will* produced.

1747   Warburton's edition of Shakespeare and William Collins's *Odes* published. Garrick and James Lacy become joint owner-managers of Drury Lane. Samuel Foote acts at the little theater in the Haymarket. Benjamin Hoadly's *The Suspicious Husband*, Garrick's *Miss in Her Teens*, Foote's *Diversions of a Morning* produced.

1748   Peace of Aix-la-Chapelle ends War of Austrian Succession. Pompeii discovered. Richardson's *Clarissa* published. Edward Moore's *The Foundling* produced.

1749   Nova Scotia founded. Westminster Bridge built. Fielding's *Tom Jones* and David Hartley's *Observations on Man* published. Johnson's *Irene*, Hill's *Meropé*, Foote's *The Knights* produced.

1750   Thomas Gray's "Elegy Written in a Country Churchyard" published. Dr. Johnson begins the *Rambler*. Opera shuts down when manager absconds with funds. Spranger Barry joins Covent Garden company. William Whitehead's *The Roman Father* and Henry Brooke's *The Earl of Essex* produced.

1751   Frederick, Prince of Wales, dies. Fielding's *Emilia* and Hume's *An Enquiry concerning the Principles of Morals* published.

1752   Acquisition of Georgia. London Hospital founded. Foote's *Taste* and Macklin's *The Covent Garden Tragedy* produced.

1753   Richardson's *Grandison* published. Opera resumes production. Moore's *The Gamester* and Henry Jones's *The Earl of Essex* produced.

1754   Hume's *A History of Great Britain* published. John Brown's *Barbarossa*, Whitehead's *Creusa*, Thomas Sheridan's *The Brave Irishman* produced.

1755   Dr. Johnson's *Dictionary* published. *Chinese Festival* riots destroy interior of Drury Lane.

1756   Seven Years' War between Britain, with Prussia, and France begins.

William Pitt becomes virtual Prime Minister. Edmund Burke's *A Philosophical Inquiry into the Origin of Our Ideas of the Sublime and the Beautiful* published. John Home's *Douglas* and Garrick's *Lilliput* produced.

1757   Hume's *The Natural History of Religion* published. Foote's *The Author* and Garrick's *The Male Coquette* produced.

1758   Dr. Johnson begins the *Idler*. Arthur Murphy's *The Upholsterer* produced.

1759   Dr. Johnson's *History of Rasselas, Prince of Abyssinia* and Voltaire's *Candide* published. Murphy's *The Orphan of China*, James Townley's *High Life below Stairs*, Garrick's *Harlequin's Invasion* produced.

1760   George II dies; George III succeeds him. George Colman's *Polly Honeycombe*, Murphy's *The Way to Keep Him*, Foote's *The Minor* produced.

1761   Oliver Goldsmith's *Citizen of the World* published. John Rich dies; son-in-law John Beard becomes manager of Covent Garden. Colman's *The Jealous Wife* and Murphy's *All in the Wrong, The Old Maid*, and *The Citizen* produced.

1762   Rousseau's *Social Contract* published. Garrick clears the audience from the stage at Drury Lane; Covent Garden management follows suit. Isaac Bickerstaffe's *Love in a Village*, Whitehead's *The School for Lovers*, Foote's *The Lyar* and *The Orators* produced.

1763   Peace of Paris concludes Seven Years' War; Canada and India ceded to Britain. Thomas Reid's *An Inquiry into the Human Mind on the Principles of Common Sense* published. Garrick begins Continental tour, leaving George Colman as manager of Drury Lane. Half-price riots. David Mallet's *Elvira*, Colman's *The Deuce Is in Him*, Foote's *The Mayor of Garrett* produced.

1764   Eight-year-old Mozart visits and performs in England. Horace Walpole's *The Castle of Otranto* published. Kane O'Hara's *Midas*, Murphy's *No One's Enemy but His Own* and *What We Must All Come To*, Foote's *The Patron* produced.

1765   Stamp Act passed, violently resisted in American colonies. Sir William Blackstone's *Commentaries on the Laws of England* published. Garrick returns to Drury Lane with new ideas for lighting and scenery. Foote's *The Commissary* and Bickerstaffe's *The Maid of the Mill* produced.

1766   The Stamp Act repealed. Henry Cavendish discovers hydrogen.

Goldsmith's *The Vicar of Wakefield* published. Foote receives patent for the Haymarket theater. Garrick and Colman's *The Clandestine Marriage* produced.

1767   John Beard sells Covent Garden patent for £60,000 to Thomas Harris, John Rutherford, William Powell, and George Colman. Colman's *The English Merchant* and Garrick's *A Peep behind the Curtain* produced.

1768   Royal Academy of Arts founded, with Sir Joshua Reynolds its first president. Laurence Sterne's *A Sentimental Journey* published. Hugh Kelly's *False Delicacy*, Goldsmith's *The Good-Natured Man*, Bickerstaffe's *Lionel and Clarissa*, John Hoole's *Cyrus* produced.

1769   James Watt invents the steam engine. Rutherford sells share of Covent Garden patent to Dagge and Leake; William Powell's widow inherits his share. The Shakespeare Jubilee at Stratford. Richard Cumberland's *The Brothers*, Colman's *Man and Wife*, Garrick's *The Jubilee* produced.

1770   Goldsmith's "Deserted Village" published. Court decision supports Colman in quarrel among Covent Garden owner-managers. Kelly's *A Word to the Wise* and Foote's *The Lame Lover* produced.

1771   Tobias Smollett's *Humphrey Clinker* and Henry Mackenzie's *The Man of Feeling* published. Cumberland's *The West-Indian* and Foote's *The Maid of Bath* produced.

1772   In a landmark case, Lord Mansfield, Lord Chief Justice, rules that slavery cannot exist on English soil. Garrick hires Phillipe de Loutherbourg as scenic designer at Drury Lane. Murphy's *The Grecian Daughter*, Foote's *The Nabob*, William Mason's *Elfrida* produced.

1773   The Boston Tea Party. Goldsmith's *She Stoops to Conquer* and Kelly's *The School for Wives* produced.

1774   Continental Congress meets in Philadelphia. Joseph Priestley isolates oxygen. The Earl of Chesterfield's *Letters* published. James Lacy dies; son Willoughby inherits his share of the Drury Lane patent. Colman sells his share of the Covent Garden patent to Thomas Hull, who becomes manager of Covent Garden under Harris. Colman's *The Man of Business* and John Burgoyne's *The Maid of the Oaks* produced.

1775   Military actions between American and British troops: Lexington, Concord, Bunker Hill. Drury Lane interior alterations by the Adam

brothers. Richard B. Sheridan's *The Rivals* and *The Duenna*,
Garrick's *Bon Ton*, Robert Jephson's *Braganza* produced.

1776   American Declaration of Independence. Charles Burney's *History of Music*, Edward Gibbon's *The Decline and Fall of the Roman Empire, Volume 1*, Thomas Paine's *Common Sense*, Adam Smith's *The Wealth of Nations* published. Garrick sells his share of the Drury Lane patent to Richard B. Sheridan, Thomas Linley, and Dr. James Ford for £35,000 and retires from the theater. Foote's *A Trip to Calais* and Colman's *New Brooms!* produced.

1777   Burgoyne surrenders British army at Saratoga. Haymarket patent leased by George Colman; Samuel Foote retires from the theater. Sheridan's *The School for Scandal*, Murphy's *Know Your Own Mind*, Colman's *The Spanish Barber*, Hannah More's *Percy* produced.

1778   Franco-American alliance. Frances Burney's *Evelina* published. Lacy sells his share of the Drury Lane patent to Sheridan for 30,000 guineas (£31,000), with a lifetime annuity of £1,000. Sheridan's *The Camp* and Colman's *The Suicide* produced.

1779   Dr. Johnson's *The Lives of the Poets, Part 1* published. Garrick dies on 20 January. Sheridan and Thomas Harris purchase opera house in the Haymarket. Sheridan's *The Critic* and More's *Fatal Falsehood* produced.

notes and references

Preface and Acknowledgments

1. *The London Stage, 1660–1800: A Calendar of Plays, Entertainments & Afterpieces, together with Casts, Box-Receipts, and Contemporary Comments,* 5 vols. (Carbondale: Southern Illinois University Press, 1960–68), 3:174; hereafter cited in text as *LS.*

Chapter 1: Introduction

1. Quoted in Richard Bevis, *The Laughing Tradition: Stage Comedy in Garrick's Day* (Athens: University of Georgia Press, 1980), 23; hereafter cited in text. Garrick himself put it somewhat more ambiguously: "When the taste of the public is right the Managers and Actors must follow it or starve" (quoted in Harry William Pedicord, *The Theatrical Public in the Time of Garrick* [Carbondale: Southern Illinois University Press, 1954], 66; hereafter cited in text as Pedicord 1954).

2. Writing about the nineteenth-century repertory, Joseph W. Donohue, Jr., asserts, "The traditional English repertory theater maintains a large
number of plays, sometimes altered, sometimes withdrawn, sometimes revived,
all to suit the changing tastes of demanding audiences. . . . As a result, the
author of a new play must compete not only with those of his contemporaries
but with works of proven merit, some of them one hundred or one hundred-fifty
years old" (*Dramatic Character in the English Romantic Age* [Princeton, N.J.:
Princeton University Press, 1970], 7). See also George Winchester Stone, Jr.,
"The Making of the Repertory," in *The London Theater World: 1660–1800*, ed.
Robert D. Hume (Carbondale: Southern Illinois University Press, 1980),
181–209; hereafter cited in text as Stone.

3. John Loftis, "Political and Social Thought in the Drama," pp.
253–85 in Hume 1980, 253; hereafter cited in text as Loftis 1980.

4. See Jennifer R. Goodman, *British Drama before 1660: A Critical
History* (Boston: Twayne, 1991), 208–10; hereafter cited in text.

5. According to Avery and Scouten, there were three older theaters in
use at the time of the Restoration: the Red Bull, an open-air playhouse rebuilt
in 1653; the Cockpit/Phoenix in Drury Lane, dating from 1609; and Salisbury
Court Playhouse, dating from 1629. The last two houses were along the lines of
Shakespeare's Blackfriars and other Elizabethan indoor, so-called private, theaters
(*LS*, 1:31–34).

6. "Such tennis courts were normally 110 feet long for a full-size court,
by 31 feet 8 inches wide. These rectangular roofed buildings had a range of
windows on each long side in the upper part of the walls, and sometimes also
across one end. Internally the building was a single great hall with a roofed
corridor, the penthouse, which ran along one side and the two end walls, and
was separated from the main hall by a waist-high partition, usually with two
openings to the court, and the roof supported on a series of posts" (Richard
Leacroft, *The Development of the English Playhouse* [Ithaca, N.Y.: Cornell University Press, 1973], 80; hereafter cited in text). If one thinks only of Shakespeare's
first Globe or the Swan as predecessors, this choice might seem odd, but Leacroft
fills in the gaps, speculating convincingly about the alteration in even the second
Globe in terms of the indoor playhouses of its time, which included a larger
stage space, stretching from side to side with side entry doors; an internal, cur-
tained acting area; and a musicians' upper gallery over the stage and balcony (see
38–50); see also Goodman, 16–17.

7. Plenty of speculation and some disagreement exist about the capacity
of these early theaters; I have used Edward A. Langhans's estimates partly because
he stresses their conjectural nature, pointing out, for instance, that "since playgoers sat on benches, the capacity of a house could vary according to how closely
people were willing to sit" ("The Theaters," pp. 35–65 in Hume 1980, 60;
hereafter cited in text as Langhans).

8. About this arrangement, Pepys complained that "there is no hearing of the bases at all, nor very well of the trebles" (8 May 1663), a situation that was probably rectified during the renovations of 1666 (*The Diary of Samuel Pepys*, 9 vols., ed. Robert Latham and William Matthews [Berkeley: University of California Press, 1970], 4:128).

9. This Drury Lane replaced the theater that burned down two years earlier; it was designed by Sir Christopher Wren, the great architect of contemporary London.

10. Side boxes alongside the stage itself were probably used, along with the King's box, for royalty; sometime during the eighteenth century, these side boxes entirely supplanted the front boxes as seating for royalty.

11. For a complete description of Garrick's Drury Lane, see Allardyce Nicoll, *The Garrick Stage: Theaters and Audience in the Eighteenth Century*, ed. Sybil Rosenfeld (Athens: University of Georgia Press, 1980), 23–34; hereafter cited in text as Nicoll 1980.

12. Richard Cumberland, *Memoirs of Richard Cumberland, London, 1806*, ed. Henry Flanders (1856; reprint, New York: Benjamin Blom, 1969), 387; hereafter cited in text as Cumberland.

13. Colin A. Visser, "Scenery and Technical Design," pp. 66–118 in Hume 1980, 70; hereafter cited in text as Visser.

14. Quoted in Phyllis T. Dircks, *David Garrick* (Boston: Twayne, 1985), 55–56; hereafter cited in text.

15. These stages, however, had only one or two such traps, as opposed to six by the early nineteenth century.

16. Curtis A. Price, "Music as Drama," pp. 210–35 in Hume 1980, 210; hereafter cited in text as Price.

17. As Price points out, "Songs and dances of this sort constitute most musical scenes in late Restoration comedies: music obviously introduced for its own sake rather than to enhance the plot; it is not completely incidental to the action, of course, being worked into the drama on some pretence" (212).

18. Sometimes literally, as Price points out: "Purcell's miniature music dramas, such as the conjurer's scene from *The Indian Queen*, resurfaced a few seasons later as entr'acte entertainments or afterpieces, rarely appearing with their original plays" (233–34).

19. Details for this section are drawn primarily from the relevant sections in *The London Stage* volumes and Judith Milhous, "Company Management," pp. 1–34 in Hume 1980; hereafter cited in text as Milhous 1980.

20. The monetary value of a patent depended on the era and the profitability of a theater: if a one-fifteenth share in the Duke's Company was worth £700 in the 1660s, the whole patent was valued at about £10,500; Garrick sold

his patent to Sheridan and others in 1775 for £35,000. Donald Greene suggests that "a pound in the eighteenth century was equal in purchasing power to between twenty and forty United States dollars in the 1960's" (*The Age of Exhuberance: Backgrounds to Eighteenth-Century English Literature* [New York: Random House, 1970], 56, n. 13).

21. After 1732, patents were not permanent in the same sense as before, but renewable each 21 years.

22. The cost of theater buildings ranged from between £2000 and £9,000 during the seventeenth century to £80,000 at the end of the eighteenth century.

23. Summing up her findings, Milhous concludes that "the more success-ful theater operations enjoyed a good deal of managerial continuity, . . . that ownership rarely shifted hands without precipitating a period of adjustment, and that when more than one or two members of a management team changed in a short time, the business was apt to fall apart" (1980, 26).

24. Milhous (1980) calculates a support staff of perhaps two-thirds the size of the performing company, for a total of some 37 to 45 persons in the mid-1670s to 128 by the 1775–76 season (excluding extra singers and dancers, who might add some 20 to 40 to the numbers).

25. According to actor Thomas Davies, "Barton Booth 'often declared in public company, that he and his partners lost money by new plays; and that if he were not obliged to it, he would seldom give his consent to perform one of them.' Back in the height of theatrical warfare (the 1670s and 1695–1700) each company often staged ten or a dozen new plays each year, and a production could be gotten up from scratch in three to six weeks. Later managers seldom had to produce more than half that number of new scripts each year, and the schedule was not so hectic" (Milhous 1980, 27).

26. Leo Hughes points out that the term *prompter* is used quite differently from today and that the role combined the functions of assistant director and stage manager as well as prompter in the narrower sense ("Evidence from the Promptbooks," pp. 119–42 in Hume 1980, 122; hereafter cited in text as Hughes 1980). After the turn of the century, a new position of stage manager or underman-ager was added to take over some of these duties, a position held by, among others, Theophilus Cibber and Charles Macklin at Drury Lane during the 1730s and 1740s.

27. These sums were not inconsiderable. Shadwell received £130 for the third night of *The Squire of Alsatia* (1688), *The Conscious Lovers* (1722) brought Steele as author £300, and *The Beggar's Opera* (1728) made its author, John Gay, rich. Publication rights were separate from production rights and could add considerably to an author's income for a given play. Richard Cumberland, for example, sold the copyright for *The West Indian* (1771) for £150 in the 1770s. See Shirley Strum Kenny, "The Publication of Plays," pp. 309–36 in Hume 1980, hereafter cited in text as Kenny.

28. Also, benefits for the sake of indigent friends, relatives, dependents, or charitable causes were given occasionally throughout the season.

29. Authors' dedications to their published editions could also be rewarded: "Cibber received £200 from the king, to whom he had dedicated *The Non-Juror*, and Steele received a munificent 500 guineas [£525] from the king for *The Conscious Lovers* (1722)" (Kenny, 311).

30. Philip H. Highfill, Jr., "Performers and Performing," pp. 143–180 in Hume 1980, 143; hereafter cited in text as Highfill. See also Alan S. Downer, "Nature to Advantage Dressed: Eighteenth-Century Acting," in *Restoration Drama: Modern Essays in Criticism*, ed. John Loftix (New York: Oxford University Press, 1966), 328–71.

31. "Today's actor has inherited no system of notation with which he might hope to imitate the onstage presence of Garrick—nothing like that accurate system by which the modern harpsichordist can nearly duplicate Haydn at the keyboard, or even the far less exact scheme by which the dancer can divine the arabesques of Noverre" (Highfill, 162).

32. A company would generally employ about twice as many male actors as female, and cast lists reflect this disproportion. Also, despite their drawing power, female actors were generally paid less than their male counterparts and, except for Betterton's comanagers at Lincoln's Inn Fields in the 1690s, Elizabeth Barry and Anne Bracegirdle, never given managerial powers.

33. See John Harold Wilson, *All the King's Ladies: Actresses of the Restoration* (Chicago: University of Chicago Press, 1958), passim.

34. "At the end of the [eighteenth] century, James Winston was able to mention some 280 theaters in circuits in England, Scotland, Ireland, and Wales. In addition, the number of provincial 'legitimate' theaters, in England alone, increased by the granting of nine royal patents: to Bath and Norwich in 1768, to York and Hull in 1769, to Liverpool in 1771, to Manchester in 1775, to Chester in 1777, and to Bristol and Newcastle in 1778" (Highfill, 156).

35. A fairly typical season, 1750–51, shows 85 different full-length pieces and 28 different afterpieces for the two companies.

36. See Pedicord 1954 and Stone, 181–209. See also Leo Hughes, *The Drama's Patrons: A Study of the Eighteenth-Century London Audience* (Austin: University of Texas Press, 1971); hereafter cited in text as Hughes 1971.

37. Harry William Pedicord, "The Changing Audience," pp. 236–52 in Hume 1980, 240; hereafter cited in text as Pedicord 1980.

38. Attempts to eliminate this deeply entrenched practice resulted in riots, the most famous being the Half Price Riots of 1763.

39. Hughes also points out (1971, 156–58) that different mixtures of audiences attended the theater on different nights and at different times of the year. On Wednesday and Saturday, for example, the upper classes tended to be

at the opera rather than the patent theaters, and these same people often were not in town at all during September and May.

40. Arthur C. Kirsch, ed., *Literary Criticism of John Dryden* (Lincoln: University of Nebraska Press, 1966), ix; hereafter cited in text as Kirsch 1966.

41. We are reminded again of Garrick's saying, nearly 100 years later, "*When the taste of the public is right* the Managers and Actors must follow it or starve" (italics mine).

42. Quoted in John T. Harwood, *Critics, Values, and Restoration Comedy* (Carbondale: Southern Illinois University Press, 1982), 2; hereafter cited in text.

43. They did, however, print "puffs": laudatory comments, gossip, and other bits of theatrical "news" that straddled the fence between criticism and advertising (*LS*, 2:93–94).

44. See Calhoun Winton, "Dramatic Censorship," pp. 286–308 in Hume 1980; hereafter cited in text as Winton.

45. For example, Nathaniel Lee's *Lucius Junius Brutus* (1680) was refused a license because of its "Scandalous Expressions & Reflections upon ye Government" (Winton, 297).

Chapter 2: The Carolean Period

1. In his *Leviathan* (1651), Thomas Hobbes posited "desire" as one of the imperatives of human nature, along with the senses and the imagination; as interpreted by the Earl of Rochester and others, Hobbes saw society as a system wherein individuals attempted to maximize their desires while recognizing the need for civil law and monarchical authority. See Susan Staves, *Players' Scepters: Fictions of Authority in the Restoration* (Lincoln: University of Nebraska Press, 1979), chapter 5 passim, and Eric Rothstein and Frances M. Kavenik, *The Designs of Carolean Comedy* (Carbondale: Southern Illinois University Press, 1988), 22; both hereafter cited in text.

2. *Secret Love; or, the Maiden Queen*, in *The Works of John Dryden* ed. John Loftis and Vinton A. Dearing (Berkeley: University of California Press, 1966), 9:113–203; hereafter cited in text as CD (California Dryden series). Unless otherwise specified, all quotations from Dryden's plays are from this series, cited in the form (act.scene.lines); other references to the series will be in the form (CD, volume: pages).

3. Nicholas Jose, *Ideas of the Restoration in English Literature, 1660–71* (Cambridge, Mass.: Harvard University Press, 1984), 1.

4. "By 1660 the principal actors of the days of James I and Charles I had died or had so drifted out of touch with dramatic enterprise that the continuity of acting had been impaired, though certainly not lost. Furthermore, most of the pre-Commonwealth theaters had been closed, destroyed, or converted to purposes other than theatrical. In addition, the playwrights of the old regime no longer were productive. And a new generation had appeared in London, one which had little intimate knowledge of acting, the drama, or the playhouse" (*LS*, 1:21–22).

5. This was particularly true of Davenant, who had received a much smaller share of the old plays when they were parceled out. (See Rothstein and Kavenik, 262–63.)

6. Robert D. Hume, *The Development of English Drama in the Late Seventeenth Century* (Oxford: Clarendon Press, 1976), 209–13; hereafter cited in text as Hume 1976.

7. For a discussion of tragic theory in general during the Carolean period, see chapter 1 of Eric Rothstein, *Restoration Tragedy: Form and the Process of Change* (Madison: University of Wisconsin Press, 1967); hereafter cited in text as Rothstein 1976b.

8. I follow the Carolean practice of calling these plays "tragedies" as opposed to "tragicomedies."

9. As I have done in previous works, I am using the word *popular* cautiously here, since production records for the early seasons are scanty. Nonetheless, such records as exist and comments made by playgoers like Samuel Pepys indicate at least moderately successful runs for the plays I have so designated (see Rothstein and Kavenik, 265–67).

10. Eugene M. Waith, *The Pattern of Tragicomedy in Beaumont and Fletcher* (New Haven, Conn.: Yale University Press, 1952), 38.

11. "While Fletcher writes episodic narrative, heroic playwrights devote themselves far more to composing displays, dramatic booths to exhibit the heroic gestures and secure the admiration of the crowd. The result is that the heroic hero seems oddly detached from the plot about him in the same way as Sherlock Holmes, say, is detached from the mystery on which he is intently working, because it exists primarily to display his deductive powers, his herohood" (Rothstein 1967b, 56).

12. Davenant, preface to *Gondibert, an Heroick Poem*, quoted in Joel E. Spingarn, *Critical Essays of the Seventeenth Century* (Bloomington: Indiana University Press, 1957), 2:36–37. H. T. Swedenberg, Jr. calls the preface a "landmark" in epic theory in England, "not because Davenant embarked on unknown seas of criticism, but rather because he brought together ideas that had appeared on the Continent, and, in scattered fragments, in English criticism

prior to this time" (*The Theory of the Epic in England, 1650–1800* [Berkeley: University of California Press, 1944], 43).

13. Ann-Mari Hedback, ed., *The Siege of Rhodes: A Critical Edition* (Uppsala: Uppsala University Press, 1973), 4. In his own "Of Heroic Plays: An Essay" (preface to *The Conquest of Granada,* 1672), Dryden acknowledged his and others' debt to Davenant and *The Siege of Rhodes* in their heroic plays: "For my self and others, who come after him, we are bound, with all veneration to his memory, to acknowledge what advantage we receiv'd from that excellent ground-work which he laid: and, since it is an easy thing to add to what already is invented, we ought all of us, without envy to him, or partiality to our selves, to yield him the precedence in it" (CD, 11:9–10).

14. Eugene M. Waith, *The Herculean Hero in Marlowe, Chapman, Shakespeare, and Dryden* (New York: Columbia University Press, 1962), 16.

15. Arthur C. Kirsch *Dryden's Heroic Drama* (1965; reprint, New York: Gordian Press, 1972), 64.

16. CD, 9:338. See also Leslie Howard Martin, "Dryden and the Art of Transversion," *Comparative Drama* 6 (Spring 1972): 3–13.

17. Even Orrery's male heroes are sometimes described as "feminine" in their passivity, loquaciousness, and devotion to strict rules of honor. Dryden, meanwhile, tends to produce either whimpering heroines (Cydaria) or warlike ones (Alibech), neither of whom resemble Orrery's strong, passionless figures such as the Queen of Hungary or Plantagenet.

18. I do not mean to imply that Philocles represents a potentially satisfying match for the Queen. On the contrary, he is being used almost symbolically in the play, as an example of the inferior objects that the heroic temper may fix upon. Although satisfactory in some respects, he is clearly of lesser stature than the Queen. Yet insofar as he represents an outlet for the more human side of the Queen's energies, his rejection requires her celibate withdrawal from passion itself.

19. For a discussion of the history of the proviso sequence in comedy, see Kathleen M. Lynch, "D'Urfé's *L'Astrée* and the 'Proviso' Scenes in Dryden's Comedy," *PQ* 4 (October 1925): 302-8.

20. John Loftis suggests possible borrowings from D'Urfé's *L'Astrée,* de Scudéry's *Cyrus* and *Ibrahim,* and Thomas Corneille's *L'Amour à la Mode* in CD, 9:340–44.

21. John Harrington Smith, *The Gay Couple in Restoration Comedy* (Cambridge, Mass.: Harvard University Press, 1948).

22. L. A. Beaurline and Fredson Bowers, eds., *John Dryden: Four Comedies* (Chicago: University of Chicago Press, 1967), 26–27, 28.

23. Anne T. Barbeau would seem to support this idea: "a gradual deepen-

ing of thought occurs between the *Indian Queen* and *Aureng-Zebe*. Toward the end of his career as a heroic dramatist, Dryden is far more interested in private moral problems and seems to skirt the broader political and historical issues" (*The Intellectual Design of John Dryden's Heroic Plays* [New Haven, Conn.: Yale University Press, 1970], 57).

24. This and successive quotations from *The Rover* are from *The Works of Aphra Behn*, vol. 1, ed. Montague Summers (1915; reprint, New York: Phaeton Press, 1967); hereafter cited in text in the form (act.scene.page).

25. *LS* records indicate seven known performances before 1700; between 1700 and 1714, with more performances of all plays recorded, there are 32 of *The Rover*, with an additional 111 performances between 1714 and 1747, after which its popularity lapsed.

26. *Epicoene* had 13 recorded performances before 1684–85, 30 more through 1713–14, and 64 more before 1779; *The Scornful Lady* had 13 recorded performances through 1685, 22 more through 1713–14, and 54 more before 1779.

27. *Sir Martin* had 27 performances through 1684–85, 17 more before 1713–14, and 10 more before 1779; *The Committee* had 10 performances through 1684–85, 52 more before 1713–14, and 314 more before 1779.

28. Seven years later, Horner would freely act out what his predecessors only pretended to. Or, as Harold M. Weber puts it, "The rake was not a static creation, for conceptions of his character changed to accommodate changes in the tastes, expectations, and composition of Restoration audiences" (*The Restoration Rake-Hero: Transformations in Sexual Understanding in Seventeenth-Century England* [Madison: University of Wisconsin Press, 1986], 11; hereafter cited in text).

29. It may indeed have been even more popular than the *LS* performance figures indicate, especially in the decade after the Restoration. In a paper given at the Midwest MLA convention in 1973, B. R. Schneider asserted that *The Committee* was "not just one of the most but *the* most popular comedy of the Restoration and early 18th Century." Before 1700, it was exceeded only by *Sir Martin Mar-all* and, Schneider suggests, perhaps not even that, since "the years of [Sir Martin's] *first popularity occurred when the record is fairly full, whereas The Committee* arrived on the stage during a very sparse period in the records" ("Howard's Misplaced *Committee*," MMLA, Chicago, 1973, 1–2).

30. By act of Parliament in 1643, the estates of royalists could be seized or sequestered by the government. If sequestered, the estate could be redeemed if its owner paid from one-sixth to one-half its value. For further details, see Carryl Nelson Thurber, *Sir Robert Howard's Comedy "The Committee,"* University of Illinois Studies in Language and Literature, no. 7 (February 1921): 40–41.

31. Some critics have tended to underrate the importance of farce in

Restoration comedy, ignoring the long and prosperous careers of actors like John Lacy and James Nokes, who made farce their business. Indeed, Leo Hughes indicates the term took its place "in dramatic nomenclature only with the Restoration" (6) and goes on to define the term: "The chief, even the exclusive, business of farce is to stimulate the risibilities of the audience. The distinction between farce and other kinds of comic drama must then rest upon the nature of the laughter elicited by each. The laugh, the smile, the smirk with which an audience receives high comedy or the laughter tinged with scorn which greets the jibes of the burlesque writer differ appreciably from the non-reflective guffaw with which the antics of the farceur are received" (19). Farce is "fitful, full of shifts and surprises, in terms of structure, episodic" (21), and its four main techniques are "repetition, disguise, . . . physical violence . . . [and] a motif peculiarly attractive to English audiences: the exaggerated or overdrawn character" (32). It is, above all, an actor's medium, dependent on stage business, comic timing, and improvisation: "Especially in farce, where everything depends upon an instantaneous and vigorous response from the audience, the skill of the actor is paramount" (153). See Leo Hughes, *A Century of English Farce* (Princeton, N.J.: Princeton University Press, 1956).

32. Borrowing, of course, was rampant throughout the late seventeenth and eighteenth centuries, and playwrights thought nothing of lifting plots and characters, without attribution, from any handy source. Occasionally, as Behn did in her defense of *The Rover*, they responded to charges of plagiarism, often disingenuously.

33. John Loftis notes that about 17 of Beaumont and Fletcher's 50 plays have Spanish sources, among them *The Chances*, *The Island Princess*, *Rule a Wife and Have a Wife*, and *The Spanish Curate*, all popular on the Carolean stage (*The Spanish Plays of Neoclassical England* [New Haven, Conn.: Yale University Press, 1973], 25–27).

34. See John Wilcox, *The Relation of Molière to Restoration Comedy* (New York: Columbia University Press, 1938), and Rothstein and Kavenik, chapter 5.

35. One should also note that at least some of these roles Molière the author wrote for Molière the actor: "He gave himself the outstanding comic part, whether as Sganarelle, Scapin, Argon, Harpagon, or Monsieur Jourdain" (Philip A. Wadsworth, *Molière and the Italian Theatrical Tradition* [Birmingham, Ala.: Summa Publications, 1977], 106–7).

36. Quoting Freud on the constitution of the "hero" who cannot suppress his instincts, Weber applies it to the rake: "such figures generate contradictory responses, for they reveal the tensions between our own conflicting desires for the security of order and the pleasures of misrule. The rake necessarily raises ambivalent responses, for the sexual energy that he represents threatens the stability of the social order even while it promises to provide the vitality that must

animate the structures of that order. These conflicting desires govern not only our responses to the rake, but the form of Restoration comedy itself, which normally asserts the efficacy of traditional notions of order—through the institution of marriage—while at the same time recognizing the power and attractiveness, even the necessity, of those forces threatening to disrupt it" (6).

37. *The Rover* is, in essence, derived from Killigrew's *Thomaso, or the Wanderer* (written in 1654), despite Behn's claims in her postscript to the published version: *"This Play had been sooner in Print, but for a Report about the Town (made by some either very Malitious or very Ignorant) that 'twas Thomaso alter'd; which made the Book-sellers fear some trouble from the Proprietor of that Admirable Play, . . . That I have stol'n some hints from it may be a proof, that I valu'd it more than to pretend to alter it: . . . I will only say the Plot and Bus'ness (not to boast on't) is my own: as for the Words and Characters, I leave the Reader to judge and compare 'em with Thomaso"* (Summers, 107).

38. "Like the male rake, the female rake commands both respect and scorn, admiration and fear; unlike the male rake, however, the female rake proves difficult to domesticate. As a projection of male fantasies about, and fears of, female sexuality, the female rake generates ambivalences even greater than those aroused by the male rake. Though she is never simply dismissed as an expression of human degeneracy and postlapsarian evil, her sexual vitality and defiance of male authority create fears that remain unresolved by the conventional resolution of Restoration comedy" (Weber, 153).

39. These and other quotations are from Malcolm Kelsall's edition of Thomas Otway, *Venice Preserved* (Lincoln: University of Nebraska Press, 1969); hereafter cited in text in the form (act.scene.lines).

40. Drury Lane's problems were mainly internal: "dissentions within the King's Company between Killigrew and his son Charles caused the Lord Chamberlain, in September 1676, to appoint as actor-managers Charles Hart, Michael Mohun, Edward Kynaston, and William Cartwright. In late February of 1677, Hart was given full authority over the others, and in July, the players achieved self-governing powers. Serious disagreements continued within the King's Company throughout the next few seasons" (Rothstein and Kavenik, 264).

41. Crowne's *City Politiques*, written in 1682, was banned and did not appear until January 1683; Lee's *Lucius Junius Brutus*, Banks's *The Island Queens*, and Tate's *The History of King Richard the Second* were also banned. For obvious reasons, the censor seemed particularly sensitive to topics such as the deposition of kings, rebellions, and advocacy of constitutional principles.

42. Sir George Clark, *The Later Stuarts: 1660–1714*, 2nd ed. (Oxford: Clarendon Press, 1934, 1956), 92–115; hereafter cited in text.

43. David Ogg, *England in the Reign of Charles II*, 2nd ed. (Oxford: Clarendon Press, 1956), 2:597.

44. Although many of the historical accounts of the crisis tend to be

either pro-Whig or pro-Tory and to highlight the adversarial nature of the conflict, Staves offers an instructive objectivity: "it cannot be stressed too often how frequently practical Whigs and practical Tories agreed on important issues, how ideology shifted with the new illuminations of new circumstances, and how fluid political alliances were throughout the Restoration. Most Whigs and most Tories protested their devotion to monarchy and to protestantism, abhorred the thought of another civil war, considered the law a relevant curb on policy, and claimed that a study of British history showed their position to rest on tradition and their opponents' position to be an innovation" (77).

45. Staves draws even finer distinctions between pro-Whig and anti-Catholic plays (79).

46. The *London Stage* records four performances in winter/spring 1682, a reprint and possible revival in 1695–96, and 23 more performances before the 1714–15 season. It was a repertory staple throughout the eighteenth century, with 260 more performances before 1779, and is perhaps the most frequently revived Carolean tragedy in modern productions.

47. See Kelsall, pp. xi–xvii; John Robert Moore, "Contemporary Satire in Otway's *Venice Preserved*," *PMLA* 43 (1928): 166–81; Aline Mackenzie, "*Venice Preserv'd* Reconsidered," *Tulane Studies in English* 1 (1949): 81–118; and Kerstin P. Warner, *Thomas Otway* (Boston: Twayne, 1982), 48–57 (hereafter cited in text as Warner).

48. Critics have often noted the Shakespearean echoes in *Venice Preserved*, for example, in Priuli's first set-speech (1.1.49–58), which resembles that of Brabantio in *Othello*, or in Jaffeir's "How cursed is my condition" (3.2.212–17), which resembles more than one of Hamlet's soliloquies.

49. J. C. Ghosh, ed., *The Works of Thomas Otway* (Oxford: Clarendon Press, 1932), 2:101–2. This diatribe is likely to have been particularly heartfelt by Otway, who was also mustered out by parliamentary order and cast upon the town.

50. Cyrus Hoy, "Renaissance and Restoration Dramatic Plotting," *Renaissance Drama* 9 (1967): 251.

51. According to Warner (87–88), these scenes were cut from productions between 1718 and 1895.

Chapter 3: The Last of The Stuarts

1. James R. Jones, *Country and Court: England, 1658–1714* (Cambridge, Mass.: Harvard University Press, 1978), 79; hereafter cited in text.

2. John W. Yolton, "John Locke," in *The Age of William III and Mary*

II: *Power, Politics, and Patronage, 1688–1702*, ed. Robert P. Maccubbin and Martha Hamilton-Phillips (Williamsburg, Va.: College of William and Mary, 1989), 155; hereafter cited in text as Maccubbin.

3. See G. S. Rousseau, "Science and Medicine at Leiden," pp. 195–201 in Maccubbin.

4. This press was not totally uninhibited, to be sure. After the expiration of the second Licensing Act in 1695, the rival parties gave moral and financial encouragement, but only moderately effective legal protection, to their own journalists, occasional pamphleteers, publishers, and printers. The judges consistently interpreted the law of libel in a way that restricted free expression by making inaccuracies as well as reflections on the conduct of government punishable. But they could not prevent either the appearance of a continuous stream of polemical (and often virulently offensive) material or its circulation and sale (Jones, 41–42).

5. Maximillian E. Novak, *William Congreve* (New York: Twayne, 1971), 24–25; hereafter cited in text.

6. "As late as 1700 . . . no more than 2 percent of the population [of London] could have attended the theater in any given week [and] probably nothing like that number of different persons ever did attend" (Pedicord 1980, 237).

7. Harold Love, "Bear's Case Laid Open; or, a Timely Warning to Literary Sociologists" (*Komos* 2, no. 2 [n.d.]:74); as quoted in Pedicord 1980, 241.

8. See David Roberts, *The Ladies: Female Patronage of Restoration Drama, 1660–1700* (Oxford: Clarendon Press, 1989), 121–26; hereafter cited in text.

9. Lois G. Schwoerer, "The Queen as Regent and Patron," in Maccubbin, 223.

10. John Loftis, *Comedy and Society from Congreve to Fielding* (Stanford, Calif.: Stanford University Press, 1959), 15–16; hereafter cited in text as Loftis 1959.

11. "In the Carolean heyday of the 1670s twenty or more new plays were mounted each year. Following the union of 1682 the United Company operated conservatively, putting on only three or four new plays per year, and those by established authors who were following proven formulas. When competition resumed after the actors' rebellion of 1695, a flood of new plays (again more than twenty each year) was an immediate result" (Judith Milhous, *Thomas Betterton and the Management of Lincoln's Inn Fields, 1695–1708* [Carbondale: Southern Illinois University Press, 1979], ix; hereafter cited in text as Milhous 1979). The percentage of new plays produced in each season is also instructive on this point. Toward the end of the 1680s, the percentage of new plays begins to increase fairly steadily, from a low of 6 percent in 1686–87 to the high 20s,

but jumps significantly with the splitting off of the second company at Lincoln's Inn Fields in 1695–96. Percentages run between 30 and 50 percent of total repertory offerings until 1702–3 and 1703–4, when they drop again, remaining in the 6 to 18 percent range through 1714.

12. For example, in actions comparable to those of studio heads during the early 1930s when Hollywood switched from silent to sound films, Rich attempted to depose older, more expensive actors by assigning their usual roles in repertory plays to cheaper newcomers.

13. Milhous 1980, 3–4; see also chapter 3 of Milhous 1979.

14. To avoid undue outside influence or any recurrence of Rich's authoritarian rule, they chose to set up as a cooperative rather than sell shares, thus losing the potential infusion of cash that outsiders might have provided (Milhous 1979, 71).

15. *The Complete Plays of William Congreve*, ed. Herbert Davis (Chicago: University of Chicago Press, 1967); all Congreve references will be to this edition and cited in text in the form (act.scene.lines).

16. Although evidence suggests that *The Old Batchelor*, produced in March 1693, was actually written in 1689.

17. "Once established in the repertory, *Love for Love* became Congreve's greatest success in frequency of performance and in regularity of revivals throughout the eighteenth century" (Emmett L. Avery, introduction to *Love for Love* [Lincoln: University of Nebraska Press, 1966], xi). See also Emmett L. Avery, *Congreve's Plays on the Eighteenth-Century Stage* (New York: MLA Press, 1951); hereafter cited in text as Avery 1951.

18. Only four performances are recorded in *The London Stage* between 1693 and 1703, although Dryden commented on an initial run of eight performances. See also Hume 1976, 105.

19. "Purged of the aggression that his alter ego [Maskwell] now bears, Mellefont moves through the play as a perfect gentleman, a man perfectly in control of his sexual desires because they are not linked to an outsized desire to conquer. Indeed, Mellefont's apparent chastity may even lead us to question his relationship to the rake tradition" (Weber, 107–8).

20. Jeremy Collier's accusation that "there are but Four Ladies in this Play, and three of the biggest of them are Whores" is, although reductive, quite true. In a play like *The Country-Wife*, this is no particular indictment (although Collier, of course, would disagree), for 1670s comedies turned on assumptions about character that placed value on gamesmanship and shared desires, and established a compromise formation to finesse them.

21. For a good overview of the critical controversy over the play, see Judith Milhous and Robert D. Hume, *Producible Interpretation: Eight English*

Plays, 1675–1707 (Carbondale: Southern Illinois University Press, 1985), 260–74; hereafter cited in text.

22. Sir John Vanbrugh, *The Provoked Wife*, ed. Curt A. Zimansky (Lincoln: University of Nebraska Press, 1969), 5; textual quotations are to this edition in the form (act.scene.lines).

23. These are essentially their authors' only original plays. Vanbrugh's *The Pilgrim* (1700) and *The Confederacy* (1705), though listed among the most popular plays of this period, are, respectively, a revision of Fletcher and a close translation, not original plays. Cibber's *The Comical Rivals* (1707) borrows substantially from Dryden's *Secret Love* and *Marriage A-la-Mode*, while his *Love Makes a Man* (1700) is a combination of Fletcher's *The Elder Brother* and *The Custom of the Country.*

24. Thomas Davies, *Dramatic Miscellanies*, III, 441, quoted in Leonard R. N. Ashley, *Colley Cibber* (New York: Twayne, 1965), 40.

25. *Colley Cibber: Three Sentimental Comedies*, ed. Maureen Sullivan (New Haven, Conn.: Yale University Press, 1973), 83; all textual quotations are to this edition in the form (act.scene.lines).

26. And please them he did; the play was acted more than 200 times during Cibber's long lifetime.

27. These and other textual quotations are from Charles Stonehill, ed. *The Complete Works of George Farquhar*, 2 vols. (1930; reprint, New York: Gordian Press, 1967), and given in the form (act.scene.page). Volume 1 contains *Love and a Bottle, The Constant Couple, Sir Harry Wildair, The Inconstant,* and *The Twin-Rivals; volume 2 contains The Stage-Coach, The Recruiting Officer,* and *The Beaux Stratagem.*

28. Quoted in Harwood, 2. Harwood's section on Collier and his respondents (chap. 2) is useful and cogent. See also Joseph Wood Krutch, *Comedy and Conscience after the Restoration* (1924, 1949; reprint, New York: Russell & Russell, 1967); hereafter cited in text.

29. "Collier's attack was not the first launched against the stage during the reign of William and Mary. The court favored . . . a general reform; and all the new young writers—Addison, Steele, Swift, and Defoe—supported some kind of regulation of the stage. In defending themselves and their plays, the playwrights were swimming against the current of the times" (Novak, 58–59).

30. William A. Speck, "Religion, Politics, and Society in England," p. 53 in Maccubbin; hereafter cited the text.

31. For example, in May 1698, the Grand Jury of Middlesex attacked plays by Durfey, Vanbrugh, and Congreve, along with printers Tonson and Briscoe for publishing them (Novak, 61). In December 1700, that same body attempted to suppress the theaters entirely (Milhous 1979, 127). In January 1704,

Queen Anne ordered that playhouses refrain from acting "anything . . . not strictly agreeable to religion and good manners" (Krutch, 184).

32. Details about Farquhar's life can be found in volume 1 of Stonehill (xi–xxxiii) and chapter 1 of Eric Rothstein, *George Farquhar* (New York: Twayne, 1967), 13–29; hereafter cited in text as Rothstein 1967a.

33. John K. Sheriff, *The Good-Natured Man: The Evolution of a Moral Ideal, 1660–1800* (University: University of Alabama Press, 1982); hereafter cited in text.

34. Maximillian E. Novak, "Love, Scandal, and the Moral Milieu of Congreve's Comedies," pp. 23–50 in *Congreve Consider'd: Papers Read at a Clark Library Seminar, December 5, 1970,* foreword by H. T. Swedenberg (Los Angeles: UCLA Press, 1971), 43.

35. See Rothstein 1967a, 44–45, for an interesting discussion of the duel as a heroic and comic device and how Farquhar redefined it.

36. Farquhar's own words in his dedication of *The Recruiting Officer* to "All friends round the Wrekin [Shrewsbury]," show he was fully aware of doing "something different": "The Kingdom cannot shew better Bodies of Men, better Inclinations for the Service, more Generosity, more good Understanding, nor more Politeness than is to be found at the Foot of the *Wrekin.* Some little Turns of Humour that I met with almost within the Shade of that famous Hill, gave the rise to this Comedy; and People were apprehensive, that, by the Example of some others, I would make the Town merry at the expence of the Country Gentlemen: But they forgot that I was to write a Comedy, not a Libel; and that whilst I held to Nature, no Person of any Character in your Country could suffer by being expos'd. I have drawn the Justice and the Clown in their *Puris Naturalibus*; the one an apprehensive, sturdy, brave Blockhead; and the other a worthy, honest, generous Gentleman, hearty in his Country's Cause, and of as good an Understanding as I could give him, which I must confess is far short of his own" (Stonehill 2:41).

37. Husbands, respectively, in Cibber's *Love's Last Shift* (1696) and Vanbrugh's *The Relapse* (1696), Cibber's *The Careless Husband* (1704), and Vanbrugh's *The Provoked Wife* (1697).

38. At the time of the play, divorce was possible only at the instigation of the husband of an adulterous wife, and involved an elaborate process of separation through the ecclesiastical court, suing the adulterer for "criminal conversation" and applying to Parliament for permission for the injured husband to remarry. As Curt A. Zimansky points out, "No woman was granted a parliamentary divorce until the nineteenth century" (introduction to *The Provoked Wife* [Lincoln: University of Nebraska Press, 1969], xviii). Martin A. Larson demonstrates convincingly that the Sullens' grounds for divorce follow closely those outlined in John Milton's *Doctrine and Discipline of Divorce,* from which

Farquhar borrowed much of the wording in their indictments ("The Influence of Milton's Divorce Tracts on Farquhar's *Beaux' Stratagem*," *PMLA* 34 [1924], 174–78).

39. Lawrence Stone would say that the "companionate marriage" was beginning to gain some ideological weight among the populace; see *The Family, Sex, and Marriage in England, 1500–1800* (New York: Harper & Row, 1977), especially parts 4–5.

40. Milhous and Hume (307–8) disagree with this interpretation because it is "not easy to stage convincingly" and feel "the action of this play really has its origin and destination in London—and its values are London values."

41. Maximillian E. Novak and David Stuart Rodes, eds., *Thomas Southerne: "Oroonoko"* (Lincoln: University of Nebraska Press, 1976); textual quotations are from this edition in the form (act.scene.lines). The editors' introduction to the volume is hereafter cited in text as Novak and Rodes.

42. Harry William Pedicord, ed., *Nicholas Rowe: "Jane Shore"* (Lincoln: University of Nebraska Press, 1974); textual quotations are from this edition in the form (act.scene.lines).

43. See Rothstein 1967b, especially chapters 2 and 5, and Kirsch 1965, chapters 4 and 5.

44. Indeed, eighteenth-century audiences and critics found that the comic scenes so degraded the tragic that John Hawkesworth excised them from his 1759 revision of the play, which became Garrick's acting version. See Novak and Rodes, xix–xx.

45. About half of Behn's novel takes place earlier, in Africa and on board the Captain's vessel.

46. Another analogue is Juba in Addison's *Cato*.

47. It is also, like *Oroonoko*, based on another form of popular literature, in this case a familiar ballad.

48. The popularity of Rowe's play may well have been enhanced by its linkage with Colley Cibber's version of *Richard III*, a repertory favorite since 1699; Cibber played Richard in both versions.

49. One of the interesting complications and ironies in the play is that, of course, Richard kills Hastings and destroys Jane for quite his own reasons, and Alicia's letter, hence her guilt, is irrelevant.

50. The questionable legitimacy of his sons, used by Richard for his own ends, adds to the portrait of a king who satisfied his personal lust even at the expense of his people.

51. One can only imagine how such a speech would sound to an eighteenth-century audience composed of "wealthy cits."

52. "The heroic play, in the hands of authors from Dryden to Durfey, relishes *invraisemblance*. It deliberately molds itself around characters of vastly expanded autonomy, characters whose choices are true as their spirits are great, whose perfection tends to destroy their humanity and to crowd aside their world as anything but an adjunct to their grandeur" (Rothstein 1967b, 78).

53. *In Restoration Tragedy*, Rothstein, discussing Banks, gives him credit for producing a new staple, "the stupid hero," who "can only live, like Banks' women, in sad religiose patience, rejecting greatness, suffering betrayal as a sure anticipation of death." He concludes that "no one can be surprised to find the distinction between male and female characters, which is at the heart of the heroic play, almost obliterated in Banks" (1967b, 96). Later he says, more generally, "Pathetic tragedy gives women more independent humanity through a new depth of feeling, and transfers chastity and fidelity (if not beauty) to men as well" (131).

Chapter 4: The Hanoverian Accession to Garrick's

1. Soon after the turn of the century, curtain time moved from 5:00 P.M. to between 5:30 and 6:00 P.M., where it remained except for summer performances and some experiments at the smaller theaters with 7:00 P.M. (*LS*, 2:51).

2. The percentage of new to old plays, which ranged from a low of 8.5 percent in 1720–21 to a high of 18 percent in 1728–9 but mostly held steady at about 12 to 15 percent prior to 1729–30, never went below 20 percent in the eight years prior to the Licensing Act and mostly stayed in the 22 to 24 percent range; afterward, it went back to 12 to 13 percent.

3. For a full discussion of opera financing, see *LS*, 2:52–53, 68–70 and *LS*, 3:68–74.

4. For a full account of Steele's role, see John Loftis, *Steele at Drury Lane* (Berkeley: University of California Press, 1952); hereafter cited in text as Loftis 1952.

5. For a complete account of the patent/license issues, and the opening of the rival theaters, see chapters 1–2 of Robert D. Hume, *Henry Fielding and the London Theater, 1728–1737* (Oxford: Clarendon Press, 1988); hereafter cited in text as Hume 1988.

6. The two theaters had very different management policies and repertories; the Haymarket under Fielding was unstable and experimental, while Goodman's Fields was well managed by Henry Giffard and "archconservative" in its repertory (see Hume 1988, 148–49).

7. The situation is roughly analogous to that in a movie theater in the 1930s and 1940s, where a standard bill would include a newsreel, travelogue, and cartoon along with the featured films.

8. Allardyce Nicoll, A *History of English Drama, 1660–1900*, 6 vols., revised edition (Cambridge: Cambridge University Press, 1952–59), 2:253; hereafter cited in text as Nicoll 1952.

9. "Pantomime, Italian opera and ballad-opera must all be taken as displaying in marked form the disintegrating elements in the eighteenth century theater. The satires considered above show quite clearly the directions in which popular taste was moving. The old had been killed, and the new was but barely born. Everything conspired towards a weakening of the drama. Sentimentalism had worn out comedy; the elements making for true tragic productivity were absent; song had come from Italy and dancing from France; the spectators were artificial and affected, seeking always after novelty. Pantomime, ballad-operas, 'Hurlothrumbos' exactly suited their tastes" (Nicoll 1952, 2:258).

10. John Gay, *The Beggar's Opera*, ed. Edgar V. Roberts, music ed. Edward Smith (Lincoln: University of Nebraska Press, 1969); textual quotations are from this edition in the form (act.scene.lines). The editors' introduction to the volume is hereafter cited in text as Roberts and Smith.

11. Edward J. Dent, *Foundations of English Opera: A Study of Musical Drama in England during the Seventeenth Century*, intro. Michael M. Winesanker (1928; reprint, New York: Da Capo, 1965); hereafter cited in text.

12. "As soon as the theaters were placed on a firm footing, there was no more need to disguise plays under the title of 'amateur representations.' The majority of the public no doubt wanted plays, and not operas; moreover actors and actresses were more easily obtained than dramatic singers. D'Avenant himself evidently had a greater interest in plays than in music" (Dent, 97).

13. Dryden also wrote *Albion and Albinius* in 1685, with music by Louis Grabu, which Dent condemns as being too masquelike with inferior music, but whose relatively poor showing on the stage was probably more the result of poor timing, its two attempted premieres coinciding with the death of Charles II and with Monmouth's uprising.

14. Dent identifies only four plays in the remainder of the seventeenth century with enough music to be considered operas: *The Fairy Queen* (1692), *Bonduca* (1695), Purcell's revised *Tempest* (1695), and *The Indian Queen* (1695).

15. Sixty-two at Lincoln's Inn Fields during the regular season, 15 at the Haymarket during the summer.

16. *Polly, a Sequel* did even better. Although refused a license by the Lord Chamberlain's office for political reasons in December 1728, *Polly* was published, partly by subscription, and Gay realized between £1,000 and £3,000

from it (Patricia Meyer Spacks, *John Gay* [New York: Twayne, 1965], 160; hereafter cited in text).

17. In addition to the 491 performances between 1728 and 1747, it had 455 performances between 1747 and 1779.

18. Hume argues convincingly that this is not a revision at all, but simply *The Beggar's Bush* retitled (1976, 471n).

19. Ten other plays on the most popular list, some of them afterpieces, qualify as ballad operas.

20. William Eben Schultz, *Gay's "Beggar's Opera": Its Content, History, and Influence* (New York: Russell & Russell, 1923, 1967), 134; hereafter cited in text. See also Bertrand H. Bronson, "The Beggar's Opera," pp. 298–327 in *Restoration Drama: Modern Essays in Criticism*, ed. John Loftis (New York: Oxford University Press, 1966); hereafter cited in text as Bronson.

21. Schultz (285–306) counts 108 such imitations, all but two before 1747.

22. Yvonne Noble, "Introduction: *The Beggar's Opera* in Its Own Time," pp. 1–14 in *Twentieth Century Interpretations of "The Beggar's Opera": A Collection of Critical Essays*, ed. Yvonne Noble (Englewood Cliffs, N.J.: Prentice Hall, 1975), 14; hereafter cited in text.

23. "When you censure the age, / Be cautious and sage, / Lest the courtiers offended should be; / If you mention vice or bribe, / 'Tis so pat to all the tribe, / Each cries, 'That was leveled at me' " (2.10.21–26).

24. Henry Fielding, *Pasquin*, ed. O. M. Brack, Jr., William Kupersmith, and Curt A. Zimansky (Iowa City: University of Iowa Press, 1973).

25. Albert J. Rivero, *The Plays of Henry Fielding: A Critical Study of His Dramatic Career* (Charlottesville: University Press of Virginia, 1989); herafter cited in text.

26. See Hume 1988, 155–99, for an elaborate account of the actors' rebellion and Fielding's role in it; see also *LS*, 3:89–96.

27. Pat Rogers, *Henry Fielding: A Biography* (New York: Charles Scribner's Sons, 1979), 71; hereafter cited in text. See also Martin C. Battestin with Ruthe R. Battestin, *Henry Fielding: A Life* (London: Routledge, 1989).

28. Hume discusses Fielding's famed anti-Walpole sentiments, and convincingly dates them no earlier than 1734, if even then (1988, 115–18). See also Hume's discussion of *Pasquin*, 209–13.

29. Fielding's plays were, of course, only part of the larger picture: "Between the end of January and late May, approximately 100 performances of plays openly hostile to the ministry were staged at three of London's four theaters— an average of nearly one per night" (Hume 1988, 240).

30. Hume convincingly puts the case that the first of these careers was financed by a substantial bribe from Walpole himself (1988, 251–3).

31. His conventionally plotted afterpieces were a different story; *The Old Debauchees*, for example, was a hit, particularly when it was reprised during the troubles in 1745.

32. "A surprising number of critics have regarded this turn of events with complacency, content that Fielding should be rid of his theatrical entanglements and free to get on with *Tom Jones*. But the catastrophic effects of the Licensing Act upon the British theater are hardly a reasonable trade for the fiction of any one novelist" (Hume 1988, 253).

33. Both versions are printed together in the Nebraska edition of *The Author's Farce*, edited by Charles B. Woods and completed by Curt A. Zimansky after Woods's death (Lincoln: University of Nebraska Press, 1966); hereafter cited in text as Woods and Zimansky. Textual quotations are from this edition in the form (act.scene.lines).

34. In the earlier version, Bookweight is a relatively minor character who visits Luckless in act 1, while the opening scene of act 2 shows Luckless's encounter with Marplay (Colley Cibber) and Sparkish (Robert Wilks) at Drury Lane. Woods and Zimansky indicate that Curll was "notorious" in Fielding's day and that many of the details in the first two acts fit Curll's practices, but admit that "much of this satire is applicable to more than one publisher" (102–3).

35. See Woods and Zimansky, 45n and Appendix B.

36. Several sexual jokes spin off from this romantic duo; presumably Signior Opera, like Senesino, is a *castrato*, and Mrs. Novel now claims she died in childbirth, although earlier she identified herself as a virgin.

37. "The King of Bantam" is a running joke dating back to Jonson's *The Alchemist*, Bantam being an exotic place whose wealth tempts fools like Sir Epicure Mammon.

38. The two Kings of Brentford are characters in *The Rehearsal*, Buckingham's parody of heroic drama and *his* contemporary theater. The play had a long life on the late seventeenth- and eighteenth-century stage.

39. John Loftis, *Comedy and Society from Congreve to Fielding* (Stanford, Calif.: Stanford University Press, 1959), 127; hereafter cited in text as Loftis 1959. See also Ernest Bernbaum, *The Drama of Sensibility: A Sketch of the History of English Sentimental Comedy and Domestic Tragedy, 1696–1780* (1915; reprint, Gloucester, Mass.: Peter Smith, 1958); hereafter cited in text.

40. *The Provoked Husband* is a rewrite of Vanbrugh's incomplete manuscript; *The Woman's Revenge* is a revised version of Betterton's *The Revenge* (1680).

41. "Steele . . . praised *The Busy Body* in the *Tatler* and *The Wonder* in

the *Lover"* (*F. P. Lock, Susanna Centlivre* [Boston: Twayne, 1979], 93; hereafter cited the text).

42. Loftis also points out how different this practice is from that of the other major dramatists of the same period, Congreve, Vanbrugh, and Farquhar: "no attractive merchant character appears in any of their plays (except for one introduced briefly in *The Twin Rivals*). In some plays the merchants are ignored; in others they are the butt of casual but derisive jokes; and in still others they are ridiculed in dramatic caricatures, sometimes very harsh ones. At no time is there an implied acknowledgment of the importance of the merchant and of trade to the nation; on the contrary, there is a tone of contempt for the business community and for the prudential virtues associated with it, which is only occasionally lightened by irony" (1959, 49).

43. Susanna Centlivre, A *Bold Stroke for a Wife*, ed. Thalia Stathas (Lincoln: University of Nebraska Press, 1968); textual quotations are from this edition in the form (act.scene.lines).

44. *The Plays of Sir Richard Steele*, ed. Shirley Strum Kenny (Oxford: Clarendon Press, 1971), 275–382; textual quotations are from this edition in the form (act.scene.lines).

45. "The quality of *The Conscious Lovers* that was felt to be most original and that proved to be most controversial . . . was not the appeal to pathos but the employment of admirable characters providing models for conduct—notably Bevil Jr., the 'fine gentleman'—rather than the traditional witty yet debauched characters familiar in Restoration comedy" (Loftis 1952, 196). Sheriff features Bevil Jr. in his chapter entitled "The Good Natured Hero as Paragon," and suggests that such portrayals are an attempt to construct character out of theory.

46. It had 190 performances before 1747 and 174 more before 1779.

47. George Lillo, *The London Merchant*, ed. William H. McBurney (Lincoln: University of Nebraska Press, 1965); hereafter cited in text as McBurney. Textual quotations are from this edition in the form (act.scene.lines).

48. Henry Fielding, *"Tom Thumb" and "The Tragedy of Tragedies,"* ed. L. J. Morrissey (Berkeley: University of California Press, 1970), preface, lines 63–64. He was suggesting that, because such writers were inept, the audiences were succumbing to "Mirth and Laughter" (line 68).

49. Although Thorowgood admits, in an aside, that he is not impervious to her charms: "How should an unexperienced youth escape her snares? The powerful magic of her wit and form might betray the wisest to simple dotage, and fire the blood that age had froze long since. Even I, that with just prejudice came prepared, had by her artful story been deceived but that my strong conviction of her guilt makes even a doubt impossible" (4.16.79–85).

50. She also dies badly, as is related by Lucy after George is led out:

"She goes to death encompassed with horror, loathing life and yet afraid to die" (5.10.5–6). Interestingly, in the fifth edition of the play, Lillo printed a further scene showing Millwood and George on the gallows, a scene his friends convinced him to suppress for the acting version. (See McBurney, Appendix B, 83–85.)

51. Though one might also say that she has learned her sense of economic reciprocity from a mercantile society. In her lust for money and luxury, Millwood is both the antithesis and the perversion of the merchant ethos.

52. For a complete discussion of these events, see *LS*, 3:48–60, and Liesenfeld.

53. Samuel Foote, for example, gave "free" performances at noon but charged money for the accompanying dish of chocolate.

Chapter 5: The Age of Garrick

1. Pedicord 1954, 17; see also *LS*, 5:209–10, and Nicoll 1980, 8–9. This does not, of course, mean that 12,000 different people attended the theater in a given week; many attended more than once.

2. Quoted in John Pike Emery, *Arthur Murphy: An Eminent English Dramatist of the Eighteenth Century* (Philadelphia: University of Pennsylvania Press, 1946), 164; hereafter cited in text.

3. It was also flourishing outside of London; Nicoll points out that theaters were springing up throughout the kingdom, in the provinces as well as Scotland and Ireland, between 1740 and 1780 (1980, 61ff.).

4. Since George Colman the elder (1732–94) is the only George Colman active during this period, his son not becoming prominent until the 1780s, I will hereafter drop the tag.

5. "Fielding in the 1730s and Foote in the 1750s and '60s, finding welcome freedom from convention in the afterpiece, developed the *short* dramatic satire into a potent weapon, simultaneously amusing and trenchant" (Richard W. Bevis, ed., *Eighteenth Century Drama: Afterpieces* [London: Oxford University Press, 1970], x–xi; hereafter cited in text as Bevis 1970).

6. Simon Trefman, *Sam. Foote, Comedian, 1720–1777* (New York: New York University Press, 1971), viii; hereafter cited in text.

7. He also mocked his own disability by playing Zachary Fungus, the social climber of *The Commissary* (1765), learning to ride a hobbyhorse.

8. In Bevis 1970, 135–61; hereafter cited in text in the form (scene.lines).

9. These and other textual quotations are from Richard Brinsley Sheri-

dan, *The Dramatic Works of Richard Brinsley Sheridan*, 2 vols., ed. Cecil Price (Oxford: Clarendon Press, 1973), 1.195–283. Volume 1 contains *The Rivals*, *St. Patrick's Day*, *The Duenna*, *The School for Scandal*; volume 2 contains *The Critic*, *A Trip to Scarborough*, *Pizarro*, *The Camp*, and *The Glorious First of June*. Further references to *The Duenna* are hereafter cited in text in the form (act.scene.lines); other material will be cited in text as *Dramatic Works*, volume: page.

10. David Garrick, *The Plays of David Garrick*, ed. Harry William Pedicord and Fredrick Louis Bergmann (Carbondale: Southern Illinois University Press, 1980), 2:97–126; hereafter cited in text in the form (part.scene.lines).

11. Samuel Foote, *The Dramatic Works of Samuel Foote, Esq.; to Which Is Prefixed a Life of the Author* (1809; reprint, New York: Benjamin Blom, 1968), 2:1.1, p. 13.

12. Another instance is another military man, the Major in Colman's *The Jealous Wife*.

13. "Foote's satirical targets were prominent persons or types of persons— the Methodist George Whitefield[;] the actor and father of Richard Brinsley Sheridan, Thomas Sheridan[;] financial profiteers who had made fortunes during the Seven Years War—not the institutions of society nor governmental policy. An acerbity in caricature of individuals was not in his case, at least not overtly, inconsistent with the social conservatism of drama in mid-century. Yet the pungent bite of his plays, characteristically short pieces of two or three acts, reminds us that not all drama of the Garrick era was bland" (Loftis 1980, 277).

14. "The distinction between the terms ballad opera, ballad farce, and burletta seem, even in the middle of the century, not to have been very clear-cut" (*LS*, 4:147), although by the end of the century, when "burletta theaters" were licensed, burlettas were defined as having no speaking parts.

15. "No dramatic piece has ever received greater countenance from Royalty than the *Duenna* has. Her Majesty after the first time of seeing it, ordered a copy of the music with the harpsichord part, to be made out for her by Mr. Simpson, and the instance of their commanding it twice successively is unprecedented" (*Morning Chronicle*, 16 December 1775; quoted in *Dramatic Works*, 1:211).

16. Other contributors included Thomas Linley, Jr., Jackson of Exeter, Michael Arne, Rauzzini, and William Hayes; see *Dramatic Works*, 1:217.

17. Martha Winburn England, *Garrick's Jubilee* (Columbus: Ohio State University Press, 1964), 4; hereafter cited in text.

18. Jean I. Marsden, "The Individual Reader and the Canonized Text: Shakespeare Criticism after Johnson," *Eighteenth Century Life*, 17, n.s., no. 1 (February 1993): 63; hereafter cited in text.

19. The procession was a popular eighteenth-century addition to certain repertory plays, and Hughes dates the phenomenon to the 1727 production of *Henry VIII* at Drury Lane (1971, 113ff.).

20. See also Jonathan Bate, *Shakespearean Constitutions: Politics, Theater, Criticism, 1730–1830* (Oxford: Clarendon Press, 1989), and Michael Dobson, *Authorizing Shakespeare: Adaptation and Canonization, 1660–1769* (Oxford: Clarendon Press, 1992).

21. Edward Moore, *The Gamester*, ed. Charles H. Peake (New York: The Augustan Reprint Society, pub. no. 14, 1948), 419–20; textual quotations are from this edition and given in the form (act.scene.page); other material is hereafter cited in text as Peake.

22. Howard's *Romeo and Juliet* had a happy ending and was played on alternate nights with the original version, according to John Downes, the Duke's Company prompter; Tate's *King Lear* also had a happy ending, with Cordelia and Edgar inheriting Lear's kingdom. See Hazelton Spencer, *Shakespeare Improved* (1927; reprint, New York: Frederick Ungar, 1963), 73–74, 241–49.

23. Peake (1–7) mentions particularly Aaron Hill's *Fatal Extravagance* (1721) as a source of *The Gamester*. But Hill's play had only 22 performances, and as in Lillo's *London Merchant*, its hero's degradation includes committing murder.

24. Not surprisingly, What is a woman? is not considered equally important, and is only implied in characters like Mrs. Beverley and Charlotte.

25. Later in the play, Jarvis tells Mrs. Beverley and Charlotte the happy news about their elderly relative's death and their inheritance by announcing, "My good master will be a man again" (5.3.488).

26. Peake points out that one of Saurin's French versions of the play had a happy ending.

27. Richard Cumberland, *The Plays of Richard Cumberland*, ed. Roberta F. S. Borkat (New York: Garland Publishing, 1982), 1:n.p.. Textual quotations are from this edition and given in the form (act.scene.page).

28. This theme also figures prominently in Hoadly's *The Suspicious Husband*, still very popular in the repertory.

29. *The Jealous Wife*, pp. 57–110 in *Plays by David Garrick and George Colman the Elder*, ed. E. R. Wood (Cambridge: Cambridge University Press, 1982), 58; hereafter cited in text in the form (act.scene.page).

30. Belcour clearly subscribes to the eighteenth-century belief that climate affects the psyche.

31. Oliver Goldsmith, "An Essay on the Theatre," in *Collected Works of Oliver Goldsmith*, ed. Arthur Friedman (Oxford: Clarendon Press, 1966),

3:209–13. Further references to the *Collected Works* are hereafter cited in text in the form (volume:pages).

32. Robert D. Hume, "Goldsmith and Sheridan and the Supposed Revolution of 'Laughing' against 'Sentimental' Comedy," in *The Rakish Stage: Studies in English Drama, 1660–1800* (Carbondale: Southern Illinois University Press, 1983), 312–55; hereafter cited in text as Hume 1983.

33. His conclusions, as he points out, are essentially shared by John Loftis in *Sheridan and the Drama of Georgian England* and Mark Auburn in *Sheridan's Comedies: Their Contexts and Achievements* (Hume 1983, 313n).

34. Ricardo Quintana, *Oliver Goldsmith: A Georgian Study* (New York: Macmillan, 1967), 142–43. A recent book on sentimental comedy has recourse to psychological, philosophical, and literary theory in trying to find a workable definition; see Frank H. Ellis, *Sentimental Comedy: Theory and Practice* (Cambridge: Cambridge University Press, 1991), 3–22.

35. Even *The Beggar's Opera* encourages its audience to empathize with and pity Macheath in a context in which he and Polly shine amid the rubble of the London underworld they inhabit.

36. *The Country-Wife* was revived briefly as an afterpiece by John Lee (1765) and as Garrick's *The Country Girl* (1766); *The Plain-Dealer* existed in a bowdlerized version by Isaac Bickerstaffe after 1765.

37. For a complete discussion, see chapter 6 of Avery 1951.

38. Sheridan, *Dramatic Works*, 1:351–443; further references to *The School for Scandal* are hereafter cited in text in the form (act.scene.page.lines).

39. Goldsmith, *Collected Works*, 5:87–217; further references to *She Stoops to Conquer* are hereafter cited in text in the form (act.scene.page.lines).

40. Sheridan produced the second version of *The Rivals* after 11 days' withdrawal of the first version from the stage in January 1775. For a full discussion, see *Dramatic Works*, 1:40–41ff.; Auburn, 32–33; and Loftis 1977, 59–61.

41. Indeed, contemporary critics most often referred to Congreve in their praise of this play: "The style of Congreve was again brought into fashion; and sentiment made way for wit, and delicate humour. That piece has indeed the beauties of Congreve's comedies, without their faults" (Robert Heron [John Pinkerton], *The Universal Magazine*, 1785; quoted in *Dramatic Works*, 1:322–23).

42. In the casting of the play from the superlative Drury Lane company, the prime female role went to Frances Abington as Lady Teazle, whereas the role of Maria ultimately went to the relatively unknown Priscilla Hopkins (see *Dramatic Works*, 1:304–5, 312).

43. I disagree, for example, with Mark Auburn's sympathy for Joseph Surface: "Joseph earns respect because he is the most intelligent character in the

play. Like the heroes of classical punitive comedy of exposure, his force of mind elevates him far above the pedestrian intellects of the other characters. Never, even in his most embarrassing exposures, is the 'man of Sentiment' at a loss. . . . Because his mind can be respected, even if his values are rejected, it is a disappointment that his attractive cleverness has to be defeated at last, and that the manner of his defeat involves circumstances over which he has no control" (109–10).

44. One of her first lines is "Wit loses its respect with me when I see it in company with malice" (1.1.364.5–6), and later she elaborates, "[I]f to raise malicious smiles at the infirmities and misfortunes—of those who have never injured us be the province of wit or Humour Heav'n grant me a double Portion of Dullness—" (2.2.382.34–5, 383.1–2).

45. See Congreve's famous statement from the preface to *The Way of the World* that he intends to cease writing for the stage because audiences could not "distinguish betwixt the charactor of a Witwoud and a Truewit" (quoted in Auburn, 140).

Chapter 6: Conclusion

1. In talking about the novel, Sheldon Sacks coins the phrase "serious actions" to define such works, in which "the final stabilization of relationships may result either happily or unhappily for the characters with whom we are most in sympathy" (*Fiction and the Shape of Belief: A Study of Henry Fielding, with Glances at Swift, Johnson, and Richardson* [Berkeley: University of California Press, 1966], 22).

2. V. C. Clinton-Baddeley, *The Burlesque Tradition in the English Theater after 1660* (London: Methuen, 1952); hereafter cited in text.

3. See Phyllis T. Dircks, "London's Stepchild Finds a Home," in *Musical Theater in America: Papers and Proceedings of the Conference on the Musical Theater in America*, ed. Glenn Loney (Westport, Conn.: Greenwood Press, 1984), 23–35.

4. Harriet Hawkins, *Classics and Trash: Traditions and Taboos in High Literature and Popular Modern Genres* (Toronto: University of Toronto Press, 1990), xiv.

selected bibliography

PRIMARY SOURCES

Behn, Aphra. *The Works of Aphra Behn*. 6 vols. Edited by Montague Summers. 1915. Reprint. New York: Phaeton Press, 1967. The standard edition; old-spelling texts.

Bell's British Theatre, Selected Plays 1791–1802, 1797: Forty-Nine Plays Unrepresented in Editions of 1776–1781 and 1784. 16 vols. Preface by Byrne R. S. Fone. New York: AMS Press, 1977. A valuable source for a number of otherwise unobtainable plays.

Bevis, Richard W., ed. and intro. *Eighteenth Century Drama: Afterpieces*. London: Oxford University Press, 1970. Useful resource for eight representative afterpieces from 1737 to 1765.

Centlivre, Susanna. *A Bold Stroke for a Wife*. Edited and with an introduction by Thalia Stathas. Lincoln: University of Nebraska Press, 1968. A good modern-spelling text, with a useful introduction.

———. *The Busie Body*. Introduction by Jess Byrd. The Augustan Reprint

Society, publication no. 19. Los Angeles: UCLA, 1949. A facsimile of the first edition.

———. *The Dramatic Works of the Celebrated Mrs. Centlivre, with a New Account of Her Life.* 3 vols. 1872. Reprint. New York: AMS Press, 1969. The only complete edition at present.

Cibber, Colley. *An Apology for the Life of Colley Cibber, with an Historical View of the Stage during His Own Time.* 1740. Reprint. Edited and with an introduction by B. R. S. Fone. Ann Arbor: University of Michigan Press, 1968. An important and lively, though not always reliable, resource.

———. *Colley Cibber: Three Sentimental Comedies.* Edited and with an introduction by Maureen Sullivan. New Haven, Conn.: Yale University Press, 1973. A useful old-spelling edition of *Love's Last Shift, The Careless Husband,* and *The Lady's Last Stake.*

Colman, George. *The Plays of George Colman the Elder.* 6 vols. Edited and with an introduction by Kalman A. Burnim. New York: Garland Publishing, 1983. Part of Garland's facsimile series in eighteenth-century English drama.

Congreve, William. *The Complete Plays of William Congreve.* Edited by Herbert Davis. Chicago: University of Chicago Press, 1967. Complete old-spelling texts of Congreve's five plays from the first editions as played onstage at the time, not the 1710 folio, with brief introductions and notes, in a readable format.

———. *Love for Love.* Edited by Emmett L. Avery. Lincoln: University of Nebraska Press, 1966. A well-edited modern-spelling edition.

Cumberland, Richard. *Memoirs of Richard Cumberland, London, 1806.* Edited by Henry Flanders. 1856. Reprint. New York: Benjamin Blom, 1969. Useful for Cumberland's commentaries on his own plays and the theater of his time.

———. *The Plays of Richard Cumberland.* 6 vols. Edited and with an introduction by Roberta F. S. Borkat. New York: Garland Press, 1982. A facsimile reprint edition.

Dryden, John. *Literary Criticism of John Dryden.* Edited by Arthur C. Kirsch. Lincoln: University of Nebraska Press, 1966. A handy modern-spelling edition of Dryden's major critical works from 1668 to 1700.

———. *The Works of John Dryden.* 20 vols. General editors H. T. Swedenberg, Jr., Vinton A. Dearing, et al. Berkeley: University of California Press, 1956–92. This multivolume work is the best available source of Dryden's plays and other works available, with comprehensive introductions, notes, and carefully researched texts.

Etherege, Sir George. *The Plays of Sir George Etherege.* Edited by Michael

Cordner. Cambridge: Cambridge University Press, 1982. The best and most recent edition.

————. *The Works of Sir George Etherege.* 2 vols. Edited and with an introduction by H. F. B. Brett-Smith. Oxford: Basil Blackwell, 1927. Until recently, the only available edition.

Farquhar, George. *The Complete Works of George Farquhar.* 2 vols. Edited by George Stonehill. 1930. Reprint. New York: Gordian Press, 1967. The standard edition for nondramatic works; old-spelling texts.

————. *The Works of George Farquhar.* 2 vols. Edited by Shirley Strum Kenny. Oxford: Clarendon Press, 1986. The best edition for the plays.

Fielding, Henry. *The Author's Farce.* Edited by Charles B. Woods. Lincoln: University of Nebraska Press, 1966. A modern-spelling edition, containing both the 1730 and 1734 versions of the play, along with indexes of the individuals parodied in the play and its music.

————. *"The Historical Register for the Year 1736" and "Eurydice Hissed."* Edited by William W. Appleton. Lincoln: University of Nebraska Press, 1967. A modern-spelling version of the two plays.

————. *The Old Debauchees. A Comedy.* Introduction by Connie Capers Thorson. William Andrews Clark Memorial Library, publication no. 258. Los Angeles: UCLA, 1989. A facsimile reprint of the 1732 edition.

————. *Pasquin.* Edited by O. M. Brack, Jr., William Kupersmith, and Curt A. Zimansky. Iowa City: University of Iowa Press, 1973. An old-spelling edition.

————. *"Tom Thumb" and "The Tragedy of Tragedies."* Edited by L. J. Morrissey. Berkeley: University of California Press, 1970. Old-spelling edition of the two plays.

Foote, Samuel. *The Dramatic Works of Samuel Foote, Esq.; to Which Is Prefixed a Life of the Author.* 2 vols. 1809. Reprint. New York: Benjamin Blom, 1968. A useful edition of Foote's plays.

————. *The Plays of Samuel Foote.* 3 vols. Edited by Paula R. Backscheider and Douglas Howard. New York: Garland Publishing, 1983. A facsimile reprint edition.

Garrick, David. *The Plays of David Garrick: A Complete Collection of the Social Satires, French Adaptations, Pantomimes, Christmas and Musical Plays, Preludes, Interludes, and Burlesques, to Which Are Added the Alterations and Adaptations of the Plays of Shakespeare and Other Dramatists from the Sixteenth to the Eighteenth Centuries.* 4 vols. Edited by Harry William Pedicord and Frederick Louis Bergmann. Carbondale: Southern Illinois University Press, 1980. The definitive edition of Garrick's plays, with spelling "conservatively modernized."

————, and George Colman the Elder. *Plays.* Edited and with an introduction by E. R. Wood. Cambridge: Cambridge University Press, 1982. A handy text of five plays: *The Lying Valet, The Jealous Wife, The Clandestine Marriage, The Irish Widow,* and *Bon Ton.*

Gay, John. *The Beggar's Opera.* Edited by Edgar V. Roberts. Music edited by Edward Smith. Lincoln: University of Nebraska Press, 1969. A useful edition of the play, containing not only a well-edited play text but also its music in the appendix. Has a good, though brief, introduction.

Goldsmith, Oliver. *Collected Works of Oliver Goldsmith.* 5 vols. Edited by Arthur Friedman. Oxford: Clarendon Press, 1966. A definitive old-spelling edition.

Lee, Nathaniel. *Works.* 2 vols. Edited and with an introduction by Thomas B. Stroup and Arthur L. Cooke. New Brunswick, N.J.: Scarecrow Press, 1954. The collected edition of the plays.

Lillo, George. *The London Merchant.* Edited by William H. McBurney. Lincoln: University of Nebraska Press, 1965. A handy new-spelling edition, well edited.

Moore, Edward. *The Gamester.* Introduction by Charles H. Peake. Bibliographic note by Philip R. Wikelund. Los Angeles: The Augustan Reprint Society, series 5, no. 1. 1948. A facsimile reprint with a useful introduction.

Murphy, Arthur. *"The Way to Keep Him" and Five Other Plays.* Edited by John Pike Emery. New York: New York University Press, 1956. Includes texts of six Murphy plays in handy format with notes.

Otway, Thomas. *Venice Preserved.* Edited by Malcolm Kelsall. Lincoln: University of Nebraska Press, 1969. A useful new-spelling version.

———. *The Works of Thomas Otway.* 2 vols. Edited by J. C. Ghosh. Oxford: Clarendon Press, 1932. The standard edition.

Pepys, Samuel. *The Diary of Samuel Pepys.* 9 vols. Edited by Robert Latham and William Matthews. Berkeley: University of California Press, 1970. An invaluable resource on the early Carolean period.

Rowe, Nicholas. *Jane Shore.* Edited by Harry William Pedicord. Lincoln: University of Nebraska Press, 1974. Useful new-spelling edition.

Shadwell, Thomas. *The Complete Works of Thomas Shadwell.* 5 vols. Edited by Montague Summers. 1927. Reprint. New York: Benjamin Blom, 1968. The standard edition.

Sheridan, Richard Brinsley. *The Dramatic Works of Richard Brinsley Sheridan.* 2 vols. Edited by Cecil Price. Oxford: Clarendon Press, 1973. The definitive edition, with valuable critical commentary from the period.

Southerne, Thomas. *Oroonoko.* Edited by Maximillian E. Novak and David Stuart Rodes. Lincoln: University of Nebraska Press, 1976. A useful modern-spelling edition.

———. *The Works of Thomas Southerne.* 2 vols. Edited by Robert Jordan and

Harold Love. Oxford: Clarendon Press, 1988. The definitive edition of the plays.

Steele, Sir Richard. *The Plays of Richard Steele.* Edited by Shirley Strum Kenny. Oxford: Clarendon Press, 1971. An old-spelling edition, with useful introductions and notes; definitive.

Thurber, Carryl Nelson. *Sir Robert Howard's Comedy "The Committee."* Urbana: University of Illinois Studies in Language and Literature, no. 7, February 1921. A good edition of the play, with notes and commentary.

Trussler, Simon, ed. and intro. *Burlesque Plays of the Eighteenth Century.* London: Oxford University Press, 1969. A good source for 10 burlesque plays from *The Rehearsal* (1671) to *Bombastes Furioso* (1810), including two each by John Gay and Henry Fielding.

Vanbrugh, John. *The Complete Works of Sir John Vanbrugh.* 4 vols. Edited and with an introduction by Bonamy Dobrée and Geoffrey Webb. 1927. Reprint. New York: AMS Press, 1967. The standard edition.

———. *The Provoked Wife.* Edited by Curt A. Zimansky. Lincoln: University of Nebraska Press, 1969. A handy modern-spelling edition.

———. *The Relapse.* Edited by Curt A. Zimansky. Lincoln: University of Nebraska Press, 1970. A useful modern-spelling edition.

Wycherley, William. *Complete Plays.* Edited and with an introduction by Gerald Weales. Garden City, New York: Anchor Books, 1966. A good, handy edition, available in paperback.

———. *The Plays of William Wycherley.* Edited by Arthur Friedman. Oxford: Clarendon Press, 1979. The standard edition.

SECONDARY SOURCES

Principal Secondary Sources

There are a number of good background sources available for the period covered by this study. For general histories of the period, see J. R. Jones, *Country and Court: England, 1658–1714* (Cambridge, Mass.: Harvard University Press, 1978), W. A. Speck, *Stability and Strife: England, 1714–1760* (Cambridge, Mass.: Harvard University Press, 1977), and Ian R. Christie, *Wars and Revolutions: Britain, 1760–1815* (Cambridge, Mass.: Harvard University Press, 1982). For social histories, see Donald Greene, *The Age of Exuberance: Backgrounds to Eighteenth-Century English Literature* (New York: Random House, 1970),

Roy Porter, *English Society in the Eighteenth Century* (Harmondsworth, England: Penguin, 1982), and Peter Earle, *The Making of the English Middle Class: Business, Society, and Family Life in London, 1660–1730* (Berkeley: University of California Press, 1989). The complete production history of the drama of this period is found in the five-part *The London Stage, 1660–1800: A Calendar of Plays, Entertainments, & Afterpieces, together with Casts, Box-Receipts, and Contemporary Comment Compiled from the Playbills, Newspapers, and Theatrical Diaries of the Period* (Carbondale: Southern Illinois University Press, 1960–68). This multivolume work is an invaluable tool, filled with performance records and other information basic for understanding the interactions and development of the repertory. The elaborate introductions to the chronological lists give an overview of the facts of production, company management, actors, and other changing circumstances that affected the theater, and were published separately in paperbacks in 1968 as *The London Stage: A Critical Introduction*. Earlier and less complete than *The London Stage* but still valuable is Allardyce Nicoll's *A History of English Drama, 1660–1900* (Cambridge: Cambridge University Press, 1923, 1965); volumes 1–3 deal with the drama from 1660 through the late eighteenth century; volume 6 contains a short-title catalog of plays. Good overall studies of the drama of the period are vol. 5 of the *Revels History of Drama in English: 1660–1750*, by John Loftis, Richard Southern, Marion Jones, and A. H. Scouten (London: Methuen, 1976), and the volume in the Longman Literature in English Series entitled *English Drama: Restoration and Eighteenth Century, 1660–1789*, by Richard W. Bevis (London: Longman, 1988). Biographies of playwrights are available in the *Dictionary of Literary Biography*, vols. 80, 84, and 89 (Detroit, Mich.: Gale Research, Inc., 1989), and of others connected with the theater in *A Biographical Dictionary of Actors, Actresses, Musicians, Dancers, Managers, and Other Stage Personnel in London, 1660–1800*, 16 vols., edited by Philip H. Highfill Jr., Kalman A. Burnim, and Edward A. Langhans (Carbondale: Southern Illinois University Press, 1973–93). Twayne's English Authors Series contains a number of books that provide a good first reference guide to major playwrights: Leonard R. N. Ashley, *Colley Cibber* (1965), Phyllis T. Dircks, *David Garrick* (1985), Clara M. Kirk, *Oliver Goldsmith* (1967), F. P. Lock, *Susanna Centlivre* (1979), Maximillian E. Novak, *William Congreve* (1971), Eric Rothstein, *George Farquhar* (1967), Patricia Meyer Spacks, *John Gay* (1965), and Kerstin P. Warner, *Thomas Otway* (1982).

Other Secondary Sources

Allen, Ned Bliss. *The Sources of John Dryden's Comedies*. 1935. Reprint. New York: Gordian Press, 1967. Useful discussion of Dryden's borrowings and translations.

Auburn, Mark S. *Sheridan's Comedies: Their Contexts and Achievements*. Lincoln: University of Nebraska Press, 1977. Discusses Sheridan's comedies in the context of other Georgian comedies.

Avery, Emmett L. *Congreve's Plays on the Eighteenth-Century Stage*. New York: MLA Press, 1951. A useful discussion of the popularity of Congreve during the eighteenth century.

Barbeau, Anne T. *The Intellectual Design of John Dryden's Heroic Plays*. New Haven, Conn.: Yale University Press, 1970. Approaches Dryden's plays as drama of ideas.

Bate, Jonathan. *Shakespearean Constitutions: Politics, Theatre, Criticism, 1730–1830*. Oxford: Clarendon Press, 1989. A study of how Shakespeare was "appropriated" by the age of George III, in the theater, in politics, and in popular culture.

Battestin, Martin C., with Ruthe R. Battestin. *Henry Fielding: A Life*. London: Routledge, 1989. The definitive biography of Fielding.

Bernbaum, Ernest. *The Drama of Sensibility: A Sketch of the History of English Sentimental Comedy and Domestic Tragedy, 1696–1780*. 1915. Reprint. Gloucester, Mass.: Peter Smith, 1958. A seminal work in the definition of sentimental comedy and tragedy, somewhat outdated.

Bevis, Richard W. *English Drama: Restoration and Eighteenth Century, 1660–1789*. London: Longman, 1989. Part of the Longman Literature in English Series; a useful and broad-based study.

———. *The Laughing Tradition: Stage Comedy in Garrick's Day*. Athens: University of Georgia Press, 1980. A fresh look at the comedy of the Garrick era that asks pertinent questions about sentimental and laughing comic forms.

Brown, Laura. *English Dramatic Form, 1660–1760: An Essay in Generic History*. New Haven, Conn.: Yale University Press, 1981. A useful discussion of the drama in terms of its literary and cultural contexts.

Canfield, J. Douglas. *Nicholas Rowe and Christian Tragedy*. Gainesville: University Presses of Florida, 1977. A provocative study.

Clinton-Baddeley, V. C. *The Burlesque Tradition in the English Theatre after 1660*. London: Methuen, 1952. A "review of critical laughter," showing the burlesque tradition's evolution over time.

Dent, Edward J. *Foundations of English Opera: A Study of Musical Drama in England during the Seventeenth Century*. 1928. Reprint. Introduction by Michael M. Winesanker. New York: Da Capo, 1965. Standard one-volume work on the subject by the acknowledged twentieth-century expert on English musicology. Embraces "all facets of the hydra-headed art form."

Dobson, Michael. *The Making of the National Poet: Shakespeare, Adaptation and Authorship, 1660–1769.* Oxford: Clarendon Press, 1992. A good discussion of the resurrection of Shakespeare after the Restoration and up to the Stratford Jubilee.

Donohue, Joseph W., Jr. *Dramatic Character in the English Romantic Age.* Princeton, N.J.: Princeton University Press, 1970. A valuable and thoughtful study.

Ellis, Frank H. *Sentimental Comedy: Theory and Practice.* Cambridge: Cambridge University Press, 1991. Along with a discussion of sentimental comedy, contains full texts of Whitehead's *The School for Lovers* (1762) and Inchbald's *Every One Has His Fault* (1793).

Emery, John Pike. *Arthur Murphy: An Eminent English Dramatist of the Eighteenth Century.* Philadelphia: University of Pennsylvania Press, 1946. A good critical biography of this prolific playwright/critic of the Garrick era.

Goodman, Jennifer R. *British Drama before 1660: A Critical History.* Boston: Twayne, 1991. The first volume in this series presents a thorough but succinct overview of the development of English drama from its earliest beginnings, along with a sense of the main critical controversies about it.

Harwood, John T. *Critics, Values, and Restoration Comedy.* Carbondale: Southern Illinois University Press, 1982. An excellent discussion of the long line of criticism of Carolean comedy.

Holland, Norman N. *The First Modern Comedies: The Significance of Etherege, Wycherley, and Congreve.* Bloomington: Indiana University Press, 1959. One of the first attempts to rescue Restoration comedies from charges of immorality and irrelevancy.

Holland, Peter. *The Ornament of Action: Text and Performance in Restoration Comedy.* Cambridge: Cambridge University Press, 1979. Discusses the intersection of theater and drama.

Hughes, Leo. *A Century of English Farce.* Princeton, N.J.: Princeton University Press, 1956. A good overview of how farce was transformed from its Italian and French origins onto the British stage.

―――. *The Drama's Patrons: A Study of the Eighteenth-Century London Audience.* Austin: University of Texas Press, 1971. A valuable assessment of audience behavior, taste, and constituency.

Hume, Robert D. *The Development of English Drama in the Late Seventeenth Century.* Oxford: Clarendon Press, 1976. An essential text for understanding the breadth of drama presented during the years 1660–1710. Hume has read and briefly analyzes hundreds of plays, fitting them into an overall view of how drama changed over time and in reaction to various external and internal forces.

―――. *Henry Fielding and the London Theatre: 1728–1737*. Oxford: Clarendon Press, 1988. A fine study of the theatrical context within which Fielding operated and his contributions to the stage.

―――, ed. *The London Theatre World, 1660–1800*. Carbondale: Southern Illinois University Press, 1980. A lively and comprehensive collection, with contributions by many of today's leading scholars in the field of late seventeenth- and eighteenth-century theater and drama.

―――. *The Rakish Stage: Studies in English Drama, 1660–1800*. Carbondale: Southern Illinois University Press, 1983. A collection of Hume's own writings on Restoration and eighteenth-century drama, most of them published previously elsewhere between 1972 and 1980.

Jose, Nicholas. *Ideas of the Restoration in English Literature, 1660–71*. Cambridge, Mass.: Harvard University Press, 1984. An interesting discussion of the intersection of ideology, mythmaking, and literature.

Kirsch, Arthur C. *Dryden's Heroic Drama*. New York: Gordian Press, 1972. An excellent discussion of Dryden's theory and practice of heroic drama, as well as those of his fellow dramatists.

Krutch, Joseph Wood. *Comedy and Conscience after the Restoration*. 1924, 1949. Reprint. New York: Russell & Russell, 1967. An important early study of Restoration and early eighteenth-century comedy, focused on the Collier Controversy and its effects.

Leacroft, Richard. *The Development of the English Playhouse*. Ithaca, N.Y.: Cornell University Press, 1973. A comprehensive and well-illustrated history of the development of the theater, including machines, from the medieval period to the present. As architect and scene designer, Leacroft provides solid commentary on the practical and social implications of changes in the physical stage and theater building.

Liesenfeld, Vincent J. *The Licensing Act of 1737*. Madison: University of Wisconsin Press, 1984. A thorough discussion of the act and its context; the index contains the actual documents.

Loftis, John. *Comedy and Society from Congreve to Fielding*. Stanford, Calif.: Stanford University Press, 1959. An excellent discussion of the changes in society and their effect on the stage during the late Stuart and early Hanoverian reigns.

―――. *The Politics of Drama in Augustan England*. Oxford: Clarendon Press, 1963. A good discussion of the intersection of politics and drama up to the Licensing Act of 1737.

―――, ed. *Restoration Drama: Modern Essays in Criticism*. New York: Oxford

University Press, 1966. A good collection, containing Bertrand Bronson's essay on *The Beggar's Opera* and Alan Downer's essay on acting styles.

———. *Sheridan and the Drama of Georgian England.* Cambridge, Mass.: Harvard University Press, 1977. A useful discussion of Sheridan's plays in the context of the times.

———. *The Spanish Plays of Neoclassical England.* New Haven, Conn.: Yale University Press, 1973. A thorough, groundbreaking work on the influence of Spanish drama, particularly on the Carolean theater.

———. *Steele at Drury Lane.* Berkeley: University of California Press, 1952. Highlights Steele's role as a critic and dramatist who sought to reform the stage; also contains complete coverage of his managerial role.

Love, Harold, ed. *Restoration Literature: Critical Approaches.* London: Methuen, 1972. A useful collection of essays.

Maccubbin, Robert P., and Martha Hamilton-Phillips, eds. *The Age of William III & Mary II: Power, Politics, and Patronage, 1688–1702. A Reference Encyclopedia and Exhibition Catalogue.* Williamsburg, Va.: College of William and Mary, 1989. Taken from an exhibition held at the Grolier Club and the Folger Shakespeare Library December 1988–April 1989, this heavily illustrated collection of essays on various aspects of life and art during the period is a valuable introduction.

Markley, Robert. *Two-Edg'd Weapons: Style and Ideology in the Comedies of Etherege, Wycherley, and Congreve.* Oxford: Clarendon Press, 1988. A postmodern analysis of the use of language in the plays of the three dramatists, incorporating Marxist, feminist, and semiotics perspectives.

Milhous, Judith. *Thomas Betterton and the Management of Lincoln's Inn Fields: 1695–1708.* Carbondale: Southern Illinois University Press, 1979. An excellent study of the crucial 13 years between the splitting of the two theaters in 1695 and Betterton's death, using copious original source material to correct a number of assumptions about theatrical development during this time.

———, and Robert D. Hume. *Producible Interpretations: Eight English Plays, 1675–1707.* Carbondale: Southern Illinois University Press, 1985. A truly original approach to eight plays that have been the source of much critical controversy. Milhous and Hume ask what interpretations would be "producible" on stage and what are merely closet interpretations.

Moore, Frank Harper. *The Nobler Pleasure: Dryden's Comedy in Theory and Practice.* Chapel Hill: University of North Carolina Press, 1963. A good discussion of Dryden's comedies.

Nicoll, Allardyce. *The Garrick Stage: Theatres and Audiences in the Eighteenth Century.* Edited by Sybil Rosenfeld. Athens: University of Georgia Press,

1980. A copiously illustrated introduction to Garrick and the theater of his time.

Noble, Yvonne, ed. and intro. *Twentieth Century Interpretations of "The Beggar's Opera": A Collection of Critical Essays.* Englewood Cliffs, N.J: Prentice Hall, 1975. A good collection of essays and excerpts, particularly the introductory piece by Noble herself.

Pedicord, Harry William. *The Theatrical Public in the Time of Garrick.* Carbondale: Southern Illinois University Press, 1954. A detailed and informed discussion of late eighteenth-century audiences, with appendices on attendance, receipts, and the repertory.

Quintana, Ricardo. *Oliver Goldsmith: A Georgian Study.* New York: Macmillan, 1967. Continues to be one of the best overall analyses of Goldsmith and his times.

Rivero, Albert J. *The Plays of Henry Fielding: A Critical Study of His Dramatic Career.* Charlottesville: University Press of Virginia, 1989. An excellent critical study of Fielding's drama in its own right, not as a stepping-stone to the novels.

Roberts, David. *The Ladies: Female Patronage of Restoration Drama, 1660–1700.* Oxford: Clarendon Press, 1989. A recent study that seeks to answer questions about the impact of contemporary women on the repertory during the late seventeenth century.

Rogers, Pat. *Henry Fielding: A Biography.* New York: Charles Scribner's Sons, 1979. A lively and well-illustrated view of Fielding's life and works.

Rothstein, Eric. *Restoration Tragedy: Form and the Process of Change.* Westport, Conn.: Greenwood, 1967, 1978. Still one of the best and most comprehensive studies of the change and development in tragic form and content from 1660 to 1700.

———, and Frances M. Kavenik. *The Designs of Carolean Comedy.* Carbondale: Southern Illinois University Press, 1988. Offers a comprehensive theoretical and pragmatic analysis of the nature of comic development from 1660 to 1685, with appropriate integration of audiences' needs with playwrights' and managers' willingness to please their customers. Uses Dryden's plays as a bridge and exemplar of various stages of comic development.

Sacks, Sheldon. *Fiction and the Shape of Belief: A Study of Henry Fielding, with Glances at Swift, Johnson, and Richardson.* Berkeley: University of California Press, 1964. Asks how Fielding's work, and fiction in general, embodies belief. An excellent and provocative work.

Schofield, Mary Anne, and Cecilia Macheski. *Curtain Calls: British and American Women and the Theatre, 1660–1820.* Athens: Ohio University Press, 1991. A good collection of essays on women dramatists, actors, and critics.

Schultz, William Eben. *Gay's "Beggar's Opera": Its Content, History, & Influence.* 1923. Reprint. New York: Russell & Russell, 1967. Covers a good deal of the contemporary reception and commentary on *The Beggar's Opera*, including material from periodicals, letters, journals, and pamphlets.

Sheriff, John K. *The Good-Natured Man: The Evolution of a Moral Ideal, 1660–1800.* University: University of Alabama Press, 1982. An excellent study of this philosophical and literary concept and its effects on the novel, poetry, and drama.

Smith, John Harrington. *The Gay Couple in Restoration Comedy.* Cambridge: Harvard University Press, 1948. An early but still provocative study of the conventional witty couple of Carolean comedy.

Spencer, Hazelton. *Shakespeare Improved: The Restoration Versions in Quarto and on the Stage.* 1927. Reprint. New York: Frederick Ungar, 1963. A useful synthesis of the versions and variations of Shakespeare staged between 1660 and 1710.

Spingarn, Joel E. *Critical Essays of the Seventeenth Century, Vol. II: 1650–1685.* Bloomington: Indiana University Press, 1957. A handy source for the important critical works of the period, including Dryden and Rymer.

Sprague, Arthur Colby. *Beaumont and Fletcher on the Restoration Stage.* 1926, 1954. Reprint. New York: Benjamin Blom, 1965. Covers the revivals and adaptations of Beaumont and Fletcher's plays from 1660 to 1710.

Staves, Susan. *Players' Scepters: Fictions of Authority in the Restoration.* Lincoln: University of Nebraska Press, 1979. An excellent study of the legal and literary changes in attitudes toward authority.

Stone, George Winchester, Jr., and George M. Kahrl. *David Garrick: A Critical Biography.* Carbondale: Southern Illinois University Press, 1979. The definitive biography of this important figure.

Swedenberg, H. T., Jr. *The Theory of the Epic in England, 1650–1800.* Berkeley: University of California Press, 1944. A useful resource for study of heroic drama.

Trefman, Simon. *Sam. Foote, Comedian, 1720–1777.* New York: New York University Press, 1971. An interesting critical biography of this figure from the "alternative theater" of the Garrick era.

Wadsworth, Philip A. *Molière and the Italian Theatrical Tradition.* Birmingham, Ala.: Summa Publications, 1977. A valuable discussion of Molière's theatrical connection to the commedia dell'arte.

Waith, Eugene M. *The Herculean Hero in Marlowe, Chapman, Shakespeare, and Dryden.* New York: Columbia University Press, 1962. Discusses the concept of the heroic hero and its roots in the older drama.

————. *The Pattern of Tragicomedy in Beaumont and Fletcher*. New Haven, Conn.: Yale University Press, 1952. An essential source and definition of the plays of Beaumont and Fletcher that formed the basis of Carolean drama.

Watson, George, ed. *John Dryden: Of Dramatic Poesy and Other Critical Essays*. *Vol. I*. London: J. M. Dent & Sons, 1962. A handy source for Dryden's critical writings.

Weber, Harold M. *The Restoration Rake-Hero: Transformations in Sexual Understanding in Seventeenth-Century England*. Madison: University of Wisconsin Press, 1986. A good discussion of the rake, male and female, as a focus of attention and value in Restoration and eighteenth-century drama.

Wilcox, John. *The Relation of Molière to Restoration Comedy*. New York: Columbia University Press, 1938. Continues to be a valuable explication of the connection between specific plays by Molière and their English versions and translations.

Wilson, John Harold. *All the King's Ladies: Actresses of the Restoration*. Chicago: University of Chicago Press, 1958. An early but still important survey of actresses during the first 30 years after the Restoration.

Zimbardo, Rose. *Wycherley's Drama: A Link in the Development of English Satire*. New Haven, Conn.: Yale University Press, 1965. An early and important study.

index

Abington, Frances, 248n42

Abra Mule. See Trapp, Joseph

Acis and Galatea. See Motteux, Peter Anthony

Actors' rebellion of 1733, 131, 242n26

Actors/acting styles, 16–19, 202. *See also* Female actors

Addison, Joseph, 66–67; *Cato*, 72–101, 111, 119, 163, 201–2, 239n46; *Drummer, The*, 119, 163; *Rosamond*, 123

Address to Persons of Fashion concerning Some Particulars relating to Balls, with Hints on Plays, Card Tables, Etc., 23

Adventures of Five Hours, The. See Tuke, Sir Samuel

Aesop. See Vanbrugh, Sir John

"After money," 20

Afterpieces, 12, 115, 117, 120, 121, 122, 161–62, 165–67, 169–71, 225n18, 245n5

Albion and Albinius. See Dryden, John

Alchemist, The. See Jonson, Ben

Alessandro Nell'Indie. See Metastasio, Pietro Bonaventura

All for Love. See Dryden, John

All in the Wrong. See Murphy, Arthur

All Mistaken. See Howard, James

Almahide. See Bononcini, Giovanni

Amorous Widow, The. See Betterton, Thomas

Amphitryon. See Dryden, John

Anatomist, The. See Ravenscroft, Edward

Andronicus Comenius. See Wilson, John

Angelo, Domenico, 10

Animal Pantomime, The, 165

Anne I, 16, 66

Apollo and Daphne/The Burgomaster Tricked. *See* Theobald, Lewis

Apprentice, The. *See* Murphy, Arthur

Apreece, 162

Arne, Michael, 246n16

Arne, Dr. Thomas, 167, 170; *Artaxerxes*, 164; *L'Olimpiade*, 164

Arnold, Samuel. *See* Bickerstaff, Isaac; Colman, George

Arsinoe, 72, 123

Artaserse. *See* Hasse, Johann Adolph

Artaxerxes. *See* Arne, Dr. Thomas

As You Like It. *See* Shakespeare, William

Auction of Pictures. *See* Foote, Samuel

Audience, 2, 19–21, 68–69, 130, 137, 158

Aureng-Zebe. *See* Dryden, John

Author, The. *See* Foote, Samuel

Author's Farce, The. *See* Fielding, Henry

Baker, Thomas, 138; *Humour of the Age, The*, 20; *Tunbridge Walks*, 72

Ballad opera, 115, 120, 124–30, 241n9

Bank of England, 66

Bankrupt, The. *See* Foote, Samuel

Banks, John, 59, 60, 240n53; *Destruction of Troy, The*, 59; *Island Queens, The*, 59, 233n41; *Unhappy Favorite, The*, 59, 72, 120, 174; *Vertue Betrayed*, 59

Barbarossa. *See* Brown, John

Barnard, Sir John/Barnard Bill, 132, 156

Barry, Elizabeth, 17, 58, 64, 70, 79, 88, 204, 227n32

Barry, Spranger, 18

Bartholomew Fair. *See* Jonson, Ben

Bate, Henry: *Flitch of Bacon, The*, 165; *Rival Candidates, The*, 166

Beard, John, 159

Beau Demolished, The, 121

Beaumont, Sir Francis, 29. *See also* Fletcher, John

Beaux Strategem, The. *See* Farquhar, George

Beeston, William, 4

Beggar's Bush, The. *See* Fletcher, John

Beggar's Opera, The. *See* Gay, John

Beggar's Wedding, The/Phebe. *See* Coffey, Charles

Behn, Aphra, 27, 74, 76, 140, 148; *City Heiress, The*, 57; *Emperour of the Moon, The*, 72, 120; *Feign'd Curtizans, The*, 56; *Oroonoko*, 101, 103; *Roundheads, The*, 57; *Rover, The*, 30, 46–55, 68, 71, 72, 75, 78, 79, 89, 90–91, 99–100, 101, 119, 125, 128, 142, 154, 167, 182, 184, 190; *Rover, Part 2, The*, 12, 46

Benefit, author's, 15, 124, 226n27

Benefit performances, 15–16, 227n28

Berlin, Irving, 208

Bernstein, Leonard, 208

Betterton, Thomas, 14, 16, 17, 64, 69, 70, 88, 118, 160, 227n32; *Amorous Widow, The*, 50, 72, 73, 119. *See also* Fletcher, John

Bickerstaffe, Isaac: *Daphne and Amintor*, 165; *Hypocrite, The*, 163; *Love in a Village*, 164; *Maid of the Mill, The* (with Samuel Arnold), 164; *Padlock, The*, 165; *Plain-Dealer, The*, version of, 248n36; *Thomas and Sally*, 166

Blackfriars theater, 224n5

Blackmore, Sir Richard: Preface to *King Arthur*, 87, 139

Bold Stroke for a Wife, A. *See* Centlivre, Susannah

Bon Ton. *See* Garrick, David

Bondman, The. *See* Massinger, Philip

Bonduca. *See* Fletcher, John

Bononcini, Giovanni: *Almahide*, 72, 123

Booth, Barton, 117

Boyle, Roger, Earl of Orrery, 34–35; *Mustapha*, 29, 30, 32

Bracegirdle, Anne, 17, 70, 79, 88, 227n32

Bray, Thomas, 68

Brecht, Bertolt: *Threepenny Opera*, 125

Briscoe, Samuel, 237n31

Britannia/Royal Lovers, The, 120

British Journal, The, 24

Brome, Sir Richard: *Jovial Crew, The*, 72, 125, 164; *Northern Lass, The*, 72

Brooke, Henry: *Earl of Essex, The*, 174

Brooks, Mel, 207

Brothers, The. See Cumberland, Richard

Brown, John: *Barbarossa*, 163, 173

Buckingham, Duke of: *Rehearsal, The*, 72, 119, 163, 207, 243n38

Bullock, Christopher: *Woman's Revenge, A*, 119, 125, 138

Bunyan, John, 174

Buona Figliuola, La. See Piccini, Niccolo

Burbage, Richard, 16

Burgoyne, John: *Maid of the Oaks, The*, 164

Burlesque, 207–8

Burnaby, William, 138

Burney, Frances, 200

Busie Body, The. See Centlivre, Susannah

Butler, Samuel: *Hudibras*, 207

Butler, Elizabeth, 152

Byng, John, 8

Caius Marius. See Otway, Thomas

Camilla. See Haym, Nicolino Francesco

Camp, The. See Sheridan, Richard Brinsley

Captives, The. See Gay, John

Careless Husband, The. See Cibber, Colley

Carey, Henry: *Contrivances, The*, 120, 165; *Dragon of Wantley, The*, 120, 165; *Honest Yorkshireman, The*, 120; *True Blue*, 166

Cartwright, William, 233n40

Carver, Robert, 10

Cary, Henry, 4th Viscount Falkland: *Marriage Night, The*, 59

Caryll, John: *Sir Salomon*, 50, 55, 76

Catherine and Petruchio. See Garrick, David

Cato. See Addison, Joseph

Cavendish, William, Duke of Newcastle: *Country Captain, The*, 37, 39

Censorship of the stage, 24–25, 88

Centlivre, Susannah, 74, 118, 138–39, 157, 205; *Bold Stroke for a Wife, A*, 119, 138, 139, 148, 163; *Busie Body, The*, 72, 80, 119, 138–39, 163, 181, 243n41; *Gamester, The*, 119; *Wonder, The*, 163, 181, 243n41

Cephalus and Procrus, 120

Chances, The. See Fletcher, John

Chaplet, The. See Mendez, Moses

Charles II, 13, 26, 27, 64

Chaucer, Geoffrey, 174

Cheats, The/The Tavern Bilkers, 120, 121

Cheats of Scapin, The. See Otway, Thomas

Chetwood, William: *Lovers Opera, The*, 120

Christmas Tale, A. See Garrick, David

Churchill, Caryl L.: *Cloud Nine*, 208

Chymical Counterfeits, The, 120

Cibber, Colley, 5, 17, 71, 74, 89, 92, 98, 117, 118, 133, 134, 135, 136, 243n34; *Careless Husband, The*, 72, 80, 94, 119, 163, 188, 190, 202, 238n37; *Comical Rivals, The/School Boy, The*, 72, 120, 165, 237n23; *Damon and Phillida*, 120, 165; *Double Gallant, The*, 119, 163; *Love Makes a Man*, 72, 119, 163, 237n23; *Love's Last Shift*, 63, 72, 73, 80, 81–82, 83, 88, 94, 119, 163, 188, 238n37; *Nonjuror, The*, 119, 227n29; *Provoked Husband, The* with Sir John Vanbrug, 119, 138, 163, 181, 190, 243n40; *Refusal, The*, 163; *She Would and She Would Not*, 119, 163. *See also* Shakespeare, William

Cibber, Susannah, 18, 19, 64, 201, 204; *Oracle, The*, 165

Cibber, Theophilus, 131, 132, 133, 134, 149–50, 226n26; *Harlot's Progress, The*, 120

Cicisbea alla Moda, La. See Galuppi, Baldassare

Circe. See Davenant, Charles

Citizen, The. See Murphy, Arthur

Citizen Turned Gentleman, The. See Ravenscroft, Edward

City Heiress, The. See Behn, Aphra

City Politiques, The. See Crowne, John

Clandestine Marriage, The. See Garrick, David

Clive, Kitty, 18

Cobler of Preston, The. See Johnson, Charles

Cockpit/Phoenix theater, 224n5

Coello, Antonio: *Empeños de seis horas, Los,* 48

Coffey, Charles: *Beggar's Wedding, The/Phebe,* 120; *Devil to Pay, The,* 120, 165

Cohan, George M., 208

Collier, Sir George: *Selima and Azor,* 166

Collier, Jeremy, 23, 85, 148, 184, 205, 236n20; *Short View of the Immorality and Profaneness of the English Stage, A,* 23, 68, 86–87

Collier Controversy, 23, 85, 86–88, 139, 205, 237n28, 237n29

Colman, George (the elder), 159, 160, 162, 181, 182, 190, 200; *Cymbeline,* 163, 172, 174; *Deuce is in Him, The,* 165; *English Merchant, The,* 163, 191; *Fairy Prince, The,* 165; *Fairy Tale, A,* 165; *Jealous Wife, The,* 163, 182–83, 191, 246n12; *Man and Wife,* 165, 170; *Mother Shipton* (with Samuel Arnold), 165; *Musical Lady, The,* 165; *Oxonian in Town, The,* 165; *Polly Honeycombe,* 161, 166–67; *Portrait, The,* 166; *Spanish Barber, The,* 164, 169; *Suicide, The,* 163

Colombine Courtezan, 120

Comedy of Errors, The. See Shakespeare, William

Comical Rivals, The/School Boy, The. See Cibber, Colley

Comical Revenge, The. See Etherege, Sir George

Commissary, The. See Foote, Samuel

Committee, The. See Howard, Sir Robert

Competitive theatrical climate, 2, 69–70, 159–60

"Compromise formation," 50–51, 53, 63, 73, 87, 99, 236n20

Comus. See Dalton, John

"Concert formula," 156

Confederacy, The. See Vanbrugh, Sir John

Congreve, William, 14, 67, 71, 74, 81, 85, 86, 87, 88, 89, 98, 99, 100, 112, 114, 135, 137, 138, 140, 148, 184, 195, 196, 197, 199, 204, 205, 237n31, 244n42, 248n41, 249n45; *Double Dealer, The,* 74–75, 76, 119, 154, 163, 190, 195; *Love for Love,* 71–72, 74–80, 85, 86, 91, 93, 99, 114, 119, 125, 129, 133, 163, 178, 181, 190, 195; *Mourning Bride, The,* 9, 72, 111, 112, 113, 119, 154, 164; *Old Batchelor, The,* 12, 72, 74, 119, 163, 190, 236n16; *Way of the World, The,* 74, 119, 163, 181, 190, 249n45

Conquest of Granada, The. See Dryden, John

Conscious Lovers, The. See Steele, Sir Richard

Conspiracy, The. See Whitaker, William

Constant Couple, The. See Farquhar, George

Contrivances, The. See Carey, Henry

Coriolanus. See Thomson, James

Corneille, Pierre: *Horace,* 173

Coronation, The, 165

Country Captain, The. See Cavendish, William

Country Girl, The. See Garrick, David

Country House, The. See Vanbrugh, Sir John

Country Lasses, The. See Johnson, Charles

Country Wake, The/Hob. See Doggett, Thomas

Country-Wife, The. See Wycherley, William

Covent Garden company, 116, 117, 156, 159, 160

Covent Garden theater, 5, illus.7, 10, 118, 204

Cowley, Abraham: *Cutter of Coleman Street, The*, 30

Cozeners, The. See Foote, Samuel

Critic, The. See Sheridan, Richard Brinsley

Criticism, theatrical and dramatic, 21–25

Cromwell, Oliver, 32

Cross Purposes. See O'Brien, William

Crowne, John, 59; *City Politiques, The*, 57, 233n41; *Henry VI*, 57; *Misery of Civil-War, The*, 57; *Sir Courtly Nice*, 72, 119

Cumberland, Richard, 7–8, 18, 168, 179–80, 181, 182, 190, 193, 200, 208; *Brothers, The*, 163, 183, 204; *West Indian, The*, 163, 180–81, 183–88, 191, 195, 226n27

Curll, Edmund, 133, 136, 243n34

Custom of the Country, The. See Fletcher, John

Cutter of Coleman Street, The. See Cowley, Abraham

Cuzzoni, Francesca, 126

Cymbeline. See Colman, George

Cymbeline. See Garrick, David

Cymon. See Garrick, David

Cyrus. See Hoole, John

Daily Courant, 66

Dall, Nicholas Thomas, 10

Dalton, John: *Comus*, 120, 164

Damon and Phillida. See Cibber, Colley

Dance, 12–13, 19

Daphne and Amintor. See Bickerstaffe, Isaac

Davenant, Charles, 69; *Circe*, 123

Davenant, Sir William, 4, 5, 8, 13, 14, 29, 70, 123, 229n5; *Gondibert, An Heroick Poem*, 32, 229–30n12; *Henry VIII*, 9, 30, 164, 247n19; *Love and Honour*, 31; *Macbeth*, 11, 12, 30, 31, 72, 119, 164, 172, 173, 202; *Siege of Rhodes, The*, 4, 30, 31, 32, 42, 123; *Wits, The*, 30, 38. *See also* Dryden, John

Davies, Thomas, 81; *Dramatic Miscellanies*, 237n24

Davis, Moll, 19

de Loutherbourg, Phillip James, 10–11

de Scudéry, Madeleine: *Artamène; ou, Le Grand Cyrus*, 34

Defoe, Daniel, 139

Dekker, Thomas: *Virgin Martyr, The* (with Phillip Massinger), 31

Demetrio, 164

Demofoonte, Il. See Metastasio, Pietro Bonaventura

Dennis, John, 87

Deserter, The. See Dibdin, Charles

Desire-based drama, 27

Destruction of Troy, The. See Banks, John

Deuce is in Him, The. See Colman, George

Devil to Pay, The. See Coffey, Charles

Devil Upon Two Sticks, The. See Foote, Samuel

Dibdin, Charles: *Deserter, The*, 165; *Quaker, The*, 166; *Touchstone, The*, 166; *Waterman, The*, 166; *Wedding Ring, The*, 168. *See also* Messink, James

Dibdin, Thomas, 207

Dickens, Charles, 207

Distrest Mother, The. See Philips, Ambrose

Divorce, 85, 97–99, 238–39n38

Dodsley, Robert: *King and the Miller of Mansfield, The*, 120, 165; *Toy-Shop, The*, 120

Doggett, Thomas, 88, 117, 118; *Country Wake, The/Hob*, 73, 120

Don John/The Libertine. See Shadwell, Thomas

Don Carlos. See Otway, Thomas

Dorset Garden theater, 5, 7, 70

Double Dealer, The. See Congreve, William

Double Disappointment, The. See Mendez, Moses

Double Gallant, The. See Cibber, Colley

Douglas. See Home, John

Downes, John, 247n22

Dragon of Wantley, The. See Carey, Henry

Druids, The, 164

Drummer, The. See Addison, Joseph

Drury Lane company, 116, 117–18, 131–34, 156, 158–59, 160, 226n26

Drury Lane theater, 5, 8, 10, 70, 88, 204, 225n11

Dryden, John, 21–22, 27, 71, 76, 140, 148, 204, 206; *Albion and Albinius,* 241n13; *All for Love,* 59, 119, 154, 163; *Amphitryon,* 72, 119, 163; *Aureng-Zebe,* 59, 72, 102, 111; *Conquest of Granada, The,* 30, 102; *Evening's Love, An,* 12, 30, 38, 40, 47, 48, 49; *Feast of Alexander, The* (with George Frederic Handel), 164; "Heads of an Answer to Rymer," 22; *Indian Emperor, The,* 29, 30, 33, 34, 35, 36, 42, 45, 59, 72, 102; *Indian Queen, The* (with Sir Robert Howard), 9, 12, 13, 29, 30, 33, 34, 35, 36, 37, 45, 225n18; *Indian Queen, The* (1695 version), 13, 241n14; *King Arthur,* 120, 123; *Marriage A-la-Mode,* 30, 46, 51, 73, 237n23; *Oedipus* (with Nathaniel Lee), 59, 72, 119; *Of Dramatic Poesy,* 22, 31, 38; *Rival Ladies, The,* 30; *Secret Love,* 28–46, 47, 49, 50, 51, 55, 58, 59, 60, 79, 90, 100, 101, 237n23; *Sir Martin Mar-all* (with William Cavendish, Duke of Newcastle), 30, 37, 47, 48, 49; *Spanish Fryar, The,* 57, 72, 120, 164; *Tempest, The* (with Sir William Davenant), 11, 12, 30, 49, 71, 72, 163, 172; *The Tempest* (1695 version), 119, 172, 241n14; *Wild Gallant, The,* 30, 38, 40

Duchess of Kingston, 162, 166

Duke of Buckingham. *See* Villiers, George

Duke of Newcastle. *See* Cavendish, William

Duel/dueling, 142–43, 238n35

Duenna, The. See Sheridan, Richard Brinsley

Duffett, Thomas, 207; *Psyche Debauched,* 123

Duke and No Duke, A. See Thurmond, John

Duke of York, 160

Duke's Company, 4, 14, 69, 225n20

D'Urfey, Thomas, 135, 237n31: *Royalist, The,* 57; *Sir Barnaby Whigg,* 57

Earl of Essex, The. See Brooke, Henry

Earl of Essex, The. See Jones, Henry

Elder Brother, The. See Fletcher, John

Elfrida. See Mason, William

Elopement, The, 165

Emperour of the Moon, The. See Behn, Aphra

English Merchant, The. See Colman, George

English opera, 123

Englishman in Paris, The. See Foote, Samuel

Englishman Returned from Paris, The. See Foote, Samuel

Entr'acte entertainments, 12–13, 88, 225n18

Epic, 32

Epicoene. See Jonson, Ben

Epsom Wells. See Shadwell, Thomas

Etherege, Sir George, 27, 46, 74, 196; *Comical Revenge, The,* 30, 31, 34, 72, 101; *Man of Mode, The,* 51, 52, 53, 72, 75, 78, 119, 128, 129, 142, 190; *She Would if She Could,* 30, 47–48, 49, 53, 72, 73

Eurydice Hiss'd. See Fielding, Henry

Evening's Love, An. See Dryden, John

Every Man in his Humour. See Jonson, Ben

Exclusion Crisis, 25, 26, 50, 56–57

Fair, The. See Rich, John

Fair Penitent, The. See Rowe, Nicholas

Fair Quaker of Deal, The. See Shadwell, Charles

Fairies, The. See Garrick, David

Fairy Prince, The. See Colman, George

Fairy Queen, The. See Settle, Elkanah

Fairy Tale, The. See Colman, George

Falkland, Lord. *See* Cary, Henry

Fall of Phaeton, The. See Pritchard, William

False Delicacy, The. See Kelly, Hugh

False Friend, The. See Pix, Mary

Farce, 9, 40, 231–32n31

Farquhar, George, 18, 71, 74, 88, 114, 118, 138, 140, 148, 184, 195, 205, 208, 244n42; *Beaux Stratagem, The,* 72, 89, 91–100, 114, 119, 125, 129, 163, 181, 190; *Constant Couple, The,* 72, 80, 88, 89–90, 91, 119, 154, 163, 182; *Inconstant, The,* 163; *Love and a Bottle,* 88; *Recruiting Officer, The,* 72, 86, 89, 90, 91, 99–100, 119, 125, 163, 181; *Stage-Coach, The,* 73, 89, 120, 121; *Twin Rivals, The,* 119, 163, 244n42

Fatal Extravagance, The. See Hill, Aaron

Fatal Jealousie, The. See Payne, Henry Nevil

Fatal Marriage, The. See Southerne, Thomas

Faustina, Sga, 126

Feast of Alexander, The. See Dryden, John

Feign'd Curtizans, The. See Behn, Aphra

Female actors, 17, 18–19, 206. *See also* Actors/acting styles

Female Prelate, The. See Settle, Elkanah

Fielding, Henry, 115, 122, 131–37, 148, 156, 157, 159, 200, 206, 207, 240n6, 245n5; *Author's Farce, The,* 120, 132–37, 157; *Eurydice Hiss'd,* 132, 137; *Historical Register for the Year 1736, The,* 132, 157; *Intriguing Chambermaid, The,* 120, 165; *Lottery, The,* 120, 121, 165; *Miser, The,* 119, 163; *Mock Doctor, The,* 120, 165; *Modern Husband, The,* 132, 134; *Old Debauchees, The,* 120, 243n31; *Old Man Taught Wisdom, An,* 120, 165; *Pasquin,* 119, 131, 132, 137; *Temple Beau, The,* 131; *Tom Jones,* 243n32; *Tom Thumb,* 120, 149; *Tragedy of Tragedies, The,* 119, 132; *Universal Gallant, The,* 132

Filosofo di Campagna, Il. See Galuppi, Baldassare

Finances, theatrical, 13–16, 158–59. *See also* Benefit, author's

Fisher, J. A.: *Sylphs, The,* 166

Fleetwood, Charles, 132, 159

Fletcher, John, 29, 59; *Beggar's Bush, The,* 125, 242n18; *Bonduca,* 241n14; *Chances, The,* 72, 163; *Custom of the Country, The,* 237n23; *Elder Brother, The,* 237n23; *Humorous Lieutenant, The,* 30, 31, 34, 72, 101; *Island Princess, The,* 72, 120; *Love Lies a'Bleeding* (with Francis Beaumont), 30; *Maid's Tragedy, The* (with Francis Beaumont), 29, 30, 31, 62; *Pilgrim, The,* 72, 119, 237n23; *Prophetess, The* (adapted by Thomas Betterton), 12, 120, 123; *Rollo, Duke of Normandy,* 30; *Rule a Wife and Have a Wife,* 72, 119, 164; *Scornful Lady, The* (with Francis Beaumont), 29, 30, 38, 47, 72, 81, 119, 125; *Sea Voyage, The,* 11; *Wit Without Money* (with Francis Beaumont), 119, 125

Fletcherian, 9, 31, 35, 36, 38, 39, 47–51, 62, 74, 151, 175, 201, 204

Flitch of Bacon, The. See Bate, Henry

Flora/Hob's Opera. See Hippisley, John

Flora's Vagaries. See Rhodes, Richard

Foote, Samuel, 14, 159–61, 190, 200, 245n53, 245n5; *Auction of Pictures,* 165; *Author, The,* 162, 165; *Bankrupt, The,* 165; *Commissary, The,* 165, 245n7; *Cozeners, The,* 165; *Devil Upon Two Sticks, The,* 165; *Englishman in Paris, The,* 165; *Englishman Returned from Paris, The,* 165; *Knights, The,* 165; *Lyar, The,* 165; *Maid of Bath, The,* 162, 165; *Mayor of Garratt, The,* 165; *Minor, The,* 160, 165; *Nabob, The,* 165; *Orators, The,* 160, 165; *Taste,* 166; *Trip to Calais, A,* 166

Fortunatus. See Woodward, Henry

Fortune Tellers, The, 120

Funeral, The. See Steele, Sir Richard

Galuppi, Baldassare: *Cicisbea alla Moda, La,* 164; *Filosofo di Campagna, Il,* 164

Gamester, The. See Centlivre, Susannah

Gamester, The. See Moore, Edward

Garrick, David, 8, 169–71; as actor, 16, 17, 19, 64, 201, 202, 227n31; as author, 19, 162, 172–73, 181, 190, 200; *Bon Ton,* 165; *Catherine and Petruchio,* 165; *Christmas Tale, A,* 10–11, 165; *Clandestine Marriage, The* (with George Colman), 163, 191, 196; *Country Girl, The,* 248n36; *Cymbeline,* 163, 172, 174; *Cymon* (with Thomas Arne), 164; *Fairies, The,* 172; *Guardian, The,* 139, 165; *Harlequin's Invasion,* 10, 165; *Institution of the Garter* (with Charles Dibdin), 165; *Irish Widow, The,* 165; *Jubilee, The,* 161, 165, 169–71; *King Lear,* 164, 173, 202, 205; *Lethe,* 165; *Lying Valet, The,* 120, 165; *Male Coquette, The,* 165; as manager, 1, 6, 9, 10, 11, 14, 158–59, 160, 162, 225–26n20; *Miss in Her Teens,* 165; *Ode upon Dedicating a Building and Erecting a Statue to Shakespeare,* 170; *Peep Behind the Curtain, A,* 165

Gate receipts, 15; *See also* Finances, theatrical

"gay couple," 38, 40, 44

Gay, John, 115, 129, 137, 148, 156, 157, 159, 207; *Beggar's Opera, The,* 5, 117, 118, 120, 121, 122, 124–30, 131, 157, 164, 168, 200, 207, 208, 226n27, 248n35; *Captives, The,* 124; *Fables,* 127; *Polly,* 130, 241–42n16; *What D'Ye Call It, The,* 120, 121, 124, 166, 207

Genii, The. See Woodward, Henry

Gentle Shepherd, The. See Ramsay, Allan

Gentleman, Francis, 201

George I, 117

George II, 117, 129

George III, 160

Gershwin, George and Ira, 208

Giffard, Henry, 6, 171, 131, 156, 240n6

Gilbert, W. S. (Gilbert and Sullivan), 207

Gildon, Charles: *Measure for Measure,* 119, 163

Globe theaters, 224n6

Glorious Revolution, 67

Golden Pippin, The. See O'Hara, Kane

Goldsmith, Oliver, 181, 189, 190, 191, 200, 201; "Essay on the Theater; or, a Comparison Between Laughing and Sentimental Comedy, An," 188–90; *She Stoops to Conquer,* 163, 189, 191–95, 200

Goodman's Fields company, 116, 131, 155, 240n6

Goodman's Fields theater, 6, 118, 156

Grabu, Louis, 241n13

Great Plague, 29

Great Mogul's Company of Comedians, The, 132

Grecian Daughter, The. See Murphy, Arthur

Grub Street Journal, The, 24

Guardian, The. See Garrick, David

Guglielmi, Pietro: *Viaggiatori Ridicoli, I,* 164

Gwyn, Nell, 17, 34

"Half-price," 20

Half Price Riots of 1763, 227n38

Hamlet. See Shakespeare, William

Handel, George Frederic, 121, 124, 204; *Judas Macchabaeus* (with Rev. Thomas Morrell), 164; *Messiah, The,* 164; *Rinaldo* (with Sacchini, Antonio Maria Gasparo), 73, 123; *Samson,* 164

Hanoverians, 16

Harlequin a Sorcerer. See Theobald, Lewis

Harlequin Doctor Faustus. See Thurmond, John

Harlequin Ranger. *See* Woodward, Henry

Harlequin Restor'd, 120

Harlequin Shipwreck'd, 120

Harlequin's Frolic, 165

Harlequin's Invasion. *See* Garrick, David

Harlequin's Jubilee. *See* Woodward, Henry

Harlot's Progress, The. *See* Cibber, Theophilus

Harris, Thomas, 159

Harris, Henry, 14

Hart, Charles, 17, 233n40

Hasse, Johann Adolph: *Artaserse*, 164

Hayes, William, 246n16

Haym, Nicolino Francesco: *Camilla* (with Owen MacSwiney), 73, 123; *Pyrrhus and Demetrius* (with Owen Swiny), 73

Haymarket company/New Haymarket company, 116, 118, 132, 155, 240n6

Haymarket theatre/little theatre in the Haymarket, 14, 159, 160

Haywood, Eliza, 135, 200

"Heads of an Answer to Rymer." *See* Dryden, John

Henry IV, I. *See* Shakespeare, William

Henry IV, II. *See* Shakespeare, William

Henry V. *See* Hill, Aaron

Henry VI. *See* Crowne, John

Henry VIII. *See* Davenant, Sir William

Herbert, Sir Henry, 25

Herculean Hero, 33

Hermit, The. *See* Love, James

Heroic drama, 28, 31, 32–37, 42–43, 44–45, 58–59, 101, 111, 123, 204, 240n52

Herring, Reverend Thomas, 126

High Life Below Stairs. *See* Townley, James

Highmore, John, 131

Hill, Aaron: *Fatal Extravagance, The* (with Joseph Mitchell), 247n23; *Henry V*, 164; *Merope*, 164; *Walking Statue, The*, 73; *Zara*, 164

Hippisley, John: *Flora/Hob's Opera*, 120, 165

Historical Register for the Year 1736, The. *See* Fielding, Henry

History of King Richard the Second, The. *See* Tate, Nahum

History of King Lear, The. *See* Tate, Nahum

Hoadly, Benjamin: *Suspicious Husband, The*, 148, 163, 181, 247n28

Hobbes, Thomas/Hobbesian, 27, 46, 111; *Leviathan*, 228n1

Home, John: *Douglas*, 163, 174, 200, 206

Honest Yorkshireman, The. *See* Carey, Henry

Hoole, John: *Cyrus*, 163, 173, 174

Hopkins, Priscilla, 248n42

House charges, 14–15. *See also* Finances, theatrical

Howard, Edward, 27; *Usurper, The*, 59

Howard, James, 27; *All Mistaken*, 37

Howard, Sir Robert, 27; *Committee, The*, 29, 30, 37, 39, 40, 47, 48, 50, 71, 72, 119, 128, 163, 187; *Surprisal, The*, 29

Hughes, John: *Siege of Damascus, The*, 120, 164

Hull, Thomas, 159

Hume, David, 138

Humorous Lieutenant, The. *See* Fletcher, John

Humour of the Age, The. *See* Baker, Thomas

Hydaspes. *See* Mancini, Francesco

Hypocrite, The. *See* Bickerstaffe, Isaac

Ibsen, Henrik, 208

Imprisonment, Release, Adventures, and Marriage of Harlequin, The, 120

Inconstant, The. *See* Farquhar, George

Indian Emperour, The. *See* Dryden, John

Indian Queen, The. *See* Dryden, John

Ingratitude of a Common-Wealth, The. *See* Tate, Nahum

Institution of the Garter, The. *See* Garrick, David

Interregnum, 32; closing of theaters
    during, 4
Intriguing Chambermaid, The. See
    Fielding, Henry
Irish Widow, The. See Garrick, David
Island Princess, The. See Fletcher, John
Island Queens, The. See Banks, John
Italian opera, 122–24, 125–26, 241n9;
    See also Opera; English opera

Jackson of Exeter, 246n16
James Street, tennis court theater in, 118,
    155
James, Duke of York/James II, 56, 65
Jane Shore. See Rowe, Nicholas
Jealous Doctor, The, 120
Jealous Wife, The. See Colman, George
Johnson, Dr. Samuel, 1, 169, 200;
    edition of Shakespeare's *Works,*
    169
Johnson, Charles, 121–22; *Cobler of
    Preston, The,* 120, 121; *Country
    Lasses,* The, 163
Jones, Inigo, 8, 123
Jones, Henry: *Earl of Essex, The,* 163,
    174
Jonson, Ben, 123; *Alchemist, The,* 30, 38,
    72, 119, 163, 202, 243n37;
    Bartholomew Fair, 30, 72;
    Epicoene, 30, 38, 47, 71, 72, 119;
    Every Man in his Humour, 163,
    181; *Masque of Queens, The,* 123;
    Volpone, 72, 119
Jonsonian, 38, 47–49, 204
Jovial Crew, The. See Brome, Sir Richard
Jubilee, The. See Garrick, David
Judas Macchabaeus. See Handel, George
    Frederic
Julius Caesar. See Shakespeare, William
Jupiter and Io, 120

Kelly, Hugh, 193; *False Delicacy, The,*
    188, 191
Kenrick, William, 201
Killigrew, Charles, 14, 69, 233n40
Killigrew, Thomas, 4, 5, 13, 14, 29, 70,

233n40; *Thomaso, or the
    Wanderer,* 233n37
King Arthur. See Dryden, John
King John. See Shakespeare, William
King Lear. See Garrick, David
*King and the Miller of Mansfield, The.
    See* Dodsley, Robert
King's Company, 4, 69, 233n40
Knights, The. See Foote, Samuel
Kynaston, Edward, 70, 233n40

La Rochefoucauld, François, duc de, 50
Lacy, James, 159
Lacy, John, 17, 48
Lacy, Willoughby, 159
Lancashire Witches, The. See Shadwell,
    Thomas
Law, William: *Unlawfulness of Stage
    Entertainment Fully
    Demonstrated,* 23, 139
Lee, Nathaniel, 59; *Lucius Junius Brutus,*
    57, 59, 228n45, 233n41; *Rival
    Queens, The,* 72, 101, 120, 154,
    164; *Theodosius,* 120, 123, 164.
    See also Dryden, John
Leiden/Leyden University, the
    Netherlands, 66, 131
Lethe. See Garrick, David
Licenses, theatrical, 14, 118
Licensing Act, lapsing of (1695), 66, 87,
    235n4
Licensing Act of 1737, 24, 25, 115, 122,
    130, 132, 137, 155–57, 159–60,
    200
Lighting effects, 10–11
Lillo, George, 157–208; *London
    Merchant, The,* 119, 148–55, 157,
    164, 175, 247n23
Lincoln's Inn Fields, rebel company at
    (1695), 15, 17, 70–71, 227n32
Lincoln's Inn Fields company (1714–32),
    116–17
Lincoln's Inn Fields theatre (1661), 4, 5,
    8
Lincoln's Inn Fields theatre (1714), 5, 13,
    116–17
Linley, Thomas, 168

Linley, Jr., Thomas, 246n16

Locke, John, 66, 138

Locke, Matthew, 123

London Cuckolds, The. See Ravenscroft, Edward

London Fire, 29

Lottery, The. See Fielding, Henry

Love, James: *Hermit, The,* 165; *Rites of Hecate, The,* 166; *Witches, The,* 166

Love a-la-Mode. See Macklin, Charles

Love and a Bottle. See Farquhar, George

Love and Honour. See Davenant, Sir William

Love for Love. See Congreve, William

Love in a Maze. See Shirley, James

Love in a Village. See Bickerstaffe, Isaac

Love Lies a'Bleeding. See Fletcher, John

Love Makes a Man. See Cibber, Colley

Love's Last Shift. See Cibber, Colley

Lover, 244n21

Lovers Opera, The. See Chetwood, William

Loyal Brother, The. See Southerne, Thomas

Lucius Junius Brutus. See Lee, Nathaniel

Lyar, The. See Foote, Samuel

Lying Lover, The. See Steele, Sir Richard

Lying Valet, The. See Garrick, David

Macbeth. See Davenant, Sir William

Machines/stage machinery, 11–12

Macklin, Charles, 17, 18, 190, 201, 202, 226n26; *Love a-la-Mode,* 165

MacSwiney, Owen. *See* Haym, Nicolino Francesco. *See also* Swiny, Owen

Magician, The, 120

Maid of Bath, The. See Foote, Samuel

Maid of the Mill, The. See Bickerstaffe, Isaac

Maid of the Oaks, The. See Burgoyne, John

Maid's Tragedy, The. See Fletcher, John

Male Coquette, The. See Garrick, David

Man and Wife. See Colman, George

Man of Mode, The. See Etherege, Sir George

Management, theatrical, 13–16

Mancini, Francesco: *Hydaspes,* 73

Marriage A-la-Mode. See Dryden, John

Marriage Night, The. See Cary, Henry

Mars and Venus, 121

Marshall, Rebecca, 17, 34

Mary II, 16, 65–66, 68, 70

Mason, William: *Elfrida,* 164

Masque of Queens, The. See Jonson, Ben

Masques, 120, 123

Massinger, Phillip: *Bondman, The,* 30, 31. *See also* Dekker, Thomas

Master of the Revels office, 24–25

Mayor of Garratt, The. See Foote, Samuel

Measure for Measure. See Gildon, Charles

Mendez, Moses: *Chaplet, The,* 165; *Double Disappointment, The,* 165

Merchant of Venice, The. See Shakespeare, William

Merchant/merchants, 138–39, 150–51, 244n42, 245n51

Mercury Harlequin. See Woodward, Henry

Merope. See Hill, Aaron

Merry Wives of Windsor, The. See Shakespeare, William

Messiah, The. See Handel, George Frederic

Messink, James: *Norwood Gypsies, The* (with Carlo Antonio Delpini), 165; *Pigmy Revels, The* (with Charles Dibdin), 166

Metastasio, Pietro Bonaventura: *Alessandro Nell'Indie,* 164; *Demofoonte, Il,* 164

Midas. See O'Hara, Kane

Middlesex jury, 25, 237–38n31

Midsummer Night's Dream, A. See Shakespeare, William

Miller, Arthur: *Death of a Salesman,* 208

Milton, John, 173

Minor, The. See Foote, Samuel

Miser, The. See Fielding, Henry

Misery of Civil-War, The. See Crowne, John

Miss in Her Teens. See Garrick, David

Mistake, The. See Vanbrugh, Sir John

Mock Doctor, The. See Fielding, Henry

Modern Husband, The. See Fielding, Henry

Mohun, Michael, 17, 56, 233n40

Molière, Jean-Baptiste Poquelin, 49–50, 195, 232n35; L'Ecole des femmes, 50; L'Étourdi, 49, 50; Les Fâcheux, 49; George Dandin, 49; Tartuffe, 195

Moody, John, 170

Moore, Edward, 208; Gamester, The, 150, 163, 171–72, 175–80, 186, 200, 204, 206; Gamester, The, French version of, 247n26

Moore of Venice, The (Othello). See Shakespeare, William

Moraliste, 50

Morrell, Reverend Thomas: Judas Macchabaeus (with George Frederic Handel), 164

Mother Shipton. See Colman, George

Motteux, Peter Anthony: Acis and Galatea, 120, 121, 164

Mourning Bride, The. See Congreve, William

Much Ado About Nothing. See Shakespeare, William

Mulberry Garden, The. See Sedley, Sir Charles

Murphy, Arthur, 158, 160, 181–82, 190, 200; All in the Wrong, 19, 163, 181; Apprentice, The, 165; Citizen, The, 165; Grecian Daughter, The, 164, 173, 206; Old Maid, The, 165; Upholsterer, The, 166; Way to Keep Him, The, 162, 163; What We Must All Come To, 166

Music, 12–13, 19

Musical Lady, The. See Colman, George

Mustapha. See Boyle, Roger

Nabob, The. See Foote, Samuel

Necromancer, The, 117, 120

New Haymarket. See Haymarket, little theater in the

Newcastle, Duke of. See Cavendish, William

Nokes, James, 48

Nonjuror, The. See Cibber, Colley

Norris, Henry: Royal Merchant, The, 72, 119, 125

Northern Lass, The. See Brome, Sir Richard

Norwood Gypsies, The. See Messink, James

Oates, Titus, 56

O'Brien, William: Cross Purposes, 165

Ode upon Dedicating a Building and Erecting a Statue to Shakespeare. See Garrick, David

Oedipus. See Dryden, John

Of Dramatic Poesy. See Dryden, John

O'Hara, Kane: Golden Pippin, The, 164, 168–69; Midas, 164; Two Misers, The, 166

O'Neill, Eugene: Long Day's Journey Into Night, 208

Old Batchelor, The. See Congreve, William

Old Debauchees, The. See Fielding, Henry

Old Maid, The. See Murphy, Arthur

Old Man Taught Wisdom, An. See Fielding, Henry

Old Woman's Oratory, The. See Smart, Christopher

Oldfield, Anne, 17, 18, 108, 118

L'Olimpiade. See Arne, Dr. Thomas

Opera, 13, 16, 101, 115, 116, 117, 120, 122, 159, 228n39. See Also English opera; Italian opera

"Opera of the Nobility," 124

Oracle, The, Cibber, Susannah

Oratorio, 164

Orators, The. See Foote, Samuel

Oroonoko (novel). See Behn, Aphra

Oroonoko (play). See Southerne, Thomas

Orphan, The. See Otway, Thomas

Orpheus and Eurydice. *See* Weaver, John

Orrery, Earl of. *See* Boyle, Roger

Othello/Moore of Venice, The. *See* Shakespeare, William

Otway, Thomas, 46, 74, 85, 149, 150, 173–74, 176, 204; *Caius Marius*, 59; *Cheats of Scapin, The*, 120, 165; *Don Carlos*, 30; *Orphan, The*, 60, 72, 101, 110, 111, 120, 154, 164, 174, 176, 202; *Souldiers Fortune, The*, 55, 60; *Venice Preserved*, 30, 56–64, 72, 81, 85, 101, 103–4, 109, 111, 120, 125, 164, 174, 175

Oxonian in Town, The. *See* Colman, George

Padlock, The. *See* Bickerstaffe, Isaac

Pantomime, 9, 13, 115, 117, 121, 122, 207, 241n9

Pasquin. *See* Fielding, Henry

Patents, theatrical, 4, 13, 139, 160, 225–26n20

Payne, Henry Nevil: *Fatal Jealousie, The*, 59; *Siege of Constantinople, The*, 59

Peep Behind the Curtain, A. *See* Garrick, David

Pepusch, John Christopher: *Thomyris* (with P.A. Motteux), 73

Pepys, Samuel, 5, 34, 68, 229n9

Pergolesi, Giovanbattista: *Serva Padrona, La*, 166; *Strattaggemma, La*, 164

Periodicals, 23–24, 66–67

Perseus and Andromeda, 120, 165

Philips, Ambrose: *Distrest Mother, The*, 119, 163

Phillips, Edward: *Royal Chace, The*, 120, 166

Piccini, Niccolo: *Buona Figliuola, La*, 164; *Schiava, La*, 164

Pigmy Revels, The. *See* Messink, James

Pilgrim, The. *See* Fletcher, John

Pix, Mary: *False Friend, The*, 119

Plain-Dealer, The. *See* Wycherley, William

Players Scourge, The, 17

Polly. *See* Gay, John

Polly Honeycombe. *See* Colman, George

Pope, Alexander, 121, 124, 129, 137

Popish Plot, 56, 57

Popular culture/drama, 1–3, 202, 203–9

Porter, Cole, 108

Porter, Mary, 108

Porter, Thomas: *Villain, The*, 29, 30, 59

Portrait, The. *See* Colman, George

Powell, George, 88

Pritchard, William: *Fall of Phaeton, The*, 120

Prometheus, 166

Prompter, 15, 226n26

Prophetess, The. *See* Fletcher, John

Proteus. *See* Woodward, Henry

Proviso scene/sequence, 41, 97–98, 230n19

Provoked Husband, The. *See* Cibber, Colley

Provoked Wife, The. *See* Vanbrugh, Sir John

Psyche. *See* Shadwell, Thomas

Psyche Debauched. *See* Duffett, Thomas

Public Advertiser, 169

"Puffs," 228n43

Purcell, Henry, 12–13, 123, 204

Pyrrhus and Demetrius. *See* Haym, Nicolino Francesco

Quaker, The. *See* Dibdin, Charles

Queen Mab. *See* Woodward, Henry

Queen's/King's theater in the Haymarket, 5, 88, 123

Quin, James, 18

Ramsay, Allan: *Gentle Shepherd, The*, 164

Rape of Proserpine, The. *See* Theobald, Lewis

Rauzzini, Venanzio, 246n16

Ravenscroft, Edward: *Anatomist, The*, 120, 163, 181; *Citizen Turned Gentleman, The*, 51, 55; *London Cuckolds, The*, 53, 55, 72, 73, 119

Recruiting Officer, The. See Farquhar, George

Red Bull theater, 224n5

Reed, Joseph: *Register Office, The,* 166

Refusal, The. See Cibber, Colley

Register Office, The. See Reed, Joseph

Rehearsal, The. See Villiers, George

Relapse, The. See Vanbrugh, Sir John

Restoration of the monarchy, (1660), 4, 26

Revenge, The. See Young, Edward

Rhodes, John, 4

Rhodes, Richard: *Flora's Vagaries,* 39, 40

Rice, Edward, 207

Rich, Christopher, 5, 6, 13, 70, 117, 123, 236n12, 236n14

Rich, John, 5, 6, 13, 14, 18, 116, 117, 121, 133, 135, 159, 160, 207; *Fair, The,* 165

Richard III. See Shakespeare, William

Richards, John Inigo, 10

Richardson, Samuel, 200; *Clarissa,* 166; *Pamela,* 138

Richmond, theater in, 118

Rinaldo. See Handel, George Frederic

Riots, theatrical, 21

Rites of Hecate, The. See Love, James

Rival Candidates, The. See Bate, Henry

Rival Ladies, The. See Dryden, John

Rival Queens, The. See Lee, Nathaniel

Rivals, The. See Sheridan, Richard Brinsley

Robin Goodfellow, 120

Rollo, Duke of Normandy. See Fletcher, John

Roman Father, The. See Whitehead, William

Romeo and Juliet. See Shakespeare, William

Rosamond. See Addison, Joseph

Roundheads, The. See Behn, Aphra

Rover, The. See Behn, Aphra

Rover, Part 2, The. See Behn, Aphra

Rowe, Nicholas: *Fair Penitent, The,* 18, 105, 113, 119, 154, 163, 173, 202; *Jane Shore,* 72, 100, 101, 105–11, 114, 119, 125, 149, 154, 164, 173, 176; *Tamerlane,* 120, 164

Royal Academy of Music, 124

Royal Chace, The. See Phillips, Edward

Royal Merchant, The. See Norris, Henry

Royal patronage, 16, 117, 227n29

Royalist, The. See D'Urfey, Thomas

Rule a Wife and Have a Wife. See Fletcher, John

Rymer, Thomas, 111; *Tragedies of the Last Age,* 22

Sacchini, Antonio Maria Gasparo. *See* Handel, George Frederic

Sacheverell, Reverend Dr., 68

Saint-Réal, l'abbé de: *Conjuration des Espagnols contre la République de Venise, La,* 58

St. Serfe, Thomas: *Flora's Vagaries,* 39, 40

Salisbury Court playhouse, 224n5

Samson. See Handel, George Frederic

Scenery/scenic effects, 8–12, 204, 206

Schiava, La. See Piccini, Niccolo

School for Lovers, The. See Whitehead, William

School for Scandal, The. See Sheridan, Richard Brinsley

Science: importance of to British society, 67; interest in, 67

Scornful Lady, The. See Fletcher, John

Scriblerus Club, 124

Sea Voyage, The. See Fletcher, John

Secret Love. See Dryden, John

Sedley, Sir Charles: *Mulberry Garden, The,* 49

Selima and Azor. See Collier, Sir George

Senesino, Francesco, 135, 243n36

Sentiment/sentimental drama, 137–38, 168, 175, 180–81, 183–84, 188–91, 193, 248n34

Serva Padrona, La. See Pergolesi, Giovanbattista

Settle, Elkanah, 59; *Fairy Queen, The,* 241n14; *Female Prelate, The,* 57

Shadwell, Charles: *Fair Quaker of Deal, The*, 72, 119, 163

Shadwell, Thomas, 27, 184; *Don John/ The Libertine*, 72; *Epsom Wells*, 51, 72; *Lancashire Witches, The*, 57, 72; *Psyche*, 30, 123; *Squire of Alsatia, The*, 72, 119, 226n27; *Sullen Lovers*, The, 30, 49; *Timon of Athens*, 72, 120; *Virtuoso, The*, 51

Shaftsbury, Anthony Ashley Cooper, Earl of, 26, 56–58, 63

Shakespeare, William; *As You Like It*, 119, 138, 163; *Comedy of Errors, The*, 9; *Hamlet*, 30, 31, 72, 111, 119, 164, 172, 234n48; *Henry IV, I*, 72, 164, 171; *Henry IV, II*, 164, 171; *Julius Caesar*, 72, 119; *King John*, 164; *Merchant of Venice, The*, 119, 138, 163, 181; *Merry Wives of Windsor, The*, 119, 163; *Midsummer Night's Dream, A*, 172; *Moore of Venice, The/Othello*, 30, 72, 103, 111, 119, 164; *Much Ado About Nothing*, 163, 181; *Othello*, 31, 177, 234n48; *Richard III* (adaptation by Colley Cibber), 105, 107, 120, 164, 239n48; *Romeo and Juliet*, 9, 151, 164, 172, 173, 202, 208; *Romeo and Juliet* (James Howard's adaptation), 247n22; *Tempest, The*, 172, 173, 181; *Twelfth Night*, 163; *Winter's Tale, The*, 163. See also Davenant, Sir William; Dryden, John; Garrick, David; Gildon, Charles; Thomson, James

Shakespeare Jubilee of 1769, 169–71

Shakespearean, 31, 183, 204

Shaw, George Bernard, 208

She Stoops to Conquer. See Goldsmith, Oliver

She Would and She Would Not. See Cibber, Colley

She Would if She Could. See Etherege, Sir George

"she-tragedies," 60, 105, 112, 173, 204

Sheppard, Jack, 126

Sheridan, Elizabeth Linley, 168

Sheridan, Richard Brinsley, 14, 159, 162, 168, 181, 189, 191, 200, 201, 208, 225–26n20; *Camp, The* (with Richard Tickell), 165; *Critic, The*, 207; *Duenna, The*, 161, 164, 167–68; *Rivals, The*, 163, 166, 191–95, 196; *School for Scandal, The*, 163, 191, 195–200; *Wonders of Derbyshire, The*, 166

Sheridan, Thomas, 201, 246n13

Shirley, James, 123; *Love in a Maze*, 30; *Traitor, The*, 30, 31

Sidney, Sir Philip: *Defense of Poesy*, 23, 86

Siege of Constantinople, The. See Payne, Henry Nevil

Siege of Damascus, The. See Hughes, John

Siege of Rhodes, The. See Davenant, Sir William

"silencing" of Christopher Rich, 13, 117

Sir Anthony Love. See Southerne, Thomas

Sir Barnaby Whigg. See D'Urfey, Thomas

Sir Courtly Nice. See Crowne, John

Sir Martin Mar-all. See Dryden, John

Sir Salomon. See Caryll, John

Sleeping with the Enemy, 208

Smart, Christopher: *Old Woman's Oratory, The*, 165

Smith, William, 69

Smollett, Tobias, 200

Societies for the Reformation of Manners, 23, 25, 66, 68, 87

Society for Promoting Christian Knowledge, 68

Souldiers Fortune, The. See Otway, Thomas

Sound of Music, The, 208

South Sea Company, 66, 129

Southerne, Thomas, 59, 67, 74, 112, 114, 149, 204; *Fatal Marriage, The*, 72, 120, 164; *Loyal Brother, The*, 57; *Oroonoko*, 72, 100, 101–5, 106, 109, 111, 113, 114, 119, 164, 184; *Oroonoko* (18th Century version of), 239n44; *Sir Anthony Love*, 113

Spanish Barber, The. See Colman, George

Spanish Fryar, The. See Dryden, John

Spanish-plot plays, 9, 29–30, 48, 49, 52, 142, 168, 204, 232n33

Spectator, The, 23, 67, 139

Spenser, Edmund, 174

Squire of Alsatia, The. See Shadwell, Thomas

Stage the Highroad to Hell, The, 23

Stage-Coach, The. See Farquhar, George

Steele, Sir Richard, 23, 66–67, 74, 91, 112, 118, 138–40, 157, 205, 208, 226n27, 243–44n41; *Conscious Lovers, The,* 23, 119, 138, 139, 140–48, 151, 155, 157, 163, 175, 177, 178, 181, 188, 190, 202, 226n27; *Funeral, The,* 72, 88, 119, 163; *Lying Lover, The,* 148; *Tender Husband, The,* 72, 119

Sterne, Laurence, 200

Strattaggemma, La. See Pergolesi, Giovanbattista

Suicide, The. See Colman, George

Sullen Lovers, The. See Shadwell, Thomas

Surprisal, The. See Howard, Sir Robert

Suspicious Husband, The. See Hoadly, Benjamin

Swan theater, 224n6

Swift, Jonathan, 124, 129, 137

Swiny, Owen. *See* Nicolino Francesco Haym. *See also* MacSwiney, Owen

Sylphs, The. See Fisher, J. A.

Tamerlane. See Rowe, Nicholas

Tancred and Sigismunda. See Thomson, James

Taste. See Foote, Samuel

Tate, Nahum, 59; *History of King Richard the Second, The,* 57, 233n41; *History of King Lear, The,* 72, 111, 119, 164, 172, 205, 247n22; *Ingratitude of a Common-Wealth, The,* 57

Tatler, The, 23, 66, 139, 243n41

Tempest, The. See Dryden, John. *See also* Shakespeare, William

Temple Beau, The. See Fielding, Henry

Tender Husband, The. See Steele, Sir Richard

Thackeray, William Makepeace, 207

Theater, 139

Theater, physical characteristics of, 3–8, 226n22; seating arrangements in, 20–21; ticket prices for performances in, 20

Theatre Royal, Drury Lane, 5, illus.6, 7; *See also* Drury Lane

Theatrical Campaign, 24

Theatrical Review, The, 24

Theobald, Lewis: *Apollo and Daphne/The Burgomaster Tricked,* 120, 165; *Harlequin a Sorcerer,* 120, 165; *Rape of Proserpine, The,* 120, 166

Theodosius. See Lee, Nathaniel

Thomas and Sally. See Bickerstaffe, Isaac

Thomaso, or the Wanderer. See Killigrew, Thomas

Thomson, James: *Coriolanus,* 163, 172; *Tancred and Sigismunda,* 164

Thomyris. See Pepusch, John Christopher

Thurmond, John: *Duke and No Duke, A* (alt. of Tate's original), 120, 165; *Harlequin Doctor Faustus,* 117, 120, 165

Tickell, Richard. *See* Sheridan, Richard Brinsley

Timon of Athens. See Shadwell, Thomas

Tom Thumb. See Fielding, Henry

Tonge, Israel, 56

Tonson, Jacob, 237n31

Touchstone, The. See Dibdin, Charles

Town Talk, 139

Townley, James: *High Life Below Stairs,* 165

Toy-Shop, The. See Dodsley, Robert

Tragedy of Tragedies, The. See Fielding, Henry

Tragicomedy, split-plot, 31

Traitor, The. See Shirley, James

Trapp, Joseph: *Abra Mule,* 72

Treasurer, 15

Trip to Calais, A. See Foote, Samuel

Trip to Scotland, A. See Whitehead, William

True Blue. See Carey, Henry

Tuke, Sir Samuel: *Adventures of Five Hours, The,* 9, 29–30, 48, 49, 168

Tunbridge Walks. See Baker, Thomas

Twelfth Night. See Shakespeare, William

Twin Rivals, The. See Farquhar, George

Two Misers, The. See O'Hara, Kane

Underhill, Cave, 70, 88

Unhappy Favourite, The. See Banks, John

Union of two companies, 1682–1695, 69

Union of two companies, 1707, 88

United Company, 14, 69–70, 235n11

United Company, splitting of (1695), 14, 65, 69, 70, 236n11

Universal Gallant, The. See Fielding, Henry

Universal Spectator, The, 24

Upholsterer, The. See Murphy, Arthur

Usurper, The. See Howard, Edward

Vanbrugh, Sir John. 5, 14, 67, 71, 74, 86, 88, 89, 92, 95, 98, 99, 100, 123, 138, 148, 204, 208, 237n31, 244n42; *Aesop,* 119; *Confederacy, The,* 72, 119, 163, 237n23; *Country House, The,* 120; *Mistake, The,* 119; *Provoked Wife, The,* 80, 82–85, 86, 88, 91, 94, 114, 119, 163, 175, 181, 190, 238n37; *Relapse, The,* 72, 73, 80, 82, 83, 88, 91, 94, 95, 99, 119, 163, 175, 190, 238n37. *See also* Cibber, Colley

Venice Preserved. See Otway, Thomas

Verbruggen, John, 88

Vere Street theater, 4

Vertue Betrayed. See Banks, John

Viaggiatori Ridicoli, I. See Guglielmi, Pietro

Villain, The. See Porter, Thomas

Villiers, George, Duke of Buckingham:

Rehearsal, The, 72, 119, 163, 207, 243n38

Virgin Martyr, The. See Dekker, Thomas

Virtuoso, The. See Shadwell, Thomas

Vittoria Corombona. See Webster, John

Volpone. See Jonson, Ben

Walker, John, 201

Walking Statue, The. See Hill, Aaron

Walpole, Sir Robert, 129–30, 132, 137, 156, 242n28, 243n30

Waterman, The. See Dibdin, Charles

Way of the World, The. See Congreve, William

Way to Keep Him, The. See Murphy, George

Weaver, John, 121; *Orpheus and Eurydice,* 120, 165

Webb, John, 8, 10

Webster, John: *Vittoria Corombona,* 30, 31, 154–55

Wedding Ring, The. See Dibdin, Charles

West Side Story, 208

West Indian, The. See Cumberland, Richard

What D'Ye Call It, The. See Gay, John

What We Must All Come To. See Murphy, George

When Harry Met Sally, 208

Whitaker, William: *Conspiracy, The,* 57

Whitefield, George, 246n13

Whitehead, William: *Roman Father, The,* 164, 173; *School for Lovers, The,* 163, 188, 191; *Trip to Scotland, A,* 166

Wild, Jonathan, 126, 129

Wild Gallant, The. See Dryden, John

Wilks, Robert, 17, 92, 117, 118, 134, 243n34

William III, 14, 16, 65–67, 70, 87

Williams, Tennessee: *Glass Menagerie, The,* 208

Wilson, John: *Andronicus Comenius,* 59

Winter's Tale, The. See Shakespeare, William

Wit Without Money. See Fletcher, John

Witches, The. See Love, James

Wits, The. See Davenant, Sir William

Woffington, Peg, 18, 201

Woman's Revenge, A. See Bullock,
    Christopher

Wonder, The. See Centlivre, Susannah

Wonders of Derbyshire, The. See
    Sheridan, Richard Brinsley

Woodward, Henry: Fortunatus, 165;
    Genii, The, 165; Harlequin
    Ranger, 165; Harlequin's Jubilee,
    165; Mercury Harlequin, 165;
    Proteus, 166; Queen Mab, 166

Wren, Sir Christopher, 6, 225n9

Wycherley, William, 27, 46, 74, 135,
    196, 197; Country-Wife, The, 30,
    51, 52, 53–54, 55, 73, 76, 83,
    119, 128, 129, 167, 190, 200,
    236n20, 248n36; Plain-Dealer,
    The, 30, 51, 55, 76, 90, 119, 163

York Buildings, Great Room in, 118

Young, Edward: Night Thoughts, 138;
    Revenge, The, 164, 243n40

Zara. See Hill, Aaron

Zucker, brothers, 207

the author

Frances M. Kavenik is associate professor of English, director of the ACCESS Program, and erstwhile director of women's studies at the University of Wisconsin–Parkside. With degrees in ascending order from Lake Forest College, Northwestern University, and the University of Wisconsin–Madison, she is a strong advocate for regional organizations: the Midwest MLA, Midwest ASECS, and the Midwest Women's Caucus for the Modern Languages. Her books include *The Designs of Carolean Comedy*, co-authored with Eric Rothstein, and *The Handbook of American Women's History*, co-edited with Angela Howard Zophy.

DATE DUE